From Impressionism to Anime

From Impressionism to Anime: Japan as Fantasy and Fan Cult in the Mind of the West

Susan J. Napier

palgrave
macmillan

First published in 2007 by
PALGRAVE MACMILLAN™
175 Fifth Avenue, New York, N.Y. 10010 and
Houndmills, Basingstoke, Hampshire, England RG21 6XS.
Companies and representatives throughout the world.

PALGRAVE MACMILLAN is the global academic imprint of the Palgrave Macmillan division of St. Martin's Press, LLC and of Palgrave Macmillan Ltd. Macmillan® is a registered trademark in the United States, United Kingdom and other countries. Palgrave is a registered trademark in the European Union and other countries.

ISBN-10: 1-4039-6213-8 (hardcover)
ISBN-13: 978-1-4039-6213-3 (hardcover)
ISBN-10: 1-4039-6214-6 (paperback)
ISBN-13: 978-1-4039-6214-0 (paperback)

Library of Congress Cataloging-in-Publication Data

Napier, Susan Jolliffe.
 From Impressionism to anime : Japan as fantasy and fan cult in the mind of the West/ Susan J. Napier.
     p. cm.
 Includes bibliographical references and index.
 ISBN 1-4039-6213-8 (hardcover : alk. paper)—ISBN 1-4039-6214-6 (pbk. : alk. paper)
 1. Animated films—Japan. 2. Europe—Civilization—Japanese influences. 3. United States—Civilization—Japanese influences. I. Title.

NC1766.J3N38 2007
303.48'25201821—dc22   2007019013

A catalogue record of the book is available from the British Library.

Design by Scribe

First edition: December 2007

10 9 8 7 6 5 4 3 2

Printed in the United States of America.

Perhaps appropriately this book is dedicated to the past, present, and future:
In memory of my parents, Julia and Reginald Phelps
And to my students over the years past and in the years to come.

Contents

Illustrations

Acknowledgments

This book is probably the most ambitious project I have ever launched myself into and I could never have accomplished it without considerable time off from teaching. I wish to thank the National Endowment for the Humanities for giving me a year off in the States, during which I was able to make use of the University of Texas's wonderful Humanities Research Center and do most of my material collecting and writing. I was also aided in this by a Faculty Research Grant from the University of Texas. The following year I received a Fulbright to Japan where I finished my writing and was also able to enjoy the resources of the International House Library and the Library at Keio University. Moreover, the Fulbright travel funds enabled me to visit Shimoda, where Japan's most recent encounter with the West really began.

I am grateful to Takayuki Tatsumi for being my academic host while I was in Tokyo. Vida Johnson, my Chair at Tufts University, allowed me a semester off before joining her department, which was crucially helpful for the final rewrite. I also received considerable financial aid through my position as Mitsubishi Heavy Industries Chair at the University of Texas. The additional funds that came with the position allowed me to travel to Giverny to see Monet's house, to Washington, DC, to look at Whistler's Peacock Room, and to Pennsylvania to see some of Frank Lloyd Wright's most characteristic architecture. Mitsubishi funds also allowed me to employ my two invaluable research assistants, Peter Siegenthaler and Michael Roemer, and to purchase books and videos. And, of course, I would like to give a special thank you to Peter and to Michael, as well. In Japan I was helped by three Keio students, Michio Arimitsu, Hideo Tsujii, and Yutaka Ebihara

Until now I have been fortunate in being able to do my work lying on the couch reading books and/or watching videos, but for this project I entered a whole new realm of research. The project combined field work, archival work, travel abroad, questionnaires, and interviews; it has left me breathless both in admiration for and gratitude to my friends, who are genuine anthropologists, sociologists, historians, and art historians. These colleagues offered me advice, direction, and readings of my work in progress. Needless to say, any errors are my own. But I would like to thank my friends and former colleagues, Mark Metzler, Tony Hopkins, Nancy Stalker, Rob Oppenheim, John Traphagan, and Robert Khan for their kind willingness to help and, in many cases, to read my material. On the anime front, Marc Hairston, Walter Amos, and Michael Johnson were invaluable and indefatigable resources. Henry Jenkins and Janet Staiger gave me excellent advice on fan studies and research.

I would also like to thank my non-academic friends who offered encouragement throughout the last five years. William Tullis read all the chapters and gave me enthusiastic comments. Deirdre and David Mendez were incredibly helpful with computer crises. Bill Barlow, an architectural preservationist, introduced me to Frank Lloyd Wright, both through the wonderful biography by Brendan Gill and by guiding me through some of Wright's buildings. Malone Hill accompanied me to anime conventions and even brought me coffee at crucial moments when I was giving presentations. My friend Tsugumichi Watanabe and my daughter Julia Napier deserve special thanks for what some might call "persistent nagging," but which they would prefer to describe as "sustained encouragement." Ko-Yung Tung was upbeat and supportive during the last painful and seemingly endless stages of page proofs and beyond.

I would also like to express my gratitude to my editor, Toby Wahl, who, once again, has displayed saint-like patience and unflappability during the occasional and inevitable moments of crisis. I would also like to thank Dale Rohrbaugh, who superintended the book's final crucial stages.

Last, but very much not least, I would like to thank all of the fans I have met and either spoken or corresponded with over the last ten years. Without them, this book would very literally not have been written. I cannot say how deeply I have been inspired, stimulated, and moved by their words in e-mails, questionnaires, or interviews. As previously mentioned, this was a very different project from anything I have ever taken on before, and, in many ways, I have learned more than I could ever have imagined by my interactions with this gregarious and creative group of people. I am only sorry that I could not have included many more of their stories but hope that the ones I do include will be at least somewhat representative of this fascinating and multifaceted culture.

Introduction

Orientalism, (Soft) Power, and Pleasure

The positive and negative transferences people make on countries are frequently just as powerful and just as "irrational" as are those they make on individuals.

—Dennis Porter, Haunted Journeys

The whole of Japan is a pure invention.

—Oscar Wilde, The Decay of Lying

It is an exquisite May morning in France. My companion and I join what seems to be a thousand or so other tourists as we walk up a slanted garden path flanked on both sides by irises. Inside the garden, flowers of all kinds overflow, but perhaps the most beautiful are the purple wisteria blossoms framing what is called the "Japanese bridge." Finally tearing ourselves away from the garden, we enter the small house, bright with spring sunlight and alive with colorful pictures, which jostle each other on virtually every wall.

This is Giverny, the home of Claude Monet, the most well-known of the French Impressionist painters. Every year thousands of tourists make the pilgrimage to this small town outside of Paris, but some come away disappointed. Inside the house, I hear mumbles of surprise and discontent: "Where are the Monets?" None of Monet's art is on the walls of Giverny. Instead, one of the greatest of all nineteenth-century European painters has chosen to festoon his house with Japanese prints and paintings—landscapes by Hokusai; birds, beasts, and flowers by Hiroshige; and costumed courtesans by Haranobu and Utamaro (see insert, Figure 7). Even the garden, although its profusion of flowers is undoubtedly Western, retains such Japanese elements as the bridge, the wisteria, and the irises.

Another vignette: This one takes place three thousand miles from France, on a hot summer day in Baltimore. I make my way to the convention center to register for a fan convention. Fortunately for me, I am a guest of the convention, so I do not need to stand in line. But as I approach the convention center my jaw drops: the line to register for the convention is so long that it snakes around the enormous civic building and goes toward the harbor. But it is not simply the size of the line that is a shock to me. At least half of the people in line are in costume. And what costumes! They range from girls in princess-style dresses with long flowing hair, to enigmatic figures in black with white masks where their faces should be, to children dressed up as cute animal figures. There are even some people in kimono or carrying Japanese swords.

This is Otakon or—to give it its full name—"Convention for Otaku Generation." Otaku is a Japanese word, which can be loosely translated as "obsessive fan," or "technogeek," although in America the word *otaku* can have "cool" connotations. Otakon is one of the biggest anime conventions in America. Like most conventions, or "cons," Otakon is a three-day extravaganza where fans of Japanese animation congregate to watch anime, buy anime and manga comics, take part in costume shows, hear Japanese pop music, and see their favorite *seiyu* (voice actors). And, of course, pose for the camera as they promenade through the convention center in their colorful outfits. I later learned that almost twenty thousand people, ranging in age from six to sixty, attended Otakon that summer.

Between Giverny and Otakon lies not only the Atlantic but also over one hundred years of history—a history in which Japan and the West have been entangled in a rich and complex tapestry of events, emotions, and religious and aesthetic movements, not to mention war, economic rivalry, and media and technological change. In the years since 1853, when the American naval officer Commodore Perry forced an isolationist Japan to open its doors, Western perceptions of Japan have gone through myriad transformations. Like a prism that emits different kinds of light and colors depending on the conditions under which one examines it, the image of Japan has been an incredibly protean one. The list of images, often wildly different but at other times overlapping, is long and sometimes surprising. At various moments "Japan," when viewed with Western eyes, has been: a nation of ascetic artists living in harmony with nature; a fascinating but faintly comic culture of ambitious men trying to beat the West at its own game; a vulnerable but erotic feminine presence eager to sacrifice herself for the Western male; a noble civilization of disciplined warriors; a brutal horde of subhuman soldiers intent on world domination; a culture of priests offering enlightenment to a world lost in material excess; a brutal horde of suit-wearing executives intent on destroying the American economy; and, most recently, a world of techno and pop culture innovation that is synonymous with the word "cool."

Throughout all these numerous changes in perception, it is difficult to find a single continuous thread: in the Western imagination, Japan has existed as an object of respect, fear, derision, admiration, and yearning, sometimes all at once. And yet, this very lack of a unified image may illuminate some of the reasons behind the depth and intensity of Western interactions with the country. Compared to other non-Western nations—such as those of the Middle East, China, or India—"Japan" seems to be harder to sum up in a few iconic words. Whereas, as Ronald Inden points out about India and China, "India" was often "understood" in terms of its caste system or its position as the land of

Imagination, and China for many centuries was characterized as the land of Reason and/or Oriental Despotism, Japan, which fully entered the Western world's consciousness much later, has been seen in a far wider variety of forms.[1]

And yet Japan also shares one major element with its fellow Eastern Others, and that is its position as an object of fantasy to the West or, more accurately, as the embodiment of a variety of fantasies to the West. I use the word "fantasy" to suggest a range of connotations. Generally, "fantasy" is interpreted in a positive light, as a wish-fulfilling dream, but it should be noted that there are dark fantasies as well. The anime fans who see in "their" Japan a place of creativity and even liberation would probably be surprised to learn that in their great-grandparents' time many Westerners saw the Japanese—along with the Chinese and other East Asian nations—as a source of terror, emblemized by the fantastic term "Yellow Peril, "a racist expression evoking a horde of Asians poised to invade the White nations of the world. Perhaps an equally important connotation is the fact that the word "fantasy" implies the imaginary, an alternative or even an opposition to reality, a reality which may be disappointing, dreary, or frightening.

To offer a psychoanalytic definition from Jean Laplanche and J. B. Pontalis, "fantasy is the *mise-en scene* of desire."[2] *Mise en scene* is a term used in theater and cinema indicating the setting and props of a performance; its use in this case suggests the constructed quality of fantasy. I might also mention the interactive nature of fantasy—though for many years fantasy was seen as a form of passive escape from the complications and tribulations of reality, recently scholars have come to realize that when we engage in fantasy, we are involving ourselves in a highly active pursuit, seeking out or even creating new worlds and new identities. Thus, when Oscar Wilde in his famous essay *The Decay of Lying* called Japan a land of "pure invention," he was talking much more about his fellow Europeans and their own needs and desires than he was about the specifics of Japanese culture.

This book is an attempt to explore the many fantasy Japans that have arisen in the eyes of the West since the 1850s. It is also an attempt to elucidate the means, motivations, and circumstances that framed the construction of these Japans. To do so, we must ask a range of questions: What factors came into play at what period? How important were politics, economics, and ideology? Did class and gender play a role, and if so, what sort of role did they play? What kind of person became fascinated by Japan? What led him or her to this fascination? And why a fascination with "Japan" as opposed to other imagined spaces?

A point I wish to emphasize is that the answers to these questions are often surprisingly complex. My reasons for highlighting this complexity have to do with my own motivations behind writing this book. Two factors were major inspirations: The first was a seminar that I taught for a number of years at the University of Texas, called "The 'Orient' in the Mind of the West." In the seminar, which was aimed at seniors in Asian studies, I tried to show students how a variety of approaches had helped to shape our conception of Asian countries and occasionally Middle Eastern countries as well. These approaches included novels and plays, such as Rudyard Kipling's *Kim* and Henry David Hwang's *M. Butterfly*; films, such as *Indiana Jones and the Temple of Doom* and *Lawrence of Arabia*; philosophical works ranging from the work of eighteenth-century Enlightenment writer Diderot to the twentieth-century semiotician Roland Barthes' book on Japan, *Empire of Signs*; and, finally, popular culture rock hits, such as David Bowie's *China Girl* and Steely Dan's *Bodhisattva*. I hoped that this array of Western responses to the Eastern Other would demonstrate to the students how complicated and fascinating cross-cultural interactions can be, issues that I wish to explore more fully in this book. Though the material varied year to year, we always started the first few weeks of the course with Edward Said's groundbreaking treatise *Orientalism*, followed by several critiques of Said by Western, Asian, and Middle Eastern scholars.[3]

I shall return to Said shortly, since his influence casts a long shadow over this book, but I also want to mention my second inspiration, which was my research on, and participation in, the world of anime fandom. In 2001 I published a book on Japanese animation, entitled *Anime from Akira to Princess Mononoke: Experiencing Japanese Animation* (revised and republished as *Anime from Akira to Howl's Moving Castle*, 2005). While *Anime* was mainly an exploration of the varieties of Japanese animation, the first edition also included a chapter on anime fandom in America. In the course of my research I became very intrigued by this phenomenon. Fortunately, my work on anime and my clear enthusiasm for the topic offered me a precious entrée into the world of fandom and, during the decade-plus that I have been involved with fandom, I became familiar with a great range of anime enthusiasts.

My contacts in the fan world and my own interest in the subject also offered a ringside seat to the surprisingly rapid penetration of anime, in specific, and Japanese popular culture, in general, into mainstream Western culture. When I began working on *Anime* in 1990, the word "anime" or the notion of Japanese animation as a genre would hardly have been recognized by the vast majority of Westerners. By the end of that decade, however, anime clubs were sprouting everywhere, in the heartland of America and Europe (I still remember walking into a small store in a village in Burgundy in 2000 and being confronted by five different magazines devoted to anime nestled on the journals shelf) and in high schools and middle schools where even boy scout troops would hold "anime nights." The terms "anime" and "manga" (the graphic novels that are frequently the inspiration for anime) had even become common enough to be used in crossword puzzles.

But it is not simply the enormous growth in anime's (and manga's) popularity that fascinated me. Rather, it was what I considered to be a genuinely unique aspect of this fandom—the fact that the "fan object" (i.e., anime) was a non-Western cultural product. I had initially believed that many fans were not particularly aware of anime's Japanese origin and were more interested in it as simply an enjoyable alternative medium. Over time, I began to realize that the Japanese aspect of anime (or, more precisely, the various aspects of anime that can be traced to Japan) was an extremely important part of many fans' overall attraction to it.

It is this last point that inspired the overall framework of this book. Anime fandom is a fascinating topic worthy of scholarly attention in itself, since the study of fan cultures in general has become a genuine academic field. As scholars of fan cultures tell us, fandom has been an increasingly important feature of industrialized society since the beginning of such mass cultural products as movies and radios. (Although we can also find earlier aspects of fandom in the feminine hysteria over the handsome musician Franz Liszt in the mid-nineteenth century or even as far back as fan-fights among Roman devotees of gladiator games.) But, in general, the fan objects have either remained tied to their country of origin or have been products of the tidal wave of American popular culture, which increasingly swept the world after World War II. With the advent of our current period of intense globalization, some commentators see American popular culture as so dominant that they fear it might end up eviscerating other local cultural products.

Enter anime. As film scholar Susan Pointon points out, anime, at least until very recently, has been uncompromisingly true to its Japanese roots, not only in terms of religious, social, and cultural references but also in relation to character conception, narrative structure, themes, and imagery.[4] But these very differences seemed to attract audiences all the more. Anime now appears throughout the world—in video stores, television broadcasts, and movie theaters, and ubiquitously on the Internet. Manga also have become enormously popular, growing from a few narrow offerings in comic book stores, to occupying increasingly large sections of such mainstream bookstore chains as Barnes and Noble and Borders, and even inspiring Western versions of the genre.

The fact that a non-Western cultural product should serve as an increasingly viable alternative to the American popular-culture dream factory is of enormous interest for a number of reasons. On a general level, it suggests that, even in the twenty-first century, the world is not nearly as homogeneous as might have been feared. Anime and manga clearly strike a chord by offering something different—stories, characters, and themes that were not only alternatives but were sometimes implicit critiques of the dominant Western entertainment industry. Furthermore, rather than being forced upon the public through mass advertising campaigns or other devices of some capitalist überestablishment, anime's popularity grew from a grassroots level, with considerable fan participation involved in its rise. Anime fandom's origins in the West are humble, beginning in the 1970s with the occasional screening in someone's room at a sci-fi convention or the excitement of a middle school student running home to catch the next installment of *Speed Racer* on afternoon television. Even now, although there are a number of reasonably established anime and manga import companies, fan involvement, particularly in cyberspace (e.g., downloading, subbing, and dubbing) is still crucial and ongoing.

But the phenomenon of anime fandom is also fascinating in terms of what it says about transcultural flows, both generally in relation to globalization and specifically regarding the history of the West's interaction with Japan. In a post-9/11 world in which interaction between different cultures seems to mainly inspire hatred and fear—be it of "French" fries or burkas—the notion that anime and other Japanese pop-cultural products have been embraced so heartily by an immense range of audiences around the world may offer one of the few benign visions of globalization currently available. Anime and Japanese popular culture have been held up by many commentators (including myself) as examples of "soft power." The political scientist Joseph Nye defines "soft power" by comparing it to "hard power," in which "military and economic might often get others to change their position." In contrast, "soft power" is seductive. It attracts; it "co-opts people rather than coerces them."[5] While Nye's initial discussions on this topic were largely confined to American power, the products of contemporary Japanese popular culture may also be seen as having a powerful seductive appeal of their own.

In relation to globalization on a historical level, anime's popularity is also thought-provoking. While some contemporary commentators tend to treat globalization as something utterly new, transcultural flows have been with us throughout human history. As I began my research into anime fandom, I became more and more aware that the anime and manga boom was not the first time that the West had become enamored of Japanese cultural products. Indeed, throughout the century-and-a-half since Japan's opening to the West, there have been a series of waves of interest in Japanese culture, a number of which have been as intense as the current fascination with Japanese popular culture. Furthermore, although some of these "waves" have been extremely negative ones, (most obviously during World War II but also during the "trade wars" of the 1980s), there were also long periods of time in which much of the attitude toward Japanese culture was frequently positive and often admiring.

This brings me back to the origins of this book. As I mentioned previously, the world of anime fandom is a worthy subject in itself, since it brings up questions of globalization, new media, and even aesthetic and philosophical values that shed light on where we are in the twenty-first century. However, it occurred to me that by contextualizing my insights on fandom within the larger historical and cultural framework of the 150 years of the changing Western perceptions of Japan, I might be able to deal with another extremely significant issue. This is the crucial question of the West's interaction with the Eastern Other, a field of study now known commonly as Orientalism—one of the most talked about theories in cultural studies today. One of the major themes of this book is that Japan, in its interactions with the West, from the nineteenth century to the present, adds some fascinating complexities to the theory of Orientalism, as developed by Edward Said.

Originally, Orientalism was a relatively neutral word referring to Western scholarship and arts related to the East, especially the Middle East and, somewhat more tangentially, South and East Asia. The Orientalist school of painters, for example, were French and English artists who specialized in picturesque renditions of the "exotic" East, from camels to casbahs. Orientalist scholars brought forth tracts on linguistics, history, and religions of the various Eastern regions of the world, while Orientalism in the arts included travelogues, such as *Flaubert in Egypt*; novels of eros and adventure in Eastern settings; and operas centering around mysterious sultans in splendid palaces, such as Mozart's *The Magic Flute*—in itself part of a long fascination for Turkey that had begun as early as the seventeenth century. As the nineteenth century wore on, it was perhaps not coincidental that most of these exotic locales were beginning to fall under the sway of European domination, either as outright building blocks in imperial Empires or as economic and political "spheres of influence" controlled by a European power.

It is this confluence of Western political and economic domination along with Western scholarship and arts in relation to the non-West that became the basic material for Said's groundbreaking book. Written in 1978, *Orientalism* has been described as a "bombshell,"[6] a bombshell that even several decades later continues to exert enormous influence on the study of non-Western cultures in general and the interaction between Western and non-Western cultures in particular. Summarizing Said's dense and complex text cannot do it justice, but its main points (and the ones particularly relevant to our discussion), revolve around Said's conception that the West's relation to the non-Western Other (in his book, this Other or "Orient" is almost exclusively Middle Eastern and/or Islamic civilization), has been built around unequal power relations in the which the West was consistently dominant and the Middle East was consistently subordinate.

While these points may seem obvious when looking at the history of military and economic exploitation by the Western powers over non-Western territories during the last two centuries, Said's most controversial emendation to this notion was his theory that all knowledge of, or even interest in, the Middle East on the part of Western civilization was inherently based on these unequal power relations. Thus, according to Said, the representation of the Middle East, or Islam, by the West—including not only scholars but government officials, writers, artists, and, potentially, film makers—was inherently prone to racism, essentializing (oversimplifying culturally specific institutions and entities), and stereotyping of the most denigrating sort. Or as Said puts it, "the essence of Orientalism is the ineradicable distinction between Western superiority and Oriental inferiority."[7]

Not surprisingly, Said's theory has been both extended and attacked since it first appeared. Scholars of other non-Western countries—particularly those of the South Asian subcontinent but also those who study East Asia and Africa—have found some, if not all, of its basic tenets extremely useful in understanding many of the [mis]representations these cultures have suffered through the years. On the other hand, many other scholars (including a number of Middle Eastern commentators) have taken Said to task for exactly some of the faults that his own book deplored, namely essentializing and misrepresentation. These include his overemphasis on binary oppositions (i.e., an "us" versus "them" mentality, with no room for admitting the complexity or ambivalence of attitudes between both "Orient" and "Occident," and which also left no possibility for a non-Western country's potential to "self-orientalize"); a lack of concern for gender and class issues; and, perhaps most importantly, an unwillingness to entertain the possibility of identification with the Other or the human need to find compensation for perceived shortcomings in one's own surroundings, which can be filled by a culture or society different from one's own. Or, as J. J. Clarke puts it, "While orientalism has undoubtedly been in some respects a means by which the West has achieved a measure of control over the intellectual and religious traditions of the East, the growth of orientalism has in other respects been marked by a growth in mutuality, in dialogue, in knowledge, and in sympathy. We must take into account that the East . . . has achieved power over the West by becoming a counter to and critique of fundamental aspects of Western culture."[8]

It is these aspects of Orientalism, or in this case what might be called "Japonisme," as critique and compensation, with which this book is particularly concerned. To give just a few examples: In the nineteenth century Japanese art challenged, and in some ways even revolutionized, European art, offering not only new ways of looking at space, light, and color but even implicitly a new value system where decorative arts and the craftsman became as important as "fine" arts and the salon painter. Visions of Japan as a pastoral utopia also served as compensation to artists and intellectuals troubled by the mounting wave of industrialization. In the late twentieth century the media of anime and manga countered the traditional notions of cartoons being only for children and may even have contributed to changing our consciousness as to what constitutes the nature of identity and reality. On a thematic level, manga and anime explorations of sexuality and romance offered not only compensation to young men uncertain about women, whom they increasingly saw as aggressive and selfish, but also a sense of liberation to gay and lesbian fans who found in the Japanese media representations of same-sex love, which were impossible in American media culture. The world of anime fandom itself can be seen as both liberating and compensating—allowing participants to try on new identities within a supportive communal space.

At the same time, however, the dark elements that Said discerns in Orientalism must not be ignored, since they occur in interactions between the West and Japan as well. These elements include unconscious and sometimes conscious racism, the frequent inability to see the Other in a three-dimensional light, the tendency to make sweeping generalizations about non-Western cultures, and frequently, a pernicious ignorance about the country of origin. Although I would contend that these dark elements are frequently balanced by positive interactions—at least on the level of culture and the arts—they still remain a fundamental element in the history of Western perceptions of Japan.

In this regard, Said's book and his subsequent writing, in which he, to some extent, modified the polemicism of Orientalism, has much to offer those of us who explore cultures different from our own. At its best, Orientalism provided a call for self-awareness on the part of scholars and commentators on other cultures, as they not only began to realize the hidden prejudices, stereotypes, and limited ways of thought embraced by previous commentators in their fields of study but also were made aware of the hidden ideological and attitudinal frameworks under which they themselves operated.

In the case of Japan, for example, there is no question racism, condescension, ignorance, and at certain points, sheer, almost mindless, hatred have eddied among the flow of discourse on the culture. This is most obvious during the period of World War II, when racist attitudes demonizing the Japanese people, and Japanese soldiers in particular, were essentially encouraged by the United States and other Western countries' propaganda. But during non-wartime periods, we can find demeaning portraits as well. For example, in Pierre Loti's popular nineteenth-century novel *Mme. Chrysanthéme*, which depicts a French lieutenant in Nagasaki, hardly a page goes by without the narrator wondering to himself whether the young *mousme* (a French derivation of the Japanese word *musume* or "young girl"), whom he has bought as his mistress, possesses a soul or even a brain.

Despite the availability of such teeth-grittingly offensive examples, when we look at the full range of Western views of Japanese culture starting in the nineteenth century, what is most striking is a relative lack of racism or belittlement, still less the "hostility and aggression" that Said claimed to invariably find when one culture [mis]represents another. Sometimes the praise for Japan, especially its aesthetics, verges on the fulsome. For example, John MacKenzie quotes the nineteenth-century British artist and critic Christopher Dresser, who, after a long journey throughout Japan where he visited sixty-eight potteries and "countless manufacturers of metalwork and woodwork, lacquer, fabrics, fans, baskets, bamboo, glass, and paper materials like wallpapers, fans, umbrellas etc." asked, "Who shall say that the Japanese are imperfectly civilized when they thus pay homage to learning and skill and prefer these to wealth? Is not their civilization rather higher than ours?"[9]

This is not to say that Japan and its culture were always represented accurately or truthfully. Many of the most enthusiastic aficionados of Japan, such as the artist Vincent Van Gogh, never even visited the country and derived their ideas about it from limited, and sometimes mistaken, information, which provided them just enough material to create imaginary Japans that fit their particular needs. Thus, what we see in the nineteenth-century conception of Japan is a complex fantasy, a living, breathing *tabula rasa* onto which Europeans and Americans projected a variety of desires, fears, dreams, and schemes. Ultimately, as we shall see, the *tabula rasa* became closer to something like an interactive video game where participants take Japanese material to construct their own playful yet complicated fantasies.

Again, I emphasize words such as "complexity" and "complicated," but other words could be used as well. Instead of the monolithic hegemonizing discourse whose only aim was to shore up "the formidable structure of cultural domination"[10] on the part of the West, which Said puts forth, I would suggest words such as "heterogeneous" "multivalent," "subversive," and (for the nineteenth century as well as the present), "soft power." Or, as J. J. Clarke suggests, "Orientalism cannot simply be identified with the ruling imperialist ideology, for in the Western context it represents a counter-movement, a subversive entelechy, albeit not a unified or consciously organized one, which in various ways has tended to subvert rather than confirm the discursive structures of imperial power."[11]

It is this counter-movement on the part of Orientalism that seems still surprisingly slow to be recognized. To return to my seminar, I should explain that my experience teaching Said in the classroom was a sobering one. Although I was careful to have the students read critiques of, and responses to, *Orientalism* by a variety of scholars, it was the power and, in certain ways, the simplicity of Said's theory that tended to stick in the students' minds. The paradigm of dominance and submission made the subsequent analyses of our texts seductively easy—perhaps too easy. It seemed to me that many of the works which we were considering, even ones from the era of High Imperialism, could not be shoehorned so easily into the paradigm. While I do not know enough about Western responses to China and India to say whether that interaction too can constitute a critique of Said's theory, my own awareness of Japan, not only as an area of expertise, but as an American who grew up in postwar America, suggested that Japan, at least, could not fit so simply into a theoretical straitjacket.

At the same time, my research into the anime-fan community was also subverting any simplistic notions of transcultural interaction and opening up ways for me to reinterpret the "Japan booms" of previous periods. As we will see in the latter part of this book, the fans, though they may not always be strictly accurate in their conceptions of Japan, are certainly not contemptuous of it nor, surprisingly, do they necessarily idealize it. Perhaps the safest assertion to make about them is that they *take pleasure* in the products of Japanese culture.

I italicize "*take pleasure*" because I think this is an element in East-West interaction that has been consistently important throughout history but has not been accorded enough significance. Perhaps this is because the word "pleasure" suggests frivolity or triviality. In a world which seems so much to be ruled by negative emotions and political and economic developments beyond the individual's control, the notion of pleasure may seem unimportant in comparison to the many complicated and painful demands of modern life.

Increasingly, however, scholars have found that what they call the "phenomenology of enjoyment" is an essential part of human life and human interaction. Often enjoyment is related to mastery and control but not in the sense of dominance and submission. Rather, as Mihaly Csikzentmihalyi describes it in his landmark book *Flow*:

> Yet we have all experienced times when, instead of being buffeted by anonymous forces, we do feel in control of our actions, masters of our fate. On the rare occasions that it happens, we feel a sense of exhilaration, a deep sense of enjoyment that is long cherished and that becomes a landmark in memory for what life should be like.... [I]t is what the painter feels when the colors on the canvas begin to set up a magnetic tension with each other, and a new *thing*, a living form, takes shape in front of the astonished creator.[12]

Pleasure, then, is something that is often experienced in relation to learning about or creating new things, thereby stimulating new emotional experiences, including a sense of mastery.

In this regard, it seems to me that the many Japan booms fit very well as manifestations of the phenomenology of enjoyment. From the Impressionists onward, the degree of active involvement with, inspiration from, and even identification with Japanese culture exhibited by many Westerners is surprisingly intense. Thus, Pissarro, Monet's fellow Impressionist, writes to his son after seeing an exhibition of Japanese prints that "Hiroshige is a marvelous impressionist. . . . I am pleased with my effects of snow and floods; these Japanese artists confirm my belief in our vision."[13] In writing in this way, Pissarro is not simply passively appreciating the beauty of the Japanese works, but also acknowledging the fact that his own labors in new aesthetic directions have been inspired and reaffirmed by artists from a very different country and culture. By calling Hiroshige an "impressionist" he consciously affirms his own identification with the Japanese artist. At the turn of the twentieth century, when martial arts and Bushido began to be exported, enthusiasts learned not only fighting techniques but also clearly culturally specific disciplines that added to their satisfaction in learning these new skills. Over a century later when anime enthusiasts tell me of how their interest in Japanese anime and manga have led them not only to learn Japanese but to translate and ultimately create their own manga, a similar sense of passionate engagement is at work.

Pleasure is, of course, also related to play, or what anthropologists call ludic activity. In my previous work on anime I developed the notion of something called the fantasyscape, based on Arjun Appadurai's theory that contemporary cultural flows belong to different "landscapes" such as "mediascapes" where communication is paramount or "financescapes," where economic activity is emphasized.[14] In the fantasyscape, play and setting are the two most important elements, creating a plethora of forms of virtual reality such as the densely constructed entertainment worlds of Disneyland and other theme parks, the intense involvements of video or online gaming, or the short-term but highly engaged gatherings of fan conventions. Fantasyscapes are inherently liminal worlds, temporary alternative lifestyles that exist parallel to the mundane, which people enter and exit when they please.

Obviously, human beings have engaged in fantasy entertainment—from telling stories, to acting in plays, since virtually the beginning of time. In a sense tribal initiations or even pilgrimages, both of which take place under otherworldly, liminal conditions, may be seen as precursors of the fantasyscape as well. But the rise of creative and interactive technology and the growing affluence on the part of the industrialized world have led, I would argue, to an increasing number and variety of these fantasyscapes, and an increasing participation in them around the world, from Indian aficionados of Bollywood cinema and its attendant stories and gossip, to the intense fan involvement in Latin American soap operas, to the passionate attachment many Americans feel toward professional sports and its subsidiary fan cultures.

The medium of anime itself—with its dazzling imagery, deeply involving narratives, and sympathetic characters—is certainly a form of fantasyscape. It is also one that has become more and more interactive over the years as fans have developed online chat rooms around their favorite series or directors and created music videos and fanfiction inspired by anime and manga. The large number of anime conventions that are virtual worlds in themselves are classic examples of concrete fantasyscapes in which the participants lose their real world identities—sometimes literally in the form of "cosplay" (costume play)—to indulge in ludic pleasures in a space securely outside mundane time and activities.

I would also suggest that the "fantasyscape," at least regarding Japanese culture, is more than just a simple escape. In a world where Enlightenment-type rationality is increasingly being called into question, aspects of Japanese culture—from the acknowledgment of the grotesque and the fantastic in woodblock prints, to the questioning of empirical reality implicit in Zen Buddhism, and even the densely encompassing world of anime fandom—have been useful in offering alternative ways of constructing or engaging with reality. As we shall see in our discussion of the Miyazaki Mailing List, for example, anime narratives or even the animated medium itself can present their audiences with different kinds of values that implicitly and sometimes explicitly call into question aspects of Western ideology.

Although one cannot draw a straight line between twenty-first-century fan culture and the waves of Japan enthusiasm beginning in the nineteenth century, I believe that the themes of pleasure, play, soft power, subversion and liberation, and the trope of the fantasyscape itself are still potentially applicable. In fact, as MacKenzie's book *Orientalism: History, Theory and the Arts* demonstrates, throughout the nineteenth and early twentieth century, Western perceptions of the "Orient" were strongly related to leisure, fantasy, and unreality. MacKenzie describes how Oriental gardens, Oriental decorations and Oriental architecture (or at least Western variations of them), were enthusiastically adopted by the Europeans. He concludes that, "By the end of the twentieth century Orientalism had certainly become the language of pleasure and relaxation."[15]

Some commentators might find the notion of the Orient's association with "pleasure and relaxation" to be a demeaning one, but MacKenzie as well as other commentators, such as J. J. Clarke, insist on its liberating aspect. He points out that "the East, however much it may have been a fabricated East, was used to unlock fresh personality traits, a richer engagement with expression, a wider scope for leisure and entertainment."[16] From my own vantage point in the first decade of the twenty-first century, where "leisure" and "virtual realities" have become a steadily more important feature of daily life, the relation between constructions of Japanese culture and ludic activity seems to be one worthy of serious consideration. "Play" and "pleasure" are now concepts that are treated with respect both on the level of society and regarding the individual. Although these activities often occur in group contexts and may be connected to outside sociocultural phenomena, it also important to remember that the participants in these activities—be they nineteenth-century French artists or twenty-first- century college students—are also individuals with their own specific backgrounds, attitudes, and tastes.

Matt Hills's remarks on the importance of "play" and "emotion" in fan culture are relevant here. He takes issue with the sociological position that often dismisses the role of individual taste and subjectivity and that chooses to emphasize outside factors, such as "cultural determinations." Instead, he suggests that "an approach is needed which preserves space both for the individual fan's psychology and for the cultural 'context' in which fan cultures exist."[17] Pointing out that it is impossible to get rid of individual subjectivity, he takes seriously the fact that the fans feel "possession," "ownership," and indeed "love" in relation to their fan objects. As he says, "Affective play 'creates culture' by forming a new tradition or a set of biographical and historical resources which can be drawn on throughout fans' lives."[18]

Throughout this book I try to pay attention not only to the historical events relating to the various waves of Japonisme but also to the individuals who became obsessed with, and even enamored of, Japanese culture. For example, although I deal with Lafcadio Hearn and Frank Lloyd Wright in the same chapter on "Collecting Japan," the enormous differences between the two men and their motivations are one of the reasons that the study of Japonisme is so fascinating. Jack Kerouac, the voice of the Beat Generation, also found something in Japanese Zen and haiku that first spoke to him on a deeply personal level, which he then tried to communicate to his readers. More recently, William Gibson, the father of the science-fiction genre cyberpunk, discovered in Japan a reaffirmation of his own views of the future. And of course in my chapters on anime fan culture I have tried to put forth the fans' individual voices and include some discussion of their background. Although it is impossible to discover any single overarching reason behind an individual's emotional involvement with another culture (be it negative or positive), a respect for those emotions is one of the bases for understanding transcultural flows.

The importance of emotional involvement with the Other is worth emphasizing because it is an aspect of East-West interaction either ignored or underrated by Said and his followers. Thus Inden, in his discussion of Orientalism, categorically privileges "knowledge" above "emotion," stating that

> A genuine critique of Orientalism does *not* revolve around the question of prejudice or bias, of the like or dislike of the peoples and cultures of Asia, or a lack either of objectivity or empathy. Emotions, attitudes and values are, to be sure, an important part of orientalist discourse, but they are not coterminous with the structure of ideas that constitute Orientalism or with the relationships of dominance embedded in that structure.[19]

In fact, I would argue that "emotions, attitudes, and values" are an *extremely* important part of Orientalist discourse, contributing mightily to "the structure of ideas that constitute Orientalism," for good or ill. As Said and other scholars have demonstrated, "knowledge" is never ideologically innocent nor emotionally objective. The knowledge that the Beat writers and poets, such as Kerouac, possessed and disseminated about Japan was mixed with inaccuracies and idealizations but it was fueled by his passionate love of Japanese haiku poetry and

Zen Buddhism, and an equally passionate hatred of the alienating modern society around him. On the opposite end of the emotional spectrum, the visions of the Japanese as "terminators of the future" embraced by some Americans during the trade wars of the 1980s was based partly on the objective facts of Japan's economic success story but at least as much on deeply nonobjective fears that frequently related to the American male's self-conception of his masculinity.

This returns me to the issue of the range of ways in which Japan has been perceived. Although the focus of this book is on the Western perceptions of "Japan" as a constructed fantasy, it is essential to remember that a real country exists at the source of these perceptions. Although, as I will argue, the enormous range of Western impressions of Japan came from specific cultural and historical needs and desires, it should also be acknowledged that events, developments, and products of Japan were the initial inspirations that stimulated Western ideas.

It should, therefore, be recognized that the immense variety of perceptions concerning Japan are very much based on the extraordinary history of Japan since its opening to the West. Over the last one hundred and fifty years, Japan has gone through an immense variety of changes. In 1853, when Perry forced open its doors, Japan was a semi-feudal island nation, which had enjoyed over two hundred years of peace under a military ruler known as the shogun. This long period of peace was probably due to a relatively rigid four-class system dominated by the ruling samurai class, a surprisingly large warrior elite who, while still engaged in military discipline, had become increasingly adept and literate bureaucrats. It was also no doubt due to the fact that during this period Japan maintained a policy of isolations vis-à-vis other nations. While the Dutch maintained a small presence on the island of Dejima outside of Nagasaki, contact with other countries was largely prohibited by the shogunate.

A few decades after Perry, this system would be totally transformed—the four-class system and the samurai caste who ran it swept away by a mammoth wave of modernization and Westernization, in which the Japanese eagerly tried to import ideas from abroad. Unusually, this was a wave that the new Japanese elite was trying to control, or at least engage with, in a wholesale attempt to avoid following the colonial or at least semi-colonial fates of its neighbors, China and India, and, ultimately, virtually all of the rest of Asia, the Middle East, and Africa. While Japan could not entirely avoid some initial Western dominance in the form of the forced opening of a number of its ports and an unequal treaty system, the country is one of the very few non-Western nations that retained its independence throughout the most intense years of Western imperialism.

A lengthy discussion of why Japan was able to remain uncolonized is outside the scope of this book, but there are a few reasons that should briefly be mentioned. One of them is luck: Because Japan was small and had few resources, it escaped the rapacious attentions of the Western powers for a long time. And when the West finally did turn more fully to Japan, the country was somewhat prepared, thanks to the disturbing models of the British Raj in India and the Western spheres of influence over China. Witnessing this cultural, economic, and military oppression, the Japanese determined to try to avoid such a fate if at all possible.

The fact that the Japanese did not fall under colonial sway might have been an important reason for the rather different attitudes held by the West toward Japan, in comparison to the contempt that was often visible on the part of the West toward its territories. Although early on the Japanese were looked at sometimes with amused condescension, even from the 1860s we can also find evidence of surprise and grudging respect as the Japanese began their attempt to modernize. For it must be said that the Japanese response to the threat of imperialism was both impressive and unprecedented. Perhaps because it had a relatively large and highly literate elite at the beginning of Westernization, the Japanese were able to put through a truly remarkable variety of reforms—including the disenfranchisement of the samurai class (although once their swords were taken, many of them became important participants in the new civil society), wholesale educational and governmental reforms based on Western models, a fervent embrace of the capitalist system, and, tragically, not only the total adoption of Western military techniques but of Western military and colonial aspirations as well.

All of these moves might be classified under the overall framework of what might be called "beating the West at its own game," a game in which, to a truly remarkable degree, the Japanese succeeded. This success spawned an even more complex variety of reactions by the Western powers. These included patronizing interest on the part of Western observers in the mid-nineteenth century as the Japanese arrived in Europe and America to try to learn more about these countries, and genuine surprise and interest as they watched the Japanese begin to appropriate and imitate Western technology (with a little help from Western advisors) by the late nineteenth century. In the early twentieth century surprise and condescension began to turn to astonished and sometimes wary respect as the Japanese first waged war against China in 1896, defeated it, and then, to the utter shock of the rest of the world, was victorious in a struggle with Russia in 1905.

Japan's hard power was bolstered by a continuous stream of soft-power successes. The tremendous admiration for Japanese arts and crafts that had been sweeping Europe and the United States since the late nineteenth century, combined with the respect toward the country's impressive military victories and the fact that they had become an imperialist power in their own right, meant that the West had to take Japan far more seriously. Soon, respect and admiration began to intertwine with a growing fear that Japan was becoming too good at following the path of Western imperialism. Ultimately, Japan's growing empire would provoke a backlash in the 1920s and 1930s as the European nations, in a panic that was partly racist and partly competitive, began to try to freeze the country out of great power status. In turn, these actions helped push the Japanese in an even more aggressive direction, the final fruits of which were their invasion of China, their attack on Pearl Harbor, and their ultimate defeat at the hands of American atomic bombs.

The overwhelming defeat led to another extraordinary chapter in Japan's relations with the West: the American Occupation, which lasted from 1945 to 1952 and in some ways further transformed the country. In all amazingly short period of time Japan went from brutal inhuman enemy to subservient little brother (and sister) in the eyes of the American occupiers. But even more intense changes were to come. In an astonishing turnaround the postwar Japanese economy revived and soon was growing well beyond prewar levels. The period of "double digit" economic growth in the 1960s eventually led it to becoming the world's second largest economy and, not coincidentally, to being perceived as a distinct and sinister threat to the American economy. Undoubtedly racist attitudes were at work here (as well as some legitimate criticisms of Japan's trade practices) and these finally reached a crescendo of panicky reactions in the 1980s as many Americans began to believe that Japan had actually "won" the war and was now threatening the American way of life.

Just when it seemed that Japanese-American relations had reached a boiling point, in 1989 the Japanese economy entered a deep recession, which they have only recently begun to climb out of. The response of the Western media seemed to involve a certain amount of celebration as commentators who had been warning of the "Pacific Century" were elbowed out by others who emphasized the "coming collapse" of the Japanese economy. In fact, these latter commentators were quite accurate about certain fragilities in Japan's success, most notably the collapse of the real estate "bubble" that, even a decade later, had still not worked its way completely through the Japanese system, but the tone of barely disguised glee and even invective in some of their descriptions can be disturbing.[20]

In any case, by the 1990s it seemed as if Japan were about to be "written off" from the world stage, a once exciting economy, which now seemed to be drowning in red ink and misjudgment. It was just at this period, however, that the anime and pop culture boom began to take off. There are many reasons behind this boom, but one of them is surely the revolution in technology, which allowed the rapid dissemination of anime across the world. As noted previously, what some commentators referred to as an "anime explosion" began very much at a humble grass-roots level and was spread initially largely through word of mouth. But this "word of mouth" was very much of the electronic kind. As early as 1995 *Wired Magazine* noted that the anime fan community was perhaps the most "wired" community of all the fan subcultures.[21] Also by the mid-1990s, the VCR explosion was beginning to crescendo, to be followed soon after by the development of DVDs. By the twenty-first century fans were downloading the latest anime directly off the Internet. Suddenly, in ways that the nineteenth-century aficionados of Japanese culture could not have imagined, the products of Japanese popular culture were ubiquitously available.

Of course, had the products themselves been mediocre or uninteresting, then the anime and manga boom would never have occurred. The last section of this book will discuss in detail the appeal in particular of anime, but for now it is worth noting that anime's dense narratives, psychological complexity, stunning visuals, and the sheer excitement of the medium itself are consistently cited by the fans to explain their attraction to it. Similarly, fans of manga mention how much they enjoy the beautiful drawing, the imaginative humor, and the heartfelt, emotionally nuanced stories of many manga narratives.

To some extent we can see these elements as being presaged in earlier Japan booms. Although, again, I wish to stress that I do not see a direct line between earlier waves of interest in Japan and the pop-culture boom of the millennial years, it is still useful to be aware that Europeans were attracted by the sheer visual beauty, different artistic techniques, and the intriguing range of subject material on display in the woodblock prints being imported from Japan. In the twentieth century readers of Lafcadio Hearn's stories derived from Japanese folklore or Arthur Waley's translation of the eleventh-century masterpiece *The Tale of Genji* were also swept away by the psychological subtlety, diverse themes, and masterful storytelling of Japanese storytellers.

It must also be acknowledged that the Japanese themselves have done much to help export Japanese culture to the world, sometimes in a fashion so eager and so self-conscious as to be labeled "self-orientalizing." This process has been going on since the nineteenth century when the Japanese chose with immense care the kind of products and architecture that would be exhibited at the many popular World Expositions that were themselves an early form of fantasyscape. Of course, other countries engaged in this kind of careful self-promotion as well, but it must be admitted that the Japanese seemed to have been particularly successful at it, on both a governmental and individual level. For example, as Christopher Benfey chronicles, early twentieth-century Boston was host to the brilliant, handsome, and charismatic Okakura Kakuzo, whose demonstrations of, and writings on, the tea ceremony helped him (and the tea ceremony itself) establish a kind of cult following among Boston ladies, even though tea had originally been a samurai activity. Benfey points out that Okakura's famous *Book of Tea* "suggested to Boston audiences that aestheticism and militarism—beauty and war—might be creatively combined."[22]

At a time when the United States was dealing with its growth as a military power, while at the same time suffering insecurities about its degree of "civilization" vis-à-vis the old powers of Europe, the tea ceremony might well have served as an attractive role model for working through some of these cultural anxieties. As Benfey also documents, President Theodore Roosevelt, himself an example of the military and the cultured, was apparently intrigued by the relationship between the martial art of jujitsu and medieval chivalry. Although it is uncertain whether Roosevelt actually read *Bushido*, the famous self-Orientalist work on the soul of the Japanese samurai, by the scholar Inazo Nitobe, he at least *claimed* to have.[23]

Having Japanese culture taken seriously by the president of the United States would have meant a great deal to the new Japanese nation, acutely aware of its anomalous position as an Asian power among Western nations. Indeed, Koichi Iwabuchi sees this tendency toward self-Orientalism in many ways as a conscious strategy to position Japan as strongly as possible in relation both the West and at the expense of its fellow Asian countries. As he says, "Japan is presented and represents itself as culturally exclusive, homogeneous, and uniquely particularistic through the operation of a strategic binary opposition between two imaginary cultural entities 'Japan' and 'the West.'"[24] When Japan did notice its

Asian connections, it performed an even higher degree of Orientalizing itself. As Jennifer Robertson points out about the wartime performances of the entertainment group Takarazuka, "[it implicitly promoted a specifically Japanese orientalism characteriz[ing] both colonial policy and revues built around the themes of Japanese cultural superiority and military supremacy."[25]

Although works such as *The Book of Tea* or *Bushido* hardly amount to a sinister plot to infiltrate the West with Japanese ideals, they do show that representatives of Japan took their role as cultural ambassadors very seriously. And this is still the case in contemporary Japanese-Western relations, as an anecdote from my own experience demonstrates. In 1989, when I was living in London, the United Kingdom in association with the Japanese government put on an enormous country-wide Japan Festival, which included everything from building a Japanese garden in Holland Park in London, to Kabuki performances in the provinces, to taking over much of the renowned Victoria and Albert Museum to stage what might be called a "Contemporary Japan Sound and Light Show," complete with pachinko machines and robots. There was one thing that was missing, however, and that was any reference to anime and manga at the Victoria and Albert. I had already become intrigued by these media and began asking where I might find anything about them. Finally, I was told that there was a small exhibition of Japanese manga at some obscure gallery across the Thames River. When I asked why so little mention was being made, I was told in confidence that the Japanese government did not want to present such a "trivial" art form to the British public! So much for contemporary popular culture.

A few years later when I returned to the United States, however, I discovered to my amusement and surprise that in the intervening period the Japanese government had changed its mind. In fact, they had issued a "white paper" strongly supporting the export of anime and manga as important representatives of modern Japanese culture. Not only that, these exports also helped make money for Japan as they became increasingly popular around the world. A few years later I was invited by the Bureau of Culture of the Japanese government to give a talk on anime and manga for an Association of South East Asian Nations (ASEAN) meeting in Tokyo. In what could be called a globalizing moment, I, an American woman, lectured in Japan about Japanese culture to representatives of Southeast Asian nations, many of whom told me afterward how much they loved the films of Japan's greatest animator, Hayao Miyazaki.

Clearly, play, pleasure, and art are essential aspects of the globalizing world we live in. They are economically and strategically important, of course, but they also might serve a deeper purpose: to release us from the irksome mental straitjackets that bind us to conceptions of ourselves as one-dimensional human beings with a narrow range of loves and loyalties. On the one hand, the history of Japan's interactions with the West is a frequently unhappy one, marred by mistrust and misunderstandings so deep as to lead to global tragedy. On the other hand, the moments of cultural liberation chronicled in this book suggest that tragedy does not always have to be the result of transcultural interaction. "Soft power" might be an ambiguous concept that carries its own potential for manipulation or abuse, but, compared to the other kinds of forces let loose in the world today, it is still a welcome addition to the weaponry of ideas.

This book attempts to span one hundred and fifty years of the West's interaction with Japan. Because both subject and time span are so broad, inevitably certain areas will be explored more than others. Often this was because other scholars have already done so much in these areas that it seemed almost hubristic to try to match their contributions, such as Christopher Benfey on the Japanese impact on gilded age America or John Dower on the fraught relationship between Japan and America during wartime and Occupation. Furthermore, since this book is primarily a cultural history, political and military events are only referred to when they seem particularly relevant to whatever cultural subject I am examining.

The book is organized into two basic parts—a chronological study of the influence of Japanese culture in the West until the 1980s, plus a chapter examining the role of the Japanese women in Western fantasy, and an in-depth study of Japanese popular culture's impact in the West, especially regarding anime and manga fandom. By organizing the book's thematic structure around play, pleasure, and soft power, I was able, I hope, to justify the amount of space I have given Japanese popular culture and anime fandom. While I do not see anime and manga fandom as emanating directly from the earlier waves of Japonisme that swept the West, I do see it as having fascinating similarities to these earlier booms, at the same time as being a unique and intriguing cultural phenomenon in itself.

The scope of this book is an ambitious one and I hope I have brought enough qualifications to it. My own immersion into Japanese and East Asian culture is perhaps illuminating in terms of explaining Japan's appeal to the West and the possible connections between a fascination with Japan and fan culture. My parents were academics, my father an historian, my mother an art historian, and, at the age of ten, they took me to Europe with them on sabbatical. Unfortunately, I did not appreciate the cultural opportunities I was offered and spent most of my year there immersed in poetry, fantasy, and science fiction.

By the next year when we had returned home to Boston, my parents had clearly despaired of my ever showing any interest in "high" culture. One day, however, we were eating lunch at a Chinese restaurant underneath a scroll of a temple with cherry blossoms. "I like that," I said spontaneously at which my mother pricked up her ears. In no time at all she had whisked me over to the Museum of Fine Arts, where I fell in love with the museum's superb collection of East Asian landscape scrolls, woodblock prints, and Buddhist sculptures. Perhaps the fact that we had returned to an America rocked by the revolution of the 1960s made the refined and reposed collection all the more attractive to me. Along with my continuing interest in fantasy and science fiction, East Asian art offered a welcome refuge from the chaos overwhelming the universities and schools around us. Soon after, I discovered the ubiquitous haiku poetry books that were floating around during that period and again fell in love with the beautiful imagery and spare lyricism of the poetry. When the head of my high school asked me what I wanted to study as a second language I replied "Japanese" and she immediately started looking for a tutor. This was long before the days when Japanese was routinely offered in high schools, but a young Harvard graduate student was found to teach me.

Throughout all of this my parents were supportive and enthusiastic. My mother who had studied the philosophy of William James as an undergraduate, gave me books on Confucius, whom she seemed to feel had developed a Chinese version of Jamesian pragmatism. My father paid for my tutoring and for the air fare that sent me to Japan to live during my senior year in high school.

Given this supportive introduction to Japanese and East Asian culture, it is perhaps not surprising that I have tended to notice the positive interactions between Japan and the West. At the same time, it must be acknowledged that Japan also served as an alternative space for me, along with popular literature. Perhaps for this reason, in my exploration of anime for my book on the subject, I became fascinated by the anime fan culture. Getting inside fan culture as both a scholar and as a participant has been an exciting and sometimes wrenching experience. Although I will probably never be a hardcore fan, I empathized with many of the fan narratives I heard and became friendly with a number of the participants.

I still recall a delightful dinner at the beautiful Hotel Fort in Des Moines which was hosting an anime convention that weekend. Tired of the nonstop intensity of the convention, I escaped into the hotel's staid dining room to find an attractive woman about my age placidly eating dinner while wearing a pink and blue costume from the popular anime series *Revolutionary Girl Utena* (Shojo kakumei utena). The other diners, all dressed in chic evening wear, hardly seemed to notice her. Over a couple of fancy desserts, however, she and I got to chatting and I discovered that she was a librarian, who had recently lost her job. "Utena is like my role model," she told me earnestly. "She's so tough and kind and brave. Wearing this costume and coming to this 'con' helps me keep going, even when I'm worried about the future." After dinner I reflected on our conversation and wondered if "Utena" could be seen as coming from "anime culture" or "Japanese culture." The rest of this book is partly an attempt to answer that question; although I should warn the reader that the answer is an ambiguous one. What is clear is that over the last century and a half "Japan" and its products have animated the Western imagination in an extraordinary variety of ways, from Impressionism to anime and much more.

Japonisme from Monet to Van Gogh: "Above All to Make You See"[1]

Nowadays even idiots and women are touched by the craze for Japanese things.

—*Jules de Goncourt*, The Goncourt Journals

Each [artist] assimilated from Japanese art the qualities that revealed the closest affinities with their own gifts and all found confirmation rather than inspiration of their personal modes of seeing, feeling, understanding and interpreting nature.

—*Ernest Chesneau, "Le Japon à Paris"*

Japonisme; A small craze that had become a huge international business.

—The Origins of Art Nouveau

She stands before us, head slightly cocked, staring out at her viewers with a charming but enigmatic smile. On the wall behind her and on the floor paper fans with designs from Japanese woodblock prints are scattered in semi-circular fashion. Her kimono, (actually a Kabuki actor's robe), is a swirl of intense red that drapes smoothly around her lithe body and makes her appear to be almost floating among the fans. On the kimono is embroidered a large figure of a Japanese warrior who seems to be in the midst of emerging from the region just below her hips. Letting our gaze travel up again, we see that the only part of her body that is actually visible aside from her face is her alabaster white arm, emerging from the deep sleeve of her robe and holding a fan, its red white and blue bands echoing the French flag, while its crescent curve makes an effective contrast to the tilted blonde head.

Yes, blonde. Despite the painting's title, La Japonaise (The Japanese Lady), the young woman depicted is definitely not Japanese (see insert, Figure 8). In fact, she is the wife of the artist, Claude Monet, perhaps the most famous of the French Impressionists, and the man whose works, from haystacks to water lillies, are among the most beloved in all of Western art. Monet and his fellow

Impressionists are justifiably known for a variety of stunning artistic innovations that ultimately changed the face of art. They departed from the stiff gloomy conventions of the officially sanctioned Academy and the grand melodrama of the Romantics to open up a world of movement, color, light, and nature that would lead in many directions, from the emotional intensity of Van Gogh and Gauguin to the experimental freedoms of the Expressionists and finally to abstract art and beyond. The influences on the Impressionists were many and varied but a major one was Japan—and not only its art, but its culture as a whole, or at least what the Europeans perceived it to be. The artistic debt the Impressionists and the artists who followed them held toward Japan has long been recognized (starting with the artists themselves and their contemporaries), but only recently has the degree of that debt begun to be fully explored.

From our twenty-first-century viewpoint, Monet's *La Japonaise* (first exhibited in 1876) can be looked at as a kind of impudent "cosplay" (costume play) of both an aesthetic and ideological type. With this picture Monet is having his wife "try on" a new identity, one that is still essentially European (after all, the lady holds a fan with the French colors), but one that is imbued with Otherness, from the controversial subject matter and the vivid colors and bold brushstrokes to the emphasis on the kimono rather than the model (leading one scholar to call *La Japonaise* a "Kimono still life").

In recent years film and art criticism has made much of the "gaze." Initially this term referred to the look directed from the audience at the subject portrayed in cinema, painting, or photography, but the term can also include the gaze of the director/artist and, until recently, was seen as usually belonging to a male. In the case of *La Japonaise*, whose gaze are we discussing? Most generally we are talking about the gaze of Western civilization, which at that period was often identified with the male. What was Western civilization to make of this strange hybrid? Why had Monet chosen to depict his wife in such a manner? What was going on in the nineteenth century that inspired the creation of such a portrait (and many others on similar themes)? And finally, what about Mme. Monet's own "gaze" (or should we say the gaze of *La Japonaise*)? Her face stares out at the viewer impudent and cheerful, as if daring the viewer to react.

La Japonaise was a brightly colored gauntlet thrown down as a challenge to the stuffy and elitist Salons that controlled the artistic world of nineteenth-century Europe. In the picture Monet was still to some extent merely playing with the exotic, but ultimately the influence of Japanese art would penetrate far more deeply and lead to a far more radical vision than a kimono and a swirl of fans. As the curators of the exhibit, "Monet and Japan," note, "It is difficult to imagine how outlandish Monet's paintings appeared to most of his contemporaries. His work embodied strange new ways of seeing, deriving from the experiences of modern life."[2]

For the viewers of *La Japonaise*, "modern life" was in many ways a very new and still disorienting experience. It involved a variety of new kinds of activities. These included new forms of transportation—particularly the train, the steamship, and, later on, the bicycle—and new forms of leisure activities, such as visiting the increasingly ubiquitous international expositions, which served as windows to a steadily widening world, or shopping in the grand new emporia known as "department stores." "Modern life" also would change the way people worked, as the individual craftsman began to be replaced by the factory worker and the newly empowered bourgeoisie would produce "captains of industry" to supervise the factories. Most fundamentally, it would change the way people looked at the world, from the new technology of photography to the new discoveries and theories of Darwin and Spenser. These latter, plus the many significant scientific discoveries of the period, would lead to what Eric Hobsbawm calls the "secular ideology of progress"[3] that would dominate the latter part of the century.

La Japonaise was part of these changes, a portrait that could not have been painted in the previous century. Even at this point, it created quite a sensation. Monet at this still early point in his career was regarded with suspicion if not contempt, as were his other fellow Impressionists. Contemporary opinion on the picture was divided. One writer exclaimed,

> What! Can this Japanese woman who stands in her blinding red robe, between fans that flutter around her head like butterflies and a fantastic character embroidered on the silk, who escapes from the folds of the material with more reality than she who wears it—be a specimen of the future?[4]

Others seem a trifle condescending. One critic describes her robe as a "magnificent dressing gown of red flannel," while Mme. Monet's head appears to be "taken from a Parisian hairdresser's window."[5] Another insists that he "won't speak of a certain woman draped bizarrely in red costume, fanning herself and framed by about thirty Japanese fans. Doubtless he [Monet] wanted to create a shock and that's all."[6]

Others felt the need to point out *exactly* where the warrior was positioned, so they could more effectively register their disgust. As one puts it, "The figure of the samurai unsheathing his sword at a suggestive part of the woman's body is certainly extraordinary."[7] Another fastidiously (and inaccurately) describes the warrior as a "monster" that is "placed we dare not say where."[8]

Perhaps the critics had a right to be disturbed. Like the warrior emerging from the red depths of the kimono, "Japanese art was alien, an irruption from an unknown, dreamlike culture and, as such it was to be a constant challenge to Monet's vision."[9] But the challenge was not simply to Monet. The artistic realm that *La Japonaise* and other, even more challenging works was ushering in would not only open up new artistic directions but would ultimately create new ways of approaching the world, a world that was changing rapidly and relentlessly. In that sense, the writer who suggested that *La Japonaise* was a "specimen of the future" turned out to be remarkably prescient.

At the time of its exhibition, however, the picture was most likely viewed as representative of current fashion, most specifically the fascination with Japan that was sweeping over Europe. This fashion was called "Japonisme" and was linked with other new words, such as "Japonaisairie" (exotic Japanese esque creations—*La Japonaise* could be included in this), "japoniserî, etc. Ultimately, the cult of Japan would spread from bohemian artists and intellectuals, who became fascinated by the new vision that Japanese culture seemed to present, to upper-class women wearing the latest kimono-inspired fashions, to the newly emergent middle class, who would decorate their parlors with Japanese curios and fans.

Monet's portrait was representative of what was already a flood of European paintings depicting women, and sometimes men, in Japanese costume or surrounded by Japanese paraphernalia. These ranged from the obvious crowd pleasers, such as James Tissot's overtly sexual *La Japonaise au bain* (The Japanese Lady at Her Bath), in which a dark-haired but obviously Caucasian woman poses flirtatiously in an untied kimono, which conceals very little of her opulent charms,(1864), to the more subtle, if intellectually provocative, such as another famous Impressionist Edouard Manet's restrained *Portrait of the Writer Emile Zola* (1867–68). This picture depicts the famous author, an avid collector of Japanese items, sitting with a Japanese screen behind him and a print of a Kabuki actor above him. Intriguingly, Manet also included a copy of one of his own most controversial paintings, *Olympia*—a portrait of a nude Caucasian woman with her black female servant—next to the Kabuki actor print, as if highlighting the revolutionary potential of both Japanese art and his own.

The fans that surround Mme. Monet in *La Japonaise* are indicative of another related fashion—the fascination with inexpensive Japanese paraphernalia, most especially the fan, as decorative motifs This fashion was not limited to artists (although such famous names as Degas, Pissaro, and Gauguin not only painted pictures *of* fans but painted *on* fans as well) but became incredibly popular with the burgeoning middle classes, looking for something inexpensive but beautiful with a touch of the exotic to display in their homes. In fact, according to Lionel Lambourne, in his book *Japonisme*, "literally millions"[10] of fans were made in Japan in the 1880s for the export market.

But the importance of *La Japonaise* lies in far more than its overtly Japanese flourishes. The subject matter itself marked an important change in what artists heretofore had usually depicted. Although beautiful women were time-honored subjects in classical and neoclassical painting, perhaps what most shocked contemporary critics was the notion of a respectable married woman posing in a fashion that was suggestive of the courtesan. The fact that Mme. Monet is clearly enjoying playing a part is also interesting, hinting at a fluidity of identity that we take for granted now but at that period would have been considered radical in a society where men and women knew their place. The picture has clearly erotic and, to contemporaries, vulgar connotations. (In fact, Monet himself years later referred to it as "a piece of filth."[11]) Not only did it show the aforementioned "monster" appearing out of the woman's hips but one fan at an angle to Mme. Monet's face has an obvious Japanese courtesan's visage depicted on it, implicitly underlining a link between Monet's wife and the pleasure quarters, or what in France was known as the *demimonde*. By the time of *La Japonaise*'s exhibtion, at least some of the audience would have been familiar with the erotic

Japanese prints known as *shunga*, which depicted courtesans and their clients, and this possible link might have disturbed (and titillated) viewers even more.

The message of *La Japonaise* and other Japanese-themed pictures from the period was far from simply salacious, however. They, and the original Japanese works that inspired them, suggested different approaches to representing the world around them. For many French artists, the willingness of Japanese artists to portray the world outside of the upper classes or historical figures had revolutionary significance. Although initially shocking, *La Japonaise*'s sense of playfulness and implicit celebration of different types of social and racial mixing were themes that would become more and more popular as artists turned away from the depiction of heroes, nobility, and picturesque peasants to celebrating what Rathbone and Halford Macleod term "the new social realities of the late nineteenth century."[12] These would include the everyday pleasures of the increasingly affluent middle class portrayed in such pictures as Renoir's joyous *Luncheon of the Boating Party* (1880–81) and *Dance at Bougival* (1883), or the increasingly explicit depictions of Paris's own "pleasure quarters" exemplified in Toulouse Lautrec's turn-of-the-century posters of dancers at the Moulin Rouge (Figures 1 and 2).

What is perhaps finally the most potentially radical aspect of *La Japonaise*, however, is its engagement with new forms of representation. This engagement is brushed upon by the critic who insisted that the warrior embroidered on the robe had "more reality" than the woman herself. By this period, the Enlightenment view of a single fixed reality was beginning to change in tandem with the new ways of seeing the world, which Impressionism and its artistic descendants would exemplify. As the catalogue for "Monet and Japan" describes it, "In the figure [of Mme Monet] two forms of representation, that of the woman and that of the embroidered warrior, seem to fight it out in the paint, while the fans speak of other more abstract modes of painting."[13]

As the nineteenth century continued and as art (and literature) began to explore avenues further and further away from classical realism, the notion of what is real versus what is fake or fantastic would become more and more ambiguous. *La Japonaise* exemplifies this. The title itself calls attention to the painting's unreality. Mme. Monet's vivid blonde head, actually a wig (which the critic who suggested that the "head came from a shop window" was clearly pointing out), shows that Monet was not even attempting to pretend that he was depicting a real "Japonaise" (in contrast to Tissot's seductive bath picture, where his model at least has dark hair and dark eyes). Indeed, the rather doll-like head suggests yet another form of reality: is Monet hinting that his model is only a puppet, strung up on the wires of the cult of Japonisme?

While *La Japonaise* calls into question our notions of representation, Japan itself would become a phenomenon that was both real and unreal; its representation would be subject to an enormous variety of approaches, as Westerners discovered and developed their own versions of the country and its culture. While many of these versions have some basis in fact, it is clear that most representations of Japan incorporated a notable degree of fantasy. A well-known quotation from Oscar Wilde sums up the special position that Japan seemed to

Figure 1
Dance at Bougival, 1883
Museum of Fine Arts, Boston
Picture Fund
Photograph © Museum of Fine Arts, Boston

Figure 2
Poster for the cabaret Divan Japonais,
published version, 1893
Museum of Fine Arts, Boston
Lee M. Friedman Fund
Photograph © Museum of Fine Arts, Boston

occupy by the end of the nineteenth century: "The whole of Japan is a pure invention. There is no such country. There are no such people If you desire to see a Japanese effect, you will stay at home and steep yourself in the work of certain Japanese artists."[14]

Of course Japan was not the only fantasy country of which Westerners had dreamed. China, India, the Ottoman Empire, Arabia (and later on Tahiti, Oceania, and Africa) all held special allures that would inspire Westerners on all fronts, from the intellectual and cultural to the economic and political. But it seems safe to say that the fascination with Japanese art and culture has been one of the most intense, most pervasive, most long lasting, and in many ways the most positive of any of the Western encounters with the non-Western other. At its most intense, Japonisme (the cult of Japan) lasted about thirty years, but, as this book will show, Japanese art and culture, both high and popular, has remained an almost continuous influence from the nineteenth century to the present.

Leaving the art world for the moment, let us turn to history. Where and how did Japonisme begin? While the closed empire of Japan had been forcibly opened by the American Commodore Matthew Perry in 1853, most commentators agree that Japan really hit Western radar screens with its participation in a series of International Exhibitions that began in the 1860s. The well-received Japanese installation at the Paris Exposition of 1867 helped to open the floodgates of interest in Japan, but perhaps the most significant Japanese success was at the 1878 Universal Exposition held in Paris, where the Japanese installation was praised beyond those of any other country's. Like today's world's fairs these exhibitions were ways in which countries could vie with each other on the cultural and aesthetic front—essentially an internationally sanctioned way to create or confirm positive images of themselves. For the Japanese this was particularly crucial. At a time when a Darwinian assessment of nations was in ascendance, the Japanese wanted to establish themselves as a culture worth taking seriously. In this regard they were notably successful, justifying the enormous amounts of effort and money expended by the Japanese government at each international fair. Thus Japan, more than most other non-Western nations, was associated with the affects of pleasure and play from almost the beginning of its interaction with the West.

The success of the Exposition of 1878 was not only an exemplar of the cult of Japonisme that was already reigning but a spur to even further fascination on the part of the Europeans. Not only were the Japanese pavilion, garden, farm, and tea house extensively admired and discussed, but the people whose culture had produced such beauty increasingly became an object of fascination in themselves.

This development is obvious in an article entitled "Le Japon à Paris" (Japan in Paris) written by the critic Ernest Chesneau, and published in the journal *Gazettes des Beaux Arts*, a magazine devoted to the fine arts. Although ostensibly a response to the Exposition, the article is most interesting for its response to the Japanese in general. It begins with the following notable passage:

There hasn't been a single day in the last ten years that we have not encountered in our major districts, on the boulevards, at the theater, young men of whose aspect we are at first taken aback. They wear with ease high hats or little round felt hats atop hair that is black, fine and lustrous with a long back parting, the randigote of woolen fabric correctly buttoned, clear gray pants, fine shoes and a necktie of a dark color above meticulous linen—from their appearance and their easy bearing one would take them for Parisians. You cross the street, you look at them: the skin tone is lightly bronzed, the beard is scarce, some of them have adopted a mustache—the mouth is large, created to open bluntly, in the fashion of Greek comedy, their cheekbones rounded and projecting on the oval of the face, the external angle of their eyes, slanted and small but black and lively. . . . These are the Japanese.[15]

The droll, slightly surprised tone mixed with both admiration and a touch of condescension continues as Chesneau describes in more detail the Japanese incursion on the West.

Since the World Exposition of 1867 and even more so since [the Exposition] of 1871, these young people, whose number increases every year, circulate quite familiarly in Paris, submitting to our customs, our morals, our language and our Arabic numerals with a flexibility worthy of astonishment. This assimilation has been accomplished by virtue of the general aptitudes of the race and the special faculties of youth. After having stayed so long shut up to foreigners—now that we have opened their doors, the Japanese, a people of initiative and action, inquisitive in quest of progress, have invaded the West. They send us intelligent generations who study our sciences, our industry and then apply them; it has been recently announced of the arrival in Marseilles of the first warship to be constructed by Japanese engineers. This is nothing more than an exchange—Japan borrows from us our mechanical arts, our military art, our sciences [and] we take their decorative arts.[16]

By 1878 Europeans had long been used to dealing with the non-Western Other. These dealings had included all the complex military, cultural, and economic aspects that made up what was about to become (and in some areas already had been) the West's domination of much of the non-Western world. Well before that, however, the cultures of India, China, Africa, and the Middle East (and, for a brief time in the sixteenth century, Japan) had hovered in the Western consciousness, being joined somewhat more recently by the cultures of the native populations of North and South America. But it was with the nineteenth century—and the rise first of the clipper ship, then the steamship, concomitant with the beginnings of the Industrial Revolution and more technological methods of warfare—that saw the most radical changes in geopolitical relationships. During that time the Europeans began to solidify their grasp over massive areas of non-Western territory, leading to the intricate sociopolitical condition that we now call imperialism and the patterns of dominance and submission that characterized much of East-West relationships.

We have discussed in the Introduction Japan's unusual entry into this complex geopolitical situation. In the long run their program of modernization would transform the country, creating the first non-Western nation to success-fully industrialize. In the short run the program led directly to the "invasion" of Paris, and other Western cities by the "young," "inquisitive," and "flexible" Japanese that Chesneau found so fascinating. Of course, the Japanese whom Chesneau describes were largely there to learn from the West, and they accom-plished this in many areas, from building the naval ships that so impressed Chesneau to creating the first non-Western parliamentary political system. In "exchange," as Chesneau puts it, the West would learn from Japanese aesthetics and ultimately its religion and art as well.

Chesneau's discussion is worth looking at closely. At a time when Europeans tended to see non-Westerners in an increasingly derogatory light (partly as a result of and partly as a justification for their own invasions of non-European countries), the tone of his essay is intriguing. Although there is a certain amount of condescension in his description of the Japanese and in his proclivity to look at them as a group rather than as individuals, the overall tone (and this becomes clearer as the essay continues) is largely one of genuine admiration mixed with a certain amount of astonishment. Stating that one could write a "solemn mem-oir" on "The Influence of the Arts of Japan upon the Art and Industry of Europe," Chesneau goes on to state that, since the first Exposition of 1867, which "made Japan the fashion,"[17] the "enthusiasm [for Japanese art] has swept through the studios [of Paris] like a flame on gunpowder."[18] Further on in the essay he admits to feeling "humiliation" and "discouragement" when looking at the products of French decorative artists. In contrast, he goes on to swoon at the "perfection" of the "sweet and lovely [Japanese] garden" at the Exposition, praises an "Imagination that is ingenious, playful, rich in surprises and of a beautiful temper,"[19] and finally laments that "when it comes to sumptuousness of materials, Paris is conquered by Kioto [sic]."[20]

Certainly some of Chesneau's words, such as "playful" and "sweet," suggest a form of belittling Japan as "childlike," linked to what would become a typical characterization on the part of Westerners. At the same time, however, an authentic tone of respect, even occasionally of envy—especially when he com-pares French art unfavorably to that of Japan—also pervades the piece. Although he praised China's installation at the Exposition, Chesneau's most interesting comparison of the two cultures comes when he speculates about the influence of Japanese art on so many contemporary French artists. At one point he passes along the well-known story that the first Japanese prints were discov-ered by an artist, who upon looking through a set of Chinese curios (Chinoiseries) became more intrigued by the Japanese woodblock prints used to wrap them than by the curios themselves. This interest thus led to the initial "discovery" of Japanese art by a Westerner. Repeating this anecdote, Chesneau wonders, "Who it was and how had he the first good fortune and penetrating sight to find among the confusions of the dead China [presumably a pun on "china" porcelain], the clarity of the living Japan.?"[21]

Chesneau was not alone in his excited privileging of Japan's artistic culture. Indeed "Le Japon à Paris" in some ways reads like a summary of the many enthusiastic comments that Japanese art and culture had garnered in the two-plus decades since Japan's forced opening to the rest of the world. If China was "dead," then Japan, as another critic put it, "was born yesterday." By the 1870s Japan had truly become "the fashion." Women paraded on the streets of Paris in kimono-esque designs, and French and English women alike entertained at home in "tea gowns," which were not only kimono-inspired but also alluded to the Japanese tea ceremony (which had spawned tea shops throughout Europe). According to one scholar, "even the way the fashionable Parisiennes stood and moved between 1860 and 1900 was, so to speak, imported from Japan."[22] Both Chinese and Japanese departments were established in places such as Le Bon Marché in Paris and Liberty in London, newly opened department stores that were themselves the latest thing in a burgeoning consumer lifestyle.

Men also owned kimono and some, especially artists, were delighted to pose in them for portraits or photographs. Operas, plays, and novels with Japanese themes flourished as well, the most famous of which included Pierre Loti's romance *Mme. Chrysanthème*, Gilbert and Sullivan's comic operetta *The Mikado*, and Puccini's operatic tragedy *Madama Butterfly*. The middle classes collected Japanese curios such as fans, parasols, and dolls, while the wealthy (and the bohemian artists who were among the first to discover Japan) began in the 1860s to collect woodblock prints and by the 1880s had progressed to screens, religious art, swords, and metal work. Japanese gardens were much admired, leading not only to Monet's garden at Giverny but to the creation of an entire teahouse and garden called "Midori no Sato" (Village of Green) by a Frenchman living near Versailles.

The Origins of Japonisme

What are the origins of what some commentators call a "mania"[23] and others called a "cult"[24] that swept though Europe and soon afterward, the United States? Was Japan simply a fashion that found the right moment? Timing was undoubtedly part of it. In an age when novelty was increasingly admired, Japan was new, exciting, and different. By this point other "Oriental" countries such as the Ottoman Empire, Egypt, China, and India had all long been part of Western "fashion." And yet, what might be called the Japonisme phenomenon was surely more than simply a matter of Japan being yet another fad.

First, it should be said that not everyone was completely enamored of Japanese art and culture. Even in the art world, some critics saw Japanese art as lacking depth or soul—as merely "decorative." It should be noted, however, that these were also the same kind of criticisms that were leveled at the Impressionists and post-Impressionists. In fact, the very "decorativeness" of Japanese art is probably a major clue to its popularity. Artists such as Monet and Manet could admire the gorgeous color patterns and designs of prints and screens without having to discover much about the history and tradition behind them. Rather than heroic scenes of statesmen or royalty, artists such as Hokusia depicted both ordinary and fantasy life, Utamaro and Harunobu showed off the pleasure quarters, and Hiroshige presented lusciously colored landscapes. All of these could be enjoyed at a purely aesthetic level. For the artists, as will be seen, the techniques and designs of Japanese art, particularly woodblock prints, would be revelatory, remaining a source of inspiration until the twentieth century and even inspiring the brilliant American architect Frank Lloyd Wright and others.

The decorative aesthetic also clearly appealed to the new middle class. In fact, it seems possible to hypothesize that Japanese art was perhaps the perfect cultural product for the new consumer culture—a culture in which women were making more and more of the decisions about what they wanted in their homes. While wealthy collectors paid exorbitant prices for ancient Buddhist statues and gold-flecked traditional scrolls, the middle classes were able to decorate themselves and their drawing rooms with beautiful and inexpensive Japanese curios. The millions of fans sold in the West at that time were an ideal vehicle for introducing Japanese art to the masses. Not only did they serve a purpose—a young lady could carry one to a ball and use the fan for purposes of coolness or flirtation, but they also were lightweight, cheap, and colorful—the perfect exotic touch on a wall or entranceway. Their subjects, often based on woodblock prints or scrolls, also put the new consumer in touch with other kinds of Japanese art.

Furthermore, unlike other non-Western nations, Japan was relatively untouched by colonialism. Europeans did not have to think about the country in particularly political or militaristic terms (at least at this point in the nineteenth century). Little was known about the culture, so it provided a particularly flexible form of fantasy projection.

The quotation from Oscar Wilde suggesting that "Japan is a pure invention" is worth recalling here. While Wilde was clearly parodying the Japan cult (and also the Art for Art's Sake movement that was connected with it), the quotation is a remarkably accurate representation not only of a general impression of Japan but particularly of what a small but deeply influential group of people, the so-called *Japonisants* and their artistic fellow travelers found in Japan as well. It was these people—writers, artists, and intellectuals—who, more than anyone else, were responsible for not only the "discovery" of Japan by the West but also for the remarkably positive attitude displayed toward Japan during that period. To the *Japonisants* Japan was important and influential, and they wrote, painted, and discussed it in a largely positive fashion. But this was also a Japan whose representation was refracted through a wide variety of needs and desires on the part of the individual Japonisant and is therefore more a phenomenon than a reality.

Who could be called a Japonisant? In its loosest definition, the term could include virtually all of the European (and some American) artists of the time who are still household names today, plus a number of major writers such as the naturalist writer Emile Zola or even perhaps the poet Baudelaire. Monet, of course, was one of them, and from early in his career had collected Japanese woodblock prints, or *ukiyo-e*, beginning with the albums of caricatures and nature studies, known as manga, by the famous artist Hokusai. Degas and Van Gogh owned fine collections of Japanese prints as did many other Impressionists. Artists such as Whistler and Tissot also collected Japanese costumes, such as kimono or *Noh* robes, a hobby emulated by such twentieth-century talents as the Viennese artist Gustav Klimt, whose impressive collection of kimono and *Noh* costumes surely influenced the flamboyant costumes worn by so many of the colorful figures in his paintings. Still others collected Japanese pottery and swords, and even dolls.

But the term "Japonisant" most specifically refers to a group of people (largely, but not exclusively, male), who were self-conscious lovers not only of Japanese art but usually of other aspects of the culture as well. These other aspects included poetry, sake, and even, later on in the century, Zen Buddhism. The *Japonisants* ranged from artists and jewelers to business people, gentlemen of leisure, writers, and journalists. Some had or would visit Japan. Many did not and, in the tradition of Wilde, saw no need to.

Generally the person credited with coining the term "Japonisme" is the art critic Phillip Burty, who in 1872 wrote several articles on the movement in the magazine *La Renaissance Litteraire*. As Gabriel Weisberg describes it, "[t]his previously unnamed fad [Japonisme] would become an influence in all areas of the arts over the next several decades."[25] As Weisberg also points out, however, the fascination with Japan had begun long before the 1870s and by the time the term was coined many of the *Japonisants*, including the writers Jules and Edmond de Goncourt and Emile Zola, owned extensive collections of Japanese art and artifacts.

Goncourt and his brother Edmond were particularly influential *Japonisants*, and, in their eccentric way, they encapsulate certain aspects of the Japonisme of the period. Coming of age in the early 1850s, a period in which both art and literature seemed doomed to being banal and imitative, the Goncourts lived through revolutions (both political and cultural) to become—through their diaries, novels, and essays—some of the major commentators on nineteenth-century European upper-class life. Associating with the bohemian fringe and very interested in the erotic life, they were also deeply misogynistic and anti-American.

Wealthy enough not to have to work for a living (although they constantly complain in their diaries over being "bankrupted" after paying for some work of art), they were also genuinely cultured and creative. Not surprisingly, their friends constituted a kind of Who's Who list of nineteenth-century French society. Hugo, Zola, and Flaubert were among their writer friends, and Monet, Manet, and Degas were among their painter and sculptor companions. For our purposes, their most interesting creative endeavor was their "discovery" of Japanese prints and their subsequent collecting of these and other objects. Edmond even claimed that he and his brother were the first to discover and promote them, stating that "we were the first to fall in love with the Japanese print and have the courage to buy them"[26] and asserting as early as 1857 that "[Japanese art] is in the process of revolutionizing Western art."[27] To the brothers, the increasing social movement toward egalitarianism would end up impoverishing art and they were strenuous believers in what would become the Art for Art's Sake movement. The beauty of Japanese art seemed an ideal foundation.

It must be acknowledged, however, that their interests were not only aesthetic. For example, in 1863 Edmund mentions how "The other day I bought some albums of Japanese obscenities. They delight me, amuse me, and charm my eyes. I look on them as being beyond obscenity, which is there, yet seems not to be there, and which I do not see, so completely does it disappear into fantasy." He goes on to speak about "the violence of the lines, the unexpected in the conjunctions, . . . the picturesqueness and so to speak, the landscape of the genital parts."[28]

The connection between Japan and the erotic is an important one, which will be discussed in more detail in Chapter 4, but it is worth remembering that the non-Western female Other has often been eroticized and essentialized. What is perhaps unusual in Goncourt's case is his pleasure in the depiction of lovemaking by both male and female, and his genuinely aesthetic appreciation of the design of the prints themselves. *Shunga*, or Japanese erotic prints, are known for their gorgeous use of costume and their detailed close-ups of enlarged genitalia, which do indeed evoke "fantasy" rather than the sweaty realities of lovemaking. Another visual trope was the image of a maid or other observer "peeking" in on a couple in the throes of intercourse—a motif which might have found its way into the post-Impressionist Degas' erotic painting. It is possible to speculate that this erotic iconography, especially its fantastic and sometimes grotesque imageries, is still very much a part of anime and manga erotica (and is still luring in new viewers).

In any case Japan was very much a part of the brothers' lives in aesthetic, erotic, social, and financial aspects. A few representative journal entries give a flavor of the degree of their fascination:

1874

   We go to Bing's [the famous dealer] where until seven o'clock in a state of fatigue verging on collapse we touch hand, and stroke more rare objects. I go to bed dead beat, my head confused, in my mind a gnawing memory of having bought some thousand francs worth of bibelots without knowing how to pay for them.[29]

1887

   [Rodin the famous sculpture comes to lunch.] He asks to see my Japanese erotics and is full of admiration before the women's drooping heads, the broken lines of their necks, the rigid extension of arms, the contractions of feet . . . all the sculptural twining of bodies melted and interlocked in the spasm of pleasure.[30]

1893

   Dinner of Japan enthusiasts at Vefours. Bing talks today about the craze for Japanese prints among various American amateurs. He tells of selling a little packet of such prints for 30,000 francs to the wife of one of the richest Yankees. . . . And we admit to each other that the Americans, who are in process of acquiring taste will, when they have acquired it, leave no art object for sale in Europe but will buy up anything.

Though the journals show their snobbish and materialistic sides they also effectively convey the sheer joy and confusion of artistic obsession. Although the brothers died a century before the anime and manga phenomenon began in the West, their intense interest and appreciation for the Japanese cultural products of their generation are perhaps not entirely different from Japanese popular culture aficionados today. In their own way, we can perhaps call the Goncourts an early example of "fan culture." Like all good fans, the Goncourts tried to pass on their enthusiasm to others. In one of their most famous novels, *Mannette Salomon*, they tell the story of how a young artist (apparently a combination of Monet and Manet) finds in the prints a "magic country," which releases him from the dreariness of a gray Parisian day.

As with many collectors and enthusiasts, the desire to share one's interest with others of the same mind stimulated regular gatherings. One such exchange of cultural capital is described by Chesneau when he discusses the first *Japonisants* at a monthly dinner of the "Japanese Society of Jingular." Apparently founded in 1867, shortly after the Exposition of 1867 made Japan fashionable, the "Society of Jingular" takes its name from the variety of sake (saluted as a "wine of mysteries!") served at the dinner. Or as Chesneau relates it,

> one eats only with chop sticks and drinks nothing but saki [sic], as witness to the title of the society, the Jingular being an informal name given to a little wine of the region which Zacharie Astruc [whom he later describes as a " poet, painter, and sculptor"] celebrated in a sonnet accompanied by charming water color illustrations. At the dinner each member received a "spiritual certificate" etched and illuminated by a certain M. Solon an elegant decorator. Both sonnet and certificate apparently affected a Japanese style.[31]

Even today the number of Japanese restaurants located in Paris may surprise visitors to this temple of French gastronomy, but the notion of a group of Frenchmen, gathering together to eat with chopsticks and celebrate the mysterious pleasures of "saki" in 1867 is slightly mind boggling. It is also a genuine pity that the "Japanese style" sonnet was not saved for posterity. By the mid-nineteenth century Japanese haiku poetry was also becoming known in Europe and it would be interesting to see if the sonnet included some haiku inspiration. In any case what is certainly clear is that, already by 1867, Japan and its products were being taken seriously by the French literati. Perhaps Chesneau sums it up best when, after enumerating the enormous growth of Japan related activities in France since the 1860s, he concludes that "This is no longer a fashion, this is a passion, this is madness."[32]

And yet, Chesneau goes on to acknowledge that this "madness" is in large part justified by the magnificent decorativeness of the objects shown at the Exposition of 1878—an Exposition which would inspire new heights of Japonisme, increasingly including a commercial approach. While artists, writers, and intellectuals remained crucial forces in the movement, it is also important to realize the contribution of commercial forces to the craze. Increasingly Japonisme would become more than an aesthete's hobby and an artistic inspiration (although it remained that as well), but it would be a noticeable part of the consumer economy as well.

In this regard, although by the 1880s there were many dealers in Japanese arts, including native Japanese experts, one name stands out above all, Siegfried (also known as Samuel) Bing. Born in 1838 in Germany, where his father managed an import-export business, Bing came to France in 1854 to help out the family business, which at that time was largely in porcelain manufacturing,—an activity that took part in the advancing industrial revolution but at the same time paid homage to the craftsmen who originally had designed the porcelain. Bing respected the significance of craftsmanship, and this respect and appreciation ultimately made him one of the most significant figures in the Japonisme movement and beyond. As Gabriel Weisberg describes his influence, Bing was an advocate of revitalizing the "appreciation of the applied arts"[33] and understood that this would require a greater awareness of new technologies, an aggressive approach to merchandising, and an openness to the integration of artistic ideas and cultures outside of France, namely Japan.

In the twenty-first-century world where Japanese crafts seem increasingly to be identified with the ubiquitous Hello Kitty or Pokemon toys, it is perhaps useful to remember that Japanese art goes well beyond the cute and cuddly. Besides the almost omnipresent fans, many other items such as combs, lacquerware, netsuke toggles, screens, tea pots, and tea were also eagerly snapped up. Many a European or American parlor was stuffed with Japanese curios and some of the wealthy even added ostentatious "Japanese rooms" to their houses. Bing tended to concentrate on the high end, with a special expertise in woodblock prints, but his activities on behalf of the Japanese arts were numerous and varied. He organized monthly "Japanese" dinner parties where collectors of several generations could enjoy eating while surrounded by Japanese arts and artifacts. Weisberg quotes Gaston Migeon, (a curator at the Louvre who would go on to organize an important Japanese print exhibition there), as recalling how, after dinner, the guests would "press around a large table, and the hours seemed to fly away as they leafed through big boxes of colour prints by wonderful Japanese printmakers."[34]

Bing clearly possessed a superb eye and a flexible imagination, qualities that would allow him to go from championing Japan to employing Japanese influences in the late nineteenth-century Art Nouveau movement that he also had a major part in developing. But he was at the same time a shrewd entrepreneur. (The Goncourts could be quite snide about his business activities.) Not only did he open what was perhaps the most important gallery of Japanese art in Paris— a veritable *Musée Japonais* (Japanese Museum) in the early 1880s, which took advantage of all the latest techniques for displaying art most attractively—but he also traveled widely in what was a largely successful attempt to engender interest in Japanese art in Europe and America. Aware that the modernizing

Japanese were also eager for European goods, he and his family also established trading offices in Yokohama.

But perhaps Bing's most important contribution to the spread of interest in Japan was the beautiful journal *Le Japon Artistique* (Artistic Japan), which he launched in 1888. Available also in English and German editions, the journal made an impact on art enthusiasts in both Europe and the United States. Even today, leafing through its century-old pages is an aesthetic pleasure. Each issue carried an article on some aspect of Japanese visual culture—such as prints, metalwork, or swordcraft—plus a luscious array of plates, both black and white and in color. Bing commissioned well-known art critics to write the articles and, although the writers sometimes veered into hyperbole, the articles are reasonably accurate and informative, especially given the period in which they were written and the relative paucity of information available to the writers. For many nineteenth-century readers, among whom included a number of Impressionist artists, they must have been an indispensable gateway into an alluring and mysterious world.

Others however, were less smitten. As Weisberg chronicles, *The Japan Weekly Mail* took Bing to task for promoting his commercial activities under cover of educating the public taste. As previously mentioned, not every art critic was as entranced by Japanese art as Bing's columnists were, and one occasionally has the sense that these nay-sayers as reacted strongly and to some extent understandably to what, in our era, we would call "hype." Bing was even accused of driving up prices on Japanese prints and art objects by featuring them so extensively in his journal. Even if this were the case (and clearly Bing was not working from totally altruistic motives), the journal performed an important educational function, including, as Weisberg notes, "identifying salient areas of research and drawing attention to works of art not widely known to [the readers]."[35]

The fact that Japanese art is still regarded today as one of the great aesthetic traditions of the world suggests that *Artistic Japan* (the title also suggests the sense that the entire culture is artistic) was on intellectual solid ground. The general tone of the articles in the journal is one of admiration tinged with genuine excitement. The noted critic Louis Gonse, for example, states baldly that "The Japanese are the greatest decorators in the world." But the articles go beyond merely describing the outer aspects of Japanese art to include some of its cultural manifestations as well, although often of the melodramatic kind. An article on the Japanese sword, for example, contains an admiring description of *seppuku*, complete with a reproduction of a woodblock print by Toyokuni of a warrior committing *hara-kiri* underneath cherry trees. In another piece the story of the forty-seven *ronin*—a group of masterless samurai who revenged their lord and then each committed suicide—is presented in respectful detail. Bing knew how to use what we would now call a "back story" to engender interest in his products, as this edition includes information on Japanese swords, in which he dealt as well. Intriguingly, however the more erotic aspects of Japanese culture are played down. For example, a description of a woodblock print depicting a crowd of youthful beauties, in the journal's sixth volume, never mentions the word "courtesan," preferring to refer to them as "figures" or "personages."[36]

Throughout all of the articles a strong sense of newness and discovery is apparent. Bing writes revealingly in his introduction to the first volume about his previous sense that the arts (presumably both European and non-Western) were "exhausted" and that there would be no chance of any novel addition. He goes on to add, however, that "all at once, from behind the barriers which a small insular people had erected around themselves with jealous care, a fresh form of art, quite startling in its novelty revealed itself."[37]

Another writer in a later volume crows, "Here is an absolutely new world which shows us some of its concrete treasures."[38] There is even a concern that the public will be put off by the extreme "novelty" of the art presented. But on many other occasions the public or at least European craftsmen are exhorted to study and learn from the Japanese example. In fact, one important aspect of Japanese artistic culture that is increasingly referred to is the lack of boundaries between artisans and artists. While some art critics saw this as exactly one of the problems in Japanese art, others saw it as an antidote to the staleness of the European bifurcation of the arts into high and low and hoped that it would provide a revolutionary impetus toward a renaissance among other kinds of arts.

To illustrate these points, the articles in *Artistic Japan* were careful to include detailed descriptions of what made Japanese art so new and worthy of study by both artisans and workers in the fine arts. In many cases, these articles would be the first European introduction of a particular Japanese art and, as such, they would influence the discourses on Japanese culture for a considerable number of years. One of the most important contributions of this sort was the two articles written by the painter Ary Renan on the great woodblock print artist Hokusai and his "Mangwa" (sic) sketchbooks. These articles and the sketchbooks themselves were to have a profound affect on French artists, including some of the most important Impressionists and post-Impressionists, such as Monet, Degas, Gauguin, and Lautrec.

To twenty-first-century readers familiar with today's manga comics, Hokusai's many-volume set (he apparently also coined the term "manga," which means something like "crazy sketches") might at first seem strange. Essentially a collection of sketchbooks containing illustrations of daily life and nature, there is no text and no story per se. On closer inspection, however, we can see that certain aspects of Hokusai's manga pertain even to this day. As Renan puts it glowingly "[The Man-gwa is] in fact, an entire review of the Japanese people."[39] According to him the sketches show "that deep sense of humor which is one of the most striking aspects of the Japanese."[40] They also contain pictures of "dragons, reptiles, recluses working miracles, wrestling contests, semi-human monsters"[41] and "chaotic landscapes and hideous combinations of the elements evolved in a delirium unknown to us, theatrical scenes, romantic pictures, wondrous studies of movement" and even "mythological figures that make the flesh creep."[42] In the second of the two articles he sums up Hokusai's work by concluding that the "Man-gwa is a whole world."[43]

Of course, Hokusai's manga are very different from those now being produced in Japan, yet much of what Renan describes seems eerily similar to what many manga and anime viewers probably first notice when they approach these media. Unlike Western mainstream comic books which, even today, are quite limited in their subject matter, Japanese manga do indeed encompass a "whole world." Just as Hokusai showed human life in all its varieties, manga genres include sports, romance, daily life, and fantasy. The grotesque and the humorous are also significant elements, features that are even more noticeable in Japanese animation. Although it would be reductive to draw a direct line between Hokusai's work (and that of other print makers) and modern-day anime and manga, in the eyes of both Japanese and Western commentators, certain connections seem obvious. For the purposes of this book what is so intriguing is the not-dissimilar effect these two forms of manga have had on audiences over a century apart. As will be detailed later, many millennium-era fans of manga and anime have also been impressed by the novelty and "differentness" of Japanese popular art versus American comics or animation.

Monet and Japanese Art

> Look at that flower with its petals turned back by the wind, is that not truth itself? . . . Here, here this woman by Hokusai, look at this bathing scene look at these bodies, can you not feel their firmness—those people have taught us to compose differently, there's no doubt about that.
>
> —*Monet in a letter to the Duc de Trevise, 1920*[44]

Hokusai's manga returns us to Monet and the Impressionists. While tens of thousands of woodblock prints were sold in Europe during this period, initially only Hokusai and two other woodblock print artists—Hiroshige, who specialized in nature scenes, and Utamaro, who was known for his prints of pleasure quarters—were the Japanese artists who were quasi-household names. Indeed, until the 1870s Hokusai was the only Japanese artist whose name was recognized among Western enthusiasts.

Monet was one of the first to appreciate the genius of the manga and these and others of Hokusai's works, particularly the Japanese artist's depiction of nature, in works such as The 36 Views of Mount Fuji, were enormously influential on his art (see insert, Figure 5). For example, some critics feel that Monet's many versions of haystacks (see insert, Figure 6) or of Rouen Cathedral at various times of day owe much to Hokusai's series of representations of Fuji. Although we began this chapter with a discussion of *La Japonaise*, in many ways the portrait—with its obvious Japan-esque aspects—is not really the most representative of Japanese art's influence on Monet. Overall, the impact of Japan on Monet was deeper, broader, and often far subtler.

In his discussion of Japanese art's influence on Van Gogh, Ronald Pickvance has identified four stages in the artist's adaptation of Japanese art, which in many ways are applicable to Monet as well (and as Pickvance acknowledges, to the Japonisme movement as a whole). As Pickvance also points out, these four stages—"discovery, appropriation, adaption, and recreation"—were actually occurring continuously and simultaneously among a variety of artists during the period.[45] For Monet, the "discovery" stage would probably have been the beginning of his interest in Hokusai, an interest that he set as far back as the 1850s, although some commentators believe it occurred a decade later. In any case, this discovery was undoubtedly similar to the one described in the Goncourts' book *Mannette Salomon*, where the young artist reveled in the different light-filled world presented by the woodblock prints in which he was immersed. In Monet's case this was also the period when he began associating with *Japonisants*. The "appropriation period" (what Pickvance describes as the "reconstruction of the oriental world") would seem to coincide with the painting of *La Japonaise*, where Monet "appropriated" Japanese objects to add an exotic (and erotic) aspect to the picture but did not substantially alter his style of painting. The third stage, "adaptation," in Monet's case probably runs directly into the fourth stage, "recreation," and this is where Monet's real debt to Japan becomes clear.

This is not at all to suggest that Monet slavishly copied Japanese art, as is obvious from even the most cursory inspection of his work compared to Japanese woodblock prints. Rather, to use Pickvance's terms, this fourth stage refers to a "a world view" that "was distilled from the language of forms and the principles followed."[46] Or as the curators of "Monet and Japan" write, "Monet was using [Japanese prints] not to construct a romanticized dream of Japan but to depict the life he knew."[47]

In Monet's willingness to depict life around him filled with color and light, rather than the subdued idealized world of Salon pictures, there is undoubtedly a direct influence from Japanese artists, particularly Hokusai. In fact, Monet was described by one contemporary critic as a faithful emulator of Hokusai. In their openness to exploring the enormous range of human and natural life Hokusai's manga and prints helped free European artists from conventional subject matter, leading them to feel increasingly free to depict the new forms of urban life. Monet's pictures from that period include street scenes, often from an unusual angle, which commentators see as reflecting the different perspectives offered in woodblock prints; boats bobbing in a harbor on a sunny, windy day; and trains crossing bridges in explosions of color, motion, and light, which contemporary commentators saw as echoing woodblock prints. Boats on the water and bridges were favorite subjects of Hiroshige and Hokusai, who would often place them at asymmetrical angles helping to frame the composition in a distinctive way. Monet's depiction of a train on a bridge is, of course, a Western interpolation, part of the "shock of the modern." In another famous work he depicts bathers at a location that one critic describes as Paris's version of the pleasure quarters, a French response to Utamaro's many depictions of bathers in the world of the courtesans.

These paintings, which twenty-first-century audiences take for granted in all of their energy and vividness, were seen as strikingly unconventional at the time they were produced. Critics complained not only about the subject matter but at the sense of their having been "dashed off" and, indeed, compared to the typical rigidly posed and carefully polished portraits of the salons. Monet's and his cohorts' pictures did seem to earn their appellation of "Impressions." That these "Impressions" would become some of the most highly evaluated pictures in modern art is something that most critics of the time never dreamed.

It is important to keep in mind that there were many other influences on the Impressionists aside from those of the Japanese and these included the influence of the Romantics and the Naturalists, who in their time had broken away from the Academy, as well as the new world of vision opened up by photography. But there is no question that Japanese art had an enormous and far reaching impact. In some ways, perhaps, Japanese art's most important function was to legitimize the variety of exploration and experimentation that the Impressionists and their followers were beginning to undertake.

As the quotation at the beginning of this chapter suggests, each artist took from Japanese art what he or she could use: a "confirmation" of their own "affinities." For this immensely talented group of people, Japanese art played into their own strengths. Monet's slightly earlier contemporary Eduoard Manet, for example, was famous for his flat planes of color creating a kind of two dimensional patterned surface, which many critics see as directly influenced by the depthlessness and love of surface detail of woodblock prints. Mary Cassatt, a slightly later member of the Impressionists, created exquisite domestic scenes inspired by the many sympathetic depictions of mothers and children in woodblock prints, while her painting of the gowns of the ladies of the house showed the same attention to detail and color as the robes of the courtesans in prints of the pleasure quarters. Degas' fascination with women bathing, while no doubt an aspect of his own personality, was undoubtedly legitimized and extended by the numerous bathing scenes of Utamoro and others, while his erotic depictions of a man watching a woman bathe or dress show distinct echoes of the voyeuristic aspects of *shunga*. On a more general level, the energy and playfulness of Hokusai's manga helped liberate Monet and his contemporaries from the need for conventionally stiff portrayals of human and natural forms.

But it was in depictions of nature or outdoor scenes that both contemporary critics and more recent scholars have felt that Japanese art was most influential. The different perspective, brushstrokes, lines, and light, as well as the overall fascination with the natural world on the part of Japanese artists clearly inspired many Westerners to create landscapes that were a far cry from those appreciated by the Salon. This was true both literally (one of the most remarked upon features of the Impressionists was their insistence on painting outside rather than in the studio) and aesthetically, as these new artists rejected the dark, and subdued colors and often symbolic landscapes of the conventional Realists or even the Romantics. Instead, they portrayed a natural world of motion and light, where an achingly bright field of poppies seems to welcome the viewer into a dazzling transient universe; a many-hued wave crashes against a seacoast of multicolored rocks in a celebration of the gorgeous ephemerality of the natural world; and even winter scenes, where the patterned and shaded snow seems to take on an aesthetic integrity all its own.

As Monet acknowledged, "We needed the arrival of Japanese prints in our midst, before anyone dared to sit down on a river bank, and juxtapose on canvas a roof which was bright red, a wall which was white, a green poplar, a yellow road and blue water. Before the example given us by the Japanese this was impossible."[48] Not only artists but writers seemed to perceive Japan as an all-embracing world. Thus, Jules Goncourt mentions on returning from a walk home that "ï felt that I was walking in one of those Japanese prints with snow covered earth, with carmine tinted trees."[49] At other times it was the Europeans who saw the Japanese as one of them. We may remember the quotation in the introduction from Monet's contemporary Pissarro, who wrote in a letter to his son after visiting a Japanese exhibition that "Hiroshige is a marvelous Impressionist—I'm pleased to have done my snow and flood effects, these Japanese artists confirm me in our visual standpoint."

But it is in Monet's varied portrayals of the natural world that critics have found some of the most interesting and subtle influences from Japanese art. Intriguingly, after 1890 the artist never again painted a human figure. The reasons for this development are open to speculation but it is interesting to note that "in the 1880s and 90s Monet became attracted to Japanese prints and paintings that had more subtle decorative effects than those that had previously influenced his work"[50] and "his own painting became ever more decorative, refined and sensuous." Although, at that period some critics used the term "decorative" in a disparaging manner (believing that "high art" should have more depth), most *Japonisants* were extremely appreciative that Japanese art was supremely decorative. They were also very much aware of the art's relation to the transition of the seasons—a connection that, in turn, was related to a perception of natural beauty as the embodiment of spiritual truths. Hokusai's *The Red Fuji* (see insert, Figure 5), for example, renders the sacred mountain in ways that are both "decorative" and suggestive of the spiritual aspect of the mountain and its relationship to the rest of the natural and human world.

How much Monet was aware of Japanese religion is uncertain, although, from the 1880s on, lectures and writings on Buddhism had begun to flow into Europe. In any case, compositionally there is no question that the Japanese depiction of the natural world had a profound effect on the way Monet portrayed nature. Recent art critics have found many obvious parallels between Monet's art of this period and specific Japanese prints. For example, many of Monet's seascapes would include huge jutting cliffs with a single lonely tree silhouetted against the background, very much like woodblock prints from Hiroshige, Kuniyoshi, and others. Furthermore, his snow scenes with their effect of putting the viewer within the landscape, almost overwhelmed by the substantiality of the winter weather, also owe debts to these and other artists.

But it is the series of paintings done by Monet near the end of his life that have particularly intrigued critics, who see in them not merely aesthetic but spiritual inspiration from Japan. These are the famous Water Lilies paintings done at the end of the nineteenth century (Figure 3). John House sees the direct influence of Japanese prints in them, noting how the first series "[e]choes Hiroshige's Wisteria at Drum Bridge" and that "the theme which dominates the later Water Lilies, of lily pads floating on the water's surface is common in Japanese prints."[51]

In addition to prints, however, another important visual force was probably inspiring Monet, and this was Japanese screen paintings (Figure 4). Far more highly regarded in nineteenth-century Japan than the mass-produced *ukiyoe*, folding-screen paintings began to penetrate European consciousness more than a decade after the more popular prints. Much larger than the prints (about the size of a wall in a conventional Western bedroom), the screen paintings used different materials and different principles of composition than the woodblocks. This is due not only to their size and breadth (basically, an "extended horizontal," as House describes them)[52] but also by the fact that the screens are broken up into panels in which "a single scene, too wide for the eye to take in at a single glance . . . is carried across all the panels."[53]

This is very much the case with the Water Lilies (and also the willows that sometimes appear at the base of the Water Lily paintings). Unlike conventional Western art, where the composition is usually framed (both literally and figuratively) by a variety of devices, the Water Lilies allow the viewer's vision to float above the canvas—as the lilies do themselves on the cloudy surface of the water. As the curators for "Monet and Japan" write, regarding the "small curved gold leafed clouds" that hover on the surface of many landscape screens, "[t]he eye seems to slip endlessly from one dimension to another."[54] While it is uncertain how many Japanese screens Monet had seen by this time, many contemporary critics sensed a strongly Japanese dimension, with one writer even pronouncing that "the whole [Water Lily cycle] is impregnated by Monet's dream of Japanese art."[55]

More than any other of Monet's works, the Water Lily Decorations were seen by critics as having a pronounced spiritual dimension. Some critics specifically saw a Buddhist aspect to the paintings, mentioning their "oriental self-effacement and impersonality."[56] Even more explicitly, Gustave Gefroy, an old friend of Monet, wrote in 1922, in the last chaper of his *La Reverie before the Water Garden*, that "the supreme meaning of [Monet's] art, of this adoration of the universe lay in ending in a pantheistic and Buddhist contemplation."[57]

Van Gogh and Japan

My whole work is founded on the Japanese, so to speak.

—*Vincent Van Gogh in a letter from Arles,* Van Gogh in Arles

The weather here remains fine, and if it was always like this, it would be better than the painter's paradise, it would be absolute Japan.

—*Van Gogh in a letter from Arles,* Van Gogh in Arles

Lack of knowledge of a foreign country is not a disadvantage for one drawn to the exotic; it is rather the precondition for utopian thought.

—*Tsukasa Kodera,* Vincent Van Gogh: Christianity Versus Nature

Figure 3
Water Lilies, 1905
Museum of Fine Arts, Boston
Gift of Edward Jackson Holmes
Photograph © Museum of Fine Arts, Boston

Figure 4
Chinese Scholars
Museum of Fine Arts, Boston
Fenollosa-Weld Collection
Photograph © Museum of Fine Arts, Boston

Though Monet's stunning late works may seem to hint at a spiritual transcendence of some sort, it is difficult to determine from Monet's own writings how consciously he was affected by Japanese spirituality. Such is not the case with arguably the other most famous artist of the nineteenth century, Vincent Van Gogh, whose intense interest in Japan was both artistic and explicitly spiritual. It was not only the country's art but also Japan itself as an ideal that stirred Van Gogh's imagination. On certain levels, Van Gogh was almost more influenced by Japan than was Monet, and it is fitting that we end this chapter with a portrait of the man whom many consider to be the greatest of the post-Impressionists.

In this case, I mean "portrait" literally. If Monet's portrait of his wife, La Japonaise, signaled the "discovery" and "appropriation" of Japanese art, Van Gogh's portrait of himself as a Buddhist priest, painted twelve years later in 1888, is a clear example of "re-creation" and the "distillation of a world view" on a profound level. While Monet's life and career, although often difficult and fraught with critical opposition in the early years, ultimately had a successful trajectory, Van Gogh's life as is well known, was deeply tragic, marred by poverty, alienation, depression, and ultimately madness.

The self-portrait, however, was created during the year that Van Gogh was living in Arles in the South of France, one of the happiest and most productive period of his life. Entitled *Self-Portrait Dedicated to Paul Gauguin*, the portrait has both a symbolic and an aesthetic role.

While Monet's wife was "trying on" the identity of a woman of the Japanese demimonde, in this portrait Van Gogh is explicitly identifying as a Buddhist priest (*bonze*). Very different from the bright colors and playful tone that characterized *La Japonaise*, Van Gogh's portrait is subdued and thoughtful, transmitting a reflective emotional tone and done in hues that are decidedly restrained. Far from gazing flirtatiously out at the world, the Buddhist Van Gogh seems to be looking inward, away from the viewer, in what Debora Silverman describes as a "steady impassive gaze."[58] As for the "gaze" of the viewer, as will be seen, Van Gogh was only hoping to reach a select few who could understand the complex spiritual depths that the painting's iconography was attempting to present.

Despite his explicit self-identification as a priest, Van Gogh is not wearing clearly Japanese clothes, instead he has donned a simple white shirt, brown waistcoat, and brown jacket. Although around his neck is a medallion, which Silverman notes "suggests a ritual or sacred vestment, signaling membership in a group bound by a common self—offering deference to the 'eternal Buddha.'"[59] There are also a few physical touches to hint at Van Gogh's self-identification as both priest and Japanese: he has shaven his head and, as he proudly noted later, represented his eyes in a slightly almond shape.

If Monet's portrait was a celebration of the exoticism and excitement of the external Japan, Van Gogh's artistic vision is of an internal Japan. This vision is on the one hand very much related to the artist's own complex and unique personality, and on the other hand an exemplar of just how deeply the cult of Japan could penetrate the European mind. In fact, *Self Portrait Dedicated to Paul Gauguin* has a fascinating history behind it, relating to Van Gogh's joys and frustrations during the year at Arles when he dreamed of establishing a Utopian community with strongly Japanese elements.

For some time Van Gogh had conceived of the idea of establishing an artist's colony in which artists lived together and shared their work. Although the notion was partially inspired by European communities, such as Dutch craftsmen's guilds and monastic orders, its most direct inspiration was from Japan, or rather Van Gogh's conception of Japan. The son of a clergyman and who had at one point been a preacher himself, Van Gogh was constantly looking for spiritual refuge in a world he saw as corrupt, shackled by technological imperatives, and headed toward ruin. In his mind Japan was the antithesis of the materially affluent but spiritually empty Western world. He believed this was especially the case with the Japanese artists, whom he idealized (rather inaccurately) as working together in supportive groups and exchanging paintings with one another while appreciating the natural world. As Van Gogh poetically described them, these "simple Japanese" are "liv[ing] in nature as though they themselves were flowers." Van Gogh derived his idea of Japanese artistic life from various sources. He had long been interested in Japanese prints. (In the 1870s he and his brother Theo had worked part time for Samuel Bing selling and buying prints.) And he had actually done some direct copies of Hiroshige prints as well as incorporate Japanese prints into portraits of friends and models. Certainly, Van Gogh read, and was influenced by, the admiring articles in *Artistic Japan*. It seems likely, however, that Van Gogh might have gotten his idea of the Japanese exchanging their works from a book by Louis Gonse, entitled *L'Art Japonaise* (1886), while his knowledge of Buddhist priests and certainly his artistic representation of them came from the description and pictures of a Buddhist funeral in Loti's *Mme. Chrysanthème*.

In any case, as Silverman acutely points out, more interesting than Van Gogh's actual sources are his own responses to them—his "projections and active remodeling of his sources according to his own preexisting values."[60] Though much of what Van Gogh knew about Japan was reasonably accurate, there is no question that he wanted to create his own "Japan," which had far more to do with his own needs and desires than any real devotion to accuracy. For example, he wrote in a letter in 1888,

> If we study Japanese art, we see a man who is undoubtedly, wise, philosophic and intelligent who spends his time doing what? In studying the distance between the earth and the moon? No. In studying Bismark's policy? No. He studies a single blade of grass but this blade of grass leads him to draw every plant and then the season, the wide aspects of the countryside, then animals, then the human figure. So he passes his life.[61]

In this passage Van Gogh is clearly envisioning the Japanese artist as a superior soul who has transcended the mundane aspects of life (here embodied as science [the distance between earth and moon], and politics [Bismark's policy]). He is also a man clearly devoted to his art, who will spend his entire life drawing "every plant." This was the kind of artistic pursuit that Van Gogh wanted to both emulate in himself and nurture in others. As a token of this desire, Van Gogh established in Arles his so-called "Yellow House," in which he dreamed of inviting other artists to join him in the communal way of life that he believed the Japanese exemplified—even going so far as to decorate the walls with Japanese prints.

Van Gogh's *Self Portrait* was in some ways a product of this endeavor. Van Gogh invited the equally brilliant, and in some ways equally tortured, artist Paul Gauguin and another mutual friend, the artist Emile Bernard, to exchange portraits of themselves with him, as part of his attempt to imitate what he believed to be a typical practice among Japanese artists. Gauguin also admired and collected Japanese prints and a number of his most important compositions were clearly inspired by specific Japanese works. However, the portrait that he sent Van Gogh had none of the spiritualism and serenity to which Van Gogh aspired in his own self-portrait. Far from identifying with a priestly ideal, Gauguin's dark pointed features look almost diabolical, and it is hardly surprising that he entitled the portrait *Les Misérables*, in an explicit homage to the outlaw protagonist, Jean Valjean, of Victor Hugo's famous novel.

Gauguin and Van Gogh both saw the contemporary world as a deeply disappointing, spiritually bankrupt place in which, among other things, artists were not appreciated. It is very likely that Van Gogh would have agreed with Gauguin's further exposition of his portrait, in which he says "As for this Jean Valjean whom society oppressed, cast out, is he not equally a symbol of the contemporary Impressionist painter? In endowing him with my features I offer you as well as an image of myself. a portrait of all the wretched victims of society."[62]

But whereas Gauguin used French literature to plunge himself into a melancholy identification with the oppressed, Van Gogh found in his conception of Japan an ideal that would help him transcend both the psychological and the spiritual pains that afflicted him. Revealingly, he compares the two portraits and finds his own picture "grave but not despairing."[63] Indeed, most of the nine-month period in Arles seems to have been among the least despairing of his adult life. Van Gogh identified Arles explicitly with Japan, even at one point telling his sister that "I don't need Japanese pictures here—for I am always telling myself that here I am in Japan."[64] Although the differences between the south of France and the Japanese archipelago might strike an objective observer as profound, there is no question that in Van Gogh's mind he had "found" Japan in this Provencal town. Perhaps Van Gogh was not totally off the mark. One truly credible example of "Japan in Arles" is an exquisite series of sixteen paintings of blossoming trees that he did that year. Although the intense and emotive brushstrokes and overall composition clearly owe much to Van Gogh's unique abilities, the subject matter, delicacy, and radiant colors exquisitely capture the spirit of the many depictions of flowering trees in Japanese art.

Van Gogh's sojourn in Arles/Japan, however, would ultimately come to an unfortunate end. In a sense, the catalyst behind his leaving, ironically and rather heartbreakingly, lay in his dream of the artistic community, which finally seemed to be coming to fulfillment. After a long correspondence, Gauguin agreed to come and live with him in the "Yellow House." Van Gogh was tremendously excited and he spent much time and effort decorating and furnishing the house in preparation for Gauguin's arrival. Not surprisingly, he wanted to decorate Gauguin's room "in the Japanese manner, [with] at least six very large canvases, particularly the enormous bouquets of sunflowers."[65] (One wonders if one of these sunflower canvases ultimately became the most expensive picture of its time when Yasuda Life Insurance paid six million dollars for it.) Whether this kind of lavish decoration was actually "in the Japanese manner" seems a moot question. For Van Gogh this invocation of Japan not only inspired him but he believed it would also inspire his friend.

Unfortunately their companionship proved dismally ill-fated. Gauguin ended up departing abruptly after the notorious episode when Van Gogh cut off part of his ear to impress a woman at the brothel the two men frequented. Soon afterward, Van Gogh ended up entering the asylum in the beautiful Provencal town of St. Remy, where he would kill himself two years later. Even in St. Remy, however, the Japanese influence seems to have lingered. From the hospital, Van Gogh painted two studies of workers mending a road, perhaps hoping, as Eliza Rathbone suggests, that this would symbolize his "own road to recovery and renewed capacity to travel along the pilgrim's road of life."[66] While the pictures treated an essentially Provencal scene, the gnarled trunks of the trees along the roadway and the powerful diagonals reveal that Japan was still part of Van Gogh's inner vision.

Monet's *La Japonaise* and Van Gogh's *Self Portrait* form the two bookends of this chapter. Each in his own way, the two artists were profoundly influenced by Japan, as were countless other artists, writers, collectors, and people who simply enjoyed the exposure to another culture. If Monet's interaction with Japan was more cerebral and Van Gogh's was more emotional, they represent only two of a multitude of ways in which Westerners interacted with what to them was a deeply Other culture.

We return to the question: Why Japan? Why so pervasive? Most books on "Japonisme" have tended to stress the how rather than the why, perhaps because these are such complex questions. One important exception to this is Elisa Evett's thought-provoking work *The Critical Reception of Japanese Art in Late 19th Century Europe*, in which she specifically deals with issues raised by the largely positive reception of Japanese art in the West. Although to do justice to Evett's ideas in a few sentences might run the risk of oversimplifying them, her primary thesis, as she states it, is that "The basic framework for the interpretation of Japanese art rested on the dominant image of the Japanese as primitive people—not uncouth savages but simple souls who intuitively understood, and were therefore in tune with nature."[67] She further links this interpretation of the Japanese to the important art movement known as "Primitivism," which would dominate the art of many late nineteenth- and early twentieth-century painters, from Gauguin to Matisse and Picasso.

It is important to re-emphasize Evett's point that by "Primitivism" she does not mean "uncouth savages" but rather "the attraction to contemporary unmodernized cultures as the idealization of the original, untainted condition of man and the fundamental purity of mentality associated with the primitive state of being."[68] In certain aspects this characterization does at first glance seem to fit how many Europeans saw the Japanese. For example, one admiring description of Hokusai envisions him living in a world "[that] is a great garden in which he plays in innocence making charming pictures and watching the flight of butterflies."[69] This description is both condescending in the idea of a major artist "playing" and deeply simplistic, showing no knowledge of the complex identity of Hokusai as an artist who lived at a time of intense social and political turmoil in Japan. And certainly Van Gogh's idealization of these "simple Japanese [artists]" also suggests that they lack the sophistication of their European counterparts. But this encomium is also based on Van Gogh's disgust with European, and specifically white, civilization. In fact, Van Gogh went so far as to excoriate "the horrible white man with his bottle of alcohol, his money and his syphilis."[70]

Evett effectively draws links between certain aspects of the period, such as the struggle on the part of some artists and intellectuals for a less elitist brand of art that would allow for craftspeople to be as admired as fine artists and the previously mentioned feeling that the decorative should occupy a higher artistic place. The fascination with Japan as a land that seemed to breathe beauty and art (exemplified by the title of Bing's journal, *Artistic Japan*) is also seen by Evett and others as expressing the desire on the part of many Europeans for a world uncorrupted by the ugliness of modern industry and technology.

Evett's argument is important and suggestive, although our emphases might be somewhat different. As Evett and others argue, the cult of Japan was linked with other cults—a celebration of the Middle Ages, a new valorization of the craftsmen and of the "Decorative" that were all part of a turning away from a perceived sense that Europe had lost its soul to materialism and technology. Or as Gauguin and Van Gogh's fellow painter Emile Bernard put it, "Industry is the natural enemy of Poetry, of Painting, of Music of Happiness. . . . [I]ndustry is the idol of the nineteenth century"—a period when, according to Bernard, "the engineer replaces the architect, the worker replaces the artist . . . the artist become[s] *useless*."[71] In contrast, Japanese culture seemed to offer a joyous world in which all Japanese were painters who loved nature and beauty.

It should be noted, however, that unlike the people typically identified as "Primitives," such as the inhabitants of Africa and Oceania, Japan had a centuries-old written culture and sophisticated artistic traditions, of which the *Japonisants* and other commentators were well aware. Thus, rather than specifically include Japonisme as part of the Primitivist movement, I would suggest that it was allied with it, especially in the European fantasy of the Japanese as living closer to nature than Westerners. This closeness to nature was seen not only in Japanese art but also in poetry and religion, and appealed to many Westerners such as Van Gogh, who believed that the ascendance of the machine led to the inevitable devaluation of humanistic and spiritual values.

In this regard, it is also possible to suggest that, beyond Primitivism, the fantasy of Japan seemed to offer humanism, a world in which individual human craft was taken seriously. As Van Gogh wrote to his brother, Theo, "I do believe in civilization but only in the kind that is founded on real humanity."[72] Certainly it is very clear that Japan existed as an attractive alternative to what many people saw as the corruption and decadence of Western civilization. Japan's perceived link with nature was used by artists such as Van Gogh and Gauguin to critique what they saw as the West's loss of its own connection to both the natural and the human. Unlike the "Primitives," however, Japan also represented a rich and complex civilization. But unlike other non-Western Others who had also inspired European admiration—such as the Middle East or India—Japan was at the same time aligned with "Nature."

There is also another aspect to Japan's prominence in the nineteenth century compared to that of other non-Western civilizations. To understand the more complicated role of the Japanese we must return to Chesneau's article quoted at the beginning of this chapter. We remember that much of the article was taken up with admiring the beauties of the Japanese pavilion at the 1873 Exposition. But the introductory section sets the exhibition and Japanese culture within a context that deals with history, politics, economics, and even technology. Chesneau reminds his readers that Japan has recently opened its doors and is eager to learn from and about the countries of the West. He points out that the Japanese are "invading" France, equipped with "intelligence, curiosity, and flexibility." And he specifically notes the Japanese naval ship that floats in the harbor of Marseilles, not to mention the fact that the Japanese are studying industry and technology.

This vision of the Japanese (whom Chesneau also, as we may remember, makes a point of describing as wearing European headgear and clothing), is a far cry from the notion of kimono-clad Japanese artists "playing" in the garden. But it is an aspect of Japan during this period that must not be forgotten. In the late nineteenth century, when notions of progress in terms of Darwinism and Spencerism dominated, Japan was beginning to command respect and fascination for its nonartistic endeavors as well. As Eric Hobsbawm states definitively, "Progress was the dominant concept of the age,"[73] which in itself linked with "the most familiar concept of the liberal economy—competition."[74] Japan began its modern relationship with the West in terms of artistic competition, offering the fresh and new to a jaded society. As time went on, Japan would become competitive in other areas, forcing the West to take notice of the country in a different way than the typical dynamic that had pervaded East-West relations by the late nineteenth century.

Not just Japanese art but also the emerging Japanese identity as a modern nation had to be taken into account. As opposed to any other non-Western nation at this period, Japan stood out as a country that was genuinely trying to compete with the West. This was not simply a nation that created beautiful woodblock prints of boats in a harbor. It was also a nation capable of creating a warship that could steam into French waters. Ultimately, therefore, perhaps Japan's most important legacy in the nineteenth and early twentieth century was not simply to help artists see new forms of reality but also to help the world see a non-Western country in a new light.

2

"Mon Semblable! Mon Frère": Collecting, Doubling, and Mirroring Japan in England and America, 1878–1941

And very naturally, we do not see our successors in the colored races we have always deemed inferior to our own. Over them we are accustomed to rule, with one exception cold blooded scientific Japan. Is she going to lead the colored races, not only to revolt but to supremacy?

—Beatrice Webb, diary entry, "Sidney and Beatrice Webb and Japan," 1920

There was more than a modicum of truth in the wry quip of a Japanese diplomat that "his people had been sending artistic treasures to Europe for some time, and had been regarded as Barbarians but that, as soon as they showed themselves able to shoot down Russians with quick-firing guns they were acclaimed as a highly civilized race."

—Ellen Conant, "Refractions of the Rising Sun Japan's Participation in International Exhibitions 1862–1910"

I was standing in some great white-walled room, where lamps were burning; but I cast no shadow on the naked floor of that room . . . and there upon an iron bed, I saw my own dead body . . . monstrous curiosity obliged me to remain: I wanted to look at my own body, to examine it closely . . . I approached it. I observed it.

"It is Myself," I thought, as I bent down and yet, it is growing queer—"It is not Myself," I thought again, as I stooped still lower,—and yet, it cannot be any other! And I became much more afraid, unspeakably afraid, that the eyes would open.

—Lafcadio Hearn, Kotto

Mike Leigh's 1999 movie *Topsy Turvy* about W. S. Gilbert and Arthur Sullivan, the hugely successful Victorian musical team, treats the viewer to a classic scene of artistic inspiration, nineteenth-century style. In the movie, as in real life, Gilbert, the librettist half of the duo is undergoing a profound case of writer's block and general disillusionment with the partnership. Wanting to do something different from their typical supernatural musicals, and "fed up with ridiculous plots and topsy-turvy situations," Gilbert is stymied for fresh ideas. A trip to the "Japanese Village" in nearby Knightsbridge, however, brings about inspiration. Having enjoyed the exotic entertainments of the "Japanese Village" Gilbert takes home a Japanese executioner's sword as a souvenir. One day, still stuck for inspiration as he paces at home in his dressing gown, the sword falls from its place of honor above the door. Leigh shows us Gilbert picking it up and examining it thoughtfully and then cuts without further explanation or preparation to a set of Western men wearing kimono, bowing and chanting the lyrics, "Defer! Defer! To the Lord High Executioner!" Music swells and an early scene of what would become Gilbert and Sullivan's arguably most successful operetta, *The Mikado*, is performed before our eyes.

As every critic who has ever written on *The Mikado* points out, the musical, while technically set in the fictional Japanese town of "Titipu," had virtually nothing to do with the realities of nineteenth-century Japan. In fact, contemporary Japanese were so offended by the many liberties taken by the operetta—beginning with its title, which refers to the Japanese emperor—that it was not performed in Japan until very recently. Its gaudy setting, gorgeous costumes, and references to death and suicide did have something to do with how 1885 Britain saw Japan, however: an exotic, highly colored fantasy world, which, despite a draconian legal system, had a disarming allure. Among the most enchanting characters are the "three little maids from school," who essentially perform "cuteness" in a manner that both satirizes Victorian girlhood and presciently anticipates the culture of cuteness revolving around school girls in contemporary Japan.

Despite its gaudy "Japanese" setting, in most regards the play is a brilliant and delightful satire on Victorian British society and also to some extent on universal human foibles. Some of these weaknesses are chronicled in the operetta's immensely popular song "As Someday It May Happen," which is sung by the Lord High Executioner and provides amusing examples of people and personalities who would "not be missed" were he to execute them. These include, ironically, "the idiot who praises, with enthusiastic tone/ all centuries but this, and every country but his own."

For by this period in England and America, as already had occurred in France, the tendency to idealize countries and centuries "not one's own" had become increasingly pronounced. Not so dissimilar to Van Gogh and Gauguin, English artists, writers, and craftsmen were trying to escape the grimmer realities of nineteenth-century civilization through idealizing other periods, other cultures, and other styles of art and life. This trend was epitomized in such movements as Art for Art's Sake, in which aestheticism reached its peak in the sayings and doings of Oscar Wilde; Pre-Raphaelitism, whose members, led by William Morris and Dante Gabriel Rosetti, idealized the Middle Ages; and also Arts and Crafts, whose adherents believed that furniture and housing design could and should be forms of fine art. These movements suggested creative alternatives to the pounding march of technological progress.

In America similar sentiments were being felt, intensified by the horrors and losses resulting from the Civil War. In his book *City of the Falling Angels* John Berendt tells the story of a prominent Bostonian gentleman who left Beacon Hill with his family for Venice, never to return. He explains, "[his] disenchantment with America was a sentiment shared by many people of his class at the same time. It was in part a reaction to the social upheavals brought on by the [C]ivil [W]ar and in part an alarmed response to the arrival of the first wave of immigrants from Ireland, who had little in common with long-established Americans."[1]

To the "long-established Americans" who made up the country's cultural elite at that point, Gilded Age America was a disappointing country that, as Christopher Benfey puts it, was in love "with prosperity alone," a far cry from the basic New England ideals of simplicity and tradition. It is not surprising that many of the East Coast elite looked beyond America and even Europe for what they perceived as a different kind of culture—purer, more rooted in the past. Unlike the English "Japanists" or the French Impressionists, many American aficionados, "all these intellectually and emotionally restless Bostonians,"[2] as Benfey describes them, actually went to Japan. Once there they began to search for everything from "Nirvana," as the artist John LaFarge put it,[3] to something even more ineffable—themselves, or, alternatively, to escape from themselves. Whether they found what they were seeking was another matter.

It is Lafcadio Hearn, an immigrant whose antecedents included the Irish and the Greek but who became the most well-known American writer on Japan during that period, who describes this complex search most eloquently. Early on in his sojourn in Japan, he explores the inner recesses of an altar at a remote Buddhist temple to find "only a mirror, a round, pale disk of polished metal, and my own face therein, and behind this mockery of me a phantom of the far sea."[4] Leaving the temple, he "descends the windy steps," and "then the mockery of the mirror returns to me. I am beginning to wonder whether I shall ever be able to discover that which I seek—outside of myself! That is, outside of my own imagination."[5]

In the passage cited at the beginning of this chapter, Hearn could not escape from a dream of a monstrous double. Now in this passage he looks for enlightenment, only to find his own face. Even the otherness of Japan cannot provide a refuge from the disappointing nineteenth-century Western self. Not only for Hearn, but also for many of the late nineteenth-century Japanists, the "real" Japan could not entirely continue to embody what they sought. While Van Gogh could peacefully ignore the warship in the harbors of Marseilles, intent on creating *his* Japan in Arles and in his "own imagination," later generations did not have this luxury.

The basic problem for the most avid Japanophile as the nineteenth century wound down was that, with modernization in full swing, Japan itself had became a kind of moving target that could not always be kept tamely inside the Western imagination. Although by the turn of the twentieth century, it was still eliciting admiration for its aesthetic qualities, these had been joined by other aspects that provoked both admiration and unease. On the one hand, Hearn, Wilde, and other artists, aesthetes, and intellectuals could still seek in Japanese arts, religion, and ceremonies, a rich and marvelous world of beauty and strangeness where they could look for their lost or other selves. On the other hand, American and British businessmen, politicians, and military strategists were waking up to a Japan that was beginning to resemble the Western nations in aspects ranging from education, politics, and trade to strenuous military adventuring, that looked remarkably like a successful Japanese version of Western imperialism.

The story of Japan in the mind of the West of this period is therefore a more complicated one than in our previous chapter. Although the culture still exerted a pervasive visual impact, it was also penetrating the Western imagination in many other forms. Thus, while for some enthusiasts, Japan continued to stand for an increasingly fragile world of beauty and elegance, for others it was the country's growing military might that overwhelmed Western perceptions. Furthermore, as they had already proved with the Impressionists and the post-Impressionists, the Japanese arts were not simply vehicles used for escape into misty traditions. By the early twentieth century, Japanese haiku would begin to invigorate poetry and help lead to radical new forms of expressing poetic experience on the part of major writers such as Ezra Pound, who would in turn inspire other writers and poets such as W. B. Yeats and T. S. Eliot, whose quotation from his groundbreaking poem "The Wasteland" is the title of this chapter. At the same time, the spatial characteristics of Japanese print and architecture would become significant inspirations for the modernist works of Frank Lloyd Wright, arguably the greatest twentieth-century American architect.

It is not surprising that as the nineteenth century turned into the twentieth, perceptions of Japan became increasingly complicated. Japan's successful war against China in 1894–95 came as a shock to the many countries who still regarded the giant Chinese empire as inherently more powerful than the small island nation. Even more significant was the Russo-Japanese War. When in 1905 the Japanese won its war against the Russian empire, the victory was like a shot heard around the world—the first time a non-Western nation had fought and won a war against a Western power. By the 1920s, Japanese industry, in the form of spinning and weaving was beginning to compete with and ultimately surpass the mills of Lancashire in England.

For better of for worse, Japan was now a country to be taken seriously in the worlds of politics, military strategy, and economics. For the first time since the West had begun to rise, a non-Western country was competing successfully with Europe and the United States. Most shockingly, Japan was beginning to play the game of imperialism and beginning to win, first annexing Formosa (Taiwan), then colonizing Korea, and ultimately pushing settlements into Manchuria. It was also sending immigrants further afield, most controversially to the United States, provoking strongly racist reactions, especially on the West Coast where the largest percentage of immigrants were ending up.

Throughout the period covered by this chapter, we see a deepening sense of uncertainty and unease mixed with genuine admiration and excitement on the part of at least some Westerners dealing with Japan. In 1902 we see the conclusion of the Anglo-Japanese Alliance, an agreement that not only had enormous political and military significance, but also possessed huge symbolic meaning for the Japanese. To the Japanese government and its citizenry, it meant that the Western nations were beginning to accept the country as a major world power, the first non-Western power to be treated in such a way since the modern era began. The abrogation of the treaty (which the British deemed necessary partly because of American pressure and partly because they themselves were concerned about the growing Japanese dominance in East Asia) several decades later symbolized not only that Japan was on its own, but that the Western powers had developed distinctly unwelcoming sentiments toward it. The fact was that Japan was now doing more than knocking on the door of the European powers, but as Roger Louis puts it, was trying to "gate-crash the white man's club of imperial domination."[6]

Ayako Hotta-Lister suggests that during this period, Japan was "emerging as an *alternative* rather than a supplementary culture, worthy of understanding on its own terms."[7] Another way to put it might be that Japan was becoming a problematic mirror to the West, reflecting America and Europe's progress and excesses in its own military and industrial triumphs. At worst Japan could be seen as a version of Hearn's monstrous double, an Asian nation threatening to beat the West at its own game. For its admirers however (and during much of this period, there were still legions), Japan remained a positive Other, whose economic and military dynamism that still (at least in some eyes) combined spirituality and aestheticism offered an alternative form of identity to disillusioned Westerners. Some socialists, falling in with the Japanese government's propaganda about how Japan would "lead" a new Asia, for a time even saw Japan as a beacon against Western imperialist depredations.

Increasingly, Westerners traveled to Japan and came back with their own discoveries and perceptions. As Christine Guth says, "Going to Japan was an excursion into history that made the past tangible in a way books could not."[8] At the same time, many were impressed by Japan's progress toward modernization, seeing in the rapid changes in society the proof of Darwinian and Spencerian theories of evolution. Americans may have felt a particular sense of fellow feeling. Guth suggests that "Americans, as representatives of a powerful and wealthy nation, saw Japan as a young nation much like their own—a land of opportunity for its inhabitants as well as themselves. They assumed that it would follow the same pattern of development as their own country and eventually 'catch up.'"[9]

By the end of the century, Americans and Europeans were coming to Japan in increasing numbers for trade, tourism, and, by the early twentieth century, even political reasons. The things they brought back from Japan were not simply curios. They ranged in the 1870s and 1880s from the Buddhist beliefs that art expert Ernest Fenollosa propagated among American intellectuals to the gorgeous tattoos on the body of the poet Longfellow's son Charley who even created a Japanese-style room when he returned to Massachusetts.[10] By the 1910s and 1920s prominent socialists would visit Japan and for a time find an alternative to Western imperialism asserting that "Japan . . . was the most gifted of the colored races."[11]

At the same time, Japan itself was beginning to work consciously to present itself as positively as possible to the Western gaze. At home, it was carrying on an all-out effort to modernize. In the short run this was an effort to force the West to get rid of the unequal treaty system that had been put into place after Perry. In the long run it was an attempt to avoid the fate of other colonized or otherwise subjugated non-Western territories, by forcing the West to accept the country as an equal.

Japan's diplomats, intellectuals, politicians, and military men were all aware of this need to perform for the Western eye. Perhaps it is no accident that the first line of *The Mikado's* libretto consists of the striking declaration, accompanied by an even more striking visual ensemble, that "We are gentlemen of Japan." Although the song continues (in a tribute to the current Japonisme craze), "We are gentlemen of Japan: / On many a vase and jar— / On many a screen and fan," the truth was that the "gentlemen" of Japan were beginning to step out of their decorative prisons to confront a complex but potentially exciting world and that the world was beginning to confront them as well.[12]

Soft Power: Japan's Performance at International Expositions

Performance, however, or at least presentation, remained an important key to how Japan was perceived. Nowadays we would probably describe this emphasis on presenting a particular appearance on the global stage as a form of soft power, a strategy of influencing world opinion without the use of force. Nowhere is this exercise of soft power clearer than in Japan's strong presence at the international expositions that became increasingly popular as the twentieth century dawned. As we have seen in the previous chapter, these expositions were started in the nineteenth century, and Japan had increasingly taken advantage of them, using its aesthetic tradition to appeal to Westerners in search of visual pleasure. By the end of the century, the expositions had become big business offering entertainment, food, shopping opportunities, and a variety of live performances, from exotic dancers to the Japanese "village" attended by Gilbert in Knightsbridge where he saw native Japanese craftsmen practicing calligraphy and was served tea by genuine Japanese hostesses. In a world before movies and television, it is hardly surprising that such entertainments were enormously popular. Between 1855 and 1914, as Carol Ann Christ points out, a world's fair was held nearly every two years. Between 1910 and 1920 alone, there were forty international exhibitions.[13]

It is no coincidence that the peak period of international expositions coincided with the high tide of global imperialism. While the fairs functioned under a vaguely educational banner, much of what the fairgoers learned was subliminal, namely a way of ordering the world in which Western superiority and progress were both implicitly and explicitly taken for granted. The fairs managed this in many ways: By showing off the technological and industrial discoveries of the West, they helped support the nineteenth-century belief in progress and tied it to Western superiority and faith in a Western-dominated future. By including exhibits from the various colonies, ranging from sports displays and craft-making to entire "villages" of native people, they arranged the world into an ordered and hierarchical collection of peoples, with whites on the top, dominating and pacifying the rest of the world. At a time of uncertainty and change, they offered, as Robert Rydell puts it, "an opportunity to reaffirm [the fairgoers'] collective national identity in an updated synthesis of progress and white supremacy that suffused the blueprints of future perfection offered by the fairs."[14]

But for non-Western and less powerful nations, the expositions played other roles. For Japan, the fairs were originally splendid opportunities to show off its sophisticated aesthetic culture as a way of proving its right to membership among "civilized" nations. As we saw in the previous chapter, the country was brilliantly successful in this strategy, beginning with its first appearance on the world stage in the London Exhibition of 1863 and reaching perhaps an artistic apogee at the Paris Exposition of 1878. As time went on, however, Japan's presence at international exhibitions began to be valued for more than its aesthetic contribution. In New Orleans, for example, the country showed off its recent technological progress in a conscious attempt to have the West see its achievements as something beyond the picturesque. And as Japan began to become a player in geopolitical military games, its presence at a fair also began to signify its political and military authority. Christ for example, quotes Blackmer, the planner of the 1904 St. Louis World's Fair, expounding to his colleagues on the need for a Japanese concession since it "would be a winner . . . because the interest of the world is centered on Japan."[15] This winning position was also helped by the strategic maneuvering of the Japanese government and businesses that made Japan's presence at a fair no longer simply due to its arts and culture. As Christ points out, "By 1904 the Japanese were accomplished exposition participants and promoters of their state and culture, intercepting aggressive Western policies with the production of their own press and exposition propaganda.[16]

How to deal with Japan's rise in the international hierarchy caused a certain amount of puzzlement on the part of the Western hosts of the world's fairs. Social Darwinism was still the organizing principle behind many expositions and indeed was the foundation of the contemporary Western world view in which the white or Aryan race was clearly at the top of the ethnic pyramid. What to do with Japan then? Ultimately the organizers of the Japan-British Exhibition of 1910 came up with an awkward but apparently satisfactory explanation. Using the popular but erroneous discipline of phrenology in which mind and character traits were determined through the study of the contours of the human skull, they graciously explained, "One curious similarity runs through the whole, that is, the striking similitude between Japs and our own people. This resemblance manifests itself in manner, physical stamp and shape of the head . . . The structural conditions are distinctive indications of considerable mental power, and are emphasized by the portraits of some of the most highly placed representatives. Taken as a whole, they constitute a good augury for the growth of sympathy between east and west."[17]

Unable to make the Japanese Aryan (something that Hitler finally accomplished when Japan and Germany became allies in World War II), the British could reassure each other through skull shape that the Japanese were closer to them than the "unprogressive" nonwhite races over which the British empire held sway. Whether this theory was universally accepted is uncertain, but it is definitely the case that the Japan-British Exposition played an important role in updating perceptions of Japan. The exhibition encapsulates the shifting perceptions of Japan during this period. Even its name (with "Japan" coming first) suggests the level of importance that Japan had attained in some ways. Taking place a few years after the Russo-Japanese victory in 1905 and the establishment of the Anglo-Japanese Alliance in 1902 to ward off the German Navy's build-up in the Pacific, the exhibition can be seen, as Hotta-Lister comments, as "an attempt to link the two empires on an equal footing."[18]

The exhibition contained all the traditional trappings that had come to be associated with Japanese installations, including fifty-two sumo wrestlers; yet another "Japanese village;" two Japanese gardens with "authentic trees, shrubs, buildings, bridges and even stones imported from Japan;"[19] models of traditional Japanese architecture; and precious and rare works of art and crafts. But it also included a "Formosan village" and, with suspicious timing, a major exhibit of Korean houses and artifacts, despite the fact that Korea had not been officially annexed until the exhibition was actually taking place. Other less traditional exhibits included a selection of Japanese created "western-style" art and dioramas, some of which emphasized recent Japanese military victories, complete with wax figures of famous military officers. Overall, the exhibition's aim seems to have been an attempt to show off modern Japan by demonstrating, as Hotta-Lister puts it, that its recent modernization was a "natural continuation of Japan's past progress and great history."[20]

How well they achieved this specific aim is open to question. Attendance figures were high, and reactions both in the press and the public were generally favorable. According to Hotta-Lister, *The Scotsman*, for example, perhaps in reference to the daily concerts given by the Japanese military band, was "genuinely impressed by how far the Japanese had come in appreciating [Western] music," suggesting that the Japanese had an extraordinarily fine sense of pitch, helped by their "vigorous faculty of poetic imagination with which no other nation is more abundantly gifted."[21] On the whole, however, visitors seemed still to be more drawn to exhibits that celebrated the Japanese past, such as the historical tableaux that they had painstakingly mounted. Most disappointingly, the exhibit of Western-style art was "greeted with contempt by European connoisseurs."[22] Despite all its efforts to show off Japan's modernity, traditional Japan still held a powerful attraction.

The increasing complexity of Japan as represented in the international fairs is an aspect that casts its shadow on the three figures particularly profiled in this chapter: Lafcadio Hearn, Arthur Waley, and Frank Lloyd Wright. All three of these men can certainly be seen to be admirers of an older and clearly idealized Japan, in the same way that Van Gogh was. Unlike Van Gogh, however, they lived and worked in a very different sociopolitical context. Each of them mourned the passing of "traditional" Japan and in some cases worked hard to ignore it (in Waley's case, at least, succeeding). Hearn and Waley created Japanese fantasy worlds in which they escaped the vicissitudes of Western society. Wright, however, was able to take inspiration from traditional Japanese aesthetics and turn it into a form of modernism that would become very much a part of the twentieth century.

The Collector: Lafcadio Hearn's Japan

The shopkeeper never asks you to buy; but his wares are enchanted, and if you once begin buying you are lost. . . . [T]he largest steamer that crosses the Pacific could not contain what you wish to purchase. For, although you may not, perhaps, confess the fact to yourself, what you really want to buy is not the contents of a shop; you want the shop and the shopkeeper, and streets of shops with their draperies and their habitants, the whole city and the bay and the mountains begirdling it, and Fujiyama's white witchery overhanging it, in the speckless sky, all Japan, in very truth, with its magical trees and luminous atmosphere, with all its cities and towns and temples, and forty million of the most lovable people in the universe.

—*Lafcadio Hearn*, Glimpses of Unfamiliar Japan

I remember as a boy lying on my back in the grass, gazing into the blue summer sky above me, and wishing that I could melt into it, become a part of it . . . Now I think that in those days I was really close to a great truth. . . . I mean the truth that the wish to *become* is reasonable in direct ration to its largeness—or, in other words, the more you wish to become the wiser you are; while the wish *to have* is apt to be foolish in proportion to its largeness.

—*Lafcadio Hearn*, Exotics and Retrospectives

Japan's impressive modernization might win respect, but not love. What continued to seduce Westerners during this period was what many perceived as the enchanting otherness of Japanese culture in terms of culture, religion, and even, for a few, a way of life. As with any prolonged seduction, however, there comes a moment (sometimes many moments) when the beloved is revealed to be less welcoming, less all-encompassing, less absolutely perfect than what had previously been thought; and disillusionment inevitably follows.

Nowhere is this pattern more obvious than in the life and writings of Lafcadio Hearn, perhaps the most intriguing of all the nineteenth-century commentators on Japan. At the risk of sounding flippant, Hearn might almost be described as the "first American otaku," a person who derived from the narrative and visual arts of Japan and ultimately from Japan itself a fascination bordering on obsession. Like today's otaku, Hearn not only loved and appreciated

Japanese cultural products, including the grotesque and the humorous, but also created his own artistic responses to them. Indeed, in the case of Hearn, his responses, in the form of his dozen books inspired by Japanese folk tales, customs, and experiences, are genuine works of art in their own right. At the time that they were published (roughly 1890 to, posthumously, 1910), they were enormously popular among English-speaking readers. In fact it would probably be safe to say that of all the many Western commentators on Japan at this period, Hearn's literary interpretations of Japan held the most sway.

Unlike the more technically learned disquisitions of such Boston writers as Fenollosa or Lowell, or the scholarly writings of English commentators such as Chamberlain or Mitford, Hearn's work was pleasurable to read in and of itself. Although his writing style may be a little flowery for twenty-first-century taste, Hearn's vivid and sympathetic descriptions and keen eye for the "weird" and the "eerie" (among his favorite words) made him a popular favorite during his lifetime. Among his literary idols was the American writer Edgar Alan Poe, echoes of whose ornate style and intense emotional affect resound clearly both in Hearn's language and in his choice of stories. Although Hearn, a former newspaper reporter, wrote on a huge variety of subjects from insect species to Japan's military preparations, a large percentage of his work deals with ghostly visitations, murders, suicides, miracles, and a variety of supernatural events. It is important to emphasize, however, that these events are often presented as wondrous or sometime humorous as much as horrifying. And while they certainly make Japan appear to be a rather eerie country, they seldom portray it in a negative light. Thus, in the story "Of a Promise Kept," two samurai agree to meet on a certain date. On the day, however, one samurai finds himself in prison. Not wanting to break his promise, he commits suicide, and his ghost appears promptly at the meeting place.

While charmingly spine chilling, the story also implicitly holds up the dead samurai as an example of honor and sacrifice, albeit of a rather unusual nature in the West, but certainly recognizable and worthy of appreciation. Other stories that Hearn collected are more amusing than admirable, such as the story of No-Face in which a farmer comes across a crying woman in the depths of night only to discover to his horror that she has no face. Running away, he encounters another person to whom he tells the story. "How awful," the person says, and then he turns to the farmer to reveal—that he too has no face. Both eerie and humorous, the story resonates as an example of universal human emotions—curiosity, shock and fear, the desire for reassurance, and finally, deeper shock and fear—that Western audiences could easily enjoy and with which they could certainly identify.

Essentially, we may describe Hearn as a collector (and in this regard he resembles modern-day otaku as well). But Hearn was a collector in both the physical and the abstract sense of the term. In the concrete sense, he enormously admired what he called "the art impulse"[23] of the Japanese. In a description from his essay entitled "My First Day in the Orient," he writes excitedly that "[On the first day] it . . . appears to [the traveler] that everything in

Japan is delicate, exquisite, admirable—even a pair of common wooden chopsticks in a paper bag with a little drawing upon it; even a package of toothpicks
of cherry-wood, bound with a paper wrapper wonderfully lettered in three different colors."[24]

Remarkably, even now, over a century later, many travelers to Japan still
express similar sentiments about what Hearn described as the "[c]uriosities and
dainty objects [that]bewilder you by their very multitude."[25] But Hearn's next
sentiment, quoted at the beginning of this section, is one that has more explicitly Orientalist implications. This is especially obvious when he confesses that
"what you really want to buy is not the contents of a shop . . . you want shop and
the shopkeeper . . . all Japan in truth and forty millions of the most lovable people in the universe."[26]

To modern readers, the intensity of this sentiment combined with the clear
urge to "possess" the Other may be disturbing. As Steven Caton remarks of a
scene in the film *Lawrence of Arabia* when Lawrence praises a Middle Eastern art
object, "[the scene suggests] the presumption that the Orient exists in the form
of beautiful and exotic specimens to be collected, extracted, and removed from
their local contexts . . . in other words the scene literally objectifies the Other,
who exists not in his or her own right and by his or her own definition but
essentially for the West's imagination and pleasure."[27]

In fact, Hearn goes even further than simple art appreciation in his desire to
ship home "forty millions of the most lovable people in the universe." Not only
the desire to own these "people," but the use of the all encompassing term "lovable" about a nation of forty million individuals smacks of acute condescension.
Looked at from another angle, however, it is possible to see that more than collecting the Other, Hearn wants to unite with the Other (although at root, "collecting" also hints at a deep urge for intimate identification with the Other). His
breathless description of the shops, streets, and scenery of Japan evokes the
same urge he mentions in the next passage: his desire to "melt into" the blue
summer sky, surely the same "speckless" sky that he now finds hovering over
"Fujiyama." By "buying" and "melting into" the Other, Hearn is clearly looking
for a path outside of himself and into an other self. This form of identity transcendence seems very different from Said's theory of Orientalism as a motivation encased in a spirit of domination. Although Hearn's romantic desire for
otherness may be interpreted as Orientalist, the impulse goes deeper than cultural condescension and could instead be considered a form of intense projection, relating to a basic human need for connection.[28]

In Hearn's case, this need for connection would undoubtedly have been
acute. At the point in his career in Japan when the first essay was written, the
country appeared as a place that welcomed him more generously than any of
the various places—from Martinique to Cleveland—that he had lived in previously. For Hearn, in certain ways, had been in exile from the time he was born.
Abandoned by his father as a baby and later on by his mother and raised in a
variety of countries and settings, Hearn became a traveler with a tendency to fall
in love with exotic places—both on the printed page and in reality—from

Martinique to New Orleans. Early on in life, Hearn also fell in love concretely with a person who at that time would have been seen in terms of the American Other, a creole woman named Mattie whom he met in Cincinatti and secretly married, although the relationship ultimately did not last.

Hearn probably first came in contact with Japan through the many Orientalist writings popular in the 1880s, but his first material encounter with the country was through an international exposition, specifically, the New Orleans World Industrial and Cotton Centennial Exposition of 1884, which he was assigned to report on. As Benfey points out, "[Although] the main effort of the Japanese exhibits was to demonstrate the extraordinary success of Japanese educational and industrial programs during the early Meiji Era . . . Hearn's first piece on the exhibits ignores this progressive slant."[29] While Hearn would ultimately acknowledge the "extraordinary success" of Japan's modernization in his later works, this acknowledgement would be tinged with sadness, even bitterness, rather than celebration.

For what Hearn, the reporter and aficionado of Japan, was "collecting" were bits and pieces (or "glimmerings," as he liked to call them) of a culture that seemed to him to be on the verge of disappearing. Hearn collected the physical elements of nineteenth-century Japanese life (including, inevitably, woodblock prints); but his importance as an interpreter of Japan was as a collector of experiences. As Jean Temple, an early writer on Hearn's work, wrote in 1931, "He was dedicated to the task of being the interpreter of experience, who ordered mystery into a system for the salvaging of hope."[30] As befits a former reporter, the experiences he collected were many and varied and included everything from a celebration of the sound of the cicada in the summer time to an acute commentary on the incredible variety of war-related souvenirs and toys produced in Japan at the time of the Russo-Japanese War (including a child's dress covered entirely in battle motifs). They also included many experiences that Hearn "collected" from the Japanese themselves.

Unlike many other commentators on Japan who wrote "about" Japan and the Japanese, Hearn imaginatively projected himself into the Japanese psyche. Some of his most moving writings were from the point of view of ordinary Japanese women. In works such as "A Woman's Diary," "Haru," and "A Street Singer," Hearn invoked the sad, sometimes tragic, situations of suffering and sacrificial women. No doubt, at some level he identified with these forlorn characters, but he writes with a delicacy and sympathy that is slightly reminiscent of the contemporary Japanese woman writer Higuchi Ichiyo. Since English translations of modern Japanese literature were unavailable at that time, Hearn's writings helped to open up a world of "real" Japanese to a curious Western public.

While Hearn tended to idealize and romanticize, he also created memorable portraits of human beings caught up in the maelstrom of change known as modernization. One of his writings in particular, "A Conservative," is a striking encapsulation of the complex psyche of the late nineteenth-century Japanese male. Essentially a composite picture drawn from a variety of Japan's new leaders, "A Conservative" follows a young Japanese man born into the samurai class as he grows up during the period of radical transformation that would change Japan from a basically feudal, isolated country to a "modern" state complete with a constitution, a full fledged bureaucracy, and the beginnings of an imperialist empire. Focusing the story through the young man's eyes, Hearn shows him meeting his first Westerner, giving up his inheritance to convert to Christianity, abandoning Christianity to become an agnostic, traveling and living in Europe and America, and ultimately coming home as a wiser, more cynical adult who looks up at his ship to see the sacred Mount Fuji, recognizing, "from long-closed cells of memory the shades of all that he had once abandoned and striven to forget."[31] In this he is rather like the traveler whom Eliot addresses in "Little Gidding," the end of whose voyaging is to "come back to the place where we started and know it for the first time."[32]

Hearn himself never returned to the West. Instead he married a Japanese woman and took a Japanese name, Koizumi Yakumo, the name by which he is still famous in Japan. According to Carl Dawson, one of Hearn's more recent biographers, Hearn's Japanese wife (he never officially divorced his American one) recounted that "[Hearn] would tell her that he was born Japanese and finally found his way home."[33]

Therefore in Japan, more than any of the other places he had lived and traveled in, two sides of Hearn merged. One was the reporter/collector, the man who wanted to take the shop and the street and finally the country "across the Pacific" and who in a sense accomplished this through his many popular publications. The other was the Hearn who wanted to merge into the" blue sky" and who wished to *become* rather than (like the collector) to *have*.

But perhaps in Hearn's case, *becoming* and *having* are two sides of the same coin. By "becoming" Japanese did he hope that he could finally "have" Japan? In this regard it is worth considering the notion of collecting in general. As Susan Stewart and others have pointed out, collecting is an activity that is intimately connected with nostalgia and longing, often of a deeply utopian kind. In many kinds of collecting, especially miniatures, the world of childhood is invoked. Also related to collecting is the notion of identity, specifically identity creation. By collecting specific objects, the collector projects him or herself onto the object. As Russel Belk says, "Collecting can lead to a symbolic self completion, [a sense] of psychological security that is most critically supplied by a collection."[34]

On the one hand, Hearn with his Japanese name, tendency to dress in kimono, and penchant for projecting his own concerns through a Japanese persona was clearly creating an identity with which he felt more comfortable than that of his own fragmented and alienated psyche. As Dawson points out, "Hearn typified many contemporaries who escaped into real or imagined exile. The Orient was a common haven for Westerners disillusioned with life at home and seeking more intense spiritual or physical experience in another culture."[35] This attempt to transcend one's national and ethnic identity is a negotiation between cultures that, at its most intense, would probably be summed up by the period phrase "going native," or what today we would now call "cultural transvestitism."

Perhaps the most famous example of a Westerner "going native" (or at least attempting to) was the Englishman who, ten years after Hearn's death, would be known by the title of "Lawrence of Arabia." Both Hearn and Lawrence were outsiders—Hearn due not only to his background, but also to the loss of an eye when he was sixteen years old, and Lawrence due to his illegitimacy and homosexuality. Brilliant and imaginative, both found, for a time at least, an escape into a world that, for them, contained utopian qualities. In Lawrence's case, this was the world of desert warfare mixed with the exoticism and eroticism of living and struggling alongside the Bedouin against the Ottoman Empire. In Lawrence's case, Said's theory of knowledge and power does have particular validity since Lawrence was working for the British military throughout his desert sojourn.

Hearn was on his own, and his attempt to transcend himself opened the gates to literary rather than military accomplishments. Hearn's Japan was a world that he described in different ways, but most frequently, as many commentators have noted, in terms of the supernatural—as full of "shadows," "glimmerings," "ghosts," and perhaps most intriguingly, "fairies" or "elves." Thus in the opening pages of his essay, "My First day in the Orient," he describes how "[e]lfish everything seems; for everything as well as everybody is small, and queer, and mysterious."[36] A few pages later, while admitting that this is a "hackneyed" description, he cannot help but use it again when he says that "the ultimate consequence of all these kindly curious looks and smiles is that the stranger finds himself thinking of fairies"[37] but justifies this as "natural," pointing out that "[t]o find one's self suddenly in a world where everything is upon a smaller and daintier scale than with us—a world of lesser and seemingly kindlier beings, all smiling at you as if to wish you well—a world where all movement is slow and soft, and voices are hushed, a world where land, life, and sky are unlike all that one has known elsewhere—this is unlike all that one has known elsewhere—this is surely the realization, for imaginations nourished with English folklore, of the old dream of a World of Elves."[38]

In one sense Hearn was quite right. Given the period in which he was writing, it was indeed "natural" that he should describe the Japanese as elves or fairies. (He seems to use the two terms interchangeably.) Even Isabella Bird, one of the few women commentators on Japan who (perhaps because of her gender) tended to write far more about fleas and dirt, at moments grudgingly also described the country she moved through in similar terms.[39] For Westerners in the late nineteenth century and turn of the century, "fairies," "elves," and "ghosts" were still very much part of the public imagination. Later on, as the casualties from World War I began to mount, the notion of an idealized supernatural world became even more attractive, with many people indulging in the occult and even celebrities like Arthur Conan Doyle, creator of the superrational detective Sherlock Holmes, being taken in by doctored photos of "fairies" in an English garden.

It was only "natural," therefore, that Japan became identified with the "fairy" world. As Benfey writes, "by the turn of the century Japan had, for thirty years, been a fantasy world for American [and—I would add—British] aesthetes."[40] Hearn himself acknowledged that he had long romanticized Japan before he actually arrived there. To a Westerner brought up on folklore and fairy tales, the "smaller," "daintier" Japanese with their "enchanting" little houses and shops might well have seen a realization of an "old dream."

A fascination with size and age bring us back to the collector. Collecting is usually connected to the past—both literally in that we remember where we acquired the object and psychologically. Belk also mentions the sense of "challenge and mastery" involved in collecting and this can also be related to a pleasant feeling of nostalgia. Not only was Hearn constantly looking for the "old" in Japan, he often equated the culture (as did many others) with that of ancient Greece, a world seen by contemporary Westerners in some ways as "primitive," but also purer and more aesthetically inspiring than their own. The ancient Japanese traditions and religions so prized by Hearn can also be seen as another route back to the Western psyche (in the case of Hearn who was half Greek, perhaps a very personal route). Similarly, fairies were also considered an ancient race, possessing mysterious magic and (like both the Japanese and the Greeks in Western perceptions) simpler and closer to nature. Furthermore, as Susan Stewart points out, "the fairies represent the animate human counterpart to the miniature,"[41] and miniatures were (and still are) some of the most popular collectibles. In fact, Stewart's description of depictions of the fairy world reads remarkably like Hearn's encomiums to Japan. As she says, "Unlike the gigantic, which celebrates quantity over quality, the fairies represent minute perfection of detail and a cultured form of nature ... the fairy is depicted as a socialized being with a culture (dress, ritual organization, economy and authority structure) particular to fairydom ... like the miniature world of the dollhouse the world of the fairies is a world of ornament and detail."[42] But Stewart goes on to comment that like the lover who emerges disillusioned from infatuation, "the observer of the fairies must 'wake up' at the conclusion of his or her encounter with these animated miniatures."[43] Both for the collector and the visitor in fairyland, time spent in their world is usually seen as outside of ordinary time.

Unfortunately for Hearn, the passage of ordinary time was his enemy. Already when he first arrived in Japan, the world of old Japan was quickly disappearing. Although he spent one satisfying year in Matsue, a remote town still attractively "old fashioned," even in the twenty-first century, most of his life in Japan was spent in the "ugly" city of Kagoshima and the soulless city of Tokyo. In a revealing letter quoted in Beongcheon Yu's biography of Hearn, he writes, "You wonder why I hate Kumamoto. Well, firstly because it is modernized. And then I hate it because it is too big and has no temples and priests and curious customs in it. Thirdly I hate it because it is ugly. Fourthly, I hate it because I am still a stranger in it and perhaps I can't get any literary material."[44]

Kumamoto and Tokyo were harbingers of the new Japan, a world that Hearn would acknowledge but never emotionally accept. In a later essay called "Strangeness and Charm," he sums up his conflicting feelings toward his Japanese experience in a typically bittersweet passage:

You will never forget the dream—never; but it will lift at last . . . Really, you are happy because you have entered bodily into Fairyland—into a world that is not and never could be your own. You have been transported out of your own century—over spaces enormous of perished time—into an era forgotten, into a vanished age . . . Fortunate mortal! The tide of Time has turned for you! But remember that here is all enchantment—that you have fallen under the spell of the dead—that the lights and the colors and the voices must fade away at last into emptiness and silence.[45]

For Hearn, "the spell of the dead" led to disillusionment and a kind of resigned sorrow. He spent the last few years of his life largely as a recluse although still writing vivid and generally sympathetic accounts of his adopted country. It is perhaps no surprise that Michael Shapiro titles his book about Hearn and other Japan aficionados *Japan: In the Land of the Brokenhearted*. Despite the fact that Hearn deplored where Japan was going, he also, more than many Western aficionados, in some ways accepted the need for Japan to change in order to ward off Western encroachment. Perhaps fortunately, his early death from a heart attack meant that he never lived to see what those changes would lead to.

The "Translator": Arthur Waley, *Genji*, and Modernism

For him there was always the Golden City. Now real now vanishing.

—*Alison Waley, "A Letter to Ivan Morris"*

For ArthurWaley, another Westerner whose writings in English would be crucial in presenting Japan to the West, the "spell of the dead" was actually an inspiring one. The spell of a long dead woman writer would lead him to translate the one-thousand-page *Tale of Genji*, the greatest classic of Japanese literature, and create an English masterpiece at the same time. In Waley's vivid prose, the highly colored eleventh-century world of *Genji* came alive to Western readers during the tense period between World War I and World War II and served as a densely textured escape from the grey uncertainties, searing memories, and political complexities of the inner war period. Like Hearn, Waley presented an exotic Japan for Western consumption. Unlike Hearn, however, what we might call "Waley's Japan" could never die because Waley totally removed himself from the country's modernity. At the same time, paradoxically, Waley's translations of premodern Japanese and Chinese literature would serve to inspire modernist English and American poets.

Waley and Hearn are striking subjects for comparison, both because of their dissimilarities and because of their similarities. Both were fundamentally outsiders, although Hearn had by far the more disadvantaged background in terms of class and economic opportunities. Waley was born in 1889 to an upper-middle-class family in the prosperous British town of Tunbridge Wells. Unlike Hearn who was self-educated and held a wide variety of jobs, Waley was educated among the elite at Cambridge University and would spend his entire career at the British Museum. The museum, in some ways analogous to a more erudite and permanent version of a world's fair, was a tremendously prestigious and powerful institution that, as De Gruchy describes, "mimicked the structure of the world by containing within its sacred, enclosed space the world's languages and styles in myriad manuscripts and artworks that were accordingly objectified."[46] People who worked in this space were also in a sense collectors or at least cataloguers of the objects representing the far-flung interests of the British empire.

Also differing from Hearn, who had a tendency to move from friend to friend as he quarreled with one person after another, Waley had a wide variety of social contacts. A Fabian socialist at Cambridge, Waley also remained throughout his life connected to the Bloomsbury Group, a collection of intellectuals, writers, artists, and aesthetes who included the writer Virginia Woolf and the philosopher Bertrand Russell and others with more marginal connections such as T. E. Lawrence. The thoughts and writings of the Bloomsbury Group would have an enormous impact on art and literature in the English-speaking world, helping to affect the transition from nineteenth-century lyricism to twentieth-century modernism.

One of the two men's most intriguing differences was linguistic. Although Hearn was known for his renditions of many Japanese legends and folktales, his Japanese remained awkward and limited until the day of his death. In sharp contrast, Waley is remembered as one of the great translators of both Chinese and Japanese in the twentieth century. This is particularly impressive when we remember that Waley never actually set foot in Asia. Rather, as he relates with typical upper-class British off-handedness, he turned to Chinese and Japanese because he disliked his reference job, found the Chinese and Japanese materials in the museum of interest, and so "got to work to learn both languages simultaneously."[47] (It should be noted, however, that Waley's language of virtuosity was largely confined to the written versions of both languages.)

This enviable casualness (anyone who has ever tried to learn either Japanese or Chinese might be excused for feeling a little jealous) concealed deeper impulses, however. Like Hearn, Waley also longed for a world outside of himself and clearly lived most intensely in his own imagination. (The anthropologist Carmen Blacker, for example, reminisces about how Waley would abruptly begin an encounter with such conversation stoppers as "The verb 'to say' in the Tao-te ching is never used transitively.")[48] The most obvious reasons for this inwardness are twofold. First was the fact that while well off in income and culturally refined, Waley's family was also Jewish. Although in prewar England, Jews were not officially discriminated against, society still contained a notable strain of anti-Semitism that would consistently render Jews as outsiders, leading to veiled discrimination and sometimes not so veiled acts of bullying and insult. Not only were they outsiders, but as De Gruchy points out, at that period Jews were seen as semi-Orientals, functioning as mediators between the white and non-White world. In this too, Waley resembles Hearn who as half Greek and half Irish never felt at home in the modern West. Consciousness of discrimination on a personal level may have led to consciousness of social injustice on a wider level, and it is perhaps not surprising that Waley was not only quiet and retiring, but also a member of the Fabian Society, the progressive socialist movement favored by such luminaries as the writer H. G. Wells and Sidney and Beatrice Webb, whose favorable attitude toward Japan may have trickled down to Waley while he was at Cambridge.

The other probable motivation behind Waley's outsider status and inner directedness lay in his homosexuality. Although many in his social set at Cambridge and in the Bloomsbury Group were also gay, or at least bisexual, homosexuality was still against the law in Great Britain, and gays and lesbians tended to lead heavily closeted lives. The memory of Oscar Wilde's imprisonment for sodomy and subsequent illness and death was still strong during this period, and neither Jewishness nor homosexuality were discussion points in polite society. Waley himself apparently never wrote about either of these aspects, but we can imagine that both these elements undoubtedly helped shape his outlook on the world from a young age.

Sexual orientation and ethnicity are not the only elements that make up a personality, however, and it should be emphasized that Waley would probably have been the brilliant and imaginative thinker he became no matter what. His brother Hubert remembers an early "anti-herd" instinct,[49] while his wife speaks of a "romantic, timid and diffident" soul who was packed off to boarding school "too early."[50] Given the hearty, Spartan nature of the typical English boarding school during that period, it is not surprising that "the small boy early learned to make escape from the humdrum and repetitive into a world of fantasy."[51]

Few worlds can be of greater contrast than the world of an early twentieth-century British male boarding school and the world depicted in *The Tale of Genji* and the other tenth-century Japanese masterpiece translated by Waley, *The Pillow Book of Sei Shonagon*. Written in both cases by women serving at one of the most glittering courts of the Heian period (800–1185), the two works privilege an ethos of sensitivity, refinement, and romance that would, in Waley's period, have been gendered as feminine and decisively set apart from the muscular masculinity that was taken for granted by elite British society. While the Heian court also contained its fair share of political ladder climbing and would ultimately face military threats, these are only vague shadows on these works where most intrigues are romantic and most amusements aesthetic rather than military.

Given Waley's background and personality, it is not surprising that he should have been drawn to this form of cultural otherness (and, it should be mentioned, the attractions of traditional Chinese poetry as well). What is particularly interesting, however, is how strongly the English-speaking elite of both England and America responded to the world of *Genji*. Almost seventy years after it first appeared in English, Waley's translation of *The Tale of Genji* appears on many reading lists as one of the world's masterpieces of literature, and is still widely appreciated despite many other subsequent fine translations. Even those who otherwise know little about Japan or Japanese culture have heard of it or have even read it (or at least parts of it). No doubt, much of *Genji*'s attraction lies in its compelling narrative, sympathetic characters, and beautiful imagery, all rendered into extremely readable English by Waley. But it is still worth speculating why a one-thousand-page romance set almost a thousand years ago in an obscure Asian country should have such an impact.

As with the previous century's obsession with Japanese culture, much of *Genji*'s appeal no doubt lay in its function as an alternative to the perceived disappointments of modern Western culture. In this case, however, these disappointments went far deeper than a vague discontent over the insidious progress of technology. For *Genji*'s first of six volumes came out in 1925, a few years after the end of World War I, at that point the most devastating conflict in European history. By the 1920s, the Western world wanted to forget about the last war and ignore any markers pointing to another one. *Genji*'s exotic and ancient provenance, combined with what the period would have seen as a remarkably liberated attitude toward sexual relationships (including the merest hint of a homosexual encounter between Genji and a page boy), was the perfect escape. Not only that, it was written by a woman, a fact that would add to its appeal at a time when women's rights were being increasingly recognized.

In *Orienting Arthur Waley*, De Gruchy does an insightful job of analyzing in some detail the reasons behind the popularity of Waley's *Genji*, calling it a "romantic escape in prose from the aftershock of war" and describing how the translation "presented to a contemporary Western audience a vision or fantasy of an alternative order, of everything the West was not; a peaceful, civilized and nonindustrial society in which natural beauty, the arts, and human relations appeared more important than politics or progress, and without a hint of militarism, almost an idealized England at some imagined golden moment of the past, certainly pre-1914."[52] In addition, as De Gruchy points out, Genji's rather androgynous masculinity may also have held a particular appeal. Although the American magazine the *Saturday Review* descried Genji as "the Don Juan of the East,"[53] suggesting a rather macho form of masculinity, the Genji that comes across in both the original and in Waley's translation would probably be described today as a *bishonen* or "beautiful youth," a popular term for the long-haired, starry-eyed sensitive youths who populate today's anime and manga. Although some English and American readers might have found Genji's type of manhood "decadent," it was precisely this kind of gentle aesthetic masculinity that seemed an attractive alternative to the muscular militarism of the immediate prewar period.

Not only is Genji thoroughly unmilitary (at one point he has to call on one of his guards to protect him from a vengeful female phantom), but he seems immersed in such traditionally female-gendered arts and interests as correspondence (as manifested in beautifully written "morning after" letters he sends to his lovers, usually attached to some delicate flower or plant) and fashion (as is shown in the many detailed descriptions of the color and cut of his robes). It is also possible to suggest, as De Gruchy implies, that Waley found in Genji a "second self";[54] but if so, it was a deeply private connection. Unlike Hearn, who exposed his search for his other self in essay after essay, Waley let the translations speak for themselves.

Waley's prose style should also be mentioned, especially in contrast to that of Hearn. By the postwar period, Hearn's florid lyricism seemed out of date. As Earl Miner critically points out about Hearn's readers, "People who turn with warm expectations to a book called *Exotics and Retrospectives* have tastes which the sober-minded find difficult to explain."[55] By the 1920s such "tastes" were disappearing as writers such as Woolf, Joyce, Pound, and Eliot were appearing on the scene with their use of minimalism and unconventional imagery and subject matter that would dramatically change the direction of twentieth-century literature. Waley's imagery and setting are of course fundamentally exotic, but the prose he uses to convey them, while still evoking romantic beauty, lacks almost all traces of Hearn's heavy-breathing romanticism and obsession with the ghostly and the strange. Furthermore, the psychological portraits of the *Genji* characters in all their three-dimensional sufferings and longings were hailed by reviewers as "strangely modern."[56]

If Hearn's work spoke to the complexity of the late nineteenth century with its lamentation of the modern and its attraction to the supernatural, Waley's *Genji* spoke to a world that was more jaded and less hopeful and perhaps precisely because of that, even more in need of a fantasy that was both exotic and yet grounded in reality. Whereas Hearn not only made a narrative of Japan but also made a narrative of himself, Waley created a totally autonomous work of art—one that may well be seen as "an English novel in its own right," as De Gruchy argues.[57]

Japan and Modernism

While Hearn and Waley were dealing directly with original Japanese material, other writers were becoming aware of Japanese literature as a source of interest and inspiration for their own work. Writers and poets such as Conrad Aiken and T. S. Eliot studied at Harvard when, according to Aiken, "[Japanese poetry] was all in the air."[58] The American poetess Amy Lowell was inspired by her elder brother Percival's journey to Japan, a voyage that had led to an important book that had stimulated Lafcadio Hearn as well.

It is with Ezra Pound, however, that we can find the most direct Japanese influence. Pound, one of the greatest poets of the twentieth century is unfortunately nowadays remembered as well for the virulent anti-Semitism and fascism expressed in both his poetry and in other writings, which would ultimately land him in prison camp after World War II. Repellent though his political and social beliefs may have been, he still must be acknowledged as one of the pioneering geniuses of modern poetry, beginning with his largely successful attempt, starting around 1910, to liberate English-language poetry from the flaccid state it had settled into by the end of the nineteenth century. In this regard, he was immeasurably aided by Japanese haiku (sometimes called "hokku") poetry, the traditional verse that, using a combination of vivid natural imagery in a seventeen-syllable structure, was able to create worlds of intense emotion and beauty.

As with Monet and the other Impressionists, Pound did not so much copy haiku as learn from it a new way of approaching reality. Pound referred to this approach as a "kind of knowing" based on images. Rather than spelling out the poem's intent in detail, Pound's poetry suggests its meaning through images, often of a discordant kind, connected to each other in a technique he called "super-position," or "one idea on top of another." Early on, Pound used this technique to create tiny intense vignettes, the most famous of these being his 1914 poem, "In a Station of the Metro," in which the entire poem consists of two lines:

The apparition of these faces in a crowd
Petals on a wet, black bough.

According to Pound, the original poem had been considerably longer but was of only "second intensity." Over a year's time he kept stripping it down; he finally made the "following hokku-like sentence." As Miner points out, by "hokku-like," Pound does not simply mean short or "somehow Japanese,"[59] although these are also aspects of the poem, but rather, I would summarize, the emotional impact of the poem that is based on a sudden epiphany—the realization that beauty can appear even in the dirty crowded metro. Pound's later poetry, most notably his famous "Cantos" would be much longer, sometimes running onto many pages, but still at least partly based on the technique of super-position and spare, carefully chosen imagery that gives the poems a tightly effective overall structure.

Not only did Japan affect the modernists through haiku, but the ancient Japanese theater known as the *Noh* would inspire another one of the geniuses of the English language, the Irish poet W. B. Yeats. Yeats's modernity lies less in his lovely lyrical poetry and more in his experimentation with the theater, where he actually created his own *Noh* plays. The *Noh* is famous for its minimalist sets, beautiful costumes, and surreal atmosphere and also poetic speeches. Yeats's plays, such as *At Hawk's Well* or his Cuchulain cycle of historical plays, were not only similar in structure and libretto to the *Noh*; they also were inspired by the traditional *Noh* subjects of ghosts, heroes, and the relentless power of the past. Writing at a time when Ireland was attempting to free itself from English domination, both culturally and politically, Yeats used heroes and phantoms from the Irish past to produce a vision of alterity that was both "eerie" in a way that Hearn would have recognized, but also "modern" in its spare and minimalist aesthetics.

Collecting Japan: Frank Lloyd Wright

Ever since I discovered the print, Japan had appealed to me as the most romantic, artistic, nature inspired country on earth."

—*Frank Lloyd Wright*, An Autobiography

What Ezra Pound did for poetry—stripping it down and zeroing in on spare intense moments of revelation to pave the road to literary modernism—the

American architect Frank Lloyd Wright may be said to have done for modern architecture. Like Pound, Wright could be bombastic and egotistical (but fortunately without the anti-semitism and fascism), but also like Pound he was an artistic genius of the first order, arguably the greatest American architect of the twentieth century. In the case of both men, their genius was fueled by exposure to Japanese culture. Unlike Pound, however, Wright had a genuinely hands-on relationship with Japan, which he visited a number of times and where he constructed one of his most famous buildings, the Imperial Hotel in Tokyo (unfortunately torn down after the war, although portions of Wright's very beautiful bar remain intact and were moved to the new Imperial building, to the edification of aesthetes and drinkers alike).

Perhaps even more than was the case with Pound, Japanese culture, specifically Japanese artistic culture, was a profound and persistent influence on Wright. Not only was Wright inspired by Japan, but he also literally collected Japan, in this case, in the form of Japanese art—in particular the woodblock prints that had inspired the Impressionists and post-Impressionists, and which became for him not only an obsession but also a business. Buying them in Japan and bringing them back to America, Wright wheeled and dealed across the United States, selling prints to wealthy mid-Western clients, using them as collateral for loans and pressing them on his employees in lieu of cash bonuses. After he became an established architect with a coterie of students, he would gather his disciples around him at Taliesin, his beautiful home in Wisconsin, for "print parties." Feasting on sukiyaki, Wright would lecture them on prints, explaining how the Japanese artists provided a "refreshment" to Western perspective and that, after looking at, say Hiroshige's treatment of rain, "you never look at nature the same way after . . . certain realistic things disappear, and the whole scene becomes more effective and simple."[60]

I began this chapter with Hearn and will end it with Wright because both men expressed their love of Japan through the collecting impulse. Undoubtedly, the Japanese curios and arts with which they surrounded themselves affected not only their work, but their approach to life in general. There are many photographs of Wright in rooms full of Japanese and other Asian antiquities, and it is surely no coincidence that Wright suggested Japanese screens, prints, and woven materials for his clients to use as decorative motifs inside his spare organic architecture. Hearn's love of small and curious Japanese decorations and souvenirs undoubtedly found his way into his writing as he emphasized the strange and the miniature.

Wright's love affair with Japan was very different from Lafcadio Hearn's heartbreaking seduction. But in both cases, their initial interest in the country came out of the currents of Japonisme that swirled through the United States in the late nineteenth century, embodied in the Japanese exhibits at two midwestern world's fairs that they both attended. We have already described Hearn's reporting on the New Orleans World's Fair, which helped inflame his interest in Japan as a mysterious Other. Wright would probably first encounter Japan through the beautiful Hooden (Phoenix Pavilion) that was especially constructed for the mammoth Chicago Exposition of 1893. Both men would also fall in love with a preindustrialized vision of Japan, exhalt the Japanese love of nature, and mourn the depredations of modernization.

At the same time, of course, what the two men did with "Japan" was very different, reflecting not only different personality types, but the different opportunities presented to them. Born in the Midwest in 1867, Wright came from a family that was substantially better off than Hearn's and deeply rooted in Midwest values that at that time were in some ways a microcosm of American society. In her book on Wright, Julia Meech quotes Vincent Scully who said of Wright that "he was the embodiment of [the late nineteenth century's] most tenacious attitudes: of its supreme confidence in the common future, and of its desperate, complementary yearning for pre-industrial, sometimes pre-civilized images and symbols to root itself upon."[61]

While Wright's "yearning" for the preindustrial echoes that of Hearn (or for that matter, Van Gogh and Gauguin), his " supreme confidence" was both very American and very much part of his own deeply egotistical personality. In many ways, however, it must be admitted Wright's confidence and egoism were well deserved. While Hearn's achievement seems largely time-bound, Wright is still referenced today as a major innovator and inspiration in the way we build the world around us. It is probably not too extreme to say that he, like the Impressionists in the nineteenth century, helped to change the way the modern world visualized space, light, and color, not to mention architecture's relationship with the natural and the organic. His achievements include the extraordinary white nautilus shell design of the Guggenheim Museum in New York and the exquisite private home, Falling Water, a house he designed to take maximum advantage of its pastoral surroundings. But perhaps his most important contribution was his creation of houses for the "common man," which included his early "prairie houses " and later his "usonian bungalows." These low-slung minimalist dwellings were inexpensive to produce, relatively easy to maintain, and, in their low key way, extremely attractive, fitting into the landscape around them with subtlety and grace.

Although Wright's genius was recognized long before he died, the extent of his indebtedness to Japan has to some extent been downplayed until fairly recently. This underplaying was surely due to Wright's own arrogant insistence that he found in Japanese aesthetics' "confirmation" of his own approach rather than "inspiration." Or as he put it once in his inimitable way, "I'm not indebted to the Japanese—the Japanese are indebted to me."[62]

Fortunately, in the last decade, two major studies reassessing Wright's relationship with Japan have appeared—one by Kevin Nute and the other by Julia Meech—which trace in great detail the many connections between Wright's art and Japan. Neither book takes away from Wright's originality and genius, but they effectively show how in many ways that genius was affected by Wright's exposure to Japanese architecture, art, and the country itself, not to mention East Asian philosophy and art in general.

Wright came to young manhood while Japonisme was still sweeping the country. Japanese curios, prints, and other forms of Japanese decoration had filtered down to American middle class parlors where they juxtaposed themselves rather awkwardly with the rather overstuffed world of Victoriana. But Japan's influence was being felt in other areas as well, including philosophy and religion and even the tea ceremony that had become quite the rage among upper class ladies in the Northeast.[63] Wright was in touch with or at least aware of some of the most important exponents of this movement, including the Bostonian collector and writer Ernest Fenollosa and the Japanese art historian Okakura Tenshin. Most famous for what might be called his self-Orientalizing writings about the unique aspects of Japanese culture, particularly his well-known *Book of Tea*, Okakura, aided by his friend Fenolossa, was at the heart of promoting Japanese culture in America during this period.

Wright was an admirer of *The Book of Tea*, but probably his first encounter with Okakura's writings was through the Japanese scholar's pamphlet on the exquisite Phoenix Pavilion at the Chicago World's Fair. Although there is apparently no actual record of Wright visiting the Hooden, the pavilion and the buildings grouped around it were on display for many years after the world's fair had ended and during the time that Wright was a young architect working for the prominent Chicago architecture firm of Louis Sullivan. The Hooden was well known and extensively admired during this time, so it seems almost impossible that Wright would not have visited it.

As Judith Snodgrass describes it, the building and the art inside it "presented an image of the sophistication and elegance of Japanese civilization from a period four hundred years before the discovery of America to the present."[64] She also points out that this "presentation" was very much for politically strategic purposes. Okakura himself was a strong nationalist, and Japan was very eager to show itself as a civilized nation in order to get the unequal treaties imposed on it by the West revised. This was so much the case that according to Snodgrass, "Japanese speeches and publications connected with the exposition, from the first introduction by the Japanese commissioner at Washington to the dedication ceremony of the Hooden, stressed the issue of the treaties and related the Japanese exhibit to Japan's desire for their revision."[65]

Whether Wright was aware of the political messages underlining the exposition is doubtful, but it is clear throughout his writings that he was ready and willing to admire Japan and its civilization without much outside prodding. It is likely that what he derived from Hooden and subsequent Japanese buildings was a very different approach to structure than that of conventional European or American architects. Some of these differences were very specific—Wright seems to have borrowed the idea of the Japanese *tokonoma*, or alcove, as the space that draws one's eye on entering the room and reinterpreted it through his positioning of fireplaces as the core element in his early prairie houses.[66] Other influences are more general and longer lasting, and some have remained influential into the twenty-first century.

One of the key aspects of Japanese architecture is the fluidity and flexibility of space. Rooms flow into rooms (separated by sliding screens) and offer a variety of uses. One of Wright's crucial ideas was to get away from the room as box, a concept that dominated Western residential building. Japanese houses and temples presented a fresh and appealing way of organizing space even in small residences. Those of us who live in houses with open floor plans today are to some extent the heirs of this attempt to get away from the box. The Japanese emphasis on restraint in furniture and decoration also offered an alternative to the overstuffed interior decoration that until recently had dominated American Victorian homes. Finally, the traditional Japanese insistence on using organic materials, mainly wood, and situating houses and temples in relation to gardens and larger landscapes was an extremely important aspect of Wright's aesthetics and one that the best architects today attempt to carry on.

It should be reemphasized that Wright consistently asserted that Japanese architecture did *not* influence him. Indeed he was already working on prairie houses before he ever set foot in Japan, but even his fellow architects at the time believed that they saw many traces of Japan in his work. Wright did, at least, acknowledge that Japanese prints were a genuine inspiration to him. One of his favorite beliefs was what he termed "the elimination of the insignificant," and Japanese prints to him seemed to offer a minimalism that in its refinement, striking use of color and space, and tolerance of unusual compositional techniques, was far more appealing than overdone Western aesthetics. Meech quotes from a booklet Wright published in 1912 in which he talks about the geometrical structures in Japanese art "structure [being here] used to describe an organic form"[67] and points out that "this could equally well be a statement of Wright's own philosophy of architecture."[68]

Not just art and architecture but Japan itself inspired Wright, particularly the city of Tokyo, which he referred to by its premodern name, Yedo. Wright particularly seemed to enjoy the night views of Tokyo, rhapsodizing about the "softly brilliant globes or cylinders the red paper lanterns patterned with strange characters in white or black,"[69] in a way that recalls Hearn's early romanticization of the country and also anticipates the French semiotician Roland Barthe's delight in the incommunicable "signs" of modern Japan. Like Hearn, Wright lamented the passing of traditional Japan, although it is possible that he might have found present day Tokyo's neon jungle an interesting form of contemporary aesthetics.

Ultimately for Wright, Japan was a fantasy that inspired real world changes. The country would leave its traces in many aspects of Wright's art in ways that were subtle but deeply influential in terms of modern architecture in general. What Wright accomplished was far more than simply creating Eastern style pleasure palaces of pagodas and domes that earlier "Orientalist" architects had spread over the European and American landscape. His work stimulated a fundamental change in the way in which architecture was approached, especially in residential houses. His gorgeous creation Falling Water, a private house in Pennsylvania actually built into a waterfall, is his most famous work that blends the organic with the manmade. But his many more workaday homes with their subdued interiors, flowing space, copious use of wood, and restrained lines offered an exercise in practical aesthetics that seem to owe a great deal to Japanese style.

In the long run, it is perhaps not necessary to decide how much of Wright's achievement was "influence" and how much was "confirmation." Wright was a genius, and part of that genius was the ability to take inspiration from a wide variety of sources, not just Japan, but Chinese and Mayan architecture as well. Wright's "collecting" of Japan, therefore, was far from the inward-looking selfish motive to possess that which we might suspect motivates the collector. In his case, the collection became the source of an outward-looking movement to teach, inspire, and ultimately change forever the way modern society constructs its living and gathering spaces.

Wright would live on until 1959, long enough to see Japan enter what they themselves called the Valley of Darkness, the era of rising militarism that led to a devastating war and the loss of much of what he loved in Japanese culture. But he always had his prints. Even late into the 1950s he would take out a variety and expound them to his students. As Meech records, he died owing money to two galleries specializing in Japanese prints.

3

Paths of Power: Japan as Utopia and Dystopia in the Postwar American Imagination

In 1962 the darkly imaginative American science-fiction writer, Philip K. Dick, published one of his first major novels, *The Man in the High Castle*. In it, Dick envisions an alternative future in which the Axis powers have won World War II, was surely conscious of, he shows the Japanese behaving like Westerners profiled in our previous chapters, searching not only for refined American antiques, but also for the "historic objects of American popular civilization."

And the Americans are eager to sell. In an early scene, Robert Childan, an antiques dealer who is one of the novel's main protagonists, welcomes an elegantly dressed Japanese couple into his shop:

> "Hello," he said and felt better. They smiled at him without any superiority, only kindness. His displays—which really were the best of their kind on the Coast—had awed them a little; he saw that and was grateful. They understood.
> "Really excellent pieces, sir," the young man said.
> Childan bowed spontaneously.[2]

In the beginning, *The Man in the High Castle*'s text seems preoccupied with the physical and the material, such as the objects of collection that the Japanese lust after, ranging from brass buttons and guns to, as Childan puts it breathlessly, "*an original signed portrait of Jean Harlow.*"[3] Ultimately, however, the novel becomes, as is typical in Dick's writings, a meditation on the meaning of what is real and the arbitrariness of fate, leaving the reader questioning his or her own perception of history. Toward the end of *High Castle*, the novel reveals the existence of another alternative history, written by a man perhaps very much like Dick himself, in which this time the United States and its allies have won the war.

As we know (or do we?), it is the second alternative history that is the correct one. But *High Castle*'s visionary world makes an excellent launching pad from which to explore some of the salient points of postwar Japan's impact on the American imagination, including the period in the 1980s when some Americans really did wonder which side had won the war. It should be noted that this chapter particularly concerns Japan and the United States because with the end of World War II and the subsequent U.S. occupation of Japan, the relationship between Japan and the United States developed particular significance, not only economically, militarily, and politically, but also in terms of culture.[4]

This chapter is about roads—physical, spiritual, and virtual. Dick's novel begins after the world had gone down the road to the single bloodiest catastrophe in human history—a war that ended with the American atomic bombing of two Japanese cities, Hiroshima and Nagasaki. The shadow of the war would permanently haunt Japanese-American relationships, although from very different angles. For the Japanese, the Americans would go from a hated and vilified memory to an ambivalent form of elder brother, or even father figure, whose economic assistance and military protection played a large part in lifting their economy on the road to recovery.[5] For Americans, Japan remained ambiguous—a defeated but grateful enemy epitomized as the self-sacrificing Japanese woman in so many 1950s movies whose distinct and appealing culture could be seen in Japanese gardens across the country or found in translations of Japanese poetry. At the same time, however, Japan still remained unalterably Other, intriguing but fundamentally different and difficult to understand, perhaps even a little uncanny.

It is probably no accident that decades after the end of the war, Americans still identified Japan with Godzilla, the voiceless prehistoric monster unleashed from the depths of the ocean through American nuclear testing. The *Godzilla* film series that began in 1953 was highly popular in both countries (and in much of the rest of the world as well), providing an entertaining way of subconsciously working through postwar nuclear trauma.[6] The American humorist Dave Barry, looking back on his childhood in the 1950s offers a characteristic account of his first impressions of Japan, which included watching "maniacal" Japanese soldiers in World War II movies on television and then watching creature features on the big screen movie theaters. As he says, "From these I learned that Japan was not just a weird foreign country that had tried to kill us, it was also a weird foreign country that was for some reason under almost constant attack by giant mutated creatures. Godzilla was the most famous one."[7]

While the Japanese grappled with rebuilding their ravaged country, Barry and many other young Americans were growing up in an increasingly affluent and materialistic culture, one that seemed to provide for all wants, except, perhaps, those of the spirit. In the contradictory and puzzling postwar world, some of these young people began to set out on the road looking for enlightenment and even new forms of identity. Dick's characters travel across the western

United States in search of the "man in the high castle" who will show them another version of history and reality. Starting in the 1950s, the Beat writers Jack Kerouac and Gary Snyder also followed literal roads up the West Coast, searching for the Zen enlightenment known as satori and finding it in nature, art, and for Snyder, perhaps, in Japan itself. The 1970s brought about a search for paths that American government and business might follow to find the secrets of Japanese economic superpowerdom, exemplified in books such as the sociologist Ezra Vogel's *Japan as Number One* (revealingly subtitled, *Lessons for America*) or the analyst William Ouchi's *Theory Z: How American Business* Can *Meet the Japanese Challenge*. The fascination with Japan's success itself brought about a backlash, as resentful American men searched for a path back to satisfying masculinity exemplified in popular culture works such as the novel and film *Rising Sun*. Finally in the 1980s, the roads led to what might be called TechnoJapan and the exploration of the mental and the virtual, culminating in the "lane to the land of the dead" in William Gibson's cyberpunk science-fiction novel *Neuromancer* and the Walled City where the *otaku* dwell in his later novel *Idoru*.

Even more than previous chapters, this chapter is also about the complexities of power. Dick's science-fictional vision takes off from the brutal memories of a recent war to show an all encompassing power reversal in which Americans obsequiously "bow spontaneously" as they put their country on sale to the Japanese. Twenty years later, in Michael Crichton's ominous thriller *Rising Sun*, a character describes an economically cowed America as "spreading her legs to the Japanese." Perhaps not surprisingly, gender plays an important role in many of the texts we will examine. By the 1990s William Gibson's cyberpunk novels would begin to anticipate Japan's new role as a purveyor of "soft power" exemplified in a virtual embodiment of the ultimate Asian woman.

Power, however, is not simply military or economic or sexual, and it is not always negatively portrayed. The relative privileging of Japanese civilization in *High Castle* echoes not only the sense of Japan as a spiritual, environmentally sensitive, and world evoked in Beat literature and poetry, but also prefigures some of the idealization of the Japanese system that occurred at the height of Japan's economic success story. By the end of the century, in Gibson's cyberpunk science fiction, Japan became a powerhouse of ideas for how all citizens of industrialized countries would soon be confronting a technologized future. As he says in an interview in 2001, "The Japanese, you see, have been repeatedly drop-kicked, ever further down the timeline, by serial national traumata of quite unthinkable weirdness, by 150 years of deep almost constant change . . . they've been living in the future for such a very long time now."[8]

By the millennium, the Japanese advancements in technology could be accepted as exciting and "cool." In Gibson's eyes, the Japanese are "further down the time line" than the rest of the industrialized world, harbingers of what is to come, a notion both heady and disturbing. For much of the postwar period, however, the response to Japan was more ambivalent. At its most negative during the 1980s, some Americans saw Japan as the enemy that had actually "won the war," a literal expression of Dick's alternative history. Japan seemed to be "conquering" America through its financial might, a turn of events that some observers felt served as a wake up call to a complacent America.

The Shadow of World War II

Even in the twenty-first century, the alignment of "Japan" and "war" is still a prevalent one, as was obvious in the many invocations of Japan's "sneak attack" on Pearl Harbor after the attacks of September 11.Over sixty years after the Allied victory, the events that constituted the war in the Pacific, and the American occupation that followed remain a defining experience in the history of both societies. While, for the Japanese, the defeat and the occupation were psychologically traumatizing, for Americans, victory over Japan and the seven years of military control that followed remain one of the most successful of the country's military undertakings.

Tens of thousands of young Americans were sent over to Japan during the years from 1945 to 1952 and came home usually with curios and swords, sometimes (as in the film version of *Sayonara*) with wives and always with recollections of a culture deeply different from their own. Unlike the problematic occupation of Iraq, the U.S. government had both the time and the impetus to prepare quite carefully for the postwar order, consulting scholars of Japan and even helping to engender the writing of what would become one of the most influential books ever published about Japan, *The Chrysanthemum and the Sword* (1946) by the anthropologist Ruth Benedict.

Chrysanthemum, which is still read today, has been described by a twenty-first-century anthropologist as "the master narrative" on Japan for the West.[9] This is not to say that the book is a flawless introduction to Japanese society. Based on Benedict's interviews with Japanese internees in America during wartime, the book, perhaps inevitably, contains oversimplifications and inaccuracies. As its title suggests, for much of the twentieth century it was easy to look at Japan in terms of binomial oppositions. The "chrysanthemum" implied the artistic and refined side of Japanese culture, while the "sword" naturally represented the militaristic and violent elements of Japanese history that had been uppermost in American minds during the recent bloodshed. Such categorization inevitably runs the risk of essentializing a complicated culture, but it should also be acknowledged that *The Chrysanthemum and the Sword* captured some of the intricacies of Japanese civilization (such as the importance of hierarchy and reciprocity) quite well. Even today, most anthropologists and sociologists acknowledge the book as a milestone in the study of Japan. A contemporary anthropologist, Sonia Ryang, while having a rather negative view of Bendict's work, sums up her idea of the work's value in the following intriguing passage: "Despite the book's many shortcomings, following the war, by the end of which Americans came to regard Japan as a subhuman monster, the significance of Benedict's work was immense: she salvaged Japanese humanity, by trying to render its monstrosity comprehensible and logical."[10]

Although Bendict herself might be surprised by such a description, since *The Chrysanthemum and the Sword* never mentions the word "monster," it is certainly the case that the book was written within a wartime context in which, to many Americans, the Japanese were indeed "monstrous." During the war, the American press and government propaganda developed truly grotesque stereotypes about Japan. While Dick's novel, written twenty-five years after the war's end, presents the Japanese occupiers in a far more favorable light than the brutal Nazis whom he depicts as taking over the U.S. East Coast, during the war itself, images of the Japanese were usually far more vicious than those depicting Germans.

These savage depictions undoubtedly had much to do with race, relating to prewar fears of a "Yellow Peril," a vision that encompassed China as well, in which the Asian "masses" were seen as potentially overwhelming the white race. But their more immediate cause was Japan's successful surprise attack on Pearl Harbor, which initiated war in the Pacific. Shocked and enraged by the attack, the American press and U.S. government propaganda rushed to fill the void of knowledge about Japan with hideous visions of the Japanese military man. As John Dower chronicles in his ground-breaking book, *War Without Mercy: Race and Power in the Pacific War*, these depictions ranged from showing the Japanese soldiers as demonic supermen in the early stages of the war when the Japanese seemed to be triumphing militarily, to later representations of them as monkey men, or else as massed hordes embodying the Yellow Peril when the war began to turn in favor of the United States.

As Dower's book makes clear, this kind of racist stereotyping was carried out by both sides during the war and is no doubt inevitable in any kind of cross-cultural conflict. What is intriguing, however, is how the myth of the Japanese superman resurfaced as another kind of war between Japan and America during the postwar period. This was the trade war of the 1980s that, despite the fact that no blood was shed, led to its own share of demeaning and demonic stereotypes that were in some ways as vitriolic as those expressed during World War II. But even during this period, counter-stereotypes also existed, from the feeling among American Zen enthusiasts that Japanese religion held a key to a superior form of spirituality and aesthetic taste, to the belief among some American academics, bureaucrats, and businessmen that Japanese efficiency could be considered a role model rather than a threat.

This chapter takes us through the four decades after World War II, a period when Japan and Japanese culture again began to become close to the lives of the average American, whether it was in the form of the little books of translated Japanese haiku poetry that were particularly popular in the 1960s, or in the shape of the well-designed fuel-efficient Japanese cars that the American consumer began to buy in the late 1970s. The country itself remained exotic and remote to many Americans, but practical Japanese products, from cars to cameras to stereos, were increasingly becoming an ordinary part of their lives in a way that they had never been in the prewar period.

This change had far-reaching economic, political, and ultimately cultural consequences. As time wore on and Japan went from being an economic basket case to an economic superpower in the 1980s, American business began to look at Japan with uneasy eyes, believing that not just Japanese goods but Japanese culture was becoming a major threat. The threat was seen as affecting both cherished American business practices and values, such as the "bigger is better" ethos that dominated the U.S. motor industry, and also cherished American icons such as movie studios in Hollywood or the Rockefeller Center in New York. The relatively benign "collecting" of American culture by the Japanese envisioned in Dick's book became the rape of America in the film and novel versions of *Rising Sun*. Furthermore, by the 1980s, Japan's economic success began to intrude itself more subtly on Western literary and cinematic consciousness. For writers such as William Gibson or Hollywood film directors such as Ridley Scott, Japan became a kind of data bank of both utopian and dystopian images.

Of course utopian aspects of "fantasy Japan" had been around for a long time. We have seen the impulse to idealize Japan previously in the visions of creative artists such as Van Gogh and Frank Lloyd Wright and writers such as Lafcadio Hearn. These tended to be strongly aesthetic visions, imagining an immensely rich culture of artists and artisans that could be "collected" in the form of cultural works from Japan and Western artistic responses to them. What might be called the postwar Utopianization of Japan was a more diverse formulation having, broadly, three aspects. The first is the idealization of the Japanese woman discussed in Chapter 4. The second is the belief in Japanese Zen as embodying at least one approach to an environmental and spiritual utopia, an approach most memorably expressed in the writings of the Beat generation. The third is what for a brief period amounted to almost an obsession among some American business people and government officials, in which the Japanese were seen as economic and technological supermen who were threatening American economic dominance through a combination of sneaky tactics and superior work ethics and strategies. Ultimately, this last vision helped give rise to the dystopian side of the coin—an image of a powerful, futuristic TechnoJapan that was both frightening yet, in some cases, uncannily appealing.

Jack Kerouac, Gary Snyder, and the Road to Dharma

> I wanta bicycle in hot afternoon heat, wear Pakistan leather sandals, shout in high voices at Zen monk buddies standing in thin hemp summer robes and stubble heads, wanta live in golden pavilion temples, drink beer, say goodbye, go Yokohama big buzz Asia port full of vassals and vessels, hope, work around, come back, go, go to Japan, come back to U.S.A. read Hakuin, grit my teeth and discipline myself all the time while getting nowhere and thereby learn.
>
> —*Jack Kerouac,* The Dharma Bums

The history of the postwar perception of Japan in the United States is in some ways as unexpected and strange as the fictional history of *The Man in the High Castle*. In 1945 Japan was simply a defeated nation, devastated by American might and seen as a potential economic dependent for decades to come. By the century's end, American perceptions of Japan would be far more complicated.

As was the case in the 1920s, Japan had once again become a kind of mirror to the West. In this case, the country at certain points became a mirror reflecting America's hopes, fears, and illusions.

The United States of the 1950s was a powerful place. Despite concerns over the cold war, the country was also enjoying an unprecedented material prosperity and satisfying sense of itself as the victor in the recent global conflict. Affluence and power allowed for grand projects. One of these was the building of the interstate system, which unified the United States in ways the country had never experienced before. Not only did the system help solidify a sense of what it was to be American (by supporting an increasingly homogenized national culture), but the cross-country road system engendered the freer movement of commerce, which helped to develop the affluent American middle-class lifestyle that would make it the envy of the rest of the war-torn world.

For Jack Kerouac, the most important writer of the Beat generation, middle-class affluence was something to be avoided, escaped from, and critiqued. In Kerouac's eyes, his fellow Americans were trapped in a prison of consumption, living in "[r]ows of well-to-do houses with lawns and television sets in each living room with everybody looking at the same thing and thinking the same thing at the same time."[11] Kerouac's antidote to this toxic state of affairs was "the road," as chronicled in his two major 1950s novels, *On the Road* (1955) and *The Dharma Bums* (1958). In Kerouac's vision, the road was both the concrete road that took him on his journeys across America and also the "eight-fold path" that he hoped would bring him Buddhist enlightenment.

But this search for enlightenment was not only for himself or his friends. Like Basho, the great haiku poet, or Hakuin, a medieval Japanese Zen priest who were among the Beat generation's inspirations, Kerouac wanted to be a traveler who enlightened both himself and others along the way. In *Dharma Bums* he offers a vision of "a great rucksack revolution thousands or even millions of young Americans wandering around with rucksacks, going up to mountains to pray . . . all of them Zen Lunatics who go about writing poems that happen to appear in their heads for no reason."[12] This vision actually belongs to Kerouac's friend and mentor, the writer Gary Snyder (refigured as "Japhy Ryder" in the novel), whose poetry and essays would also serve as important means of introducing aspects of Buddhist culture to Americans lost in the desert of materialism.

Kerouac and his friends were not the first group of Americans to become interested in Buddhism. Earlier American Buddhists in the nineteenth century ranged from Ernest Fenollosa, the Boston art collector who wrote a long poem called "East and West" extolling the virtues of syncretism, to middle-class women in the Midwest, to a small circle of college students in at the University of South Dakota.[13] In general these adherents seemed to be in search of a philosophy that would run counter to the late nineteenth-century American trend of what J. J. Clarke describes as the "prevailing mood of Western triumphalism."[14]

In many ways these early followers were not so different from the Beats (nor from the European Japanophiles profiled in previous chapters). Although many appreciated Buddhism for possessing what they felt was lacking in Christianity— such as tolerance or even a rationalism that might accord better with the new theories of Darwin and Spencer—many also seemed to have experienced what an American scholar of the time called "the pleasure . . . arising from the strangeness of the intellectual landscape [of Buddhism] . . . so different from anything to which I have been accustomed that I feel as all the time as though I were walking in fairyland."[15]

In their growing attraction to Buddhism, Americans were helped along by various Japanese commentators, the most famous of whom was Daisetsu T. Suzuki, a teacher, scholar, and proselytizer whose long career (he was born in 1871 and died in 1966) and enormous output (he published over one hundred books on Zen) allowed him to become the major promoter of a Zen Buddhism that was strongly linked to certain stereotypes about Japanese culture. Suzuki is appropriately seen as a master "self-orientalist," helping to develop an image of Japan as a mystic country of unique traditions, most of which he related to Zen and also to the spirit of bushido, or "the samurai spirit."[16] Far from being abstract in the way of many religious texts, Suzuki's writing also contained many concrete examples and anecdotes making Zen appear to be a particularly approachable kind of religion. In his classic work, *Zen and Japanese Culture*, he included many poetic images to evoke a mystical spiritual Japan but at the same time played on the Western (and by then Japanese) fascination with the cult of the samurai sword, offering two long chapters on the relationship between the sword and Zen that would presumably help explain the religion to Western men and women.

Suprisingly, neither Kerouac nor Snyder seeem particularly interested in the samurai ethos. But it still clear in *Dharma Bums* in particular that Kerouac's and Snyder's attraction to Buddhism was not simply philosophical but cultural as well, an interest in a "strange" remote world that seemed to offer a rich and fascinating way of life. As the quotation at the beginning of this section makes clear, Japan itself, with its "golden pavilion temples" and its "big buzz Asian port" of Yokohama, was part of the allure. Ultimately Snyder would spend years in various parts of Japan, integrating his experiences there into both his poetry and his essays and marrying a Japanese woman. Kerouac never went to Japan, but his writing, especially his poetry, was clearly inspired by the Japanese poetic form known as haiku, while his work in general contains references to such Japanese Zen masters as Hakuin (1686–1769) or the Zen version of enlightenment known as satori. In the mid-1950s, Kerouac began making notes on Buddhism and adding responses and poetry, compiling them in a long volume that would be published after his death as *Some of the Dharma*.

Like many adherents, Kerouac's interest in Buddhism was not only in Japanese Buddhism per se, but in the religion as a whole. Born and raised a Catholic in an immigrant family in Lowell, Massachusetts, he discovered references to Buddhism in the early 1950s in the writings of Henry David Thoreau (another New England nonconformist). Although ultimately his Catholicism would prove impossible to wholly reject, Kerouac, for at least a decade, immersed himself in Buddhist teachings.

This complex and profound religion emerged in India in the fourth century and was carried across Asia, flourishing in Tibet, Japan, and Southeast Asia. Zen, the sect most well-known in America, was actually developed in China but decayed there and eventually became most associated with Japan, partly because it was the favorite discipline of the samurai. Zen's emphasis on enlightenment through meditation and through the enigmatic riddles known as *koan*, plus its concern for the cultivation of both military and aesthetic arts, appealed to both the warrior and the poet. Rather than relying on difficult texts, Zen, at least as it was taught in the West by Suzuki and others, thrives on intuitive leaps, quirky parables, and an emphasis on simplicity and the fundamental relationship between humanity and the cosmos.

In medieval Japan, there arose a cult of the hermitage celebrating Zen believ-ers who would retreat to mountain refuges, far from the turmoil of daily life to paint, meditate, and appreciate the beauties of nature.[17] As such, what might be called the "Zen lifestyle" was about as distant from the materialism of the American 1950s (what Japhy in *Dharma Bums* sums up as "martinis every night and all that dumb white machinery in the kitchen")[18] as it could possibly be. Kerouac himself was initially contemptuous of Zen, insisting in *Dharma Bums* that he was a "serious Buddhist . . . an old fashioned dreamy Hinayana coward of later Mahayanism," and calling it a "*mean*" (his italics) religion of "Zen Masters throwing young kids in the mud because they can't answer their silly word questions"[19] (presumably a reference to the *koan* riddles). *Dharma Bums* follows Kerouac's (or rather his alter ego Ray's) gradual embrace of what he calls "Zen Lunacy" and revolves around two mountain journeys in California—the first being one that Ray takes with friends and the second a sojourn alone on a mountain known as Desolation Peak.

The "Zen Lunacy" that Ray and his friends follow seems to be an exuberant and eclectic embracing of a variety of Buddhist beliefs, but also including an appreciation of the power of the road, nature, literature, and art, and a sponta-neous and uninhibited enjoyment of life. Ray follows this road through his con-nection with "Japhy," whom he meets in Berkeley and whom he depicts as a kind of combination poet/scholar/visionary. In fact, Japhy is in some ways an even more important figure in the novel than Ray, since it is he who guides Ray on the road in search of enlightenment, often quite literally, as in the memorable early section of the novel when Japhy takes Ray and (for part of the trip) another friend, Morley, on an overnight excursion to climb Mount Matterhorn in the beautiful California wilderness.

This journey is perhaps the novel's most hopeful and engaging section, as the young men bound up Mount Matterhorn quoting various Buddhists sages (as well as Cervantes), "feeling fine and . . . talking a blue streak about anything, lit-erature, the mountains, girls, Princess [one of Japhy's lovers], the poets, Japan, our past adventures in life."[20] Ray goes on to exult that "walking in this country you could understand the perfect gems of haikus the Oriental poets had written, never getting drunk in the mountains or anything but just going along as fresh as children writing down what they saw without literary devices or fanciness of expression."[21]

While the phrase "fresh as children" may remind us of Van Gogh's and others' condescending idealization of the Japanese artist (in fact, haiku does have its fair share of "literary devices"),[22] Japhy and Ray are correct in that freshness and spontaneity of experience is a crucial aspect in both haiku and Zen. For Ray in particular, their mountain journey seems to provide him with a number of moments of enlightenment. These include the solemn, as when he and Japhy watch the sunset from a high promontory above "America's steel mills and airfields" until the "pinkness vanished and then it was all purple dusk and the roar of the silence was like a wash of diamond waves going through the liquid porches of our ears."[23]

But there are also moments of excited intensity that perhaps best exemplify their doctrine of "Zen Lunacy." This is especially obvious when Ray, exhausted at trying to keep up with Japhy, thinks of quitting on the last stage of the mountain. Instead, he inspires himself by "the famous Zen saying, 'When you get to the top of a mountain, keep climbing.'"[24] What had seemed like "cute poetry" back in Berkeley now makes his hair "stand on end."[25] Rather than force himself up the last bit of the mountain, however, Ray finally realizes that "you don't have to prove anything." No longer trying to compete with Japhy, he ends up "flying down"[26] the mountain with great leaps and screams of joy.

Dharma Bums ends with Ray once again on a remote mountain top, having taken a job as a fire lookout for the summer at Japhy's suggestion. It is the end of summer, and he is taking his leave of Desolation Peak where he has lived a hermit's existence in a tiny hut for months. By this time, Japhy is thousands of miles away in Japan "answering the meditation bell," but in Ray's mind he stands before him on Desolation Peak and witnesses Ray's farewell to him and to the mountain. Ray says out loud, "Japhy . . . I don't know when we'll meet again or what'll happen in the future, but Desolation, Desolation, I owe so much to Desolation."[27]

In the end, while Kerouac's writing contains clear moments of what might arguably be called satori, the dark undercurrent in his work reaches back to Mahayana Buddhism and the doctrine that all of life is suffering due to our inability to rid ourselves of desire. In Kerouac's own life he searched the country, the arts, and his own mind to escape from desire and achieve enlightenment, but it is doubtful if he ever found true spiritual peace for long. He died in his mother's house in Florida, racked by alcoholism and buffeted by fame at the age of forty-seven.

It is Gary Snyder whose life seems to closer approximate certain aspects of the Zen ideal. When we first meet Japhy in *Dharma Bums*, Kerouac describes his new friend as living "the simple monastic life . . . with his Japanese wooden pata shoes . . . pad[ding] around softly in over his pretty straw mats,"[28] and goes on admiringly to mention "the slew of orange crates all filled with beautiful scholarly books, some of them in Oriental languages, all the great sutras, comments on the sutras, the complete works of D. T. Suzuki [the Japanese scholar who was most responsible for introducing Zen to the West]and a fine quadruple volume edition of Japanese haikus."[29]

Actually, Japhy's "monastic" life has its sybaritic pleasures, including wine, women, and peyote, as Ray discovers when (in a scene that would have been quite shocking for the 1950s) Japhy introduces him to "Zen Free Love Lunacy" with a young woman known only as Princess. How much of these sensual explorations are actually Zen-inspired seems open to question, but other parts of the novel, especially in the scenes of their mountain journey when he and Ray exchange haikus or when Japhy expounds to Ray and others on joys of the simple life, do indeed bear a resemblance to Zen monastic life.

In Japhy's case, his philosophy is clearly deeply related to his interest in Japan in general. In one instance, for example, he tells his friend Alvah (actually the poet Allen Ginsberg), "Get yourself a hut house not too far from town . . . clap your hands at shrines, get supernatural favors, take flower arrangement lessons and grow chrysanthemums by the door."[30] While the "hut" certainly has Zen connotations, Japhy's references to "shrines" and "supernatural favors" actually invoke Japan's indigenous Shinto religion, while his mentioning of "flower arrangement lessons" and "chrysanthemums" call to mind traditional Japanese aesthetics that are not exclusively Zen inspired.

How much Kerouac's characterization of Japhy is accurate in regards to the real-life model of Gary Snyder is of course uncertain, but reviewing Snyder's life and writings, it is clear that Japan and Buddhist philosophy were major influences on him, although he was also fascinated by other civilizations as well. A practicing Zen Buddhist who lived in Japan for a number of years, Snyder is widely read in Japanese poetry. (He invokes Basho "roving the coast up and down"[31] at the opening of one of his most beautiful poetry books, the 1968 *Back Country*). He was also influenced by the *Noh* Theater and various *Noh* themes such as journeys, history, and vengeful ghosts, which appear in his work as well. Although the short haiku form inspired him, most of his poems are considerably longer.

More than a Zen or even a Buddhist poet, Snyder is an environmentalist poet, an activist who believes in what he calls "bioregionalism" and the need to go beyond "contemplation and utopianism to put thought into practice."[32] As he says in one of his essays, he feels the need to develop a sense of place to counter "the alienation of people from the cancerous and explosive growth of Western Nations during the last one hundred and fifty years."[33] Snyder's longest stay in Japan was during the 1960s, a period when Japan was suffering from major environmental problems in response to which arose major popular movements attempting to deal with the toxicity (both literal and spiritual) of modern Japanese life.

Ultimately these movements would fail, as the Japanese came increasingly to embrace economic growth at all costs, and Sndyer brought his family back to America to live and farm in the Pacific Northwest. But his art and life clearly remain strongly influenced by Japan as well as other non-Western cultures, particularly those of ancient India, China, and Native Americans. Buddhism has been perhaps the most important single influence on him, allowing him in his cosmos-embracing environmentalist poetry to paradoxically "create a sense of insubstantiality, like the nothingness of the universe."[34] At the same time, Snyder's poetry is also often joyous, reveling in the organic connection of all things. Thus, in "Spring and the Ashura," he writes:

> I am one of the Ashuras
> (chalcedony clouds flowing
> Where is that singing, that spring bird?)
> Sun Wheel shimmering blue
> ashura echoing in the forest ...
> a thing in the golden meadow:
> just a person.
> Farmer wearing a straw cap looking at me
> Can he really see me
> At the bottom of this shining sea of air?
> ... breathing anew in the sky
> lungs faintly contracting
> (this body totally dispersed
> mixed with atoms of space)

Ashura is a Buddhist term for the types of malevolent beings who inhabit the six realms of existence, but this poem has an exultant quality, a joy in the interconnections of space, time, nature, and humanity that offers a vision of hope. In contrast, Kerouac's haiku poems are often more measured and quiet and sometimes more pessimistic:

> In my medicine cabinet
> The winter fly
> Has died of old age.

Yet, perhaps even more than Snyder, Kerouac seems to have grasped one of the most fundamental aspects of Zen, the paradox of being and nothingness. This elucidation seems contained in a passage toward the end of *Dharma Bums* when Kerouac invokes for a second time the phrase "roaring silence," a phrase reminiscent of one of the greatest haiku ever written by Basho:

> The stillness
> Stinging into the stones
> The voice of the cicadas

Whereas the Japanese poet on one of his many trips is contemplating the white noise of cicadas on a hot summer day in northern Japan, Kerouac is also on the road again but bedding down in the Texas desert. As he says of the desert night:

The silence is so intense that you can hear your blood roar in your ears but louder by far is the mysterious roar which I always identify with the roaring diamond of wisdom, the mysterious roar of the silence itself which is a great Shhh reminding you of something you've seemed to have forgotten in the stress of your days since birth. I wished I could have explained it to those I loved, to my mother, to Japhy, but there just weren't any words to describe the nothingness and purity of it. "Is there a certain and definite teaching to be given to all living creatures?" was the question probably asked to beetlebrowed snowy Dipankara, and his answer was the roaring silence of the diamond.[35]

The writings of Kerouac and Snyder were crucial in introducing their many young American readers to Buddhism (especially Zen), haiku, and Japanese culture. While *Time* magazine in its review of *Dharma Bums* snipingly described the book as "How the Campfire Boys Discovered Buddhism,"[36] the book appealed to a generation of young Americans eager to find meaning in their lives at a time when Western capitalism seemed to be only bringing about materialism, emptiness, and spiritual corrosion. Ultimately, the way of life exemplified by *Dharma Bums* would become a key model for millions of Americans searching for peace, love, and enlightenment during the 1960s, one of the most culturally tumultuous periods in the nation's history.

In the twenty-first century, Zen remains the best known of Buddhist doctrines in the West, although other Buddhist sects, most notably Sokka Gakkai, have also made inroads into the American heartland. But even today, professors of Japanese religion often complain that many students come into their classes believing that Zen essentially equals Buddhism and being disappointed when they learn how much else the religion has to offer. Even more intriguing, in the last few decades, the term "Zen" has crossed into American culture to become an iconic word, suggesting a special quasi-mystical approach to the complexities of modern life.

This process probably began with another "road" book. Robert N. Pirsig's bestselling *Zen and the Art of Motorcycle Maintenance*, which had very little to do specifically with Zen except for the notion of a journey toward spiritual enlightenment, involved both literal traveling and, yes, careful attention to tuning up one's motorcycle. *Zen and the Art of Motorcycle Maintenance* at least supported the spiritual aspect of Zen by concentrating on the interrelationship between the spiritual and the concrete and celebrating nature. But subsequent "Zen" titled books diverge almost ludicrously from any religious qualities. As Shoji Yamada, a Japanese scholar, chronicles, these newer titles range from *Zen and the Art of the Internet: A Beginner's Guide* (Kehoe, 1992) to *Zen and the Art of Casino Gambling* (Stabinsky, 1995) and even such gems as *Zen and the Art of Changing Diapers*.[37] How close this is to "real" Zen is rather dubious, as are the numerous references to a Zen lifestyle to be found in glossy magazines focused on upscale living.

Haiku too has etched a distinctive path into American popular culture. While the early 1960s brought many charming English translations of the Japanese masters (often illustrated with pictures of temples and cherry blossoms), haiku in English soon became mainstream. Elementary school teachers eased their students' entry into poetry by having them compose the seventeen-syllable poems in class on subjects ranging from nature to baseball. Nowadays, any bookstore will contain interesting varieties of English-language haiku, such as *Haikusine*, a book of culinary haiku,[38] or my personal favorite, *Redneck Haiku*, advertised as "What Happens When Bubba Meets Japanese Verse" and containing memorable compositions such as the following on a seasonal theme:

> Bobby's spring break trip
> Cost him five hundred dollars
> And clinic visit.[39]

While the gentle charm of haiku and the spiritual allure of Zen still remained a part of the Japanese image in the 1960s and 1970s, by the late 1980s a very different vision of Japan was building. This was one based on money and power although, intriguingly, it was often expressed in sexual or at least gender terms.

Mirrors and Shadows: Japan "Conquers" America

What can you do? [The Japanese] are ahead of us every step of the way. And they have the big guys in their pocket. We can't beat 'em now. . . . They're just too good.

—*Michael Crichton*, Rising Sun

This country is at war and some people understand it, and some other people are siding with the enemy.

—*Michael Crichton*, Rising Sun

Philip Kaufman's 1993 movie *Rising Sun* opens with a magnificent and puzzling scene: What appears to be a red rising sun turns into a circle surrounding an anthill in what seems to be the desert of the U.S. Southwest. Indians ride slowly down a trail with a young female hostage on horseback. A dog runs out of a doorway, jaws locked around a severed human hand. By this time the viewer could be forgiven for thinking that she has come to the wrong movie theater and is unaccountably watching a spaghetti Western. But there is more. Suddenly a heavily accented male voice starts to croon off camera an old Cole Porter song, "Don't Fence Me in." As he gets to the line about "I want to ride to the ridge where the West commences," the camera pulls back to show a louche looking Japanese man standing in front of a video screen and singing into a microphone while the words to the song crawl across the Western scene on the screen next to him. Behind him to his left, a group of thuggish looking Japanese men in sunglasses croon along to the chorus. The camera pans to his right, showing a stunning blond in a revealing black dress leaning against the bar and looking annoyed. Losing patience she starts to walk out, whereupon the singer abandons his microphone and rushes after her. He remonstrates with her for leaving and she snaps, "I was bored," and tries to walk away. He hustles her into a red Ferrari, hissing at her, "Don't you *ever* do that again. Or else. . . . "

This opening scene brilliantly telegraphs *Rising Sun*'s main theme: The Japanese are taking over. They take our land ("don't fence me in"), our movies, our music, and most painful of all, *they are taking our women.* Or, to put it another way, the Japanese economic juggernaut of the 1980s not only threatened American financial and political power, but also American identity, specifically, its masculine identity. When Americans looked at the Japanese during that period they saw an exaggerated version of themselves—aggressive, materialistic, sexually potent, and, as the British once complained of American soldiers on English soil, "over here." Both the film *Rising Sun* and the 1989 novel by Michael Crichton on which it is based are extraordinary pop-culture testaments to a profound American fear of invasion—not by soldiers or terrorists, but by an army of executives and workers who were beating America at its own game.[40]

Looking back from a twenty-first-century perspective, the American hysteria over the Japanese threat seems almost incredible. In the space of a few decades Japan had gone from savage enemy to grateful war-torn nation whose charming culture could inspire gardens and poetry, back to being a savage enemy again who, in the words of one of the characters in Crichton's book, deserves "another bomb."[41] What happened?

The simplest explanation is that, for a while at least, Japan did indeed beat America at its own game. With one tenth the area of America and virtually no natural resources, Japan, at the time that *Rising Sun* was written, had become an economic superpower, roughly the third largest economy in the world. A devastated and traumatized nation in 1945, Japan by the 1960s became the first country in history to experience double-digit economic growth. This growth was fueled by exports. Whereas Japan goods had once been known for their cheapness, now they were known for their quality and for their threat to American industries. Stereos, cameras, watches, television, and, most iconically, cars—all industries in which American or European quality had traditionally dominated—were falling to the Japanese.

American reactions were intense. Japan was accused of unfair trade practices, especially dumping (selling goods for export at a low cost in order to get market share and drive out competitors), getting a free ride on defense because of American military protection, and creating unfair barriers to entry making it difficult or impossible for Westerners to enter the Japanese market. Some of these criticisms were justified—many Japanese companies did charge lower prices abroad than they did at home, and, thanks to Article 9 renouncing war in their (American-designed) constitution, they spent far less on defense than most other countries. And barriers to entry certainly existed, ranging from the incredible amount of bureaucratic red tape that anyone trying to sell in Japan had to deal with, to such frustrating practices as claiming that Japanese snow was "different" from that of America or Europe, so that skis made in the West were not considered "suitable" for the Japanese market. It must also be acknowledged that the Japanese government and business leaders insisted on displaying a rather tactlessly dismissive attitude toward the West during this period. This attitude was understandable as a reaction to Japan's prolonged dependence on the United States in the postwar period but it shocked Americans used to thinking of their own culture as superior.

But those who saw only deception, arrogance and dirty tricks behind the Japanese success were missing a great deal of the story. The fundamental reason why American consumers turned toward Japanese goods was their high quality. The most obvious example is the story of the American automobile industry's struggle with Japanese cars. Small Japanese automobiles became popular during the oil crisis of the 1970s because of their fuel efficiency but Americans also discovered that the cars were well made and had fewer problems than domestically produced automobiles. Even after the oil crisis faded, therefore, Americans went on buying cars from Toyota, Nissan and Honda, despite the protests from Detroit.

This produced some ugly reactions. To Americans, cars were more than simply means of transportation—they were tied to American identity. At one point a group of congressmen was photographed destroying a Japanese car. Far more seriously, a Chinese man named Vincent Chin was murdered in Detroit by workers who mistook him as Japanese. The American press frequently described the Japanese in monstrous terms, inevitably invoking the monster Godzilla, but also adding new epithets such as the caption to a photo in *Newsweek* suggesting that the Japanese might be the "economic 'terminators' of the future,"[42] a reference to the monstrous robot in James Cameron's *Terminator* movies.

The robot references were almost more popular than the Godzilla ones, satirizing Japanese efficiency, discipline, and training. The pop group Styx composed a song, "Mistah Roboto," whose first line was in Japanese, "Domo arigato, Misutah Roboto" (thank you very much, Mr. Robot). Another pop song, "Turning Japanese," by the Vapors was even more vicious. Not only is the term "turning Japanese" slang for autoeroticism, but the song contained such memorable lyrics as "no sex no drugs no wine no women no fun no sin . . . that's why I'm turning Japanese, turning Japanese, I really think so."[43]

Not all Americans resented the Japanese. The 1985 comedy *Gung Ho* directed by Ron Howard depicted a group of small-town Americans who had lost their industrial base coming to Japan and wooing a Japanese company to "save" them. The resulting cross-cultural confusion can be imagined, but the film ends in an atmosphere of good will on the part of both the Japanese and Americans. The late 1970s and 1980s saw a slew of books aimed at American executives, purporting to reveal the secrets of Japanese success with titles like *Theory Z* or *The Enigma of Japanese Power*. Of these, *Japan as Number One: Lessons for America* by the Harvard sociologist Ezra Vogel in 1979 is one of the more sober and thoughtful examples.

The book is a careful look at certain aspects of Japanese society, such as education, law enforcement, and management, in an attempt not only to discern the secrets of Japanese success but also to see what elements might be fruitfully copied in America. What is most striking about *Japan as Number One* is that Vogel, a respected Harvard academic, saw Japanese society as in some ways superior to America and the implicit (and sometimes explicit) condemnation of American society that the book contains. As he says in the preface, "On the American side our confidence in the superiority of Western civilization and our desire to see ourselves as number one makes it difficult to acknowledge that we have practical things to learn from Orientals."[44]

In the multicultural world of the twenty-first century, asserting the need to learn from non-Western others seems like simple common sense, but a generation ago, Vogel felt that he had to emphasize and even reemphasize the notion. Although the book has been criticized for playing into the myth of Japanese uniqueness, Vogel acknowledges that "Japan to some extent shares the full range of problems found in every modern society."[45] The first chapter of *Japan as Number One* is titled "A Mirror for America," suggesting that Japan is a useful mirror in which American society can explore both the problems and solutions for certain universal issues of modernization.

The problems that Vogel points out are not just economic or political ones. At the time of writing the book, American society seemed mired in complex social challenges. These included a deteriorating industrial base, crime-ridden inner cities, and a national psyche still traumatized by the wounds of social chaos in the 1960s and the mishandled Vietnam War. Vogel notes the rise of alienation and the lack of social cohesion, pointing out that American individualism comes with a cost: "In the guise of pursuing freedoms we have supported egoism and self-interest and have damaged group or common interests."[46] In contrast, what Vogel sees as the Japanese emphasis on consensus, "fair share" rather than "fair play," and a commitment to creating a harmonious working environment suggests a society that effectively elevates the common good.[47]

Interestingly, Michael Crichton's sometimes venomous, occasionally laudatory portrait of the Japanese in his best seller *Rising Sun* at least pays lip service to the notion of learning from the Japanese. If, as both book and movie constantly remind us, the Japanese believe that "business is war," then America's response would have to be to wage war on all fronts, including a willingness to study the enemy's strategy. To help us in our studies, Crichton introduces his hero, the police detective John Connor (played by Sean Connery in the film) who has lived in Japan but is known for having a "balanced approach" to the Japanese. It is Connor who explains "the Japanese" to reader and viewer through eloquent and detailed lectures to his sidekick, Lieutenant Peter Smith (played by Wesley Snipes in the film).

Rising Sun's narrative begins with a politically sensitive crime: The Los Angeles Police Department brings Connor back from retirement to investigate the murder of a beautiful young blond woman (the same one who appears in the opening scene of the movie). The young woman, Cheryl Lynn, is found strangled to death on the boardroom table of the powerful Nakamoto Corporation's gigantic new company headquarters in Los Angeles. Fearing political repercussions because the event occurred at a gala party full of American VIPs, the police call in Connor to "handle" the Japanese. All evidence initially points to a Japanese "perp," most likely Eddie Sakamoto, her sometimes boyfriend, who in the movie is figured as the louche young man singing Cole Porter in the opening sequence.

But Crichton, like all good thriller writers, makes things increasingly complicated as multiple suspects appear and disappear to the point where the reader or viewer may be forgiven for becoming quite confused, especially since the identity of the criminal differs between movie and book. The fact that the murderer's identity changes between book and movie is revealing, suggesting that the point of *Rising Sun* is not really the explication of a murder mystery. Instead, both book and to a lesser extent the movie may be seen as an almost over-the-top call to arms to save America, not only from the Japanese, but also from itself. America, as we are constantly reminded, has "allowed" the Japanese to take over its financial markets, its entertainment franchises, its cities, even, through funneling money to laboratories, its research aims. What in Vogel's book comes across as suggestions for improving American society through learning from Japanese examples, becomes in *Rising Sun* a strident indictment of American laziness and greed and a revelation of threatening Japanese machinations.

Throughout the novel, the Japanese are seen as all-powerful, all-knowing, and fundamentally sinister, appropriate denizens of a country that Americans disparagingly had begun to call "Japan Inc." Early on in the case, for example, Connor explains to a clueless colleague how Nakamoto Corporation has been able to slow down the investigation telling him, "Don't kid yourself. They know exactly who was on call tonight. They knew exactly how far away Smith would be and exactly how long it would take him to get there."[48] Later on he explains that "everything *works* in Japan."[49] In contrast, Americans are "incompetent,"[50] "eager to sell [their own country] to the Japanese,"[51] and "dependent"[52] on Japanese money and expertise.

It is little wonder that, according to Connor, the Japanese have created a "shadow world"[53] inside major American cities like Los Angeles, New York, and Honolulu. This shadow world refers explicitly to the bars, clubs, and residences exclusively for the Japanese, but it is also a metaphor for what Connor intimates is Japanese management, even control, of America through influencing the U.S. economy, government, and educational system. Increasingly, the shadows are lengthening across America, a prognostication underlined in both book and film by the almost preternatural expertise of the Japanese in every area.

This fearsome picture, although containing certain accuracies, was an immensely exaggerated, distorted, and arguably a racist one. Throughout the 1980s many other countries influenced and bought into the American economy, but since they were usually Western, they were treated with far less fear mongering. What is ultimately most fascinating about *Rising Sun*, however, is the way gender and sexuality became insistent metaphors for the American engagement with Japan during this period in a way that is even more suggestive than the privileging of Japanese women during the immediate postwar period.

Both film and book abound in sexual imagery that consistently shows the United States as a weak-minded and vulnerable female who is "spreading her legs"[54] to vicious, even bestial Japanese. In one of the film's most over-the-top images, for example, viewers are treated to a scene in which Japanese men in suits enjoy eating sushi served on the body of a naked blond. In both book and movie it is made clear that the murdered Cheryl Lynn was a high-class prostitute, kept by a Japanese *yakuza* (gangster) in one of the shadow world residences. One of the murdered girl's fellow prostitutes hints at some length to Connor and Smith about the depraved tastes of their Japanese keepers, suggesting that pressure from Japanese rigid social customs leads to an explosion of perverted tastes (some apparently related to the samurai tradition) on the part of the men when they are in America: "I mean, I don't mind a little golden shower or whatever, handcuffs, you know. . . . But I won't let anyone cut me. I don't care how much money. None of those things with knives and swords. . . . But they can be . . . a lot of them, they are so polite, so correct, but then they get turned on, they have this . . . this *way*. . . . They're strange people."[55]

But American women are also "strange people," as becomes particularly clear in the book version. It turns out that Cheryl Lynn also had perverse tastes—she enjoyed the sensation of near strangulation while having sex. The image of her on the boardroom table of the Nakamoto Corporation being strangled while having sex suggests an America that is out of control, giving in to its own perverse desires and literally laying itself open to Japanese invasion.

Cheryl Lynn is not the only problematic American woman, however. In a subplot that seems unnecessary from the point of view of the narrative, Lieutenant Smith's ex-wife is presented as the archetypal evil women's libber. A monster of selfishness and self-involvement, Smith's ex-wife abandons her husband and baby girl to become a high-powered lawyer, often failing to take the little girl even on weekends and when she does, failing to play any maternal role. In one gratuitously unpleasant scene, Smith reminisces about how his ex-wife at one point brings back their daughter still stained by feces from an unchanged diaper.[56]

In the long run, however, *Rising Sun* apportions blame to both American males and females, as is evidenced in the real identity of the criminal. In the book, the perpetrator is an American senator, originally a patriotic defender of America against the Japanese, whose involvement with Cheryl becomes a means for the Japanese to blackmail him and ultimately leads to him shooting himself. In the film, after massive numbers of red herrings, it turns out that the real perpetrator is the pompous American liason who works for Nakamoto, implying a generalized indictment of anyone who "sells out "to the Japanese by working for or with them.

Rising Sun, especially in novel form, hit a nerve with the American public and engendered rave reviews, stressing the seriousness of the Japanese threat. As we now know, such concerns were highly exaggerated and misplaced. Ultimately the Japanese threat against America suggested more about Americans themselves and their own fears and confusions during this period. It is no accident that one of the running themes of both the book and movie is surveillance technology. Japanese recording devices are everywhere, filming the reality of events such as Cheryl Lynn's death and then being tampered with to create alternate versions of what actually happened. Americans were looking at themselves through Japanese eyes, and they did not like what they saw, a tawdry picture that mixed both fact and fantasy but, in any case, underlined the country's vulnerability to the "conquering" Japanese perspective.

Rising Sun was not the only popular culture work to engage with American fears of Japan during the 1980s. *Die Hard* (1988), the first film of the popular Bruce Willis action series, also takes place largely inside a giant Los Angeles skyscraper owned by the Japanese. Interestingly, in this film, the villains are "Eurotrash" terrorists, hinting at a more generalized sense of American inadequacy. The image of a barefoot and bleeding Bruce Willis taking on dangerous Europeans in a Japanese-owned building suggests a deep level of masculine anxiety vis-à-vis all the Others that seemed to be threatening America during this period.

A more metaphorical, but perhaps even more subtly disturbing take on America's anxieties about identity and "Orientalization," is Ridley Scott's brilliant 1982 science-fiction film *Blade Runner* (based on the novel *Do Androids Dream of Electric Sheep* by Philip K. Dick). A tech noir vision in which a world-weary detective named Deckard (played by Harrison Ford) tracks down a group of powerful "replicants" (androids) who have gotten loose in a near-future Los Angeles, the film contains a number of images that are either generically Asian or specifically Japanese. The voiceover to the original version even opens with a Japanese word: "Sushi—raw fish—that's what my ex-wife called me," reminisces Deckard as the camera captures him sitting down at a sushi bar in an area that looks like an old-fashioned Chinatown mixed with contemporary Tokyo. High above the bicycles, coolie hats, and chopsticks, however, is a glittering holographic sign in which a beautiful Japanese woman in kimono beckons the denizens of Los Angeles to a better life in an "off world" colony.

The use of the traditionally dressed Japanese woman to link to a utopian world is an interesting one, perhaps subliminally aligning Japan to a superior civilization, or at least life style, in comparison to the grubby world around Deckard. Even more interesting in that regard are the replicants themselves. While they are figured as Caucasian (the leader, played by Rutger Hauer, is almost a parody of Aryanness), the replicants also come across as smarter, more powerful, more effective, and more passionate than their human counterparts. They are also insidiously infiltrating the human world and threatening their creator, the head of the massive Tyrell corporation. Perhaps it is not too much of a stretch to see the replicants as the Japanese, who seemed on the point of besting their American "father" throughout most of the 1980s.[57]

The Road to Walled City: Cyberpunk Visions of Japan

And here, gone so fast she was never sure she'd seen him, through one window like all the rest, was a naked man, cross-legged on an office desk, his mouth open as wide as possible, as if in a silent scream.

—*William Gibson,* Idoru

Written two years after *Blade Runner*, William Gibson's 1984 science-fiction novel *Neuromancer* opens with the following memorably bleak lines: "The sky above the port was the color of television tuned to a dead channel."[58] Like *Blade Runner*, *Neuromancer* may also be called a tech-noir work. These works envision a near future in which technology, far from bringing about the utopian world promised in golden age science fiction, simply coexists with the tawdry realities of global capitalism, sometimes offering a temporary escape, at other times actually adding to the alienation experienced by sad urban dwellers caught in a fast-paced world where mass media, mass consumption, and globalization have taken the place of human connection. *Neuromancer* ushered in what came to be know as the cyberpunk genre, the most important movement in recent science-fiction history and one that, especially in the works of Gibson, would be heavily indebted to a certain vision of contemporary Japan that might be called TechnoJapan.

Far from the Japan of light, poetry, and art that animated previous Western visions, TechnoJapan incorporates both utopian and dystopian elements. As in *Rising Sun*, the country is still viewed as a society capable of great technological innovation that is often extremely creative and imaginative. As Gibson says, "Japan is the global imagination's default setting for the future."[59] The fact that this "future" is exciting but also chaotic and alienating gives Gibson's fiction its gritty edge. All the innovations he chronicles seem to add little to the sum of human happiness in a world where drugs, sex, and cyberspace seem to be the only forms of pleasure still available. Case, the novel's American protagonist, is a former hacker who has lost his ability to "jack into the net" and wanders the "port" looking for a way back in, no matter how risky or illegal.

The "port" is actually the Japanese city of Chiba, in Gibson's vision a city of garish light and ominous shadows of yakuza gangsters, coffin hotels, and stores selling the star-shaped Japanese weapon known as *shuriken*. Although much of the subsequent action of *Neuromancer* takes place on the Moon or in the "Sprawl" (the U.S. East Coast), it is significant that Gibson decides to open his narrative in this unlovely Japanese urban milieu. No longer is Japan a threatening conqueror; instead it is an example of the worst aspects of globalization, a country whose aesthetic tradition is summed up by a traditional weapon and the occasional invocation of ninja warriors and *yakuza*. By the time that Gibson wrote the novel, the Western image of Japan had changed markedly from the temples and mountain dream world of the Dharma bums to one that contained only a few elements of the traditional exotic (the shuriken) coexisting uneasily in a dreary urbanized world where pollution and crowds hold sway. This world is Japan, but it is also the nightmare future of any industrialized country. In TechnoJapan, Western readers could venture half a step into their own ominous technological future.

In *Neuromancer*, Case is able to escape temporarily (but still by technological means) into the "lanes to the land of the dead," as explained to him by the Artificial Intelligence (AI) program known as Neuromancer. The "lanes" are actually his own nerves ("neuro"), which, through technological advances combined with memory, allow him to call up a dead lover from his past for a brief respite from the nightmarish world his hacking abilities have plunged him into. Ironically, the novel privileges the physical (nerves) and language (the "romance" in Neuromancer) over the technological.

In Gibson's 1994 novel *Idoru*, however, escape is based more on the blending of the visual with the technological and comes, perhaps not surprisingly, in the figure of a Japanese woman who is in some ways the ultimate feminine embodiment of TechnoJapan. Rei Toei is an *idoru* (based on the English word "idol"), a "Japanese girl who isn't real."[60] But Gibson is not speaking metaphorically here—Rei really *isn't* real. As one of the Japanese characters helpfully explains to Laney, the novel's male protagonist, "She is a personality-construct, a congeries of software agents, the creation of information-designers."[61] At other times, she is described as a "big aluminum thermos bottle,"[62] hardly an appealing characterization.

And yet Rei enchants another character in the novel, the pop singer Rez, a Chinese-Irish pop star residing in Tokyo, enough to make him publicly announce his desire to "marry" her. This sets in motion the novel's convoluted plot. Disturbed by Rez's bizarre decision, his handlers bring in Laney, a typical Gibson techy loner, who has unique skills of pattern recognition in regards to celebrities, which he describes as seeing "faces in the clouds."[63] Rez's management hopes that Laney will help them understand what is going on and, if possible, disrupt the romance. At the same time, Rez's pronouncement has disturbed his fans, including a chapter of young girls in Seattle who decide to send a representative to Tokyo, Chia Mackenzie, to find out what is going on. Chia's and Laney's quests are told in parallel stories as the two innocents abroad try to learn to deal with the complicated and, to them, often weird world of near future Japan. This allows Gibson the chance to create a rich and detailed vision of TechnoTokyo, which, in the best tradition of science fiction, is as Fredric Jameson says, "a defamiliarizaton"[64] of our own present rather than a vision of some unknown future.[65]

By the time he wrote *Idoru*, Gibson had visited Japan a number of times and clearly found it a fascinating and stimulating site for ideas and images. In *Idoru* he pulls out the stops, imagining a future post-"Quake" Japan where nanotechnology has filled the void of the ruined city with buildings that constantly seem to move out of the corner of one's eye. In one particularly imaginative scene, he has Laney visit a bar whose staircase is made of processed (and deodorized) urine, a relic from the day the Quake hit and people were trapped in upper story rooms with no bathroom facilities. Both Laney and Chia also have to deal with the complexities of high-tech Japanese toilets (a clear extrapolation of the sophisticated toilets currently in use in Japan) and confront confusing Japanese sex toys. The closest that Laney gets to what might be called "traditional" Japan is watching a competition for wooden top spinning on Tokyo television.

But it is Chia who really engages most with TechnoJapan and its denizens. Fortunately for her, the president of the Tokyo chapter of the Rez's fan club has a brother, Masahiko, who is, as her computer translates, "a pathological-techno-fetishist-with-social-deficit"—in other words, a dyed-in-the-wool otaku. Masahiko grudgingly introduces Chia to something called the Walled City, a dense multi-user domain that is both intimidatingly high tech and reassuringly gritty and down to earth. The Walled City is described to Chia as "a hole in the net,"[66] an urban construct created by rebels who wanted a part of cyberspace that would be free of government or corporate intervention. Using data from a real but now vanished urban site near Hong Kong, they create a city with no laws.

Idoru's images of the Walled City and of the otaku subculture take us into a Japan at great variance from the vision of well-dressed, hyper-efficient supermen that dominated the ten-year earlier *Rising Sun*. While still technologically proficient, the scruffy otaku are seen as outsiders improvising under-the-radar lives that intersect very little with the conventional vision of Japan Inc. It is not surprising that another one of Masahiko's otaku friends, Gomi (trash) Boy, takes an anime character as his avatar in the Walled City.

Gibson's knowledge of contemporary Japan extends even to a particularly unique feature of modern Japanese life, the love hotel, hotels that provide not merely rooms for couples by the hour but rooms that are highly decorated fantasies of escape in their own right. In the novel's climactic scene, all roads converge on a love hotel in Tokyo, the Hotel Di, with a white wedding cake design, heart shaped fluffy furniture, and a variety of sex gizmos (some cute, some strange) in the bathroom medicine cabinet. Chia and Masahiko are not interested in sex, however, but enter the hotel in order to connect into Walled City from an undetectable site. Menaced by Russian Mafiosi who believe that Chia has unwittingly stolen a powerful nanotechnology device from them, Chia is saved partly by the arrival of Rez, Laney, and company to whom the device is actually a facilitator for the "marriage" between Rez and the Idoru. Even before the arrival of the Rez entourage, however, the hotel is invaded by a different type of rescuer, girl fans of Rez who converge on the hotel thanks to a well-timed rumor that Rez has died there.

In his vision of love hotels combined with nanotechnology, multi-user domains, otaku, gangsters, and tear-stained phalanxes of girl fans, Gibson conjures up a unique vision of Japan that is both imaginative and believable. Although *Idoru* does not attain the heights of such Western novels of India as Kipling's *Kim* or Forster's *Passage to India*, with their moral conflicts and three-dimensional native characters, Gibson at least grasps some the fascinating complexities and intriguing dynamics of Japanese society with a wider range and depth than virtually any other Western fiction writer on Japan. A master stylist, Gibson makes Tokyo come alive in its unique mixture of nightmare and dream, mass culture and technoculture, escape and entrapment, to provide an impressively textured vision of one possible future for industrialized societies.[67]

Idoru could have been even better if its eponymous title character had been more fully realized. Gibson has been taken to task by feminist critics for his tendency to create binary worlds of male hackers "penetrating," "jacking in," or "invading" what they see as the suspiciously passive world of cyberspace. This is of course not so different from the literary and pop-culture visions we have seen of Western men engaging with a feminized Japan. Cyberspace is essentially data, and in Gibson's world (and that of many other cyberpunk writers), it is the men in particular who have the power to "read" data, as is the case with *Idoru*'s Laney and his special skill at pattern recognition. Frequently in Gibson's work, his hackers will encounter a sinister female presence lurking in cyberspace, "information that talks back," as Stockton puts it.[68]

In the case of Rei Toei, the "idol," she is literally information that talks back. As the epitome of virtual womanhood, she could have been an intriguing character. Unfortunately, she falls quickly into the stereotype of the exotic Asian woman. When Laney first sees her, he "falls through her eyes"[69] into a vision of sunset and clanging bells in the Mongolian mountains, which turns out to be images from her most recent music video. The vision is beautiful, even ethereal, but it also enhances Rei's one-dimensional otherness.

To his credit, Gibson does offer the female protagonist, Chia, who is the most fully realized character in the novel. Through the course of *Idoru*, the fourteen-year-old girl grows from being a one-note fan who sees Rez as simply a possession of his fan clubs, to a more mature young woman who begins to grasp the complexities of fandom and stardom and even the ambivalent lure of the various virtual realities presented in the book. It is fitting that we should end this chapter with Chia. As a member of fandom who in encountering Japan discovers some truths about herself, she makes the perfect bridge to the world of anime fandom that we will explore in the second part of this book.

The virtual words of *Neuromancer* and *Idoru* at first seem to have little in common. But in a sense, cyberspace and idol worlds are also worlds of otherness in which enlightenment may be sought. Gibson's pioneering vision of cyberspace (a term he is credited with coining) as a "consensual hallucination" is perhaps not so different from Kerouac's many Buddhist references to life as a dream. Both visions privilege the mind over physical reality. Case's temporary escape into the lanes of the land of the dead where he calls up his deceased girlfriend may bring to mind a passage from *Dharma Bums*. In this scene Ray on a mountain trail feels as if "there was something inexpressibly broken in my heart as though I had lived before and walked this trail under certain circumstances with a fellow Bodhisattva. . . . The woods do that to you, they always look familiar, long lost, like the face of a long dead relative in an old dream, like a piece of forgotten song drifting across the water, most of all like golden eternities of past childhood or past manhood and all the living and the dying and the heartbreak that went on a million years ago and the clouds that passed overhead seemed to testify (by their lonesome familiarity) to this feeling."[70] Perhaps the AI that is

Neuromancer is the millennial version of the Bodhisattva, an entity that acts as bridge between heaven and earth, the unreal and the worldly. In *Idol*, Laney's talent of seeing "faces in the clouds" suggests the ephemerality of twenty-first-century idol culture, while the planned union between Rez and the idol, "shadows among other shadows,"[71]anticipates a world where dreams and reality create a new plane of existence.

4

The Dark Heart of Fantasy: Japanese Women in the Eyes of the Western Male[1]

To sum up, the country is more plentifully supplied than any other with these sort of means [prostitution] for gratifying the passion for sexual indulgence.

—*Francesco Carletti*, They Came to Japan

In the Katsuhiro Otomo's 1995 science-fiction anime *Magnetic Rose: Kanojo no omoide* (*Her Memories*), a group of interstellar "salvage agents" are lured to an isolated space station by an unusual distress call, the aria from Puccini's opera *Madama Butterfly*, which wafts powerfully across the lonely reaches of space. Once they arrive at the station, however, the group discovers that it is they themselves who must be rescued. Pursued by the vengeful hologram of a dead opera singer named Eva Friel, two of the men, Manuel and Heinz, ultimately meet frightening fates trapped inside the simulacrum of a nineteenth-century villa where the dead singer manipulates their romantic fantasies and their longing for home to create seductive but ultimately fatal images. Manuel dies searching for a beautiful phantom woman, while Heinz is caught in a shower of rose petals, running after a projection of what appears to be his little daughter, while the music from *Madama Butterfly* swells around him.[2]

Magnetic Rose is of course a variant on the "Madame Butterfly" myth, a myth that many commentators see as one of the archetypal stories in Japanese-Western or, more generally, East-West relations. Both *Magnetic Rose* and *Madama Butterfly* revolve around the power of illusions and how they distort relationships between men and women. But Puccini's opera also pivotally involves illusions between cultures, both within its own narrative and in terms of its audience reception, where it has been seen as a kind of iconic embodiment of the West's engagement with the Eastern Other. As with so many archetypal narratives, the Puccini opera tells a relatively simple story: An American man, Lieutenant Pinkerton, arrives in Nagasaki, takes a Japanese woman as his temporary wife, and abandons her, only returning to take back their child while she commits suicide in an inner room of their little house. *Madama Butterfly* was

first performed in 1904 and quickly became (and remains) one of the most popular operas of all time, overwhelming audiences with the richness of its music
and the power of its simple, tragic narrative. In recent years, however, the story
has been seen in considerably darker terms. Theresa de Lauretis describes the
opera as the "ultimate Orientalist fantasy based on hierarchies of gender, race,
and political domination."[3] Or, as Dorinne Kondo says, "In Puccini's opera, Men
are Men, Women Women, Japanese Japanese, Americans Americans, as defined
by familiar narrative conventions. And the predictable happens: West wins over
East. Man over Woman. White Man over Asian Woman. Identities too are
unproblematic in Puccini's opera."[4]

This chapter largely agrees with these assessments, although I might suggest that the American male lead, Pinkerton, is rather satirically presented as a
bumptious Yankee oaf. Overall, however, more than any other dynamic examined in this book, the one between Japanese women in relation to Western
men, or to the Western male gaze, seems worthy of being described as
"Orientalist" in its most problematic form involving Western dominance and
Eastern submission. This is most obvious in the case of *Madama Butterfly*.
While Puccini's opera is without doubt a beautiful and moving piece of theater (helped enormously by its gorgeous music), it is also simplistic, racist,
and melodramatic, offering a stereotypical vision of the submissive, sexually
available Asian woman who sacrifices everything for the love of a (rather
boorish) Western man. Furthermore, this vision has had remarkable staying
power. Even today, according to David Henry Hwang, the author of the
play *M. Butterfly*, a contemporary deconstruction of Puccini's original, within
the Asian community, women are still sometimes described as "doing a
Butterfly."[5]

Even more than Japonisme in general, The *Madama Butterfly* archetype is
based on fantasy, desire, projection, and illusion (or, sometimes, delusion). It
should be noted that these emotional states are not confined only to the Western
male. Butterfly, as Kondo notes, wants to be "American,"[6] even giving up her
faith to do so, but is cruelly disappointed in her fantasy of assimilation.
Pinkerton sees her as a magical creature, a "butterfly" in a "fairy dwelling," but
talks presciently about "pinning" her. Both engage the other in an ecstatic
romantic dream that obscures the nasty reality that Butterfly is a commodity
that has been bought and paid for and that Pinkerton will inevitably go home
without her. The Western female is involved as well. She exists as an enthusiastic consumer of these stories, but also as a foil within the narratives to show the
Japanese female in a particularly positive light.

Given the very obvious unequal power relations that occur in the Western
male–Eastern female dynamic, it is not surprising that many of these narratives
belong to the genre of melodrama. At its simplest, melodrama is defined as a
"play full of emotional suspense in a sensational and emotional style,"[7] but in
recent years literary critics have noted the importance of gender relations at the
heart of melodrama, specifically, the fact that women, usually in a passive or victim mode, were often the heroines of melodrama. As for the main male character,

he is often seen as in some ways suffering an "impairment in masculinity."[8] In many of these dramas, as we will see, it is the (relatively) passive Japanese female who saves the insecure Western male.

It is important to realize, therefore, that even something that seems as basic as the *Madama Butterfly* archetype can have many permutations, adding up to a more complex dynamic between male and female, East and West, than might originally be suspected. The *Magnetic Rose* anime, with its turning the tables on the men and exploiting *their* romantic fantasies, is one of the most extreme variations, but the works we will explore in this chapter all contain visions that include surprising twists on the dynamic of dominance and submission that is the dark heart of Orientalist fantasy. These include most obviously issues of power and perception but also questions of spectatorship, spectacle, and performance. The stereotype of the submissive Japanese woman does not exist in isolation but, to the Western spectator, also seems to offer a glimpse into a secret world of beauty, sensuality, and titillation, within a fictional context that emphasizes the spectacle and the performance.

Dancing Dogs: Pierre Loti's Silver Coin Romance

> There is actually some expression in her glance and I am almost persuaded that she—this one—thinks.
>
> —*Pierre Loti*, Madame Chrysanthemum

All of these issues surface in the work that was one of the inspirations for *Madama Butterfly*, a novel or, perhaps more accurately a memoir, by the French writer Pierre Loti entitled *Madame Chrysanthemum* (*Madame Chrysanthème*). Published in 1887, the story tells of the month-long sojourn with a "temporary Japanese bride" that Loti, an officer in the French navy, experienced while his ship was stationed off of Nagasaki in 1885. Although Loti had a long career in the navy, his true profession was that of a writer of exotic romances based on his many sea journeys. Of these, *Madame Chrysanthemum* was among his most popular. Translated into many languages and esteemed by both male and female readers (including Lafcadio Hearn and Van Gogh), the book's presentation of an exotic and ultimately unknowable Japan, embodied by Chrysanthemum, added another dimension to the nineteenth-century fascination with Japan.

To a twenty-first-century reader, however, *Madame Chrysanthemum* can seem truly disturbing. From the very beginning, the Loti character seems determined to denigrate his host country, describing the Japanese in terms that either evoke the animal, such as the "human hedgehog" of a rickshawman or Mr. "Kangaroo" who sets up the initial meeting between Loti and his "wife," or the artificial, as when he describes Chrysanthemum and her friends as "little Nipponese dolls"[9] and after the wedding refers to her and her family as a "set of puppets."[10] He also frequently contrasts his relationship to Chrysanthemum and to Japan in general to an earlier romance in Turkey (on which he based his first novel, the 1877 *Aziyade*), making clear his preference for "far away night-shrouded Stamboul."[11]

Although in later writings on Japan, especially in regards to Japanese noble-women, Loti is more admiring (suggesting a strong degree of snobbism in his personality), *Madam Chrysanthemum* reeks of condescension and contempt, with the Western male watching in patronizing amusement the antics of a race that he insists on seeing as childlike and grotesque. For Loti, everything in Japan is some form of spectacle or performance—his "little Japanese comedy,"[12] as he refers to his sojourn. This includes the way his bride and her friends appear when they walk in front of him, about which he exclaims, "Seen from behind, our dolls are really very dainty, with their back hair so tidily done up, their tortoiseshell pins so coquettishly arranged. . . . Moveover, they are very funny, thus drawn up in a line. In speaking of them, we say: 'Our little dancing dogs,' and in truth they are singularly like them."[13]

Loti's patronizing condescension for his Japanese "wife" would seem to have much in common with the unequal power relationships described in *Madama Butterfly*. Unlike the idealized vision of *Butterfly*, however, Loti's novel shows a more complex emotional subtext than a simple dominance and submission paradigm might suggest, most notably a sense of frustration with and perhaps even fear of the Other. Throughout the book we see Chrysanthemum and her people through Loti's gaze, and this gaze is not only condescending but seems puzzled and even fearful as well. A sense of (literal) darkness is constantly evoked. In discussing the religious habits of the Japanese, for example, Loti metaphorically throws up his hands in perplexity, resigned to merely saying, "These customs, these symbols, these masks, all that tradition and atavism have jumbled together in the Japanese brain, proceed from sources utterly dark and unknown to us,"[14] echoing an earlier comment made at a festival when he was "surprised by incomprehensible conceptions which seem the work of distorted imaginations."[15]

Even the landscape, which Loti sometimes praises, is ultimately presented as dark and unknowable. In one particularly revealing comment, Loti speaks of looking down from on high at a "terrible somber tear" in the mass of large green mountains, and "further still, quite low down on the waters which seem black and stagnant are to be seen, very tiny and overwhelmed, the men-of-war, the steamboats and the junks, flags flying from every mast."[16] Unlike "night shrouded Stamboul" where Loti feels at home, the "mass " of mountains and the "black and stagnant" seas of Japan are threatening, even "overwhelming."

Furthermore, these landscapes seem remarkably female, at least from a Freudian point of view. Not only does Loti present the reader with the image of a "tear," he also describes Nagasaki as lying inside a "yawning abyss,"[17] while the harbor itself appears as a "dark and sinister rent, which the moonbeams cannot fathom . . . a yawning crevasse opening into the very bowels of the earth, at the bottom of which lie faint and small glimmers, an assembly of glow-worms in a ditch—the lights of the different vessels lying at harbor."[18]

While undoubtedly some of the vessels described by Loti are Japanese, the overall impression from this series of quotations is that of Western man or indeed Western manhood (the "faint" and "small" "assembly of glow-worms in a ditch") being overwhelmed by the darkly feminine "rents," "tears," "crevasses," and "abysses" that make up Loti's conception of Japan. While for later observers, such as Hearn and Wright, the darkness of Japan was clearly seductive, even, perhaps, comforting. It leads Loti to this final despairing assertion shortly before he leaves: "How far are we from this Japanese people! How utterly dissimilar are our races!"[19]

The key to Loti's almost frightened incomprehension may well lie in the character of Chrysanthemum herself who, in many ways, comes across in remarkable contrast to Butterfly. Technically, Chrysanthemum fits the submissive Orientalist mode very well. She is young (only fifteen years old), pretty, and initially at least appears as simply the object of Loti and his friend Yves's lustful gaze. She is also a chattel, sold by her family (or perhaps "rented" would be more accurate) for the handfuls of silver coins Loti promises she will receive when she leaves. All these elements would make her seem an archetypal Butterfly. And yet, very much unlike the opera, Loti's narrative leaves us with the sense that Chrysanthemum also has power in terms of her emotional and psychological impact on him. While Loti continually attempts to disparage her, calling her "childish" (hardly an insult considering her age!) and wondering, "Does she possess a soul? Does she think she has one?"[20] these comments only emphasize his lack of success in reaching her. That Loti himself is subliminally aware of this failure is clear in his repeated assertions that he does not care if she loves him, while at the same time wondering if "her appearance of sadness"[21] at his leaving was on Loti's own account or for the sake of his friend Yves, or worse—perhaps she is not really sad at all.

Matters come to a head on the day before his departure when the narrator has just about persuaded himself that Chrysanthemum is genuinely melancholy at the idea of his leaving. Startled by a noise coming from the upstairs room in his house, Loti listens more closely and begins to distinguish a jangling sound, "a metallic ring as of coins being flung vigorously on the floor."[22] Reaching the top of the stairs, Loti opens the door and silently observes Chrysanthemum from behind: "On the floor are spread out all the fine silver dollars which . . . I had given her the evening before. With the competent dexterity of an old money changer she fingers them, turns them over, throws them on the floor . . . singing the while I know not what little pensive bird-like song.[23]

Loti's reaction to this disillusioning encounter is perhaps even more intriguing. He describes the scene as "even more completely Japanese than I could possibly have imagined—this last scene of my married life!" and feels "inclined to laugh. How simple I have been to allow myself to be taken in by the few clever words she whispered yesterday."[24]

Far from being seen as a delicate and vulnerable creature, Chrysanthemum is compared to an "old money changer," metonymically associated with the impressions of toughness and coldness that the ringing sound of the "fine silver dollars" evokes. The fact that Loti describes the whole scene as "completely Japanese" is also interesting, indicating that the piece of theater that was his "marriage," whose "last scene" he has just witnessed, was far from being the romantic and exotic spectacle that the archetype of East-West romance usually suggests. For example, in his earlier novel *Aziyade* the Turkish lover of the Loti character crushes a cup that causes her to bleed on the night before his departure, suggesting her vulnerability and forecasting her subsequent death. Chrysanthemum, in contrast, seems hard and untouchable. While, as in the "dancing dogs" scene she again presents her back to him, she is no longer the "dainty" child who pleased him that day, but has become instead a forbidding, walled-off presence.

Madame Chrysanthemum does not overtly challenge the power relations inscribed in the Orientalist dynamic between Western man and Eastern female. But the reader's final view of Chrysanthemum, sitting erect and counting her money while singing happily, serves as a useful corrective to the more typical scene of the Eastern woman left prostrate and probably suicidal at her lover's departure. Far from being a romance or a melodrama, Loti's tale, especially in its final chapters, seems closer to the often cynical naturalist fiction of such contemporaries as Zola. It is perhaps little wonder that, as his ship leaves Nagasaki harbor, Loti picks up some faded lotus petals that were his last souvenir of Japan and throws them into the sea. Neither Japan nor the woman he knew there have given Loti what he seems to have wanted and, with this final rueful action, he acknowledges that the play is at an end, the performances gone wrong, and the spectacle deprived of its power to excite.

"One Fine Day": Madame Butterfly Gets It Right

They say that in your country / if a butterfly / is caught by a man / He'll pierce its heart with a needle.

—*Butterfly to Pinkerton*, Madama Butterfly

It would be up to Puccini to get the play right—by giving Western audiences the romantic, indeed tragic denouement that Loti seems to have craved. Based on a short story by John Luther Long written in 1898, roughly the same time as Loti's novel, the story of Madame Butterfly became a play in 1900 and was seen by Puccini while being performed in London. Puccini developed his own libretto and composed music that incorporated some genuine Japanese elements to create in *Madama Butterfly* a gorgeous spectacle of love, sacrifice, and devotion. The opera pulls out all the emotional stops, plunging its audience into a tidal wave of intense emotionality and exotic spectacle that leaves little room to question the inherently racist and condescending dynamic that animates the plot.

That this dynamic is one based on fantasy is clear from the beginning. In the opening scene the curtain rises to show Pinkerton and his Japanese associate

Goro walking around the little house that Pinkerton and Butterfly will occupy. Goro demonstrates the fluidity and flexibility of the Japanese structure, where walls can slide to create different rooms, in response to which Pinkerton describes the house as a "fairy dwelling" that "comes and goes as by magic."[25]

Just as the Japanese house is flexible, accommodating, and "fairy like," so too is Butterfly who, despite her misgivings, enters into the marriage with the American believing in the power of their mutual love. She is, of course, ultimately mistaken. While Pinkerton lacks the poisonous condescension of the Loti character in *Madame Chrysanthemum*, he still considers her simply a " gossamer creation"[26] and (in a clear echo of Gilbert and Sullivan) something that has "stepped straight down from a screen,"[27] while it is he who is the one who will "come and go." Unlike Chrysanthemum, however, Butterfly plays along, referring to herself as Pinkerton's "baby." While, in Loti's eyes, Japan was an "abyss" that "even the moonbeams cannot fathom,"[28] in Puccini's opera Butterfly herself takes on the role of the "Moon's little goddess, the little Moon-Goddess who comes down by night from her bridge in the star-lighted sky."[29] Where Chrysanthemum/Japan is all impenetrable darkness, Butterfly is all light and radiance, reflecting back to Pinkerton an idealized version of himself wrapped in her obsessive love.

Although Pinkerton too seems to love Butterfly in his fashion and appears genuinely guilt ridden at forcing her to give up her baby (so that he and his wife may raise it in America), the opera's tragic and melodramatic construction leaves no room for a nuanced ending. Consistent with the tragic construction of most nineteenth-century operatic narrative, Butterfly *must* sacrifice herself by giving up her child and then committing suicide, and her Japanese identity is the useful engine that drives the plot to its inevitable denouement. Although it is possible to imagine up to a point a similar plot involving a Western man and woman,[30] the issue of the child's mixed race is what causes the final romantic blow to fall, while the Japanese tradition of honorable suicide (of which Puccini was aware) gives her the means to transcend her fate. Convinced that her child will have a better future if she relinquishes him, Butterfly becomes the epitome of both maternal and romantic sacrifice, allowing her American lover to return home with a conscience that might, at most, be only slightly clouded by her sad but beautiful death.

Ironically in 1900, the year that the play version of *Madame Butterfly* was first being performed in America, the country also had the opportunity to witness a real Japanese actress in a real Japanese play—the brilliant performer Sadayakko who, as Leslie Downer recounts, depicted "Japanese women to be as complex as Americans."[31] Unfortunately, Westerners refused to believe in that characterization, and later on, when Puccini saw Sadayakko perform in Europe, he based the character of Butterfly on what he believed to be the actress's true personality—quiet, retiring, and submissive. In fact Sadayakko was a strong and creative personality who became, for a while, the darling of Europe. It is significant, however, that this fascinating and complex woman has almost disappeared from history, and it is Butterfly's simple archetype that has remained fixed in the mind of the West.

Admittedly, Butterfly's staying power was probably aided immeasurably by the beauty of Puccini's music and what, to turn-of-the-century viewers, would have seemed the nobility and depth of her love. When she sings in one of Puccini's most beautiful arias how "one fine day" she will see her man's ship appearing while she "waits . . . never weary of the long waiting,"[32] she seems to embody the essence of romantic love, a fantasy that of necessity can never be fulfilled, but always hovers just out of reach, like the exotic fantasy that was Japan itself.

Although both *Madame Butterfly* and *Madame Chrysanthemum* can be read as pandering to male fantasies (with Loti's being frustrated and Pinkerton's fulfilled), it is useful to remember that both opera and novel were appreciated by a female audience as well. *Madame Chrysanthemum*, in fact, is fawningly dedicated to one of Loti's many aristocratic female fans, the Duchess of Richelieu. While Orientalism is often described in terms of the Western male's gaze at the East it is worth speculating on what the Western woman obtained from these cultural products. Is it possible that female readers might have vicariously enjoyed Chrysanthemum's refusal to live up to Loti's fantasies? Or did they, along with the Western male readers, simply enjoy the exotic setting and the titillating hints of a legitimized form of unmarried sexual liaison? In *Madam Butterfly*'s case, it is likely that the Western female spectator was able to enjoy a double form of identification—the breathless pleasure of Butterfly's romantic and erotic position in the first act of the opera and the epic but satisfying anguish of her ultimately sacrificial maternalism in the second act. This masochistic act, as Gina Marchetti points out, also underlines Butterfly's "moral superiority"[33] to the male, a trait that for turn-of-century Western women, steeped in their own tradition of female purity, would also have deemed laudable. Indeed, by presenting the audience with the character of Pinkerton's American wife at the end of the opera, Puccini allows for yet a third form of identification on the part of his female viewers: that of the triumphant but guiltless Western woman who "rescues" the baby from its potentially tragic fate.

Sayonara (I): The "Secret"

Men with wives back in the States talk about Junior's braces and country club dances and what kind of car their wife bought. But the men with Japanese wives tell you one thing only. What wonderful wives they have. They're in love. It's that simple.

—*Airman Kelly,* Sayonara

Marchetti suggests that *Butterfly*'s appeal to women viewers may have been partially in relation to the confusing array of possibilities that women were experiencing at the beginning of the twentieth century, where calls for women's rights were increasing while Victorian traditions still held sway. By the time that the opera was made into a movie in 1915, the period had beome a "a time when female sensual self-expression and Victorian notions of the power of sentiment were vying for ascendancy in women's daily life."[34] Very unlike the emancipated "flapper" who would come to dominate the image of women in the 1920s, Butterfly seemed to offer a model of patient endurance whose sexuality was ultimately subsumed through sacrifice.

The function of the *Butterfly* archetype as, in some ways, a warning to emancipated women surfaces again in the years after World War II. This was a time when women's roles were again in flux as millions of men flooded back from combat, displacing women from the jobs they had held during the war years and offering them instead a vision of the contented suburban housewife who lives only for her husband and family. The fact that some women appeared disinclined to submit to this vision serves as the subtext for a popular novel and film of the 1950s, James Michener's *Sayonara*.

Sayonara, published in 1953, may also be seen as emblemizing America's attempt to come to terms with both defeated Japan, occupied until 1952 by its American conquerors, and postwar American masculinity itself, using occupied Japan as a foil. In this regard the novel's protagonist, Lloyd "Ace" Gruver is an interesting characterization. While hardly the rebellious teenager that was becoming a staple of American popular culture during that period, Gruver is allowed to have moments of self-doubt, passion, and despair that make him somewhat more intriguing than the stereotypical image of the conquering American hero. This is even more obvious in the movie where Marlon Brando's rich performance creates a genuine three-dimensional personality.

What we would today call Gruver's "issues" seem to stem from a lack of confidence vis-à-vis his father, a four star general who never actually appears in the book but hovers over the story as a rigid but respectworthy paternal presence, in some ways suggestive of the American ideal that Gruver seems unable to live up to. Gruver's lack of confidence ends up turning into hostility toward American women on both a personal and a general level. Indeed *Sayonara* comes across as an unusually personal novel, a kind of love letter to Japanese womanhood that is also a surprisingly blatant harangue against American females. In the novel, Japanese women are depicted as oases of nurturing warmth who have a secret: they simply "love" their husbands or boyfriends, as opposed to American women whose demanding personalities tear down rather than restore the male ego.

As contemporary critics noticed as well, *Sayonara* shows a clear debt to the *Madama Butterfly* scenario, offering star-crossed lovers, suicide, and sacrifice against the exotic setting of Japan in the immediate postwar period. We first see Gruver in Korea, however, where he is experiencing mild battle fatigue after having shot down his seventh Russian MIG. When asked by the army doctor if he wants to "tangle with those beautiful Japanese dolls at Tachikawa,"[35] Gruver is unenthusiastic, remembering an earlier trip to Japan where all he saw was "dirty streets, little paper houses, squat men and fat round women."[36]

The rest of the novel is essentially the story of Gruver's gradual change of heart, partially toward Japan whose "picture book landscape"[37] and ancient artistic traditions he comes to appreciate, but especially toward Japanese women. The impulse behind this change can be seen as being engendered by three women: The first is Katsumi, one of those "fat round women" whom

Gruver initially despises but who, in marrying Airman Kelly, one of the more troublesome members of Gruver's outfit, and redeeming him through her love, becomes a symbol of all the best aspects of female nurturance in Gruver's eyes. The second is Hana-ogi, the beautiful Japanese dancer specializing in male roles with whom Gruver falls in love, not so coincidentally, when he first sees her performing as Pinkerton in a burlesque of *Madama Butterfly* offered by the Japanese women's theater troop of which she is the star. Hana-ogi embodies the mystery and sensuality that is the other side of the Japanese female fantasy and, as with Butterfly, is associated with an artistic commodity, in this case woodblock print portraits of the Edo period courtesan whose name she has taken (see insert, Figure 7). The third woman is Gruver's fiancé Eileen Webster, also beautiful, a general's daughter from Tulsa and ultimately (along with her battleaxe of a mother) the symbol of everything that is wrong about American womanhood in Gruver's eyes.

These differences are summed up in one of the novel's major visual and emotional tropes—the Japanese bath. At one point Gruver is discussing the allure of Japanese girls with his marine friend Mike Bailey who asks him, "You ever had your back scrubbed by a Japanese girl . . . a girl who really loved you?" and then follows up with the question, "Can you imagine Eileen Webster scrubbing your back?"[38] Gruver's response is a long mental monologue inspired by his having witnessed Katsumi giving her husband a bath after Kelly had had a particularly bad time with a racist American officer:

> It was a crazy question, a truly hellish shot in the dark, but I could immediately visualize fat little Katsumi Kelly . . . taking her sore and defeated husband into the bath and knocking the back of his neck and getting him his kimono and quietly reassuring him that her love was more important than whatever Lt. Colonel Calhoun Craford had done to him and I saw runty, sawed-off Joe Kelly coming back to life as a complete man and I had a great fear. . . . that Eileen Webster would not be able to or willing to do that for her man . . . for my mother in thirty years of married life had never once, as far as I knew, done for my father the simple healing act that Katsumi Kelly had done for her man the other night.[39]

The trope of the Japanese bath with its implicit erotic qualities was very much in evidence in Hollywood films about Japan in the 1950s, from Samuel Fuller's *House of Bamboo* (1955) to the Jerry Lewis vehicle *Geisha Boy* (1958; director Frank Tashlin). By that point most of the Western audience would know that Japanese often bathed together, an occurrence that would have seemed strange and undoubtedly titillating to most non-Japanese. What is interesting in *Sayonara*, however, is how assiduously Michener's novel works to downplay the erotic associations of the bath and instead suggests its nurturing aspects. The literal hands-on qualities of the bath in terms of its comfort and reassurance are what seem to be appealing to Gruver, just as Katsumi's cooking for Kelly "laboriously, by hand" with "no can openers, no frozen foods"[40] implies a traditional maternalism that American women, in their preoccupation with "country clubs" and "Junior's braces," seem to have given up. The book's explicit emphasis thus is on a "love" that incorporates more than sexual attraction. Although the novel does contain (for its time) a quite erotic scene where Gruver is transfixed by Hana-ogi's "golden breasts,"[41] *Sayonara* is clearly a novel of romance rather than sex. Gruver's love for Hana-ogi makes him a deeper and more tolerant person, while Hana-ogi's love for him helps her transcend her previous hatred of the Americans who had killed her brother and father. Perhaps even more romantic are Katsumi and Kelly who, when told that Kelly cannot bring his bride back to America, find that their only way out is double suicide.

As a novel of romance, *Sayonara* no doubt was particularly meant to appeal to a female audience who would have enjoyed the erotic touches but, during the conservative 1950s, probably appreciated even more the passion and tragedy of the principle characters. It is this female audience, one assumes, who would be receiving the lessons of love and nurturing that Katsumi and Hana-ogi seem to exemplify and might be expected to shift their identification away from the demanding Eileen to the self-sacrificing Japanese women.

It should be acknowledged that the portrait of Eileen is not totally one dimensional. Even Eileen, we are given to understand, could be passionate too, given the right circumstances as when she suggests to Gruver that he "drag her off to a shack somewhere."[42] But nowhere is it suggested that she could be sacrificial, tender, or nurturing.[43] In the novel's final lines, it is her sinister shadow that waits for Gruver after he has finally abandoned his plan to marry Hana-ogi. Caught in the maze of obligations and rewards that constitute modern life, Gruver is told by Eileen's father that he has just been promoted and that "Eileen wants to drive us to the airport."[44] This final sentence puts the American woman literally in the driver's seat, ruthlessly conveying her man out of the fairy tale country and life that had absorbed him so intimately and so passionately.

To be fair to *Sayonara*, the novel is clearly promoting a worldview that, for its period, would have been considered quite liberal. For example, Michener allows Hana-ogi to have a self-respecting profession and for *her* to be the one who actually turns Gruver down, thus reversing one of the basic tenets of the *Madama Butterfly* archetype by giving the Asian woman some element of control. Gruver and Hana-ogi's respective change of heart toward one another and toward each other's country evidences the importance of mutual understanding and indeed love between the races. To make this point even clearer, Michener has Gruver muse, toward the end of the novel, that "I lived in an age . . . when the only acceptable attitude toward strange lands and people of another color must be not love but fear."[45]

Earlier on, Gruver had tried to explore his romance in terms of transcending racial and national barriers as when he insists that "you find a girl as lovely as Hana-ogi and she is not Japanese and you are not American."[46] In fact, however, Michener undermines this race-transcending ethos throughout the novel. Hana-ogi and Katsumi are desirable precisely because they *are* Japanese "girls," linked to a unique country and possessing (apparently) uniquely un-American qualities. Although, unlike Pinkerton in *Madama Butterfly*, Gruver is able to see in the woodblock prints of Hana-ogi's namesake a variety of Hana-ogi's rather than a single stereotype, in the final analysis he cannot take Hana-ogi out of her Japanese frame.

"Tell them we said 'Sayonara'": Ace Gruver in Joshua Logan's film *Sayonara*

While it argues for cross-cultural understanding, Michener's novel gives off a slightly sour smell of misogyny and condescension that undercuts its message of tolerance.[47] Surprisingly, the movie version of *Sayonara* (which won an academy award for best picture in 1957) can be seen as a work of genuine liberalism on both the cultural and the gender front. Indeed, the movie contains an explicit valorization of interracial marriage in the movie's happy ending and an implicitly positive vision of gender bending in its privileging of both male and female crossdressing performances that make it almost subversive for its period. Furthermore, the movie seeks to move Japanese-American relations beyond simple mutual recrimination about the war, although this attempt is a somewhat timid one.

In all these areas, the film moves beyond the book, helped by the fascinating performance of Marlon Brando, who plays Gruver not as the rather bland upstanding young Southwesterner of Michener's vision, but instead, as a contemporary *New York Times* review puts it, as a "shut-mah-mouf-talking Southerner with a good-humored sort of impish nature underneath his standard West Point crust."[48] Given that this was the period when the civil rights movement was beginning to stir across America, Brando's decision to push his character's "Southernness" had clear ideological implications suggesting that Gruver's growing appreciation of Japan could be a model for cross-cultural and, implicitly, cross-racial reconciliation. Even more obvious in this regard was the decision (apparently at the insistence of Brando) to change the book's rather awkwardly manufactured tragic ending to a happy one where Gruver convinces Hana-ogi to marry him, and the two walk away together saying "Sayonara" to a crowd of insistent reporters.

Another intriguing aspect, given the period's conservative ethos toward gender construction, is the fact that not only does the film not downplay Hana-ogi's position as an actress of men's roles, it actually adds a potential romance between Gruver's ex-fiancee, Eileen Webster, and a Kabuki actor, Nakamura, who specializes in women's roles. The film does not take its subversiveness as far as it might, since Nakamura is played by the Caucasian actor Ricardo Montalban (similar to the casting of Yul Brynner as Thai royalty in *The King and I*), but even more than the interracial marriage promised by Gruver and Hana-ogi, the notion of romance between a white woman and a non-white male would have been considered transgressive by many audiences of that time.

Gruver's attraction to the "mannish" (as the novel describes her)[49] Hana-ogi is also implicitly transgressive. Gina Marchetti has suggested that Gruver's wooing of Hana-ogi "turns her into a woman," and thus defuses this potential subversiveness. And it is certainly true that at the end of the movie, Hana-ogi is only seen in feminine clothing, including a Japanese wedding gown in her final performance on stage. But the fact that Gruver is initially attracted to Hana-ogi when she is wearing men's attire, rather than falling in love with the typical "geisha girl" stereotype of most Orientalist fantasies, also suggests that both film and book are at least trying to present the Japan-West dynamic in a more complex fashion than the *Madama Butterfly* archetype offers.

The film also contains a surprisingly even-handed vision of war guilt that is not in the novel. In one scene early on, for example, Hana-ogi refuses to meet with Gruver because, as Kelly reports, "We shot her brother and dropped bombs on her father," to which Gruver responds, "Well shoot . . . I didn't do it." But Gruver's marine friend, Major Bailey, who is presented as an even more typical soldier type than Gruver, suddenly interjects, "We *all* did it." The notion of a marine in that period explicitly acknowledging America's responsibility in the bombing of Japan is truly surprising. Perhaps to ensure that Japanese guilt is also acknowledged, the film contains a scene later on where Hana-ogi apologizes to Gruver for having believed him and all Americans to be "savages" for having destroyed her country, and asks his forgiveness. To this, Gruver responds, "Well, I guess I feel maybe I should apologize too."

This is not to say that the film radically subverts the basic dynamic of American paternalism and Japanese dependency. But it does go out of its way to show how Japan and Japanese culture can jolt Americans out of their complacency and at least marginally destabilize the overall attitude of condescension taken by Americans. It achieves this effect at least partly through Brando's performance, which, in its off-key way, helps the viewer to look at Japan in a more intimate and relaxed fashion than the more reverential attitude taken by the novel. The movie provides a number of scenes of pure Japanese spectacle of a largely stereotypical kind, from the many flamboyant dance revues performed by Hana-ogi, to several ostensible Kabuki performances by Nakamura, to the highly traditional triumvirate of the *Noh* Theater, puppet theater, and tea ceremony. What keeps them from being simply exotic fillers is Gruver's genuinely amusing reactions to them.

Brando plays Gruver here as a man out of his depth but willing to learn, even when his legs give out during the tea ceremony or when he cannot resist standing up and bowing in appreciation of Hana-ogi's performance at her theater. Not only comic but also revealing is when Gruver (with Eileen) first sees Kabuki and comments when Nakamura comes out dressed in a lion costume: "Good lord! That's my father!" Since part of Gruver's problem, as he explains in a conversation with Bailey, has been his desire to please his father by never questioning the military lifestyle, this humorous remark suggests the beginnings of the loosening of the parental bond.

Even more obvious and also relating to freedom from parental control is Eileen's developing interest in Nakamura. Although she and the Kabuki actor are only shown as potentially developing a romance, the film highlights the erotic tension between them when Nakamura, during a stroll in the garden, tells her, "I am not *necessarily* making love to you." The audience's last view of Eileen (very different from the one in the novel) is after Gruver announces that he is going to marry a Japanese woman, and her furious mother tries to get her to stay and "talk" about Gruver's decision. Instead, Eileen angrily leaves the room, telling her mother as she leaves that "there's only one person I want to talk to and, oddly enough, he's Japanese!"

In her acute and provocative analysis of the film version of *Sayonara*, Marchetti points out a number of these subversive aspects but sees them as ultimately being subsumed by the "very traditional view" offered by the film of "femininity, masculinity and romance as a bulwark against the other fundamental social and ideological changes alluded to within the film."[50] Certainly, the film's ending, with Gruver whisking Hana-ogi away from the reporters to start the marriage process, suggests the film's inherently conservative subtext. Yet even the ending allows for a slightly more liberal interpretation: the film makes sure that it is Hana-ogi rather than Gruver who speaks for the couple, as she emphasizes when beginning her speech by saying that "It is very unusual for a Japanese woman to speak in public," and also when she affirms that she would "hope to keep on dancing," underlining her commitment to her professional art.

Rather than turning Hana-ogi into a butterfly, it might be said that Gruver seems to be turning her into an American woman, perhaps even the kind of woman that the Gruver in the novel version feared the most. That this is paternalistic (smacking of America's attempt to democratize Japan) should still not obscure the fact that, compared to many contemporary film visions of the Japanese woman, *Sayonara* presents her in a relatively powerful position.

Marchetti also castigates the film for its many subplots that "do not seem to be wrapped up at the end,"[51] but this lack of closure may also be viewed as a strength, provoking the audience to wonder about other possibilities. At the very least, the Japan of *Sayonara* is a far more complicated place than is the case in most postwar films about the country. The director Joshua Logan uses the spectacular and exotic aspects of Japan not simply for entertainment, but also to suggest possible alternative ways of finding meaning—an aspect that Marchetti clearly appreciates. As she says, "Japanese theatrical tradition seems to offer . . . the promise of a world in which culture, racial and gender boundaries can be toyed with or aestheticized rather than fought over and upheld through war."[52]

It is possible to suggest that *Sayonara*, with its romance, melodrama, and scenes of sacrifice, may be associated with the genre of women's films that were popular particularly in the 1940s and 1950s (although, unlike the classic women's picture, the action takes place through a male point of view). The fact that the movie allows Eileen at least potential sexual agency and emphasizes Hana-ogi's commitment to her dance may have been added (either consciously or subconsciously) to please the female audience. It can also be argued that Hana-ogi "saves" Gruver from his restrictive American masculinity, and this salvatory aspect of femininity has been traditionally highly valued by both male and female audiences. On the other hand, Eileen's unconventional exploration of other kinds of romance may well have seemed exciting and even empowering to the female audience.

Geisha Girls and Boys: Jerry Lewis's *Geisha Boy*, *Miss One Thousand Spring Blossoms*, and *Memoirs of a Geisha*

While *Sayonara* at least tries to present a more complex picture of Japanese femininity, most Hollywood films of the 1950s and 1960s remained fixated on the image of the geisha, with titles like *My Geisha* (1962; director Jack Cardiff), *The Barbarian and the Geisha* (1958; director John Huston), and even *Geisha Boy*, a 1958 film starring and produced by the comedian Jerry Lewis. However, although the geisha image remained largely fixed, the image of the Western male vis-à-vis the Japanese female began to change, perhaps even as early as the film version of *Sayonara*. While "Ace" Gruver in Michener's novel was still rather woodenly conceived as a duty-bound West Point man, Marlon Brando played him as "emotionally immature as a teenage boy" in the assessment of the reviewer for the *New York Times*.[53] This "emotionally immature" teenager contrasts to the stereotype of the all-powerful American conqueror and may perhaps have been a more accurate emblem of American masculinity in the confusing postwar climate of the 1950s as America tried to work out its new position in the world. The confused adolescent hidden beneath Gruver's topgun mystique hinted that underneath all the bellicose cold war posturings, a sense of uncertainty existed in how best to construct the postwar American identity.

Despite its title, *Geisha Boy*, which appeared a year after *Sayonara*, only presents one scene of a genuine geisha. Rather, the film's title seems to reflect one of its subtexts: the destabilizing of the postwar stereotype of the powerful American male rescuing defeated Japan. In *Geisha Boy*'s rather anodyne vision, the American male also needs rescuing, and the film presents a feel-good resolution in which both sides are empowered through their relationship. The title itself could refer to Lewis's character, Mr. Wooley, a peculiarly hapless American magician who comes to Japan on a USO tour as a last ditch attempt to save his flagging career. As a performer, Wooley is no geisha, being continually upstaged by his clever and manipulative white rabbit, Harry. Another candidate for *Geisha Boy*'s title is Watanabe, a young Japanese orphan who becomes entranced by Wooley's incompetent antics to the point that, as his beautiful aunt notes, he is able to laugh for the first time since his parents' death. Wooley ends up bonding with the boy and his aunt and in the film's finale is seen creating a successful magic show at last, with the help of his new Japanese wife and adopted son who, along with Harry, virtually steal the show.

Described in this fashion, the movie sounds like another Orientalizing vision, this time one in which the paternalistic American male saves a dependent and grateful Japan. Certainly the relationship between Wooley and Watanabe is shown in terms that seem to reinforce the stereotype of the American male helping the little Asian brother. In one heartrending scene, for example, a tearful Watanabe tries to stow away on Wooley's plane home only to be discovered and sent back to Japan. Furthermore, the film also seems to be echoing *Sayonara* in its privileging of the Japanese woman over the American female. In *Geisha Boy*, American womanhood is shown, at best, as misguided, in the persona of a young WAC (member of the Women's Army Corps), who has lost her boyfriend to a Japanese girl because she did not treat him well enough, and at worst, as emasculating, in the form of the glamorous Hollywood star heading up the tour who is a monster of self-absorption and selfishness. In contrast, both Watanabe and his aunt are sweet, accepting, and loving toward Wooley, once again echoing *Sayonara* in that it is their confidence in him that helps him to reconstruct his shattered self-image.

Here, however, we come to an intriguing difference in comparison to the earlier film. Not only is Wooley no geisha, but he is no Marlon Brando either. Unsexy, unattractive, and incompetent, Wooley is a singularly unprepossessing specimen of American manhood. In fact, he almost appears to be a foreshadowing of the otaku characters that appear in so many Japanese manga and anime. Sincere, honest, but hopelessly pathetic with woman (and with most of the world around him), it is Wooley's very helplessness that allows him to win the girl (and the boy). This is a formula that has subsequently been repeated many times, especially in the so-called "magical girlfriend" genre of anime, although of course in that case the characters are Japanese. While *Sayonara* shows an American male beginning to question his identity but still ultimately staying in control, *Geisha Boy* is interesting in that it is willing to show the American male as needy, even desperate. Although the film has clearly paternalistic elements, with Wooley "saving" the young Japanese male through making him laugh again, it is also clear that the boy and his aunt save Wooley too. This is most obvious in the film's ending when the viewer sees Wooley, grown more polished and sophisticated, but clearly grateful for the support of his Japanese family.

In *Geisha Boy* the spectacle is less Japan (although there is a section where Wooley and Watanabe travel around Japan visiting various picturesque places), than the abortive magic show that the American tries to create, initially unsuccessfully. Perhaps Wooley's incompetent magic may also say something about a fundamental unease underlying America's performance as a world power, suggesting that any such performance always requires smoke and mirrors, plus the need for a credulous audience.

Intriguingly, throughout the film, the second World War is barely mentioned, except in a brief interlude when the boy's grandfather (played by Sessue Hayakawa, famous for his brilliant portrayal of a rigid Japanese general in the 1957 prisoner-of-war movie *Bridge on the River Kwai*) suddenly appears to the sound of *Kwai*'s popular theme music. This episode is played for comedy, however, emphasizing once again that this is a movie of reconciliation in which boundaries are transcended rather than solidified. Instead it is the Korean War that is highlighted in a sequence when Wooley and Harry are sent on a "private tour" to entertain the troops in Korea. Here too, neither Wooley nor the American soldiers he "entertains" come across in any way powerful, as is clear in a darkly comic sequence when an extremely hungry-looking soldier starts pursuing Harry with a knife. Not surprisingly, when Wooley returns from his tour he appears relieved to be back in Japan, an Asian country in which the recent past seems to have magically disappeared.

Geisha Boy is of course a comedy, in contrast to *Sayonara*'s tragic dimensions; but it is interesting that by the end of the 1950s, the portrayal of Japanese-American relations, at least regarding male-female relations, was shifting to comic mode. Comedy, albeit of a very gentle sort, is also the preferred mode in the 1968 novel *Miss One Thousand Spring Blossoms* by John Ball, an author whose previous book, *In the Heat of the Night*, was made into an Academy Award–winning movie about black-white race relations. *Miss One Thousand Spring Blossoms* is a much more romantic work than *Geisha Boy*, but it also highlights an unsexy, rather hapless protagonist who builds up his masculine identity through the love of a beautiful Japanese woman. In this case, the woman is a real geisha, Masayo, "Japan's Number One Geisha," as she is proudly introduced by the Japanese executives who hire her for the evening to entertain the novel's protagonist, Richard Seaton. Seaton is a straight-laced, slightly puritanical engineer from Boston, sent over to work with a Japanese company on a technical problem.

The novel's plot revolves around Seaton's misunderstanding of Masayo's profession: he falls in love with her and invites her out on dates, not realizing that her time is being paid for by his increasingly unhappy host company. Eventually, he loses his virginity to Masayo, only to discover soon afterwards the truth of her geisha profession. Convinced that she, or at least her geisha house, was simply using him, he goes on a drunken bender then loses himself in an engineering project that ends up saving the Japanese company he has been working with. All ends happily, however. Seaton learns that Masayo herself paid the geisha house out of her savings for their erotic interlude because she has fallen in love with him. Relieved that he need no longer to see her as little more than a prostitute, Seaton finds out where the geisha house has hidden her and convinces her to marry him.

Despite its many stereotypical moments, *Miss One Thousand Spring Blossoms* is actually quite a charming story, thanks to the way that Ball manages to make his male characters reasonably three dimensional. Unusual for a work of this sort, the male Japanese are described sympathetically as intelligent, humane people who are truly concerned when Seaton makes his anguished discovery. Seaton himself is another prototype otaku, although with more depth than Wooley—good-hearted and sincere, but fumbling when it comes to women and human relations in general. As usual, it is the Japanese woman who is the agent of his salvation. In this case, both the erotic and the nurturing elements are seen as major facets of his transformation: a scene with Masayo in the bath when he first sees her in the nude is lovingly described, as is the scene when Seaton loses his virginity.

Perhaps the most interesting aspect of the novel is its ending, presaging what would eventually become a genuine shift in the Japanese-American power dynamic by the 1980s. Unlike *Sayonara*'s romantic couple, Seaton stays in Japan, accepting an offer from the Japanese company he has been working with. Scenes toward the novel's end show Seaton settling into his Japanese-style house and discussing with his fellow engineer, Shig Fujihara, the need for him to learn Japanese. While unusual for its time, Seaton's trajectory would become an increasingly common one by the late twentieth century when Americans and other Westerners would begin to come to Japan as professionals rather than tourists.

Although in that regard the novel is rather ahead of its time, in other aspects *Miss One Thousand Spring Blossoms* remains deeply mired in the old stereotypes. For example, after Seaton "saves" the company, its president writes a haiku poem in his honor. The novel's presentation of women, both American and Japanese, is also depressingly familiar. While the one American woman, Norma Scott, is depicted as interested in and engaged with Japan—she is, in fact, a judo player—she also comes across as materialistic and (in interesting contrast to Masayo) sexually promiscuous. Reiko, the quiet little secretary who secretly falls in love with Seaton, is shown as submissive and self-sacrificing with little will of her own. And Masayo herself is represented almost entirely in visual terms, a spectacle of eternal beauty with less personality even than the aunt in *Geisha Boy*, much less the driven Hana-ogi in *Sayonara*.

The world of Japan at work that *Miss One Thousand Spring Blossoms* forecasts was becoming an increasingly important aspect of both the reality and fantasy of Japan in the Western mind during the 1970s and 1980s. As Japanese companies made inroads into American manufacturing and technology, the image of Japan as the dependent little Asian brother changed considerably. Instead of the geisha, Japan began to be likened to far less attractive images, including robots, the Terminator, and of course Godzilla. These images were discussed more closely in Chapter 3, in relation to what I call the science fictionization of Japan in the mind of the West.

While much has changed in the dynamic between America and Japan over the last several decades, the 2005 film *Memoirs of a Geisha* still seems firmly intent on relaying traditional stereotypes. *Memoirs* was directed by Rob Marshall, famous for having previously directed the Academy Award–winning musical *Chicago* about two female murderers. It is instructive to compare the two works. Both films revolve around women and what might be called "secret worlds"—in the case of Chicago, the women's prison, in the case of *Memoirs*, the geisha houses of Gion in Kyoto. The two films are also both intensely melodramatic, offering highly colored portraits of women at their most vengeful and emotional. But *Memoirs* is ultimately far more subdued than *Chicago*, privileging sacrifice and submissiveness over vengeful raging.

The obvious reason for these differences is the fact that *Chicago* is based on a musical play that emphasized the hard edges of a distinctively American time and place—Chicago in the 1920s (itself as much of a fantasy, of course, as Japan). *Memoirs of a Geisha*, on the other hand, is based on the bestselling novel by Arthur Golden, which, from its opening description of the heroine's "tipsy house" by the seacoast, evokes the misty world of fairy tales. This unreal quality is aided by the movie's mise-en-scene. Unable to find places in Kyoto, in which most of the film takes place, that retained the traditional air of prewar Japan, Marshall built his own elaborate set in California. In doing so, he ended up with a beautiful filmic world that, while based on Japanese settings, also borrowed elements from Chinatown or else made up its own—such as the stunning but sometimes inauthentic costumes worn by the female leads—to create an overwhelming impression of claustrophobic female space. Furthermore, this is a space that is almost entirely Asian, although Marshall mixes Chinese with Japanese actors.

Consequently, this is the first film about Japan discussed in this chapter that has virtually no Western male gaze beyond that of the director himself (except for what might be termed the "obligatory" bath scene when Sayuri is offensively treated by an officer in the American military). In an article in *Vogue* magazine, the movie is described as a "throwback to old Hollywood: a woman's epic" and "a ravishing swirl of costumes and sets that offers a glimpse into what Marshall calls 'a mysterious, hidden forbidden world.'"[54] This mysterious world is of course both the world of the geisha and the world of women. Women, in one sense, dominate the movie: they include Sayuri, whose story we are hearing/seeing, the cold and calculating "mother" of the geisha house who buys Sayuri, and the beautiful older geisha Hatsumomo whose jealous machinations provide one major element of the plot. The other element, however, is very much dominated by the male gaze, but this time by that of a Japanese male, "the Chairman."

Sayuri first encounters this man, played by Japanese actor Takakura Ken, when, still a young girl, she finds herself crying alone on a bridge in Kyoto. Accompanied by a beautiful geisha, the Chairman stops to console her, noting her unusual colored eyes and giving her his handkerchief and a bit of money for ice cream. Not only does Sayuri fall deeply in love with the Chairman after this encounter, but she realizes that by becoming a geisha, she can bring herself closer to him. By what seems like luck at the time, she is taken up by an older geisha, Mameha, a rival to Hatsumomo, and eventually becomes one of the most famous geishas of the pleasure quarters, ultimately winning the Chairman's love and becoming his official mistress for the rest of their lives.

Both the book and movie are almost startlingly regressive. While they retain the standard fairy-tale plot of an orphan going through training to achieve empowerment over a complex and frightening world, Sayuri's achievements are seen only in relation to the men who desire her. In fact, her first "success" is when her virginity is sold at the highest price ever recorded, leading Mameha to exclaim triumphantly, "Tonight all the lights in Gion burn for you!" Even more obviously, at the end of the novel/movie when Sayuri and the Chairman finally declare their love for each other, the Chairman reveals that it is he who financed Mameha's takng her on as a disciple. Sayuri's tale is thus both a fairy tale and a melodrama—although on the one hand she is active in learning the arts of the geisha, and on the other hand she is totally a pawn to the whims of fate and male desire.

If *Memoirs* is a women's film, it is interesting to note that it did not have great success either in America or the rest of the world. Perhaps this may simply have to do with the quality or lack thereof of the film itself, since the novel was extremely successful and the image of the geisha, as embodied in the pop singer Madonna's appropriating of the persona or in the fact that Banana Republic created a line of "Geisha-inspired clothing," seems still to have much appeal. The fans of the book, although usually decrying Sayuri's regressive lifestyle, seemed very much to enjoy the novel's fairy-tale aspects and its satisfyingly romantic ending (an ending that would be most unlikely in a realistic depiction of geisha life).

The desire for romance and love is a basic human yearning that should not be made light of. Furthermore, it is not an emotion that is exclusive to the female gender. The otaku types appearing in Geisha Boy and Miss One Thousand Spring Blossoms have their real life prototypes among the many contemporary male fans of romantic Japanese anime and manga, in particular the so-called magical girlfriend genre. In my research on favorite fan entertainments, I have noticed that many young American men are not embarrassed to say how much they enjoy series such as Oh My Goddess (about a young male student who calls out for pizza and gets a loving nurturing and beautiful goddess delivered to him instead) or Urusei yatsura, whose sexy and magical female protagonist is also utterly devoted to her rather mediocre human boyfriend.[55] While many of my respondents also admitted to enjoying sexually explicit material, by far their most eloquent appreciations were reserved for these kinds of shows where sexuality is subsumed by emotional interaction.

In her article, "Magical Girls and Atomic Bomb Sperm," Annalee Newitz suggests a number of reasons for this trend among young American males, all of which connect with the explorations in this chapter. As with Gruver, Seaton, and Wooley, part of the reason may be a "nostalgia for the kind of social situations made possible by traditional gender roles,"[56] (i.e., before American women began to assert their authority outside the home). But perhaps even more importantly, Newitz points out that "the American otaku's pleasure in romantic comedy anime goes beyond simply experiencing nostalgia for male domination. While traditional gender roles in America are associated with various kinds of social oppression and prejudice, they are also linked to an idealized notion of romance," explaining that "relationships between young men and women in romantic anime are based upon sexual innuendo and deferral . . . rather than sexual consummation and its aftermath (a common theme in American romance)."[57]

The ability of manga and anime to explore more nuanced human emotions than is seen in typical American popular culture products will be discussed at greater length in later chapters, but for now I would like to emphasize Newitz's findings concerning the need to, as she calls it, "escape the hypersexuality of American culture by reimagining romance as going beyond the purely sexual."[58] Sometime this desire on the part of the male can seem regressive and patriarchal, but in other ways it can be seen as an understandable reaction to the jaded and cynical culture around them.

In my courses on anime, the most intense (and sometimes most tense) discussions among students have been around the magical girlfriends series that we view in class. Not surprisingly, many female students are offended by what they see as the oppressive stereotypes that these magical girlfriends seem to convey: virtually all of these women, without exception, are powerful (or certainly magical) and totally focused on their boyfriends. Often these fixations lead to comic and chaotic moments, but the fundamental dynamic of the adoring female doing everything for her man is seldom really questioned. In reply, however, my male students have tended to point out that the male protagonist usually loves and, at some level, treasures the woman. Furthermore, they ask, what is so bad about wanting to be loved?

Gruver, Wooley, and Seaton (and perhaps Sayuri or even Pinkerton as well) might ask the same question. The fantasy of Japanese womanhood that the West has constructed (with massive help from Japanese culture, at least in regards to anime and manga) is one with deeply regressive and genuinely Orientalist aspects. At the same time, however, the fundamental emotions that prompt these fantasies are worth taking seriously. Even in these sometimes disturbingly simplistic works, pleasure, play, and love are parts of a fantasy that is not entirely without its basic human attractions.

5

The 1990s and Beyond:
Japanese Fantasy Takes Wing

Cultural consumption is not merely a form of self-indulgence but an avenue for self-definition.

—*Heide Fehrenbach, "Persistent Myths of Americanization"*

In *Idoru*'s image of the fans rescuing Chia and Masahiko from the Russian Mafia, Gibson gives a memorable vision of "soft power," the kind of power that Japan in the new millennium would come to be most identified with. By the 1990s, Japan's influence on popular culture worldwide would come in many forms including music, fashion, and horror movies. It is probably safe to say, however, that anime and manga and the fan culture that they engendered have had the most penetrating impact on a global cultural scale.

I begin this chapter with an Otakon anecdote. It is a hot summer night in 2003, time for a lot of Con participants to begin enjoying the partying side of Con attendance. But various panel sessions are still going strong. A motley group of us files into a panel entitled "Anime: 1983," a panel looking back over the growth of anime fandom over the past twenty years. At the head of the room stand three middle-aged men in regular clothes. They are the speakers. One of them, a distinguished-looking African American, begins to talk about the genesis of Otakon. Otakon began in 1993 when a group of students at Penn State University decided to hold a convention at State College Pennsylvania that would be free of commercialism and industry pressure, a convention simply for anime enthusiasts. Ten years later, Otakon has become one of the biggest, if not the biggest, anime conventions on the East Coast, bringing in music groups from Japan, an immense variety of guests, and providing a vast range of anime related entertainment and panels.

The speaker goes on to talk about a period even earlier than that, when anime was only being shown as a small part of science-fiction conventions. During one such event, he relates how he had been part of one of the first groups of Americans to bring the *Uchusenkan Yamato* movies, known at that time as *Star Blazers*, to a sci-fi convention in the early 1980s. Originally a television series that spawned several movies, *Yamato* is credited with being the main impetus behind the beginning of anime fandom in Japan, occupying roughly the position of *Star Wars* in the hearts and minds of many Japanese fans. Unlike *Star Wars*, however, *Yamato* is far darker. Although it is technically for children, the series explores such issues as the apocalypse, historical memory, and the fundamental need for human connection, as its crew rockets across the universe in an attempt to save an Earth menaced by overwhelming alien forces. Quite often, the "bad" side wins.

In its dubbed version on American television, *Star Blazers* has made inroads into some young Americans' imaginations, although many did not realize they were watching a Japanese product. The showing of the movie *Yamato*, with its clear Japanese origins, was a watershed, an iconic moment remembered forever by any fan lucky enough to be there. On that evening in Baltimore, I realize that I have heard this story before from my friend Walter Amos, another older anime aficionado, and the accounts dovetail quite neatly. Apparently, *Yamato* was to be shown after a screening of *The Right Stuff*, the new American movie about NASA. But *The Right Stuff* proved so popular that fans clamored to see it again, setting up a confrontation with the *Yamato* fans waiting for their turn. According to legend (or Walter), *The Right Stuff* fans sneered at the very notion of the *Yamato* series, asking why anyone would want to see "some militaristic Japanese cartoon." Ultimately, a compromise was reached, and the *Yamato* film was shown well after midnight. And then it was shown again, and again. Many members of the audience had never seen anything like it. As Robert Fenellon recounts in his article "Talkin' 'Bout My Star Blazers Generation," "American viewers unused to this kind of high drama must have found themselves saying, 'Wait a minute! Aren't you supposed to end every cartoon with the good guys laughing about their victory? Aren't the HEROES supposed to win? What are the BAD GUYS doing?'"[1]

Thus, anime fandom was born, although at that time the fans would not have described the object of their interest as "anime" and could never have guessed that in the not-so-distant future anime cons would be far more numerous and well attended than science-fiction conventions. At Otakon, the speaker noted that many die-hard sci-fi fans at the initial *Yamato* screening had scoffed at its unexpected popularity and predicted that the interest in Japanese cartoons would soon fade away. At this point, the speaker stopped for a minute and looked around the room at us. "That was twenty years ago," he said, "*And we are still here.*" Several members of the audience cheered. The speaker's words are a quotation from the second film of *The Matrix* trilogy, *Matrix Revolution*, (2003; directed by Andy and Larry Wachowski), when Morpheus, one of the main characters, tells the citizens of Zion, the last human city in a world almost completely taken over by machines, that despite the formidable obstacles against the human race, "We are still here."

Of course anime audiences were far from facing the obstacles that the humans in *The Matrix* had to deal with, but the use of this quotation from the film does raise an interesting question: How is it that anime fans are "still here"? In fact, not only are they still here, but over the last decade they have grown enormously in number and include fans of manga and consumers of Japanese popular culture in general.

Concurrently, anime's influence has become increasingly ubiquitous, not only in America, but also throughout the world. To give just a few examples, a Brazilian civil servant, upon learning what I do, told me that he often sees his younger countrymen engaging in "cosplay" (costume play) and not in a convention setting but out in the street. The son of the man who fixes my cable television tells me that while his real name is Alejandro, he prefers to be known as "Hideki," since he and his friends in Mexico City are all obsessed with anime. South African television has its own anime station. Korean television, which banned Japanese imports for a long time, now airs anime and Korean cartoons inspired by anime. On a recent trip to Paris, I ended up at the Musee de la Monnaie, which, belying its neoclassical architecture, was featuring an exhibition comparing the art of the Japanese animator Miyazaki Hayao with that of the famous French cartoonist Moebius. Although there were few tourists at the exhibition, the halls were crowded with young French people.

Overall, in the last two decades, Japanese popular culture has gained a strong global foothold. Some of the reasons behind this will be explored in more detail in subsequent chapters, but for now, let me present a brief overview. We have seen how Japan in the 1980s became known principally for its astounding economic rise. This rise, based on a number of factors but including the ability to produce excellent technological products and what at the time appeared to be a highly successful management system, also influenced the way the rest of the world saw Japanese culture. Rather than haiku poetry, art, or Zen Buddhism, people around the globe and perhaps Americans in particular saw Japanese "cultural" exports in terms of advanced technological devices and impressive management techniques that included such buzz words as "quality circles" (ironically, originally an American conception), "consensus," and "just-in-time inventories." As we have seen, this success story stimulated both admiration and resentment on the part of the West, but it also engendered mixed emotions on the part of the Japanese. Especially as the economic boom began to fail, many Japanese commentators began to bemoan the fact that their country was known as "Japan Inc." Haruki Murakami, a major Japanese writer, went so far as to lament in a public lecture at Berkeley in the 1990s that the most well-known exponent of contemporary Japanese culture was Sony.

All this would change enormously by the end of the next decade as Japanese cultural products that ranged from Hello Kitty to Pokemon to Japanese fashion began to flood the world. By the millennium, Japan was "cool." The pop star Gwen Stefani would have a hit record singing about "Harajuku Girls" (the Tokyo neighborhood with the most cutting-edge fashions). The rock group Linkin Park would win an MTV Viewer's Choice Award for "Breaking the Habit," their bleak, anime-style video recorded in Japan by a well-known Japanese animator. Quentin Tarantino would feature a fifteen-minute violent anime-style sequence in his 2003 hit film, *Kill Bill*. Even the American hit cartoon series *South Park* got in on the action with a typically offensive (although humorous) episode that satirized what they perceived as Pokemon's sinister takeover of the minds of American children. And just about everyone was eating sushi (except for those sophisticates who had graduated to drinking rarefied sake along with the nutty-tasting little green soybeans known as edamame).

Scholars and journalists took note of course. In a watershed article published in *Foreign Policy* in 2002, Douglas McGray coined the term "Japan's Gross National Cool" and introduced the article with the telling sentence, "From pop music to consumer electronics, architecture to fashion, and animation to cuisine, Japan looks more like a cultural superpower today than it did in the 1980s when it was an economic one."[2]

McGray's argument was based on Joseph Nye's book *Soft Power*, discussed in the introduction. But McGray extends Nye's initial argument beyond the United States to Japan and to popular culture. (It should be noted that as early as 1990, Nye had presciently suggested that other soft power hubs might well arise globally.)[3]

Purveyors of Fantasy: Kitty, Pokemon, and the Culture of Cuteness

The reasons behind the growth of Japanese soft power are many and varied, but perhaps the most fundamental one is that over the last two decades, Japanese manufacturers, engineers, and creative artists have been increasingly adept at competing with American popular culture in purveying a variety of appealing fantasies to a hungry world. It is worth noting that the last decade of the twentieth century was a time when fantasy became extremely popular throughout the world. The West offered such blockbusters as *Harry Potter* and *Lord of the Rings*. Japanese fantasy was more varied—ranging from the child-oriented tsunami that was the Pokemon media mix to the erotic world of beautiful boys available to fans of *yaoi* manga and anime. Building on a superb hardware base, Japanese software and soft power began to make inroads as early as the 1980s. Although American popular culture is still dominant globally, Japanese products are serving more and more as both additions and alternatives to it.

While it would be reductive to try and characterize either form of popular culture in a totalizing way, certain elements can be distinguished. Although Fehrenbach and Poiger assert that "there is no monolithic 'American culture' but perhaps only a stream of image-ideals,"[4] certain of these image-ideals have clearly exercised a great deal of global influence. Among these would surely be a fascination with portrayals of power, dominance, and violence and what might be described as a rather flashy form of sexuality, all presented without a great deal of nuance or subtlety. This proclivity is on display in any number of postwar Hollywood films, ranging from the 1980s *Indiana Jones* series where the protagonist is portrayed as seeking "fortune and glory," as he refers to it in *Indiana Jones and the Temple of Doom* (1984; director Steven Spielberg) at all costs, to the 2004 *Mr. and Mrs. Smith*, where virtually the entire action of the film consists of the two sexy and beautiful title characters opening up enormous and sophisticated arsenals in their heartfelt attempts to murder each other.

Of course Hollywood would not create so many productions of this sort if they did not sell to a broad audience. Clearly, overwhelming violence and black-and-white adventure stories strike a chord throughout humanity, as the global reach of Hollywood attests. Furthermore, it must be acknowledged that Japanese culture contains its own traditions of extreme violence and power plays, not to mention an erotic tradition that, while arguably more creative and imaginative, is also sometimes far more grotesque than most of the sexuality on offer in American film and television.

On balance, however, it seems safe to say that the fantasies that contemporary Japan purveys are quite different from what American popular culture offers. Subsequent chapters will deal in more detail with Hollywood in comparison to Japanese animation, but the entertainment media are not the only areas of difference. We might compare Hello Kitty with Barbie, for example. Launched in 1974, Hello Kitty initially did not have much of a following and was almost dropped by the late 1970s. However, as Woodrow Phoenix relates, "Fans started asking questions: Did she have any brothers or sisters? Where was she born? . . . From the questions Sanrio gradually developed her character, choosing London for her birthplace because in the seventies this was a place young Japanese girls dreamed about."[5] In other words, Hello Kitty's creators developed a "story" for her, a crucial ingredient in the making of a successful fantasyscape. Of course Barbie had a story too: she was a teenage fashion model trying to get ahead in the competitive worlds of both high school and modeling. Barbie was also a doll who spoke uniquely to the needs and desires of young girls, becoming aware of their femininity in the newly emancipated culture of the 1960s. As is well known, she was the first doll to have breasts, and her figure is extremely sexually delineated in a hard and angular sort of way.

In contrast, Kitty is cuddly, soft, fluffy, and extremely nonthreatening. In sum, she is "cute." While cuteness is also an attribute that can be found cross-culturally, it is one that Japanese society over the last couple of decades has particularly excelled at producing. Besides Hello Kitty, cute examples range from the myriad other toy "characters" such as Tare Panda, a droopy bear with a sweet expression, to childlike clothes for grown women marketed as "Lolita fashion," to the many adorable heroines of anime and manga. As both Anne Allison and Sharon Kinsella explain,[6] cuteness is not only nonthreatening, but it is actively reassuring, and both are attributes that may seem particularly attractive in a world that appears increasingly chaotic and dark. Cute characters and toys are also generally quite small, colorful, and inexpensive, lending themselves to the collecting impulse. As we saw in Chapter 2, collecting can be a means of control, of creating a safe and comforting fantasyscape, separate from the demands and complexities of modern life. Cuteness, then, is a fantasy that is particularly appealing in the new millennium culture.

Another aspect of Hello Kitty's appeal may well be the fact that she does not appear to be particularly "Japanese" and can be seen as more of a generic fantasy of cuteness. In this regard, she resembles a number of Japanese pop-cultural products, most famously, the characters of Pokemon, perhaps the most successful video game and related products phenomenon in history. Originally a video game designed for children, Pokemon spawned a variety of other related products, from the immensely popular television series and movies, to the equally popular card game, to the cuddly stuffed toy monster known as Pikachu.

In its most basic conception as a video game, Pokemon seems like the very model of modern Japanese entertainment technology—well-made, inexpensive, and accessible, not to mention imaginative and engrossing. Although video games are not exclusive to Japan, many of the most well-known ones are created by Japanese designers, and the devices on which they are played are virtually always made in Japan. Pokemon built on this successful tradition but went well beyond the average video game, becoming a genuine social phenomenon as, for a brief time, children's playgrounds and recess hours were dominated by an obsession with the game in all its manifestations.

The story of Pokemon's rise (and decline) has been well documented in such texts as *Pikachu's Global Adventure*, edited by Joseph Tobin, and in chapters in Anne Allison's book *Millennial Monsters: Japanese Toys and the Global Imagination*. Although the scholars brought together in Tobin's book differ somewhat among themselves in their explanations for Pokemon's popularity, it seems clear that one major aspect of Pokemon's appeal was the density and complexity of the story and game (so complicated that adults sometimes gave up on trying to understand it) and its highly interactive quality. The Pokemon fantasyscape offered a colorful world of adventure, risk, and competition and even, according to some scholars, a vision of personal maturation. Buckingham and Sefton-Green go so far as to describe its narrative trajectory as "a kind of bildungsroman" or else a "quest."[7] Even more intriguingly, they suggest that "Pokemon is centrally about acquiring knowledge."[8] Throughout this book we have seen knowledge and mastery as forms of cultural capital that have been an essential part of the West's relationship with Japan.

This returns us to the question of Pokemon's "Japaneseness." Were the children who fell in love with Pokemon also falling in love with Japanese culture, or simply with a generic entertainment designed to please as many children worldwide as possible? According to Koichi Iwabuchi, much of Pokemon's popularity is due to the fact that the phenomenon has little relation to its Japanese national origin. He points out that the American producers who arranged for *Pokemon* to be shown on American television made changes so that "a relatively ambiguous portrait of good and evil was changed into that of clear black and white confrontation between characters"[9] (presumably in order to cater to what might be perceived as a more fundamentalist American sensibility). He also mentions how the producers of *Pokemon* were at pains to suppress any Japanese "odor" by creating a generic setting with characters who do not look recognizably Japanese. In this regard, they resemble not only the "London-born" Hello Kitty, whose last name is "White," but also one of the first and most popular of Japanese computer games, Super Mario Brothers, whose main characters' appearances and names were "stereotypically Italian."[10]

From another point of view, however, it can be argued that both Hello Kitty and the Pokemon characters still possess certain distinctively Japanese characteristics, even if they are not as obvious as facial or landscape features. One of them is the aforementioned attribute of cuteness. Although some scholars point out that the American Pokemon distributors made an effort to have the Pokemon figures appear more "cool" than "cute," it is certainly the case that Pikachu himself was very much in the line of cute, cuddly, and nonthreatening, and also extremely popular among American boys and girls alike.

Another possible ur-Japanese characteristic is what Anne Allison terms "techno-animism," a trait that she suggests links traditional Japanese culture and its contemporary popular culture products. By "techno-animism," she means the way consumers seem to imbue inanimate objects with a kind of soul. Again, this is not a concept unique to Japan, as anyone who has tried to separate a child from her beloved blanket knows well, but Allison makes an excellent case for certain aspects of traditional Japanese religion and customs as being particularly conducive to this practice. As she says, "This is more of an aesthetic proclivity, a tendency to see the world as animated by a variety of beings, both worldly and unworldly, that are complex, (inter)changeable, and not graspable by so-called rational (or visible) means alone. Drawn in part from religious tendencies in Japan, these include Shintoism (an animist religion imparting spirits to everything from rivers and rocks to snakes and a the wind) and Buddhism (a religion adhering to notions of reincarnation and transubstantiation)."[11]

The world of Pokemon is, on the one hand, a world of material things—trading cards, beeping GameBoys, and brightly colored cartoons. But it also one that, particularly in the card game, seems to be infused with life and soul that draws children deeply into it. Adults may have winced when they heard the slogan "Gotta catch 'em all!" which conjured up visions of consumer culture gone wild. But the children I observed when the fad was at its height reacted as if they were genuinely imbued with the thrill of the quest for actual creatures, a quest that was also related to a "story," in this case not only the adventure narrative created by the manufacturers, but also the foundation story of how the creator of Pokemon based the game on his own love of collecting unusual insects as a child. Again, it is important to acknowledge that animistic qualities imbue to goods in Western culture as well, but it appears safe to say that the Pokemon and other Japanese toys and goods were particularly effective in creating an interactive fantasyscape that effortlessly transcended material reality.

The "Japaneseness" of Pokemon also cropped up in American adult reactions to the craze. Often these reactions were negative to the point of implicit racism. As Christine Yano relates, some commentators suggested sinister connections between Pokemon and a "samurai" ethos at odds with the American way of life. She discusses a right-wing Christian publication that, as she describes it, seems to view Japan as a "pagan country, mired in occultism, mysticism and martial arts."[12] These publications seem particularly concerned with Japanese violence. Yano give such quotes as, "The game reflects Japan's warrior past in its violence, with the object being to conquer other Pokemons through physical force or sorcery."[13] Other, more up to date critics suggest that Pokemon playing may turn young Western children into Japanese-style otaku beings with no social or inner life who live only to accumulate.[14]

Perhaps the most creative, memorable, and offensive attack on Pokemon was the infamous *South Park* espisode, "Chimpokomon." In this episode, the creators of *South Park* (one of whom, Trey Parker, was a Japanese major at the University of Colorado), pull out the stops to create what Matthew Allen describes as a manipulation of "pre-existing stereotypes of Japan into slightly paranoid, orientalized, and ultimately emasculating images of Japan that place it in the role of the world's leader in the promotion of (immoral) global consumer ideology."[15] The episode follows *South Park's* main characters—four elementary-school boys and their hangers on—as they are seduced by the evil Chimpokomon Corporation (a pun combining "Pokemon" with a Japanese slang word for "penis"),who have produced a game of such power and appeal that it literally brainwashes the children who play it into mindless automatons, bent on acquiring more and more Chimpokomon goods. At this point the satire is a fairly conventional extrapolation of what many adults truly feared about the consumerist implications of the Pokemon craze.

What follows next, however, is a vitriolic satire on certain cultural and historical stereotypes related to Japan. These include the attack on Pearl Harbor (rather bizarrely, the *South Park* episode shows the children being taught Japanese and informed that they must prepare to attack Pearl Harbor as a revenge for the Japanese sneak attack in World War II), the ambiguous role of the Japanese Emperor Hirohito during the war (in the episode the Chimpokomon chief executive is named Hirohito and dresses as a samurai), and finally and most offensively, an extended satire on American and Japanese stereotypes involving penis size. In *South Park's* satirical vision, the wily Japanese executives are able to get around the simple-minded Americans by flattering them about the size of their penises. Ultimately, however, the parents of the South Park children are clever enough to think of a way to turn the children away from the craze by pretending to embrace it themselves and thus rendering Chimpokomon "uncool."

In *South Park's* parodic vision, Japan is a combination of old and new stereotypes—samurai warriors and World War II sneak attacks are set beside the overwhelming force of Japanese technocapitalism. How much of this parody would be understandable to *South Park's* viewers is debatable. As Allen suggests, much of the episode's historical and cultural satire would likely have been lost on younger viewers. But the jokes about penis size are hard to ignore. In certain ways, the Chimpokomon episode lays bare the subtext of films such as *Rising Sun*—that in contests between countries, masculine potency becomes a subconscious issue. Allen points out that "in a quite literal interpretation of Freud's theory of the phallus as a symbol of power, the writers highlight the popular perception that penis size equates with political power."[16]

South Park is famous for its evenhanded offensiveness that takes virtually everything as its target. Even its most offensive attacks can also make compelling points. The "Chimpokomon" episode's treatment of such issues as global capitalism and obsessive consumerism is clever and certainly addresses aspects of the commercialization of American society in an original and memorable manner.

From that point of view, we might even see it as continuing in the line of satire that Gilbert and Sullivan established in *The Mikado*—that of playing off a craze for the Japanese Other in a way to make satirical points about one's own culture. Even the comparisons of penis size can be seen as having as much to do with American masculine insecurity as they do with offensive racial stereotyping. It is also probably the case that the generation of viewers targeted by *South Park* is used to this kind of humor, although it would be interesting to see how young Asian Americans would react to what most older viewers would probably find a truly poisonous degree of stereotyping.

In any case, the "Chimpokomon" episode does a good job of capturing the truly remarkable sway exercised by the Pokemon phenomenon on a global scale. Although the craze has ultimately abated, Pokemon's descendants, most notably the Yugi-oh game, remain both popular and influential in the lives of children around the world. The hardware aspects of Japanese gaming have also continued to dominate electronic entertainment, as the waves of frenzy concerning the most recent Nintendo and Sony products easily attest.

Pokemon was not the only Japanese cultural phenomenon that generated mixed reactions in the West. Anime and manga also had to suffer certain negative connotations and stereotyping. Although aimed at younger children and created as a mass commodity, Pokemon could be considered a form of anime and indeed was taken that way by certain American commentators, usually in a negative fashion. Yano quotes one such writer, Bloch, who asks, "Do parents need to be concerned about Pokemon? Does the visceral Japanese animation called anime, which has found quite a following in American subculture, prompt violence in viewers?"[17]

This kind of reaction was quite typical in the early days of anime and manga's rise in popularity. The degree of sexual content in both media also produced strong responses. For Americans in particular, the idea of cartoons containing nudity and sexuality was genuinely hard to encompass, since both animation and comics have been traditionally seen as children's entertainment and therefore "innocent." Certainly at the beginning of the phenomenon, both anime and manga had to struggle with some extremely negative stereotyping. Much of that has changed, however, in the last decade, as the public perceptions of what constitute art have begun to change, and the Japanese imports have become more ubiquitous. Nevertheless, the success of the two media was hardly assured. It is worth reiterating that manga and anime are two resolutely non-Western cultural products. Far more than Hello Kitty or even Pokemon, they brought with them a variety of what Iwabuchi calls "cultural fragrances" that differed in many ways from domestic Western products. These "fragrances" included not only different approaches to design, action, or narrative, but also different forms of representing gender relations and even different value systems as well.

High Tech Meets Grass Roots: The Rise of Anime and Manga

The rest of this chapter will provide an overview of the rise of anime and, tangentially, manga fandom in the West. Further chapters will go into more detail as to the specifics on fan interactions with anime and manga, but for the moment, I would like to concentrate on some of the broad outlines behind the phenomenon. Certainly one of the key factors that helped anime fandom to develop was the increasing advancement in technology that Japanese companies helped to engender. In some ways, this is ironic. Technology is often seen in an negative light. Even if it does not create the sinister machine world envisioned in *The Matrix*, recent technological advances in particular have been criticized as isolating and alienating individuals from community. At least in the case of Japanese popular culture, however, the development of both recording and communications technology, not to mention ever more sophisticated techniques of mass production and marketing, have helped to bring about a form of soft power that thrives on interconnections between cultures and individuals. Rather than adding to the dehumanization of society, it can be argued that Japanese cultural products, from toys to anime, are actually surprisingly effective in promoting a sense of community or at least a sense of identification with something outside of ourselves.

This is especially true in the case of anime, which is a fascinating example of how growing technological sophistication can combine with a truly low-tech grassroots movement to create a genuine community. As the earlier anecdote from Otakon indicates, Japanese animation was initially very hard to come by in the West. A few series like *Star Blazers* crossed into American television, but they were almost always Americanized beyond recognition with infelicitous dubs, American names, and sometimes, mangled plot lines. Somehow, however, a few of the viewers began to recognize that they were seeing something different from American television fare and ultimately became aware of the Japanese origins.

By this point (in the late 1970s), private individuals were beginning to use VCRs. Anime began to establish a limited beachhead at science-fiction conventions, the usual scenario being that someone would put a sign up on the notice board announcing showings of "Japanese cartoons" in their hotel rooms. The cartoons would often have been recorded on a third or fourth generation videotape and usually would not provide much in the way of translation. If the viewers were lucky, there might be someone there who had learned a bit of Japanese, perhaps in the army, or who had received some basic plot description from a Japanese pen pal. Undoubtedly, however, part of the fun was in the incomplete understanding and the enjoyment of the pure visual pleasure of anime. There was also, according to older fans with whom I have talked, the particular pleasure of being part of a small and very specialized community of cognoscenti. The vision of a small group of fans gathering around a scratchy videotape at a science-fiction convention also suggests a form of ritual, something that commentators on fandom have frequently mentioned as an important part of the appeal of fan subculture.

While twentieth-century anime fans are a long way from the Japonisants of Paris, there is perhaps some similarity in the pleasure with which they recount how each discovered such a little known art form and perhaps the even greater pleasure of sharing it with a few like-minded friends. Even more than the woodblock prints that flooded Europe in the nineteenth century, it also must be said that the quality of what was being seen was often haphazard at best. Obviously, science fiction and fantasy (major genres in anime) were highlighted, and the sci-fi fan viewers enjoyed the Japanese "take" on familiar subjects such as space exploration, high-tech weaponry, and fantasy worlds. It is probably also safe to assume that the far more open approach to sex and nudity displayed in anime played a part in the initial reception of anime, as it still does today (and which was, of course, a component behind the popularity of Japanese art in the nineteenth century as well).

In some cases, the erotic content of anime had a notably deleterious effect in terms of spreading an appreciation for the medium. This was most clear in the United Kingdom where the tape of a *hentai* (sexually perverse) epic known as *Urotsukidoji* (Legend of the Overfiend), with scenes of extraordinarily violent, even apocalyptic sex between humans and monsters, was imported early on. The film's genuinely shocking content seems to have caused a moral panic on the part of the public that affected anime's reception in the British Isles for years to come.[18]

On the whole, however, most older fans remember the culture of videotaping with fond nostalgia. The culture produced its own rules and codes of behavior. A longtime participant in the fan world described to me how one of the most important activities at early anime conventions was swapping videotapes. Fans would arrive from all parts of the country with their own tapes and VCRs and record other fans' anime on their own tapes. Usually no money was exchanged, except perhaps, the price of a blank tape. During this period, anime tapes would usually come with a subtitle added on: "Recorded by Fans FOR Fans." My informants will dwell eloquently on the intimacy of the exchanges, the pleasure of finding something new and different, and the almost total lack of commercialization during that period, a far cry, many suggest, from what it is like now.

The VCR revolution was important in other ways as well. From the Japanese creators' point of view, it was now technologically and economically feasible to create, record, and sell not only anime television series with many episodes but also shorter series created for video alone—the so-called OVAs (Original Video Animation). This may have also helped the explosion of creative energy that seemed to take place among Japanese animators in the 1980s and 1990s. Although Japan had once been known for its superb film industry, by the 1970s the industry had been greatly overshadowed by Hollywood blockbusters, and young directors increasingly turned to television and animated series to make their marks. By the 1990s economic recession, artistic talents became increasingly disillusioned with corporate culture, a trend that, as McGray suggests, may have helped to empower a generation of young creative artists. This may be even more true in the field of manga, since the start-up costs of becoming a manga artist are so much lower.

In any case, Western fans benefited enormously from this combination of technological availability and creative artistic energy. Anime, it turned out, offered far more than science fiction and fantasy—popular series included historical epics, romantic comedies, mysteries, psychological thrillers, and coming-of-age stories. Western anime fans began to clamor for more and different varieties of anime and were increasingly able to obtain them. As time went on, subtitling became ever more sophisticated, as fans began to make more connections with the Japanese producers, and some fans began to learn Japanese themselves. Manga's popularity developed more slowly, possibly because of the difficulty in translating the many slang and onomatopoeic expressions used in manga and the perception that the market for reading as opposed to viewing Japanese cultural products would be smaller. Still, manga began making its way into American and European comic bookstores (in fact, the Europeans in general have a higher regard for comics as art than did Americans). And during the 1980s, *Mangajin*, a magazine to help teach Japanese to students by using manga graphics, had quite a successful run over a number of years.

Even with these developments, however, it is possible that anime and manga would have remained niche phenomena had it not been for the Internet. Early Western anime fans often tended to come from the scientific and technological fields and were thus early users of the Internet; and the earliest fan clubs used mimeographed newsletters and "zines," anime-related Internet chat groups developed with impressive rapidity. In 1994, *Wired* magazine ran an article on anime fans that suggested that they were the most "wired" fan subculture in existence. The Internet allowed fans all over the world to get in touch with each other, to spread news about conventions, to trade tapes, obtain anime-related paraphernalia, and to organize clubs of like-minded souls in the same area. As we will see in our chapter on Miyazaki, the Internet helped to sustain interest in certain kinds of anime and in certain kinds of discussions. All in all, it was probably the single most important instrument in creating the anime fan "community," what media scholar Henry Jenkins describes as "a cultural community, one which shares a common mode of reception, a common set of critical categories and practices, a tradition of aesthetic production and a set of social norms and expectations."[19]

In the twenty-first century, fan communities are omnipresent; but it is worth reemphasizing the fact that, unlike the fan cultures existing around *Star Trek* or *Star Wars*, non-Japanese fans of anime are coalescing around a nondomestic fan product that until quite recently did not even appear in English. Therefore, anime fandom tends to be a particularly self-conscious kind. Even now, as anime becomes more and more mainstream, fans are still highly aware that they are participating in activities surrounding a culture very different from their own, which may well be one of anime's central attractions.

There is no question that anime's popularity was helped by fortuitous timing—both in terms of the VCR and then the DVD revolution, and perhaps even more so by the rise of the Internet. The improvements in telecommunications and the ability to broadcast over many channels also undoubtedly helped to feed the appetite for all kinds of entertainment. The stage was set for a revolution in transcultural flows around the globe. But the question then becomes, Why anime and not, for instance, Hong Kong martial arts films or Bollywood cinema?

Although we will delve more deeply into this in subsequent chapters, a few suggestions are worth keeping in mind. One I have already mentioned: the breadth of anime. Unlike most Western cartoons that are usually expected to be child-oriented and comical, anime explores the same thematic ground as Hollywood. Its modes and genres are universal ones—from horror to romance to slice of life—and viewers all over the globe can empathize with and enjoy them. At the same time, almost paradoxically, anime is also deeply distinctive and, at this writing, still very culturally specific. Although there is no single anime-viewing experience, certain elements are often found. These include longer narrative trajectories where the characters' personalities build up over time, a more nuanced approach to the question of good and evil, a willingness to use silence and lack of motion (as opposed to the frenzied nonstop action in most American cartoons), story lines that range from anarchic craziness to heartbreaking tragedy, and, of course, an extremely distinctive use of color and design.

The "look" of anime is very significant. Fans frequently mention the aesthetic pleasure they find in the visual images presented to them. Another visual aspect that is important is the fact that these are, after all, cartoons in which characters are depicted in a distinctive "anime" (or manga) style. Some commentators feel that anime and manga characters look "White," but in fact they exhibit quite a range of characteristics that are not really Caucasian or Japanese, such as the huge eyes and often strangely colored hair that have come to be visual trademarks of the media. Unlike Bollywood or Hong Kong martial arts films, which are both live action, the viewer can easily identify with anime and manga characters. This is especially true of the younger generation of anime and manga fans who grew up not only on *The Simpsons* and *South Park*, but also on computer games and computer graphics. The anime fantasyscape truly is an Other world, one that older viewers with stereotyped notions of what cartoons should be may have trouble entering, but for younger viewers, a world that may even feel more comfortable and familiar than the "reality" around them.

It is also worth remembering that the 1990s saw a huge rise in the popularity of fantasy and science-fiction narratives, the most prominent being the breathtakingly successful *Harry Potter* books that had a worldwide impact. In cinema, *The Lord of the Rings* trilogy broke many box office records. Even when anime is at its most realistic, its visual style offers a form of fantasy imagery that may become increasingly appealing as the world becomes ever more polluted, urbanized, and overrun by modernization.

Who Are the Fans?

We will conclude this chapter with an exploration of one final question: who are the anime fans? Again, this will be discussed subsequently in more detail, but for now I would like to introduce anime fandom at a general level. My observations are based on six years of interviewing fans, going to conventions, and collecting responses to a questionnaire that I first developed for the first edition of my anime book in 2000 and have refined continually since that time. Overall, I received around 350 responses to the post-2000 questionnaire, which ranged over several thousand pages as the fans were prolific and thoughtful. I also developed a separate questionnaire for the Miyazaki fans, from whom I received sixty-four additional questionnaires in response (see Chapter 8). Although I cannot claim that this is a "definitive portrait" (college students are probably overrepresented because I gave many lectures on college campuses) I believe that geographically, and to some extent demographically, my findings can serve as a reasonably accurate introduction to this fascinating subculture.

When I first began researching anime fans in the mid-1990s it was fairly easy to categorize them. As discussed in the supplement to the first edition of my book *Anime from Akira to Princess Mononoke*, the majority of anime fans were male (70 percent of my respondents), and a majority were in science- or technology-related fields (or if they were students, were majoring in those areas). These findings reflect the fact that so many anime fans came out of science-fiction fandom, traditionally a male-dominated subculture (with the interesting exception of *Star Trek* fandom) and one in which, not surprisingly, people with science and technology backgrounds were common. This is not to say that one could not find lawyers, humanists, or artists among the fans—indeed artists were probably the second highest category after those in technology fields—but they were proportionately far fewer. Racial and ethnic characteristics ranged fairly broadly, but the preponderant identities were white and Asian American. The age range was also on the older side; although I met some high-school students, the majority of my respondents were in their twenties and thirties.

Less than a decade later, the composition of anime fandom has changed enormously. The most obvious development has been the increase of younger fans and the enormous rise in female fandom. Children's involvement is undoubtedly linked to the popularity of Pokemon and Yugi-oh, although other factors such as increasing proliferation of manga and the publication of the large manga journal *Shonen Jump*, which was particularly marketed for young people, were also factors. Older fans also began having children and taking them to cons with them, which increasingly provided family-friendly activities. There is even a Houston-based convention called Chibicon (*chibi* in Japanese means "little runt") that is specifically targeted at children.

Female Fandom: The Shojo

The rise of female fandom is also due to a variety of factors. Many of my fem-interviewees mentioned the *Sailor Moon* anime and manga series as a crucial factor. Enormously popular in Japan, the anime was brought over to America and Canada in 1995–96. Although the series never achieved anything like the audience it had in Japan, many of the young girls who did see it became avid fans. *Sailor Moon* was considered unusual even in Japan because it followed the adventures of an all-girl group of superheroes, known as the Sailor Senshi (Sailor Soldiers), rather than the usual all-male or mixed groupings. Furthermore, these girls, particularly Sailor Moon herself (Serena or Usagi [Bunny] in Japanese), were far from being the omnicompetent heroic type common in American comics and even some manga. Serena, in fact, could be described most appropriately with the adjectives ditzy or klutzy.

Of course, the very humanness (and cuteness) of the senshi was the secret of their appeal. Young girls enjoyed the daffy humor of the series, the surprisingly realistic tensions among the senshi, and the mixture of fantasy and slice-of-life reality (Serena is always having trouble with her homework) that made the series so fresh and appealing. Compared to American cartoons, the plots were surprisingly complicated and involving, keeping the viewers' interest from episode to episode.

While *Sailor Moon* never became the hit its distributors had hoped it would be, it not only enticed many female viewers into anime, but also opened the way to wider distribution of the translated versions of the manga-for-girls genre known as "shojo manga." These incredibly popular manga have been a staple of the Japanese industry for decades, appealing not only to girls but to grown women as well. Shojo manga are like nothing ever produced in the West (at least until recently when American publishing houses have started to manufacture their own versions). They are beautifully drawn in a distinctive gauzy style, which includes such features as (literally) starry eyes, careful attention to clothes and hair, and exceedingly attractive, often rather androgynous-looking male love interests.

But it is not only the "look" of shojo manga, but the strongly developed characters and narratives that draw in viewers. The story lines emphasize emotional interaction and delve quite deeply into the characters' psychology, at the same time as they offer fantasy and romance. As Evelyn Dubocq, a representative of the American manga publisher Viz, explains, "In shojo, many of the struggles depicted have to do with day-to-day issues like love, family responsibility, and identity. Regardless of the level of fantasy and artifice, most shojo stories remain endearingly grounded in universal concerns."[20]

While the themes are definitely universal, it is safe to say that the approach is still Japanese. Just as Japanese literature offers impressive psychological complexity, the manga are willing to dig deeper into the characters' psyches than most American popular fiction would ever do. Not dissimilar to the magical girlfriend genre discussed in Chapter 4, there is an emphasis on cuteness and a relative lack of adolescent cynicism or jadedness that is quite different from the characterizations of most teenagers in American popular culture in general.

Female Fandom: Yaoi

The sex brings you in but the stories and the art are what keep you.

—*Tran Nguyen, founder of Drama Queen*

Beside shojo manga, another kind of manga (and anime) has helped to capture female fans in the West (and other parts of the world too). This is the so-called *yaoi* genre, which in recent years has become increasingly popular. *Yaoi* shares the conventions of shojo manga in that its characters are beautifully drawn (and beautiful physically), and its plots are romantic and complex. The crucial difference, however, is that the main characters are almost invariably male, and the main focus of the stories is on male/male sexuality, a focus that runs the gamut from gauzy romance to hardcore erotica. Narratives are often highly baroque, taking place in exotic European countries among wealthy and noble people and often featuring evil older men attempting to seduce romantic *bishonen* (beautiful boys).

Yaoi's popularity in America is intriguing. To some extent it shares certain elements with the Western "slash" genre in which women fans "rewrite" popular television shows or books, such as *Star Trek* or even *Harry Potter* to make the male main characters gay and romantically involved with each other.[21] Many *yaoi* fanfiction writers also base their writings on established series, but *yaoi* also includes original fiction as well. The *yaoi* fiction that I have read also seems more explicitly sexual than most of the slash material with which I am familiar. This is not to say that *yaoi* resembles the kind of narratives found in men's pornographic magazines. Usually there is an enormous amount of description and suspense before actual sexual activity is engaged in.

Yaoi is popular enough not only to have its own panels at anime conventions (often restricted to fans ages eighteen and over), but to even have its own convention, YaoiCon in San Francisco. As at most conventions, cosplay, panels, and dealer rooms are staples (see Chapter 6), but the convention also includes such distinctive highlights as a "Bishonen Auction" where attractive young men are "sold" for a few hours to the highest bidder. When I asked what the bidder actually did with her bishonen, I was told that the activities were quite innocent, mainly dressing him up and taking pictures, apparently.

Yaoi fandom strikes me as a particularly interactive form of fandom, or what Jenkins calls "participatory culture."[22] The panels I have attended at various conventions were packed, mainly with women (although there might be one or two aesthetically pleasing young men in posing mode), most who were either *yaoi* writers themselves or hoping to get tips on how to become one. Translating *yaoi* fiction has also become a popular pursuit that even offers financial gain at the same time as emotional and intellectual satisfaction.

I spoke to two fans involved in the translation business, both of whom struck me as remarkable young people with a strong work ethic, creative intelligence, and impressive streak of entrepreneurial enthusiasm. I met "Gabriel" in person. An attractive blonde wearing a dark suit, Gabriel sees himself as transgender, but was originally female. He had been working at IBM but found it "boring" and had the good fortune to find employment with a Houston-based translation company known as Drama Queen, which specializes in *yaoi*. Gabriel became interested in Japan in elementary school when he found a book on the country and later on became a fan of anime and manga and watched all the "staples," such as *Neon Genesis Evangelion* or *Cowboy Bebop*. His first major *yaoi* discovery was a series called *Yami no matsue*, which had not been fully translated. Desiring "instant gratification," Gabriel started learning Japanese and halfway through his first year of his Japanese language course began translating.

Anyone who has ever struggled with the Japanese language, especially its complex grammar and system of ideograms, will know what an impressive challenge he had taken on. Rather then giving up, as most students might, Gabriel continued, scanning the Japanese manga, whiting out the original language and putting in the English.

Eventually, things got easier as he developed more fluency and knowledge, and he ended up translating a five-volume series that helped him to land the job at Drama Queen.

When asked what appealed to him about *yaoi*, Gabriel was very frank, replying that he liked "the novelty of not having to read about relationships that don't interest me [i.e., heterosexual ones]." He also mentioned the "aesthetic level," the pleasure of looking at beautiful boys, "analagous to why guys like lesbian porn."

Clearly on some level, reading *yaoi* was a liberating experience and one that was not offered by American culture. Gabriel has also taken a course on Japanese literature and spent two weeks in Japan. While he does not idealize the country (the actual Japanese attitudes toward homosexuality are, in their own way, quite repressive), he did see Japan as much more open to homosexuality, at least on a moral level. His impression of Japan is of a "high energy materialistic society where religion doesn't have much of a place," adding, "you don't see people there getting up in arms about moral issues."

I also spoke by telephone to Tran Nguyen, Gabriel's employer and founder of Drama Queen. In some ways Tran is unique with a fascinating background, but she also seems to me to represent a new kind of fan: someone with the savvy and experience to transform her own particular enthusiasm into a genuine business that employs fifteen people. A child of a Vietnamese mother who grew up in Houston, Tran had always loved fantasy and science fiction, particularly such classics as C. S. Lewis's *The Lion the Witch and the Wardrobe*, which awakened in her a "sense of adventure" and the importance of being able to "carve one's own destiny." After majoring in philosophy at Fordham University, she came home for a while and developed an interest in Buddhism, which led to a desire to serve the community. Deciding that Law School would be the best avenue for such an endeavor, she enrolled at the University of Texas, only to be shocked and disappointed by the "competitive spirit" of her fellow students.

Needing something to do for relaxation, she took up reading manga, which she had enjoyed in college; but this time she wanted something "with an edge." As befits her role of a publisher of *yaoi*, Tran was eloquent and enthusiastic on the pleasures of *yaoi*, describing it as a "genre of wonderful sexy men having sex" and pointing out that "as a voyeur, you don't have to engage in anal sex, but you can fantasize about the cutest guys all you want."

Ultimately, Tran moved from the law to the entrepreneurial, founding Drama Queen. Drama Queen is clearly more than a business enterprise, however. At this point, it is the only all-female manga translation company in the West, employing translators in England and Holland as well as in the United States, and Tran sees it as having a genuine mission. As she says, "We are feminists, pioneers . . . who want to build a *yaoi* global community." There is definitely an element of social criticism when she asks "[if] it's acceptable for guys to fantasize about girl on girl, why is it unacceptable for women [to do the same]?" She is also frank about the pleasure of being able to "direct the action . . . peeping into someone else's sexuality—and they're pretty!"

From Tran's point of view, *yaoi* is not simply an escapist fantasy world but one that brings up profound questions such as, "What is normal? What is healthy?" She also enjoys the fact that this "appreciation of beautiful men" transcends cultures, drawing together women around the world who can find themselves and others in *yaoi* chat rooms or reading and writing *yaoi* fiction.

Like Gabriel, Tran sees Japan as more receptive to this form of sexual aesthetic. As she says, "Nowhere in the Western world can women write about this kind of thing and, even if it's kind of taboo in Japan, there are still a lot of women who love it."

One thing that may differ between Japanese and Western fans is the fans' sexuality. At least one researcher on *yaoi*, Alexis, believes that many *yaoi* fans in the West may occupy a broader sexual continuum than the purely heterosexual. Actually, Alexis questions whether the Japanese *yaoi* enthusiasts are as exclusively heterosexual as they claim to be.

Questions of fans' sexuality aside, it seems clear that the *yaoi* community offers something important and perhaps unique to female anime fandom: the chance to explore a very different form of erotic interaction and even perhaps to take on a very different form of identity, not just in terms of gender, but in terms of culture as well. It also provides the sense of a community within a community. What Sharon Cumberland says of women's erotic fanfiction in general effectively applies to the world of *yaoi* as well: "The sum of this activity is community . . . a place where the cultural offerings of a detached and commercialized world are manipulated and 'shaped to our taste.' Women are using erotica not only to explore their inner lives, but also to expand their outer connections with the world."[23]

A Composite Fan Portrait

I would like to offer a few profiles of what might be called "typical" anime fans if it were possible to describe a "typical" anime fan. Ten years ago, I might have been able to give an example of such a species with some confidence. At this point, however, with the explosion in fandom and the evolution of age and sex, such typecasting would be impossible. Anime fans come in all shapes and sizes, from all walks of life and with a wide range of approaches to both fandom and to life in general. That caveat being stated, I would like at least to introduce the reader to three fans whom I feel are in some ways representative of their gender and generation. I also add additional examples from other interviews I have conducted to give what I hope is as reasonably three dimensional a portrait of fandom as possible.

Marc

Let me start with the oldest and most longtime anime fan, Marc. Marc is an academic, a physicist who teaches at the University of Texas, North Dallas (UTND) and specializes in analyzing data about the Earth's ionosphere. He also has a humanist side. One of his favorite books is Thomas Pynchon's *Gravity's Rainbow*, and he is about to tackle Pynchon's latest book. When not teaching physics, Marc has also helps to develop a course with Pam Goosen, a member of the English Department at UTND, on nature and the environment that has increasingly contains a strong anime and manga component.

I met Marc and his colleague Pam for the first time when they invited me to give a lecture for their course on Miyazaki Hayao, the director and manga artist whose ecomasterpiece is the epic manga and anime, *Nausicaa of the Valley of the Wind*. Since then we have become friends and colleagues, serving together on the board of *Mechadamia*, an academic journal devoted to Japanese popular culture. I have visited Marc and his wife at their house in Dallas and have had the pleasure of viewing their wonderful collection of anime and manga-related paraphernalia. Slender, fit, and bearded, Marc is also highly energetic and articulate. Although knowledgeable about many things, he is clearly thrilled to talk about his hobby to anyone who has an interest.

Marc's story in many ways encapsulates the older fan's entrance into anime fandom (although other fans of my acquaintance, such as Walter Amos, were more into science-fiction cons and costume play). He began in the days of tape swapping, word of mouth, and small clubs and is now part of a world of con going and Internet chat groups. Marc explains that he watched *Speed Racer* as a child and liked it and animation in general. In the mid-1980s he and his wife started watching *Robotech*, another iconic anime series that galvanized many peoples' interests. Curious about anime but unsure how to obtain it, he noticed a store in San Franciso that sold videotapes. Not only did he buy his first "bootleg" videotape there, but he also found an English-language magazine about Japanese animation that introduced him to what would become one of his favorite anime, *Nadia: The Secret of Blue Water*. As he sums up the beginning of his immersion, "About half a year or so later we finally got Internet access at UT Dallas and I discovered the usernet bulletin boards about anime. And it's been downhill ever since."

Marc's explanation as to what appeals to him about anime is also not unfamiliar: "Well, I have to confess that one of the first things that attracted me to anime (and still does) is the cute girls. I confess that the first time I saw the images of Nadia, even though I knew almost nothing about the series, I thought, "this character looks fascinating. I want to know more about her." As discussed in Chapter 4, a staple of anime's appeal to young men has been the many adorable, playful, and sometimes surprisingly complex young female characters who are so ubiquitous in anime. In relation to this, Marc adds another interesting point, which is his enjoyment of *shonen* romance, "a love story where the protagonist and the point of view is the lead male. . . . It's something of a surprise to find out how many anime/manga are sentimental love stories aimed at males and told from the male viewpoint. Being the hopeless romantic I am I rather like them."

In some ways, Marc's (and other males') appreciation of the fact that anime allows him to indulge his "romantic" side is the flip side of the female *yaoi* fans who appreciate the openness to sexuality they find in *yaoi*. For both types of fans, Japanese media has allowed them to explore a side of themselves in a way that they feel would be impossible in American cultural products. Marc's other anime favorites, such as the quietly moving fantasy *Haibane Renmei*, which he describes as a slice-of-life story, or *Aria*, a science-fiction tale that he puts into the category of *iyashi kei* (healing type), neither of which genres are particularly popular in American popular culture.

Marc's fandom is clearly a major part of his life and will continue to be so. His love of the more thoughtful and subtle anime and manga is typical of his age and sophistication. Not surprisingly, he is also a great fan of Miyazaki's work, whose films, as we will see in Chapter 8, combine idealism, warmth, and humor to create a compelling universal appeal. Interest in anime has made Japanese friends for Marc and has brought him and his family to Japan where perhaps their favorite excursion was a trip to the Studio Ghibli Museum outside of Tokyo (see the adorable photo of him and his family with Totoro in Figure 10).

Anime has also affected him professionally. Although his "real" career lies in physics, over the years he has taught, lectured, and written about anime (particularly Miyazaki's work). What was once a single week of readings for an environmental course has now become an entire course on anime and manga. As Marc says about the course, "Some of the students [in the first course in 1999] were leery about using a manga as part of the reading material and there was only one student in the class (of about forty) who knew anything about anime and manga. 'How am I supposed to write a college level paper about a comic book?' one of them asked. A year later when we did the class again, we had about seven or eight fans in the class. And now we're about to start teaching a class of 138 students, all of whom are fans!"

Marc has lived to see what was once an esoteric hobby become a genuine cultural phenomenon, all in the space of his young son Betto's lifetime. On the one hand, he is delighted that so many younger people are becoming interested in anime and manga. Sometimes, however, a slight note of wistfulness creeps into his voice as he talks about the days when anime fandom was a more intimate and personal kind of experience.

"Maya"

The younger fans I profile will never know this kind of time. My next portrait is of adolescent girl fandom. In this case, I have made "Maya" into a composite because some of the revelations that I have heard from young women are more personal and disturbing than those of the other fans profiled here. I meet Maya at an anime convention in the Midwest. When I originally began my work, I had assumed that most cons would be on the East Coast and West Coast. In fact, cons are spread all over the country with one of the largest being Animefest, occurring in Atlanta. Midwest conventions tend to be smaller, but in some ways more fun as they are less overwhelming in terms of not only numbers of participants but of scale. As with most anime fans, people are friendly and happy to help me in my interviews.

Maya comes to my hotel room with her mother. She is seventeen but looks younger, slim, and slight with long brown hair. She is clutching in her hands her portfolio of manga-related drawings. She and her mother both participate in the interview. Divorced, Maya's mother makes a living as a magician and entertainer for parties. She is clearly proud of Maya and very concerned about her happiness.

Maya became interested in anime through friends in middle school. At first she did not want to be thought of as "weird," but she soon got over her hesitation when she became attracted to what she considered to be the beautiful art and draughtsmanship on display in manga and anime. A little too young for the Sailor Moon craze, she loves *Revolutionary Girl Utena*, which is by the creator of *Sailor Moon* but more flamboyant and with more adult themes. Set in an imaginary boarding school where students wander around in flowing gowns and military uniforms engaging in sword fights, intrigue, and romance (sometimes of a homoerotic nature), *Utena* developed quite a following among young women fans. When asked why she liked *Utena*, Maya replied, "I like the fact that Utena stands up for other people. She's willing to lay herself on the line for her friends. And I really like all the costumes!"

Maya likes fantasy. Her favorite novels are the *Harry Potter* series, and she is interested in doing cosplay—probably because of *Utena*—but needs to convince her friends to participate, as "it's scary to do it alone." We talk about what anime means to her, and she is very forthcoming in her answers, saying that "it really saved my life in middle school. It gave me something outside of myself to think about and got me away from all the . . . you know . . . gossip and stuff. I really liked learning how to draw manga and making my favorite characters come alive."

In Maya's case she does not literally mean anime or manga "saved her life," but one other young female interviewee actually did mean it when she used those words. A school rebel who had to be sent to an alternative school for adolescents with challenges, this young woman told me how during eighth grade when her parents were breaking up, she had come close to suicide. Luckily, as she explained, her older brother had gotten into anime through video games, and he introduced her to the hobby. Not only did anime become a passion to share with her brother, but it became her escape outlet—"a whole different world from what was happening at home," as she put it. In particular she loved *Escaflowne*, a dense fantasy anime with many episodes and sympathetic characters.

Anime and manga's function as a safety valve for troubled young people is, of course, not unique to the media. Throughout human history people have sought solace in the arts, after all. But it is clear that the highly colored worlds they offer, especially the series with long involving story lines, can be particularly engaging, perhaps all the more so in that the cartoon element takes them even more securely away from the "real world." Anime fandom may also work as a safety valve, something that Meri Davis, the organizer of the A-Kon Convention in Dallas, alludes to (see Chapter 6).

Maya and I end our discussion with a look through her portfolio. She is clearly talented but surprisingly quite restrained. Much of her work is done in charcoal with a few flashes of color. As we peruse the pictures, she tells me that she is also taking Japanese lessons at her high school, which she says is "pretty fun." When I ask her to say something in Japanese, however, she says that she is "too shy." The interview concludes with her giving me one of her pictures of an elf maiden in a green robe. On the way out she hesitates and looks back, and then performs a perfect, Japanese-style bow.

Saman

Saman is my youngest interviewee. Even at fifteen years old, however, he is articulate and engaging. Normally he wears Led Zeppelin T-shirts, but "in my honor," as he explains, he is wearing a checked shirt that goes well with his dark eyes and curly black hair. The child of Iranian parents, Saman was born and grew up in Manhattan and goes to the United Nations School. Cosmopolitan, knowledgeable, and confident, Saman might be the typical Manhattan teenager, except that he radiates enthusiasm and vitality rather than the jaded sophistication one might expect. When not watching anime or playing video games, Saman is fond of soccer and plays the electric guitar.

Like so many of his peers, Saman became interested in anime through the Pokemon craze, which lasted for him from the time he was seven until he was ten years old. As he says, however, "I don't really consider Pokemon an anime, though. It was during that time when my mother introduced me to *Totoro* and all the Studio Ghibli movies. That's what really started it." Saman's love of Ghibli movies is not surprising. The studio products are remarkably appealing to a wide range of audiences and can be enjoyed on many levels. Like Marc, another Ghibli fan, Saman has made the pilgrimage to the Studio Ghibli Museum.

Saman is proud of his Persian heritage and speaks some Farsi. He and his older sister have also studied Japanese. When he and his family visited me in Tokyo in 2006, he seemed equally at ease among the temples of Kyoto as in the shops of Akihabara (Tokyo's center for anime- and manga-related merchandise). Not as broad a collector as Marc, Saman preferred to look for his favorite anime and manga series and video games such as "Kingdom Hearts" and "Final Fantasy."

Like Jim, a cosplayer interviewed in the next chapter who felt that anime had given him a good preparation for the "real" Japan, Saman found Japan pretty much what he expected. He credited the slice-of-life series *Love Hina* for giving him a "pretty realistic picture." When asked his impressions of Japan, Saman replied, "I found a society torn between tradition and modernity. On the one hand, there was the crazy Tokyo youth who dye their hair strange colors and dress up as anime characters who have futuristic technology. On the other, there is a solemn traditional Japan with temples and tea ceremonies."

In recent years, perhaps Saman's favorite series has been Rumiko Takahashi's long-running medieval fantasy *Inuyasha*. One of the most popular manga and anime series of all time (in both the West and Japan), *Inuyasha* concerns the adventures of a young half-demon, half-human boy in the fourteenth century. Saman especially enjoys the myths and legends that Takahashi weaves into her narratives and also the fact that Takahashi "creates a certain empathy for the 'evil' villains."

As with most of the anime parents I have come across, Saman's parents, a financier and a history professor, are supportive of his interest. In particular, his mother the professor, "likes to make connections about some anime stories to historical events and analyze what specific undertones they might have to today's world." His friends are on the whole supportive as well. "The few who don't [like anime] crack jokes about some of the stereotypes of the genre (peace signs, big eyes, big mouth, etc.), but not vehemently."

As must be obvious, Marc, Maya, and Saman are all very different personalities, and it is probable that they obtain somewhat different satisfactions from their interests in anime and manga. At the risk of overgeneralizing, I would say that they share a certain depth of insight and intellectual inquisitiveness that may not fit the stereotype of the incurious, parochial American. Maya and Saman are clearly creative types, and Marc and Saman share a love of reading. I have encountered repeatedly these two characteristics in my interviews. A truly impressive number of my younger interviewees enjoyed reading very much. Although many of their favorites were fantasy works such as *Harry Potter* and *Lord of the Rings*, one young seventh grader in Austin, Texas casually announced to me that he was reading the eight-volume translation of the medieval Chinese masterpiece *Journey to the West*. (He had developed an interest due to his fondness for the anime and manga *Dragonball Z*, which is loosely based on *Journey*.) Artistic interests ranged over a wide variety from making music videos to designing and sewing costumes.

As I have said, it is impossible to sum up anime fandom in a few stereotypes. What follows in the next chapters will show even more clearly the range of people involved in this subculture. At the very least, however, these portraits should suggest that anime fans as a group are far from the stereotype of the fan as an outsider who sits in his or her room communing only with the fan object. These are people who are passionate and involved and enjoy communicating their enthusiasms, whether it is through teaching courses, sharing art, or sharing words. Contrary to the stereotype of the insular American, they are unafraid of different cultures and actively seek to engage with them.

These proclivities, I would suggest, may be rubbing off into mainstream culture. It is perhaps no accident that the major new television hit of fall 2006 was the series *Heroes*, about an enigmatic group of young people with strange powers. This is hardly a groundbreaking narrative device, but what is genuinely fresh is that the most popular of the heroes is a Japanese otaku who speaks frequently and lengthily in his native language. It is difficult to say whether when Maya and Saman are Marc's age, if anime and manga will still have as much of a following. But it is probably safe to say that in the short term, their impact has been a profound one, both on an individual and a countrywide scale.

Figure 5
Fine Wind, Clear Weather (Gaifū kaisei)
Museum of Fine Arts, Boston
William S. and John T. Spaulding Collection
Photograph © Museum of Fine Arts, Boston

Figure 6
Grainstack (Sunset)
Museum of Fine Arts, Boston
Juliana Cheney Edwards Collection
Photograph © Museum of Fine Arts, Boston

Figure 7
Hanaōgi of the Ōgiya (Ōgiya Hanaōgi,
in rebus form)
Museum of Fine Arts, Boston
William S. and John T. Spaulding Collection
Photograph © Museum of Fine Arts, Boston

Figure 8
La Japonaise (Camille Monet in Japanese Costume),1876
Museum of Fine Arts, Boston
1951 Purchase Fund
Photograph © Museum of Fine Arts, Boston

Anime Nation: Cons, Cosplay, and (Sub)Cultural Capital

[Laney] saw that the quantity of data accumulated here by the band's fans was much greater than everything the band themselves had ever generated.

—*William Gibson*, Idoru

In our previous chapters we explored the rise of Japanese popular culture on a global scale and the development of anime fandom in particular. This chapter approaches anime and manga fandom with a different question: What are the elements that give anime fandom meaning? We have seen how anime's differences from Western cinema and television have appealed to people on an individual basis. This time we ask what institutions or acitivities draw fans together and make them continue in their enthusiasm. What kind of power dynamics are involved in fandom, and what is the relationship between anime fandom and Japan? Although this chapter is concerned with the pleasurable and ludic activities of fans at play, there are still hierarchies and power plays hidden in the heart of the most appealing fantasyscape. Japanese soft power also plays a role here as well.

In terms of what gives the most meaning to fans, a variety of possibilities comes to mind. Is it watching anime with one's friends at a weekly anime club meeting? Is it writing fanfiction inspired by one's favorite manga, or creating music videos based on scenes from one's favorite anime? Is it dressing up as one's favorite anime, video game, or manga character and parading and posing at a convention? Is it traveling to Japan to make a "pilgrimage" to Akihabara, Tokyo's electric city where popular-culture action dolls jostle against shelves crammed with the latest DVDs and manga serials? Or is it another kind of pilgrimage—traveling to the Ghibli Museum on the outskirts of Tokyo to commune with the creations of Japan's greatest animator Hayao Miyazaki? Perhaps it is simply the pleasure of encountering another fan of one's favorite shojo manga series in the manga section at Borders or Barnes and Noble, or the opportunity to find a rare action figure that will complete a collection.

Any and all of the previous examples are value-laden activities to fans, part of the "mattering maps"[1] that Lawrence Grossberg suggests we construct to give our lives meaning and framework. Although the importance of each example differs from fan to fan (some fans will never go to Japan, others would never dream of engaging in cosplay), there are two crucial aspects that the aforementioned pursuits possess in common. The first is the highly active, indeed interactive nature of these pursuits. As we saw in previous chapters, anime fandom from its beginning has always been a strongly grassroots activity, deeply dependent on fan input. Even today, despite the rise of commercial companies that license, translate, and sell anime and manga, anime and manga fandom is far from the passive consumer culture that early commentators on popular and mass subculture feared might develop. Club activities, internet postings, convention going, and creative production all indicate a high degree of fan involvement on a psychological, social, and artistic level.

The second common element that gives meaning to fan activity is what I have called subcultural capital—the knowledge and expertise that one gains about the object of one's enthusiasm that allows one not only to feel comfortable with other like-minded fans, but also to gain status among fellow enthusiasts. Often it is this subcultural capital that truly animates and sustains fandom. The quotation at the beginning of the chapter from William Gibson on the fans of his fictional pop group is relevant here. His narrative suggests that it is "the quantity of data *accumulated by the band's fans*" (emphasis added) that ultimately inspires the fans, allowing them to create their own pleasurable and meaningful world from their own varieties of knowledge and experience vis-à-vis the band.

In the case of anime and manga fans, subcultural capital can include a wide variety of "data"—experiences such as con-going, club attendance, or trips to Japan, expertise that allows one to win anime trivia contests online or at a convention, and the creative abilities that enables fans to make a remarkably accurate costume from a couple of pictures of their favorite anime character or to produce fanfiction so compelling as to develop its own set of fans. Knowledgeable and creative fans win the respect and admiration of their peers, inspiring still more interest and enthusiasm.

Subcultural capital is also related to the experiences of pleasure and mastery discussed in the introduction, in themselves highly active forms of involvement. The cosplayers who spend days creating their costumes, the con organizers and staff members who work long hours to achieve a successful convention, and the enthusiasts who learn Japanese so they can better appreciate their favorite manga or anime series are experiencing the joyous sense of "flow" that comes from gaining experience and expertise in a particular area. Often this feeling of flow is missing in their mundane lives, making it all the more attractive when they experience it in fan-related activities. Of course this kind of subcultural capital is hardly exclusive to anime fandom or even to fandom in general, but for the purposes of this book, what makes it particularly intriguing is that in regards to anime and manga fandom, knowledge of and experience with Japanese culture is an important component of it.

The rest of this chapter concentrates particularly on cons and con-related activities. I emphasize the con because it is the nexus point where flow, play, cultural capital, and Japan all meet to create a genuinely distinctive experience, a fantasyscape that is concrete but also emotional, in which fans immerse themselves to an intense degree. My discussion of the cons is based on my own participation in twelve conventions over the last decade. Because I had written a book on anime, I was invited to speak at a variety of cons as a guest panelist and to meet other guests. When not speaking, however, I was free to soak up the con atmosphere as a participant observer.

This dual status gave me excellent access to the intriguing textures and threads that make up the con experience and allowed me to get to know many con organizers, some of whom who I have interviewed for this chapter. Unfortunately, I have never participated in cosplay, so my discussions of this aspect of con attendance are largely based on interviews and viewing. Again, however, my dual role as both a genuine enthusiast and a scholar helped, I think, to obtain honest and thoughtful responses from my interviewees.

Con Culture

[The con atmosphere] is one of unconditional acceptance and support—people feel like they have found a real family, a family that doesn't reject them for being "geeky" or into weird things . . . spending a weekend with people living, sleeping, eating in the same space with them (and going through sleep deprivation) and partying and watching lots of anime creates that "instant family" feeling.

—*Shannon (graduate student and fan)*

The surest indication of madness is that you want to run a convention.

—*Walter Amos (fan and con organizer)*

For a few brief days the world of the con is a world in itself. Part spectacle, part learning experience, part social gathering, fan conventions can be all consuming to the participants, many of whom who stay for the entire two or three days, putting up at the convention hotel and wandering from activity to activity in an increasingly sleep-deprived haze. In a sense, anime cons (and other fan conventions) partake in two traditions. One of them is the world's fairs and expositions that, as we have seen, played such an important role in introducing Japanese culture to the West. As at an exposition, there are exhibits to be viewed, special food to be eaten, and the sheer pleasure of wandering through a special festive space, taking in a wide range of sights and circumstances.

Anime conventions in particular may be seen as carrying on the international aspects of the world's fair tradition, since they always feature performances and exhibits specifically related to Japan. At Anime Iowa, for example, I enjoyed hearing about and subsequently participating in a tea ceremony demonstration, whose basic framework has probably changed hardly at all since the first performances of tea ceremonies for non-Japanese audiences over one hundred years ago. Exhibitions of Japanese martial arts and swordsmanship also pop up frequently from convention to convention. And at every convention I attended, certain favorite and hard-to-obtain Japanese foods, such as the candy snack Pocky, were extremely popular with convention audiences.

Anime conventions, at some level at least, may therefore be seen as acting as cultural ambassadors, offering participants a taste (and sometimes much more) of Japanese culture. Obviously, these "tastes" are somewhat idiosyncratic—as most anime and manga fans acknowledge, their favorite media do not necessarily represent the "real" Japan. Yet through the highly colored prism of anime and manga available at the con, certain genuine elements of Japanese culture do shine through, ranging from the importance of college entrance exams seen in the ubiquitous anime and manga devoted to high-school stories, to the differing attitudes toward sexuality and technology that appear throughout the media, offering a far more richly textured picture of Japan than those of the traditional world's fair exhibitions would have been able to do. Furthermore, non-anime- and non-manga-related elements such as the tea ceremony or language lessons allow participants to gain a deeper and more multifaceted appreciation of Japanese culture.

The other tradition that cons partake in is that of the professional conference/convention. Anyone who has been to an AMA (American Medical Association), MLA (Modern Language Association), or any large organized gathering around which working people frame their lives will recognize certain common aspects with con culture. The most important of these is the social element. Many fans tell me that over the years, as their involvement in fandom has ebbed and flowed, they have come to appreciate conventions above all for the chance to see old friends. This is all the more true as anime fandom has evolved, and increasing numbers of fans could look back at years of involvement with anime. For young fans, it is a place to make new friends with similar interests and, ideally, meet up again at other cons. While cons vary greatly in size and geographic reach, most of them occur once a year in the same spot. As with any professional gathering, participants will plan months ahead to meet up with friends from different locations whom that they see only rarely otherwise.

Other aspects of con culture mimic professional gatherings as well. At every con, panels on a wide variety of topics are important staples. These range from discussions of a particular "hot" anime—such as a question-and-answer session on the enigmatic science-fiction blockbuster *Neon Genesis Evangelion*—to the care and maintenance of Japanese swords, to panels on the relative merits of dubbing versus subbing. Guest panelists include academics and other writers on anime and manga culture; people in the industry whose decisions on what anime and manga to distribute help to shape the markets; and guest artists, including American actors who dub the English voices in anime, manga writers, anime voice actors, and musicians from Japan. There are also the celebrities, writers of particularly famous manga or directors of particularly popular anime.

There is also the opportunity to learn of the latest developments in the "field"—seeing the latest anime, hearing discussions of trends in anime and manga, and being able to buy the most recent anime and manga paraphernalia. Recently, with the rise of Bitorrent and other Internet engines designed to help download global entertainment and the rise of eBay and other online market-places, this aspect of con culture has become somewhat less important. But there are still fans who proudly boast of finding something special in the dealer rooms that they were unable to obtain online. Furthermore, the so-called Artist's Alleys where fans exhibit and sell their own work are places to find unique objects unattainable in the electronic world. Finally, as with professional conventions, there is the opportunity to exchange ideas, share enthusiasms, and even to network. While conventions are on the whole not concerned with career advancement, there are increasing numbers of panels and workshops on every-thing from how to draw manga to how to get into voice acting for English-lan-guage dubs.

That being said, it is important to remember that the main point of a fan convention is pleasure, what I have referred to as ludic activities. The vast majority of the fans are there to have fun. The atmosphere at a typical anime convention, therefore, is fundamentally different from a professional conference where participants are always to some degree or another aware that their partic-ipation is related to improving their career possibilities. While fans do enjoy sharing (or showing off) their knowledge, they do this secure in the conscious-ness that if they make a mistake, this will not have an impact on their roles in what one conference organizer calls the "Muggle World" (a reference to the "real world" as opposed to the fantasy one in the *Harry Potter* series).

At its most fundamental level, therefore, the fan convention is a fantasy world. For a few days, fans throw off the burdens, responsibilities, and roles of ordinary life to take part in a liminal world that, while it intersects with reality at certain moments, in other ways subsumes reality to create a densely textured utopian environment in which, as Victor Turner says about liminality in gen-eral, participants can "don the masks of liminal masquerade."[2] In some cases this is quite literal, as we will see in our discussion of cosplay, but in other cases "masquerade" simply means the chance to assume a somewhat different iden-tity than one's normal workaday self. For some fans this "identity" may be more positive or even truer than the one they show in the workplace or at home, as it is one based on feelings of love and pleasure, feelings that may be misunder-stood or even insulted in the outside world. One con organizer describes the pleasures of the con as including the fact that "[fans] can discuss favorite char-acters, shows, game, novels and so on ad nauseam with people who can actually follow the discussion."

For other fans the pleasures are deeper than simply sharing enthusiasms. As Shannon says, "The con atmosphere is one of unconditional acceptance and support." Meri Davis, the chair of A-Kon, one of the longest running and most successful cons in the South, emphasizes the supportive nature of the con even more explicitly. In answer to my question, "What are the pleasures of organizing a con?" she replied, "Seeing the happy faces of all the fans once they get there. Knowing that for some people (and we've actually had letters to this effect), it's saved their lives. Giving 'square peg' people a place to fit in, a place to find friendships (and sometimes more—mates, jobs etc.). . . . Seeing all the people who normally wouldn't even know each other, find each other and work together, is a big joy." She continues in this vein on being asked, "What has been your favorite con moment?" She replied with an answer that mixed the personal with the interactive: "Being proposed to on a stage in front of 1,100 people was a pretty shining moment for me, that's for sure! Hearing from people that literally [if] A-Kon [had] not been someplace for them to go, they were very close to suicide (and seeing in their eyes that they meant it)."

This aspect of con or anime culture—that it can literally "save" participants from the indifference or trauma of the Muggle World, suggests that involvement in fandom can be genuinely therapeutic. In the fantasyscape of anime and manga and the fandom surrounding them, the fan can leave behind the complexity and disappointments of the real world. Although this involvement is inherently transitory, it seems that many fans emerge refreshed and more able to deal with real life thanks to this temporary immersion in alternativity.

While I have used Victor Turner's term "liminality," which he defines as a "betwixt and between space,"[3] to describe the world of the con and of anime fandom in general, it is important to realize that there are some differences between these worlds and the more traditional form of liminality that Turner is talking about. Turner bases his theory on "threshold" experiences (the term liminality literally means "threshold"), periods when young men or women are taken out of society to undergo certain ritualized communal experiences, often organized by tribal or community elders. They are then returned to society and expected to take their place in it once again but on a more experienced and mature level than before.

The fan convention experience is a little different from this, although there are certain rituals involved—for example, the opening and closing ceremonies, the masquerade ball, or simply the viewing of new products. (These are, I would submit, alternatives to reality—ways of escaping for a while the feelings of alienation and isolation that so often seem to be part of contemporary life, rather than groundwork for a return to reality.) Like all forms of enthusiasm, play, or fantasy, fandom can be seen as a form of resistance to a disappointing outer world. As media scholar Henry Jenkins puts it, "Fans, like all of us, inhabit a world where traditional forms of community life are disintegrating, the majority of marriages end in divorce, most social relations are temporary and superficial, and material values often dominate over emotional and social needs."[4]

Anime fans are clearly highly aware of their own ambivalent relation to the real world. While in recent years, anime viewing has become more mainstream and with far less of a stigma attached to it, many fans still acknowledge that they enjoy the pleasurable escape that anime represents. This escape can be from an identity that they find disappointing. Even in my more recent surveys, some fans still referred to themselves with such terms as "your typical geek" or "instant otaku." Sometimes they use self-deprecating humor as, perhaps, a way to reveal themselves in as nonvulnerable a fashion as possible. I remember at one convention seeing a rather shy looking young girl sporting a T-shirt that said, "Talk Nerdy to Me." Anime conventions therefore offer even more of an escape than anime itself, since they allow fans to be relaxed and open about who they are in relation to a significant enthusiasm in their life.

Of course the desire to escape from the mundane and the miserable is hardly restricted to contemporary society. We may remember the nineteenth-century protagonist of the Goncourt novel *Mannette Salomon* who finds in the rich hues and exotic designs of Japanese woodblock prints a marvelous escape from the gray Paris winter, or the Japonisants exclaiming with delight as each produced some exciting new Japanese curio for the dinner party's delectation. But what anime and other forms of fandom offer is a more organized and all-encompassing form of fantasyscape, or what might even be called "alternativity."

The Creation of the Con Fantasyscape

When I became a man, I put away childish things, including the fear of childishness and the desire to be very grown up.

—*C. S. Lewis*[5]

It is worthwhile spending some time on the mechanics behind the construction of the cons in order to understand the complexity of the enterprise. Although cons vary enormously in size and location, some elements are common throughout. First and foremost is the amount of work involved. Anime cons rely largely on volunteers—another indication of their grassroots foundation—and recruiting and organizing volunteers can be almost a full time job in itself. As Dan, an organizer at Anime Iowa, puts it, "One of the toughest parts is recruiting staff, as anime enthusiasm and attendance grows you need more staff. You have to be able to weed out the people who want to be on staff so they can have free reign of the guests or the dealer rooms and [those] who genuinely want to see the convention be successful and grow." Once recruited, he continues, organizers and staff must "work on budgets, negotiate hotel contracts, work with local law enforcement, schedule monthly meetings and organize feedback forms."

Anime conventions present special logistical and cultural problems in that many of the most sought after guests are coming from Japan, which raises not only financial issues but questions of inviting, negotiating, and entertaining in Japanese. Inevitably misunderstandings can occur, sometimes caused by the unwillingness of hosts or guests to be frank about their expectations. At one con, for example, I recall an autograph signing and a question-and-answer session that seemed to go on forever, or at least, well after the dinner hour. While a couple of American voice actors continued a lively discussion on the mechanics of voice subbing, a Japanese guest cartoonist grew increasingly hungry and tired. Unable or perhaps unwilling to voice his discontent out loud, he ended up drawing a detailed picture of dinner, including an extremely realistic looking cheesecake, and hanging it on the edge of the table in front of him. Unfortunately for him, the picture was visible to the audience rather than the panel organizers, and he was kept waiting quite a while longer.

Perhaps the most vital component of con organizing is managing financing. Cons are expensive and complicated affairs, and the potential for financial slip ups always exists. Off the record, I heard the occasional horror story about con funds being mismanaged. Even without these problems, things can go wrong if money is poured into an unprofitable venture or guests renege at the last minute or, almost as bad, suddenly decide to bring along their entourage as I was told one Tokyo pop group did.

As Meri of A-kon graphically explains, "The normal 'fan on the street' does-n't even think that somebody paid more than their year's salary to hang a light-ing rig so 'Group X' can have lights, and another year's salary to rent drums, guitars, special music equipment. . . . In some cases every single thing has a price involved including every plug in the wall, every table, chair, extension cord (if you don't have your own), tablecloth, telephone hookup so a vendor can use their credit card machine, every piece of curtain used to block off areas, trash pickup after the show, the myriad of 'little charges' that add up is enormous."

Besides financial headaches, there are also structural and political problems. Heather, who has worked on both sci-fi and anime cons, acknowledges that while the fans are enjoying themselves, certain elements of hierarchy and inter-nal politics can crop up behind the scenes. Heather calls these problems "reality interference," an intriguing choice of words that underline the fantasy nature of the con. Sometimes the reality interference can simply be difficult personalities. As she puts is succinctly, "It's amazing the number of people who never mas-tered the preschool notion of playing nicely with others." Since some fans con-sider themselves outside the mainstream, this tendency may be even more pronounced than in most organizations. As Heather says of anime fans versus science-fiction enthusiasts, "Most anime fans are younger than sci-fi fantasy fans with the energy, rebelliousness, idealism and (sometimes, not always) irre-sponsibility that go with the age." As with all organizations, power bases are important, with groups forming cliques that break down and reconstruct them-selves in alternative ways. Personal feuds can also happen, sometimes damaging enough that one person may simply leave the fan community.

Most fans are happily unaware of these behind-the-scenes elements. Certainly, every convention I have attended has been extremely well run— equipment was always ready, helping hands were always available, and everyone seemed to know where to go. This enabled the con-goers to relax and truly enjoy themselves in an atmosphere that contained elements that recalled the spon-taneity of the festival and the carnival within a smoothly operating framework.

The organizers seem to recognize this and are proud of their accomplish-ments in creating this special atmosphere. Despite their complaints, the con organizers that I interviewed seemed generally happy with their experiences. For them, the successful running of a convention appeared to evoke the sense of mastery and accomplishment that we have referred to as "flow." For a volunteer such as Heather, con organizing gave her the opportunity to learn useful skills and to network, not to mention "a certain, almost giddy satisfaction to be found in watching people come and enjoy what you've worked so hard to make happen." Meri also was pleased that she had created at A-kon a "place to make new friends and to hopefully find a place where [the fans] are welcome because of their diversity, not in spite of it."

Japanese Culture at the Con

Not only are the fans diverse, but the cons themselves offer an impressively diverse set of activities. In a sense, since they are all related to anime and manga, these activities are inherently related to an appreciation of Japanese culture. But the degree of awareness of Japan differs from event to event. Not surprisingly, many con activities concern anime or manga knowledge. Anime- and manga-related games abound, such as the "25,000 Yen Pyramid" where "contestants are paired with an anime celebrity in order to make it up the pyramid for top prizes." Often these are trivia games in which fans compete at the most basic level of fan subcultural capital—knowing what new character is introduced in episode 49 of the popular anime and manga series *Inuyasha*, for example, or what is is the favorite costume of a particular anime princess. One organizer marveled at the fans' "amazing ability to quote character stats, plotlines, and astoundingly in-depth trivia about their favorite series."

Other activities relate to the culture behind anime and manga. For example, one very interesting panel I attended at Otakon was called "A Parent's Guide to Anime." It was described in the convention guide in the following manner: "What do you do when your child starts showing an interest in anime? After all, isn't anime just cartoons depicting sex and violence? Learn the different genres and what to look for on a DVD case to make an informed decision on what your child watches. Anime doesn't have to be a scary word any more!" The description of the panel is intriguing, evoking the debate on anime's supposed propensity for sex and violence that was its stereotype through much of the 1980s. But the last sentence is deliberately reassuring, and the actual panel discussion, in which both parents and panelists (who were usually parents themselves) participated to about the same degree, was thoughtful and nonalarmist. Inevitably Japan's different cultural norms came up, especially the different cultural attitudes toward nudity and sexuality in general, but these were discussed calmly and rationally. Indeed the relative lack of moral panic or disparaging judgements was impressive.

I was able to contribute an anecdote from my own experience in which the *Dallas Morning News* asked my opinion of an incident in which a father had bought a manga from Toys "Я" Us for his son. The book included scenes of a little girl lifting her dress to pacify a nasty old man. What had surprised me at the time was the relative *lack* of fuss that ensued around the incident. Toys "Я" Us simply agreed to discontinue stocking the comic book, and the father went home apparently satisfied. A similar nonjudgmental attitude was on display at the Otakon panel with the parents merely asking for information on the DVD rating systems in order to make certain that they were buying their children age-appropriate material.

On the whole, the parents I talked with on that panel, and at other times and places, were generally positive about anime and manga's effects on their family. Several mentioned how pleased they were that anime and manga gave their children a creative outlet. This was particularly true for the parents of children who drew their own manga, and many of them proudly showed me examples of their children's work. Some parents seemed slightly confused about this rather different world that their children were so passionate about; but most were tolerant, and some were genuinely enthusiastic. Others were humorously resigned. I recall one father at a convention indulging in his own unique form of cosplay: he had a rueful expression on his face and a sign around his neck that read, "Anime Parent—Please Help."

The relative acceptance of anime culture on the part of fathers and mothers suggests a welcome trend toward a more sophisticated attitude toward other cultures on the part of contemporary Americans. Although it may go too far to say that anime and manga contribute to intercultural tolerance on a wide scale, it is still probably safe to suggest that children's broad-based enthusiasm for products from another culture has opened many parents' eyes to the possibilities of genuine intercultural interaction.

Each con provides many opportunities to get to know Japanese culture on a deeper level. Besides Japanese language classes and panels such as "Learn About the Japanese Origins of Manga," the cons also include programs for children, such as making and hanging koi (Japanese carp), making headbands using Japanese characters, paper making, origami, and making paper lanterns. Besides hands-on activities, some convention booklets include articles about Japanese culture.

One particularly thoughtful article I found was called "What's so Japanese about Anime?" Written by two nonacademics who had clearly given much thought to the topic, the article first eliminated some stereotypes, pointing out that the "big eyes" so common to anime and manga are actually derived from prewar American cartoons. It then went on to discuss the distinctive Japanese traditions of storytelling, pointing out the narrative and visual links between anime and manga and Japanese theater. Besides talking about the "exaggerated faces" of anime characters and the possible connections with Kabuki actors' makeup and *Noh* masks, the article confronted the issue of sexuality and violence, pointing out that rape and suicide were common fare in Kabuki and puppet theater.

Anyone reading this article would come away with a genuine sense of the continuity of cultural tradition in Japan. Knowledge of and information about Japan thus becomes another form of subcultural capital for fans, a little different from knowing which episode of a famous anime introduces a particular character, but for some fans at least, perhaps equally satisfying. Other articles included hints to learning Japanese, such as concentrating on action narratives in manga, and offered a list of dictionaries and textbooks that the writers found to be particularly useful.

Accumulating subcultural capital can also be a gustatory experience. Anime Iowa offered a highly enjoyable and genuinely intellectually stimulating discussion of Japanese snack food, guided by a young American named Evan who had just come back from a year in Japan. Wearing a *happi* coat (a short Japanese jacket), he ushered in the audience with fluent expressions of welcome, "*irrashaimase*" (greetings of welcome that a store keeper would give), and "*furii fu-do*" (free food). Evan went well beyond the famous foods such as ramen or even Pocky, however, to give examples of traditional snacks, such as senbei crackers wrapped in nori seaweed. These kinds of snacks allowed him to discourse on Japan's isolated island geography and how it gave rise to unique snacks such as nori or dried squid. He also mentioned the importance of Chinese influence, explaining that chestnuts and sweetened tofu were originally from China. While a volunteer went through the room offering different items to the eager audience, Evan casually read out loud in Japanese the various ingredients on the boxes and just as casually translated them into English. At the end of the discussion he brought up the topic of food in anime and manga, such as the ubiquitous okonimiyaki (Japanese pizza), which many youthful characters are seen eating in series such as *Ranma 1/2*. Evan went beyond the anime references to mention that *okonimiyaki* became popular after World War II when people struggled to survive by opening simple *okonimiyaki* stands among the ruins of the war-torn cities. In a similar vein he displayed the nostalgic Sakura candy drops that were an important symbol in the affecting Studio Ghibli film *Grave of the Fireflies* (*Hotaru no haka*), about two children trying to survive during wartime. Again, the drops were related to both anime and to events in Japanese history.

The whole panel was a kind of cross-cultural tour de force. Evan's ease with the Japanese language; his knowledge of history, geography, and local customs; and even his donning of the happi coat made him an excellent example of a genuine transcultural figure. The fans saw an American who was clearly at ease with his own nationality (he made jokes about his home stay in Japan where "people's idea of a wild fun time is a bottle of sake and a mahjong game"), but also comfortable in and enthusiastic about the Japanese environment.

The discussion on food crossed another "culture" as well: that of the real versus the virtual. The discussion linked the fantasy worlds of anime and manga to the solid realities of food, survival, and hard work, all through the homey medium of tasty snacks. Ultimately, the discussion allowed the fans to enter into a different world where another nation's memories of a lost war became connected, not only to the entertainment that the fans enjoy, but to the foods that they consume as well.

Cosplay: Of Mimicry and Fans

The single most obvious intersection point between the real world of modern American life and the fantasy world of anime and manga is undoubtedly cosplay. The word itself is a classic example of hybridity. Coined in Japan from the

English words "costume" and "play" (and said in Japanese as *cosupurei*), the term was enthusiastically taken up by Western anime fans who appreciated its evocative minimalism. In Japan, cosplay is performed not only at conventions, but also in various urban areas as well, most notably, the Tokyo neighborhoods of Harajuku and Akihabara. Recently, it has been particularly popular with young women, and it is not necessarily related to anime characters. The streets of Akihabara and Harajuku are full of young women dressed as maids in black and white or in the frothy but slightly sexy fashion known as *Rorigosu* (Lolita plus goth). Although a few Americans may venture into these guises, on the whole, cosplay in the United States still largely involves favorite anime and manga characters.

For first-time visitors to a con, the cosplayers are undoubtedly the most memorable visual experience that they will take home with them. Even more than at a science-fiction or fantasy convention, the variety is stunning. Anime is like Hollywood cinema in that it covers all modes and genres that live-action film does, and fantasy, horror, and science-fiction modes are particularly popular and perhaps even more so among non-Japanese fandom. As I have argued elsewhere, animation is an especially appropriate medium for fantastic representations because it is inherently nonreferential. As opposed to live action film, there is no "need" to represent something "accurately." In animation the imagination is unbound, producing worlds in which the unexpected, the unusual, and the surreal mix together in creative free flight.

This imaginative fluidity leads to marvelous creations on both manga pages and anime screens. Some characters may remind us of Hokusai's manga or even of creatures from traditional Japanese art in general. Throughout their history, Japanese theater, dance, and traditional arts such as scrolls, woodblock prints, and screens have produced memorable visions of other worldly characters, including ghosts, ogres, goblins, and demons that are both remarkably grotesque and uncannily beautiful (see end of chapter, Figure 9). Many artists, most famously Takahashi Rumiko, the creator of *Ranma 1/2*, *Inuyasha*, *Urusei Yatsura*, and other immensely popular manga, have drawn from the wellsprings of Japanese folklore and mythology to manufacture an array of unforgettable characters. These range from adorably evil characters—such as the conflicted young demon who is the main protagonist of Takahashi's medieval fantasy *Inuyasha* and whose long silver hair, red robes, and pointed ears make him strangely appealing to audiences everywhere—to the enchantingly strange—such as the sexy female *oni* (ogre), Lum, of *Urusei Yatsura*, whose green hair and horns make an attractive contrast to her very human figure clad in a tiger-skin bikini (traditionally *oni* wear tiger skins and have horns, but they are far from attractive).

Not surprisingly, both Lum and Inuyasha are extremely popular cosplay subjects, appearing ubiquitously at virtually every convention I have been to. But they are hardly alone. Walking through an anime con, one feels as if one is in a cross between a dream, a fairy tale, and a carnival. The variety is endless: a long-legged girl in a futuristic uniform strides along carrying an evil-looking gun, accompanied by a brawny-looking man with strangely metallic eyes—both are playing the cyborg protagonists from the cyberpunk film *Ghost in the Shell*. Girls swish by in Japanese kimono and Chinese gowns, sporting little furry cat ears in their hair. Young men in black robes carrying huge paper-mache crosses on their shoulders pace ominously. What seems like dozens of little boys decked out as the rebellious young ninja Naruto run by in excited throngs. Even smaller children dressed as Pokemon or perhaps a Ghibli character scurry around, trailed by parents in dazzlingly colored masks and swirling capes.

Quite often a "crossplayer" will appear—someone trying on a character of a different gender. Inuyasha with his ambiguous red outfit and long silver hair is one frequent example. Occasionally one may see a female samurai warrior, modeled on the androgynous hero of the popular historical series *Rurouni Kenshin*. Other characters are genderless. After Miyazaki's fantasy, *Spirited Away*, won the academy award for best animated picture in 2002, many people dressed as No Face, the silent and enigmatic ghost who brings chaos to the bathhouse of the spirits. Perhaps most impressive are the group efforts, where sometimes as many as a dozen fans will dress up together as characters in their favorite series, spending the whole day in costume and in character. Cosplay provides an almost literal example of "flow" as the players parade up and down through the convention halls, stopping for other fans to take their photos in dynamic poses, and then moving back to join the river of players and fans.[6]

For the pleasure is not simply in creating the costumes or even posing for photos, although that is of course an important element in convention cosplay. There is also the excitement of getting into the persona of the character one admires. This can happen either as part of the parade through the convention halls, when strangers will greet you familiarly by the name of your character, or more formally in the skits that fans perform for the masquerade competition.

The pleasures of cosplay are on the whole obvious—stemming from the basic human impulse that is especially strong in childhood of "dressing up." Halloween is the ultimate American fantasy of costume play, and it is hardly surprising that for much of the postwar period, popular costumes were particularly "American," or at least Western ones. Although the more universal guises of witches and devils were perennial favorites, many other children chose to be cowboys, astronauts, sports figures, nurses, and brides.[7] But cosplay is more than simply dressing up. Of course, the transformation and the motivations behind the desire to transform are perhaps more complex than simply "dressing up" suggests. To transform is to change one's identity, to become Other, if only for a little while.

I had the chance to interview a number of cosplayers about their hobby and found their answers intriguing and enlightening. There are three in particular that I would like to profile: James, Lorelei, and Gretchen. Each had a distinctively different personality and profession. Lorelei was an exotic dancer who had just come out of the air force. James worked at the University of Texas in computers. And Gretchen was a homemaker who had previously worked at IBM. Each had their own reasons for being involved in cosplay, but they also had certain interesting elements in common. Perhaps the most salient and, in a way, least surprising element that they had in common was their love of sewing. They were all creative people (Gretchen had gone to graduate school in art history, Lorelei writes fiction, James had built his own haunted house for Halloween at the age of five) who enjoyed the chance to go beyond the drawing or writing to actually produce a material object. James mentioned his pleasure when he saved up enough money for his first sewing machine, while Gretchen went into elaborate descriptions of her adding gold detail and special buttons ("which took me forever to find") to transform a white bodysuit into the uniform of Dio Eraclea from the series and video game *Last Exile*. Lorelei not only made costumes for cons, but also created Lolita outfits to wear on the streets.

All of them were happy to explain about how much time they spent on creating their outfits—usually at least one week per costume, but sometimes much more—and how much money they spent as well. All three of them explicitly stated that the process of creating their (and sometimes other peoples') costumes was at least as much fun as the actual moment of displaying themselves at the convention. Each of them also spontaneously commented on the "newer" fans who sometimes bought their costumes and seemed only to care about "showing off" and "winning prizes" rather than the creative process itself.

Another, perhaps more surprising, commonality was that they all loved to read. In a previous chapter, I discussed how a (to me, unexpectedly) large number of anime fans enjoyed reading, and these three cosplayers obviously shared this enjoyment. James was reading *Atlas Shrugged*, by Ayn Rand, while Lorelei enjoyed Victorian literature. Since they were all relatively young (between the ages of twenty-one and thirty-four), this fondness for reading in an increasingly visual world struck me as particularly interesting. It is possible to speculate that the enthusiasm that they bring to the costume-making process, which is clearly a form of immersion into an intense state of consciousness, is similar to the feeling of "getting lost" in a good book.

Another intriguing similarity was that all three they were all fascinated with and knowledgeable about Japan. Lorelei has taken a year of Japanese, decorates her bedroom in Hello Kitty, and was well informed on the more arcane points of Japanese cosplay, pointing out that Japanese cosplayers "don't do wigs." Gretchen and her husband (who speaks Japanese) go to Japan every other year, straying far away from typical anime-style activities to take in the beauty of Kamakura temples or the excitement of a plum-blossom festival. Gretchen was eloquent about the pleasures of seeing the ancient cities of Nara and Kyoto, "which [she] had studied about," presumably in her art history courses. James had taken so many Japanese courses that he was able to double major in Japanese and computer sciences.

In contrast to Gretchen, James's one trip to Japan was spent almost entirely in Tokyo, where he and his brother (also a fan) made the pilgrimage to Comiketto, the enormous bi-annual convention (attended by three hundred thousand to four hundred thousand people) for manga lovers. Intriguingly, James, for whom this was his first trip out of the country, spontaneously volunteered that Japan was "exactly the way [he] thought it would be" from the manga and anime he knew. Aside from Comiketto and the pleasures of Akihabara, he and his brother enjoyed walking the Tokyo streets, riding on public transportation, drinking the innumerable variety of drinks from the omnipresent vending machines, and generally enjoying the differences between Tokyo and Texas. Clearly, James's immersion in anime and Japanese culture (on the way over on the plane, he even watched the in flight movies in Japanese) allowed James to feel at ease in this new country.

In their fascination with Japan, these three cosplayers may remind us of the Japonisants and other enthusiasts profiled in previous chapters but with the important difference that, though positive about the culture, they were hardly starry eyed. Japan and its products were important aspects of their lives, but there were clearly many more. Their varied motivations for cosplay reflected this complexity. While all three loved the process of making costumes, their actual attitudes toward the cosplay performance itself varied to some degree. James seemed to prefer working and performing in relative anonymity, enjoying seeing the fruits of his labor without necessarily loving the exposure. His proudest achievement so far in cosplay-related activities was when he brought together a group of about thirteen people to cosplay the series *Haibane Renmei*. This must have been a truly impressive accomplishment. A magical, understated drama created by Abe Yoshitoshi, *Haibane Renmei* is a tale of young people who awaken after a curious dream in a strange walled town to find themselves wearing haloes and wings, although they are not able to fly.[8] After awakening, they take on names that are related to the dreams they had before their arrival. They are controlled in mysterious ways by a group known at the *Haibane Renmei* (Gray Feathers Federation), who wear robes and masks. Occasionally they have encounters with a strange people known as the Touga, who come from outside the walls and wear strange and colorful clothing.

James told me that had he made costumes for each of the main characters plus *Touga* and *Haibane Renmei* outfits, using clothes and materials found in thrift shops because "[in the series] the Haibane aren't allowed to wear anything new." Not only did he create all the costumes, but in a final highly creative touch, he also asked each participant to make up an appropriate dream and then created individual books for each of them, with their Haibane name based on their dream. The books themselves held coupons that were the equivalent of Haibane currency, and James proudly told me that a few of the dealers at the con even took the currency instead of real money!

In a sense we can see James as a director or designer as much as he is a performer, although he also mentioned to me how much he and his brother had enjoyed their first con when he made "generic bad guy" costumes for the two of them. James described how he created "ominous shoulders" made out of sheet metal (taped over so they would not be dangerous) and mentioned the pleasure he felt when "people would stand back from [them]" as they made their way through the con. At a slender five feet and seven inches, James clearly enjoyed how a simple change of costume could change the reactions of people around him.

The pleasure of taking on another identity was obviously of importance to the two women cosplayers. Self described as "a little shy," Gretchen related how "the first time was a little scary but it was also kind of fun because you're not you—you're a different person, so to speak." And of course this is not just any "different person," but a specific anime manga or video game identity chosen by the cosplayer. When asked why she thought cosplaying was so appealing, Gretchen replied that it revolved around "love for the character. You want to show that to other people." She also mentioned the "empowering nature" of some of the costumes, as when she crossplayed for the first time, not simply because she had changed genders but that the costume itself, "a big cloak and white makeup," made her "noticed" wherever she went.

Gretchen also mentioned the allure and the challenge of staying "in character." On the one hand was the pleasurable feeling of communing with a character one admired; on the other hand she discovered that strangers would "presume a relationship with her" since "they already have a relationship with the characters, even though they don't know [her]." She recalled being startled at one con when someone came up to her and said, "Oh, you're Dios. My sister hates you. May I take your picture?" Other moments were extremely positive, however, as when "a little kid cried out, 'Dios' and gave [Gretchen] the biggest hug saying, 'I love you Dios.'"

Lorelei's first cosplay had been as Sailor Moon, her favorite anime character, at Halloween in fifth grade. Like Gretchen, she too enjoyed the option of trying on a different identity. Self-described as a tomboy, Lorelei related how much she enjoyed "getting to feel like a girl." Her photos from various cosplays show her wearing beautiful sexy clothes. As she says, "I like the fact that I can be someone else for the weekend and wear something outrageous."

The question still remains however, why do so many young Americans like to dress up as characters from a culture that is not their own? On the one hand, the answers are simple: as we have seen, anime and manga provide a plethora of colorful possible identities, more even than Western science fiction and fantasy, which are on the whole less visual. Obviously, fans of *Star Trek*, *Star Wars*, and *The Lord of the Rings* have a good deal of material to choose from, but they are still bound by the limits of live action cinema. In contrast, animation and comics are the perfect sites for imaginative visual fantasy. Furthermore, as we have seen, anime and manga characters come out of an exceptionally creative visual tradition that goes back to at least the tenth-century scrolls of hungry ghosts and playful beasts of Japanese court culture. Finally, it must be acknowledged that Japanese art education seems to be better than that in America. Although anime and manga art may seem simple, they are usually based on a long discipline of drawing and painting from early childhood that endows many artists with an authority and effectiveness of technique that is often unmatched in the West. Cosplayers often comment on the imaginative detail and style they find in anime and manga characters' costumes, aspects that are both a challenge and an inspiration to their creativity.

But perhaps there are deeper motives than simply the pleasures of trans-forming oneself into an imaginative artistic creation. Does the fact that these creations are from another culture lend a particular interest to the proceedings? Or is it that fantasy worlds of anime and manga are so dense and rich in them-selves that they are particularly effective in providing imaginative material? And how important is the Japanese origin of anime to all this?

In an important essay entitled "Of Mimicry and Man," Homi K. Bhabha dis-cusses the fraught relationship between the dominant Western colonizer and the colonial subject in terms of what he calls mimicry—the attempt by the non-white colonized to imitate the white authority figure. In the dynamic sketched by Bhabha, the attempt at imitation is always doomed and simply underlines the powerlessness of the colonial. One reason for this inevitable failure is the "gaze of otherness" by which the dominant Westerner only sees the non-white as a collection of degraded fragments. As Bhaba writes, "Black skin splits under the racist gaze, displaced into signs of bestiality, genitalia, grotesquerie."[9] In other words, the non-Westerner imitating the Westerner is always fated to be "not quite / not white."[10] Imitation, when springing from an unequal power relationship, can never really be effective.

But what of Westerners who imitate the non-Western Other? Previous chap-ters discussed Lafcadio Hearn who took a Japanese name and dressed in Japanese costume in an ultimately failed attempt to become one with Japan, and Vincent Van Gogh who identified so strongly with his idealized vision of Japanese artists that he too dressed up at one point as a Japanese priest. On a more general level, we may recall that at the height of imperialism, nineteenth-century Westerners performed their own form of mimicry, dressing up in kimono, posing with fans, and acting in "Oriental" tableaux vivants ("living pic-tures" in which individuals dressed up to represent exotic scenes). In the case of those middle-class Westerners, mimicry was clearly a form of pleasure when dressing up as the exotic Other, with perhaps a hint of the pleasure of feeling like a member of the dominant culture. To these nineteenth-century "cosplayers," Japan was all surface, a country that produced beautiful and unusual garments and objects that one could array oneself in without dealing with the culture at any depth.

Hearn's and Van Gogh's stories are far more complex. In both cases we have a clear desire to identify with the Other, but not a specific individual Other. Rather, it is the world that Japan represented to them that was so alluring. For Hearn, dressing in Japanese costume and acquiring a Japanese name allowed him for a time to indulge in the fantasy that he too could partake in the fairy land, which he initially took to be the Japanese nation, and, of course, escape his own inadequacies and discontents. To Van Gogh, his imitation of a Japanese priest was partly ideological, a way to rebel against the ominous advance of industry and science that seemed to be destroying all the best elements of nature and art. It was also, of course, a way for him to escape his own fears and psy-choses in a vision of a peaceful, civilized society of supportive artists.

The Westerners who engaged in dressing up were in their own ways perhaps seeing the Japanese in fragments, while Hearn and Van Gogh at least had a more holistic (if extremely idealized) view. In all cases Japan was their source of inspiration. This is less certain in the case of the anime fans. Although there is no question that the cosplayers I interviewed were extremely aware of and quite knowledgeable about Japan, in their actual cosplay, they did not seem to be trying to be "Japanese" so much as to be "Anime." This was not always the case, since to some extent it depended on which character one was playing. One Rurouni Kenshin cosplayer I talked to had an excellent knowledge of the tumultuous historical period that his character was based on, while a couple of Inuyasha players I met discoursed quite learnedly on certain aspects of Japanese folklore. The popular Naruto ninja character inspired an impressive amount of knowledge about ninja and martial arts from some of the young boys I talked with. For others, however, the Japanese origins of their cosplay were far less important than the particular story they were trying to recreate. While these stories were created by Japanese artists and usually occur in Japanese settings, it was the characters' interactions, adventures, and personalities that were of the most concern and with which the cosplayers identified.

I will discuss the question of fan identification in the next chapter, but for now it is worth contemplating the meaning of cosplay in a larger context. In many ways, the appeal of cosplay is a testament to the quality of anime and manga narratives, many of which, such as *Haibane Renmei*, are just as involving and exciting as any work of literary fiction. For some players a close identification with the character is very important. For example, Lorelei's favorite persona to cosplay is Shiranui, a female character in the anime and video game *Fatal Fury*. Shiranui is a female superhero who uses fans as weapons, which she keeps in her décolletage. Lorelei showed me photos of herself as Shiranui in several outfits looking both beautiful and happy. But it was clearly not simply Shiranui's outfits that attracted Lorelei, but her persona as well. Lorelei discussed her character's complicated emotional history and added that she had even written a story about her.

The appeal of cosplay is also a testament to the increasing importance of fantasy in the world around us. Unlike some subcultures of dressing up, such as vampires and goths, who have been described as "rejecting pink femininity,"[11] anime cosplaying seems to have little to do with rebellion, at least against an older generation or against any clear societal norms. Indeed, as we have seen, anime cons in particular seem increasingly to draw whole family groups. At twenty-one years old, Lorelei was the youngest cosplayer I interviewed, but she indicated that her parents did not have a particular problem with her fan enthusiasms. Lorelei was also the only fan I interviewed who cosplayed outside of con walls. The day I interviewed her she was dressed in a" Lolita" outfit, a white ruffled skirt with strawberries on it and shiny low-heeled shoes (it should be noted that the Japanese "Lolita" style is frilly rather than sexy). Here again, though, the motivation seemed to be to have fun being feminine rather than rebel. In fact, she mentioned to me that elderly women come up and compliment her, telling her, "It's so nice to see a skirt the right length on someone your age."

The very plethora of identities one can assume in anime or manga costumes may militate against making any particular social or ideological statement. Whereas the women who dress in black clothing as goths or vampires see themselves as a particular form of outsider (since the gothic and the vampire styles have very specific cultural connotations), anime offers an entire realm of identity possibilities. One can display the body in a thong and fans; one can augment the body with wings, such as the *Haibane Renmei* cosplayers; or one can disguise the body in the black robes and white mask of No Face. The fact that these personae are all drawn from a non-Western society with fewer specific cultural connotations (at least to the Western fan) may also add to the sense of liberation and empowerment that seems to be part of the cosplay experience.

In the period of imperialism, the colonized non-Westerners had to deal with the bleak realities of power in a world in which whites dominated. In our millennium culture, at least among those lucky enough to live in affluent industrialized societies, power may no longer have such a clearly racial or national base. Once again, we return to the question of soft power and its relative importance. The anime and manga fans swirling through the cons as Pikachu or Inuyasha, monsters or cyborgs, goddesses or samurai, are attesting to the power of contemporary Japanese culture to create incredibly dense and involving fantasy worlds.

It is also of paramount significance that these characters are cartoons—caricatures and fantasy creations existing in a separate dimension from the real and even from the human. Anime costume play gives the fans the opportunity to transcend the limitations of human bodies, to explore new frontiers where the genetic inheritance with which one was born can be cast away. At its best, anime cosplay suggests a world that is almost the opposite of the one delineated in Bhaba's analysis—a world in which one is finally liberated from the power dynamics of race, sex, gender, and nationality and even of species. That this is a fantasy world cannot be stressed enough, but it is probably no accident that at a time when national and ethnic concerns seem to be growing more and more oppressive, a countermovement toward emancipation from these very concerns should appear as well.

Figure 9
One Hundred Ghost Stories in a Haunted House (Shinpan uki-e bakemono yashiki hyaku monogatari no zu)
Museum of Fine Arts, Boston
Gift of C. Adrian Rübel
Photograph © Museum of Fine Arts, Boston

Differing Destinations: Cultural Identification, Orientalism, and "Soft Power"in Twenty-First-Century Anime Fandom

What matters is not the destination defined by the text. Equally important is the identity one assumes for the trip, what one takes along and what one brings back.

—Elihu Katz, "Viewers Work"

Suddenly there was a new media that looked essentially similar but exotic with its own stylistic conventions, and moreover even the stereotypes were different from the ones [Americans] had grown up with. These Japanese cartoons could push the limits of animated storytelling, including philosophy, moral dilemmas, deep characterization, tragedy that isn't easily resolved and other more mature themes.

—Female USC student

Japan is an interesting culture and fascinating as it is so alien to my own. I think so many young Americans are captivated by it as our own culture, that of the melting pot, is so amorphous. As Americans it's really hard to pin down what really makes us whole and Americans. What rituals mark our lives? What ceremonies? . . . How may of us can say, "We're American and we do things THIS way?" when our popular culture encourages us to forget our roots and ourselves. . . . Is it a shock that our youth cling to the rituals and patterns of another culture for this reason?

—Twenty-three-year-old female Republican, computer science major, Texas

[Anime] is something that is new and familiar at the same time.

—Twenty-three-year-old Muslim male, psychology major, Texas

The previous chapters explored the rise of Japanese popular culture and anime and manga fandom on a general level. In this and the following chapter, we go into the hearts and minds of fans on an individual level—specifically, what do the fans find in anime that they do not find in the dominant popular culture of Hollywood and other products of American society? To understand this, it is useful to put fandom in the context of the postwar rise of American popular culture on a global scale.

In 1989 in an address given at the founding conference of the Commission of the European Communities, French president, Francois Mitterrand, warned that he did not want to see a time of "American pictures combined with Japanese technology overwhelming Europe."[1] The "American pictures" to which Mitterrand referred were, of course, the American television programs that seemed to be becoming increasingly dominant throughout the world at that period. In response to this trend, the European intelligentsia and bureaucracy reacted in horror, as if threatened by a cultural tidal wave. Their sense of threat, as Schroder and Skovamand explain, no doubt stemmed from "the fear of being Americanized, dating back to the beginning of the twentieth century, [a fear that] has persistently seen American materialism and vulgarity washing over an authentic, aesthetically sophisticated cultural heritage."[2]

Ironically, Mitterrand's speech occurred the same year as the Japanese animated film *Akira* was released in Europe and the United States. A brilliant dystopian science-fiction work, *Akira* was a groundbreaking film, not only because of its imaginative cyberpunk plotting and cutting edge animation, but also because it was the first anime to be taken seriously as an artistic work in both Japan and in the West. Even now almost two decades later, it is still considered a "must see" among fans of both animation and science fiction. With its artistic depth and dark contemporary sensibility, *Akira* helped to usher in a new era, in which Japanese animation and its related medium manga would gain viewers and readers worldwide to become a thriving alternative to American popular culture. Initially (and to some extent even now) anime's reputation was controversial. Due to certain high-profile works such as the violent sci-fi porn film *Urotsukidoji* (*Legend of the Overfiend*), the general audience associated anime with bizarre sex and violence, unaware that anime, like Hollywood cinema, spans an enormous array of genres.

Unpleasant though it was to imagine American cultural dominance over Europe, it was clearly simply impossible for Mitterrand (and others) in 1989 to imagine a world in which *Japanese* pictures would ever play a significant role in shaping global popular culture. Perhaps it was fortunate that Mitterrand and other cultural commentators could not look into the future. In fact, as we have seen in the last decade, Japanese visual and popular culture have become virtually synonymous with the term "soft power." Prevented by its constitution from possessing an army and yet wielding increasing economic dynamism globally through its pop cultural products (which ranged from video games, anime, and manga to the cuddly "billion dollar feline" Hello Kitty), Japan has come to seem the quintessential example of soft power. Moreover, soft power itself increasingly seems to be the quintessential late-millennium mode, a force created through a unique nexus of circumstances (the rise of technology in particular, developments in recording and communication; the development of an increasingly affluent and sophisticated consumer culture; and the opening of markets worldwide) that are now seen as integral parts of the larger phenomenon of globalization.

In previous chapters we have seen the rise of earlier forms of Japanese soft power that had swept over Europe and America. Of course there are major differences between the two waves of influence, some obvious, others less so. On the obvious side, we can cite the rise of technologies that were simply unheard of in the nineteenth century, most importantly the development of recording technology such as videos and DVDs and the rise of the Internet. These developments have allowed Japanese cultural products to attain global reach with a speed and efficiency that would have been unheard of even a few decades ago. More subtly, the kind of culture that spawned these developments is in certain respects qualitatively different from the more stratified world of the nineteenth century, where the distinction between "high" and "low" culture was still important. In a sense, the artistic era that the importation of Japanese woodblock prints (themselves mass cultural objects in Japan) would help bring in with a new openness of subject matter, material, and audiences would eventually lead to the contemporary world in which anime and manga (if not Hello Kitty) can be seen as genuine art form.

These changes took place over a century ago, however, at the same time as myriad other changes were transforming industrial society and one's place therein. One potentially significant difference between the two eras pertains to the construction of identity in an increasingly transnational world. In their book, *The Postnational Self*, Hedetoft and Hjort discuss how what they call "globality" has affected "the cultural landscapes of belonging" through the fact that "[globality] changes the contexts (politically culturally and geographically), . . . situates national identity and belonging differently and superimposes itself on 'nationality' as a novel frame of reference values and consciousness [leading to a challenging of the] organicism and essentialism of national identities."[3] In other words, our current era is in some ways a paradoxical one in which nationalist, ethnic, and religious identities are reaffirmed at the same time as transcultural flows incite more openness to and enthusiasm for different cultures.

In contrast, the European and American nations that embraced Japanism in the nineteenth century were, in general, culturally secure entities whose citizens, although capable of genuinely admiring and in some cases—especially among artists such as Van Gogh or writers such as Lafcadio Hearn—identifying with aspects of Japanese culture, were also still situated in a world of firm national boundaries that included a strong sense of the East as being the West's Other. Of course there were stereotypes and tensions among Western nations too: we may remember the anti-Americanism of the nineteenth-century Goncourt brothers or Puccini's satire on American power in *Madama Butterfly*. But it is certainly clear, as we have repeatedly seen, that the West often identified itself in relation to the East and often to Japan.

Aspects of Orientalism certainly continue to operate in the increasingly transnational world of the twenty-first century, but some of the cultural flows that are involved in globalization have helped to problematize a simple us-versus-them opposition. Of these flows, the dynamic of soft power must surely be one of the most important. Products like Hello Kitty are not necessarily perceived as related to Japan (after all, Kitty's backstory is that she is from London), but fans of anime and manga are very aware of these products' culturally specific origins. Indeed, as will be seen, the "Japanese" aspects of anime and manga can be part of the allure for many fans who enjoy the opportunity to get to know another culture. While there are still viewers like the twenty-two-year-old woman quoted at the beginning of this paper, who see Japan as fundamentally alien (but "fascinating"), the vast majority of the anime fans I have surveyed over the last ten years maintain a more complex relationship to Japan and its culture. This attitude encompasses the notion that the culture, or at least its products, is both familiar and different, as the previously quoted male psychology student noted. Or as a Spanish member of the Miyazaki Mailing List (MML) put it, "Different cultures but the final human feelings are the same."

This chapter attempts to situate soft power in relation to Orientalism by examining the reasons behind the popularity of Japanese animation and the ways in which this popularity has influenced the construction of cultural identity among the Western fans of anime. As the only major non-Western form (indeed, as one of the very few non-American forms) of global popular culture, anime and manga occupy a fascinating place in the exploration of contemporary notions of culture, nationality, identity, and even the construction of the self on a deeper level. For not only does anime challenge Western television and film in terms of its national origin but also, as a nonreferential medium (as opposed to live-action film and television), it offers different destinations and paths to the construction of selfhood.

To understand the significance of anime's impact as a global cultural influence, it is useful to once again go back in time to the 1980s to the situation rued by Mitterrand when he spoke disparagingly of "American pictures." In the 1980s the most popular television program in the world was *Dallas*. An American prime-time soap opera set at the mythical Southfork Ranch and peopled by larger-than-life Texan characters, the series was at one time seen in *ninety* countries. There was one major country, however, where *Dallas* did not succeed, and that was Japan. Although other American television shows and, of course, American films had garnered great popularity in Japan over the years, *Dallas* was cancelled after six months. In 1988 the Israeli researchers Liebes and Katz set out to find the reasons behind *Dallas*'s worldwide popularity and also why it had failed in Japan. Their resulting book, *The Export of Meaning: Cross Cultural Readings*, includes reports from a variety of focus groups throughout the world, including a chapter on Japan. From the point of view of studies of cultural identity, the responses are illuminating.

While other respondents, ranging from Germans to Israelis, found aspects of *Dallas* not only familiar, but sometimes nostalgic and often became emotionally engaged with the saga, the Japanese viewers saw the series as a "remote world" with a story that was "not possible."[4] Based on their findings in countries other than Japan, the researchers felt that at many levels viewers were able to identify with certain universal aspects of the program and suggested that this was due to what they called the "primordial" quality of the narrative(presumably meaning something akin to mythic), comparing it, among other texts, to *Genesis* and less specifically to "an old fashioned family saga."[5] The Japanese audience, on the other hand, criticized not only the narrative but also the characterization, suggesting that the characters needed "shading" and that "even the bad guys should have some weak points."[6] Overall, Liebes and Katz summed up the negative reactions as follows: "The characters are too stereotypically good or bad, strong or weak, without being tempered by the contradictory elements that characterized human beings in Japanese eyes."[7]

Ironically, the reasons behind *Dallas*'s failure in Japan suggest some of the reasons behind anime's success in America (and in the rest of the world as well). The Japanese reactions to *Dallas* are a provocative mirror image of what fans worldwide believe they find in anime—stories that, far from being "remote," have universal appeal and characters that are complex and three-dimensional. As such, anime, despite its Japanese origin and frequent culturally specific references, easily crosses boundaries to become a cultural force that may have particular appeal in an increasingly complex transnational world. Whereas two decades ago, global audiences were satisfied with situations and characters that were larger than life and usually drawn in black and white terms, in recent years a substantial minority of viewers has begun to want to see a popular art that acknowledges and even embraces the complexities of life. That this art was manifested in the form of what many older viewers (especially in America) would disparage as "cartoons" is one of the central ironies involved in the spread of anime's popularity. I will also examine this phenomenon specifically in regards to the fans of Studio Ghibli works, but in this chapter I would like to devote my analysis to anime fans in general, concentrating particularly on fans in the United States.

To appreciate some of the particularly intriguing aspects of anime fandom, it is useful to see them in relation to fan culture in general. Anime fandom, both in America and worldwide, represents one facet of the explosive growth of fan culture in general over the last few decades. Both fandom and the study of fandom have become a growth industry, leading, among other things, to documentaries, newspaper articles, and scholarly books attempting to explain, or at least to explore, the phenomenon.

In academia, fan culture is studied as a liminal realm of shared emotional intensity, a kind of "imaginary community" grouped around what are called fan objects. In the fan community, the true fan is deeply engaged with the object of his or her fandom, which can range from soccer teams to Elvis Presley; and this engagement can evolve into, or even be based on, a feeling of identification with the object. As Sandvoss notes, this can be a narcissistic form of identification in which the fan sees the object of his or her engagement as "an extension of the fan's very self."[8] Examples include when a fan believes that Bruce Springsteen must have been "reading his mind"[9] when Springsteen wrote a particular song, or, more subversively, when a fan object expresses an attribute that the fan had heretofore not recognized as part of his or her conscious personality. For example, Liebes and Katz mention a woman who suddenly admits that she appreciates the domineering side of J. R. (*Dallas*'s main villain), because it expressed a side of herself that she usually preferred not to acknowledge. The "identificatory fantasy," as Cornell Sandvoss and others call it, can therefore be a complicated and ambiguous process, revealing aspects of oneself that one may not even previously be aware of.

Furthermore, identification in fan culture can be more than simply identification with a desired Other. It can also include identifying with the world of fandom itself or, more specifically, the sense of community that the world of fandom promises. As Roger Aden chronicles in *Popular Stories and Promised Lands: Fan Cultures and Symbolic Pilgrimages*, the late-twentieth-century growth of fan culture may well be related to the increasing deterritorialization and decentralization of modern life, where one may work and live far from relatives and other social and emotional roots and one's "sense of belonging is diminished."[10] In Aden's view, fandom offers an attractive alternative to our normal "habitus," the term coined by French sociologist Pierre Bourdieu, meaning the combination of economic, cultural, and social factors that make up a specific modern human life.

Aden sees fandom's appeal in its spiritual and emotional aspects, as do many fans themselves who are highly conscious that being a fan offers a kind of comfort and community that is increasingly difficult to find in the modern world. But fandom also has strong commercial aspects as well. The commercial realm offers stores, online merchandise, and also the conventions, which may or may not be run by fans but are usually a money-making enterprise. At the cons, fans may buy enormous amounts of merchandise that, in the case of Japanese popular culture fans, can range from DVDs, soundtracks, and figurines to kimono and junk food such as the popular candy Pocky. In this regard, then, we see that anime and manga fandom (as opposed to anime and manga texts) is a form of economic soft power in itself. As a twenty-year-old art student in Minnesota commented on "younger fans," "There is a newer and younger group that enjoys the action aspect of anime, the *Yu-Gi-Oh* and *DBZ* (*Dragon Ball Z*) fans, and enjoys the million bits of merchandise as much as they enjoy the show."

Having established the validity of anime and anime fandom as a form of soft power, it is now time to return to the issues raised by what this power means. More specifically, what does it mean when growing numbers of people from all over the globe become involved on a deep emotional level with a form of non-Western popular culture? Are the same factors that attracted the rest of the world to American mass-culture items like *Dallas* (such as what Liebes and Katz refer to as "primordiality") at work here as well? Or are there new elements involved? In the twenty-first century where, on the one hand, the world seems to be growing more localized and "tribal" in response to the seemingly overwhelming tide of globalization, can the worldwide development of anime fandom be seen as a kind of countermovement, one that uses the energies behind globalization to create a new form of communal identity that has both local and global elements? Or is it still possible to suggest that the current anime boom is simply a new form of Orientalism, in which anime is one more product in a long line of "exotic" Japanese objects put on display for Western consumption?

This last question is complicated importantly by the animated medium itself. Unlike earlier Japanese art products that, Westerners believed, accurately represented Japan (although this Japan was itself a Western fantasy), and also unlike other popular fan objects such as *Dallas*, the cartoons and caricatures that make up anime and manga are fundamentally nonreferential. They may be related to or even based on the real world and real humans, but they also may be a completely fantastic creation, without any specific relationship to the world around us. In the world of animation, natural laws such as gravity do not necessarily apply. Animation artists can do whatever they like with their characters and with the realm they create. This very flexibility may be why many older viewers accustomed to realism still feel uncomfortable watching cartoons. Animated images, like dreams, may be linked to the subconscious or to childhood in which fluidity and transformation are the norm before the rigidities of the "real" take over. Perhaps a forty-nine-year-old male librarian from the MML says it best:

> It may be that I am trying to re-create myself as an adult by first going back to an imaginary childhood where I was not a victim or an object or a consumer, in other words rebuilding my foundation. . . . [T]here is something refreshing about the freedom of anime: the freedom to show a beautiful young woman like Chiyoko from *Millenium Actress* turning into a beautiful old woman (live action cannot do this without burying actors under mountains of face-concealing plastic). Live-action cannot realistically show a pair of children starving to death as in the film *Grave of the Fireflies*.

Furthermore, I might add that apocalyptic themes, which are very popular in anime, are also well served in animation, which in works such as *Akira*, *Neon Genesis Evangelion*, or *Metropolis*, can create images of destruction that can be both terrifying and sublimely beautiful.

This freedom from natural constraints also gives rise to an aspect of anime and manga often noticed by non-Japanese viewers, which is the fact that many, if not most characters, do not look "Japanese." Many commentators feel that the characters look Western, but in fact, a more accurate analysis to my mind is that they look "anime" or "manga." Although each artist has his or her own unique approach, there are certain elements—most notably the huge eyes, certain movements and gestures, and sometimes strangely colored hair or distorted body types—that are virtually standard aspects of "anime style." But anime style is not necessarily off-putting. As commentators such as Scott McCloud have pointed out, a caricature inevitably has a more pared-down quality than a photograph and is therefore more universally accessible.[11] Indeed, many older anime fans recalling their first involvement with anime will fondly remember racing home in the afternoon to watch their favorite shows *Speed Racer* or *Star Blazers*, not knowing that the programs they loved were Japanese but simply aware that they seemed "different."

The issue of "difference" returns us to the issues of Orientalism and identification. In comparison to *Dallas*, which was a product of an American culture that by the 1980s was well known if not well liked, anime came from a country that during this period of time, was known more for its technology than its cultural products. Furthermore, *Dallas* was a live-action program with readily identifiable human characters and settings. In contrast, anime is "different" (by being both Japanese and an animated medium), so we might wonder whether viewers can still participate in the identificatory fantasies that are so much a part of fandom. Alternatively, it is possible to argue that it is anime's "difference" that appeals to viewers. In fact, as I have suggested in my previous research, probably the fundamental reason behind anime's appeal is that it *combines* both difference and universality. This difference actually comprises a variety of elements. The young viewers who rushed to see *Star Blazers* were attracted not only by the interesting visuals, but also by the unusually complex and gripping story lines.

In fact, what may be most surprising to those unfamiliar with anime is that for most fans, the important difference is not between cultures per se, but between the quality of the cultural products. Most anime fans when questioned about why they liked anime answered in terms of what they perceived as Japanese superiority (in terms of narrative, range of subject matter, character development, and quality of animation) versus American inferiority (stale plots, one-dimensional characters, limited intellectual interest, unimaginative or unaesthetic visuals). Furthermore, for most young viewers at least, the fact that the medium was an animated one seemed to be a relatively unimportant factor. Thus, the difference in quality was seen not simply in relation to American cartoons, but to American television and cinema in general.

The Appeal of Anime

Although anime still to some extent carries the stereotype of being sexually explicit and violent, as previously mentioned, these were far from the major factors behind its appeal, according to my respondents. In fact (to my mind) a surprisingly strong minority (30—35 percent) of the respondents mentioned how they were turned off by the explicit sexuality and lack of morality in *American* culture. Even for those who specifically cited "adult content" as part of the appeal, this was often in the context of the overall anime "experience." As one male respondent mentioned, "The Japanese just do more with animation than most American animators do. They can use nudity, language, violence, graphic images, or whatever they really want and society doesn't have an uproar like Americans tend to, if it's something outside of what they're used to."

Others noticed and approved of the relative frequency of homoerotic interactions in anime, beginning with the child-oriented fantasy *Sailor Moon*, whose homoerotic aspects were carefully edited out when the series was broadcast on American television. As one twenty-one-year-old female put it, "I also think that some of the anime characters are more liberal and appeal to the gay community for the fact that there are more gay characters and situations represented." Regarding violence, a male student at USC wrote eloquently that "Many kids/teenagers who do not watch anime for its philosophical complexity simply love its creative and visually stunning violence and action," favorably comparing the quality of the anime film *Ninja Scroll* with two American live action films, *The Matrix* and *Terminator 2*.

The aesthetic allure of anime and its innovative style in relation to American works were also frequently mentioned. As one respondent said of two recent films that used cutting-edge animation techniques, "*Steamboy* and *Metropolis* are works of art." Another simply pointed out that "Anime does something with its art that U.S. cartoonists have never tried: make the characters attractive in appearance." To fans used to *Sponge Bob Squarepants* or *The Simpsons*, the idea of attractive human-looking animated characters seems to have come as a pleasant revelation.

For the majority of my respondents, however, anime's major appeal was in its thematic complexity and three-dimensional characterization. Compared to American entertainment, fans found anime both more thought provoking and more emotionally involving. In fact, some of the critiques offered by fans might usefully be read by Hollywood moguls. For example, one fan summed up Hollywood's failings in the following vivid manner: "U.S. action movies become straight journeys of explosion and violence. Romantic comedies become tired long repetitions of the same simple problems with no variations. Strange art films are getting more and more strange. . . . [In contrast] anime characters are able to grow and change, as opposed to a constant static role (the reluctant hero, bumbling romantic) or a sudden reversal (reformed bad guy, jealous rival becomes supporter)." Another critically aware fan, a Muslim premed student, explained, "The reason I watch anime . . . and also read literature is to remove myself from the real world and experience the world in someone else's imagination. I want to have the satisfaction that is gained from reading a beautiful poem or passage from a book. Television shows and movies can evoke such feeling but few in the U.S. now do. I get the feeling that some television networks have simply given up on such a concept and we see that in the proliferation of 'reality' television."

Anime fans clearly had the sense that with their favorite anime they were watching a work that was both carefully crafted and thought provoking. As one respondent said of the science-fiction series *Cowboy Bebop*, "It is not simply a good anime, it is arguably the best television program ever made. . . . It adheres to a level of cinematic complexity almost incapable of being achieved on American television." An aspiring artist wrote that "[anime] delves into topics that may not be taken up by Western society nearly as quickly because of marketability." Another respondent, a male in his late twenties, appreciated the challenging nature of certain anime, suggesting rather crankily that " believe it or not, not everyone is stupid and there are people who want to see material that truly affects and tests them."

Other respondents discussed their reactions on a more personal basis. A male high school student described anime's special quality in the following memorable passage: "[I love] the way it can psychologically take you apart and make you think about things a lot more deeply. I broke down and just started crying after I saw the first two episodes of *Eva* [shorthand for the apocalyptic television series *Neon Genesis Evangelion*]. It totally broke me . . . it made me realize that animation is not just for children any more. . . . It's just so exciting." A Hmong college student from the Midwest wrote simply, "No American cartoons ever show me that life is not all pretty."

From the aforementioned responses it seems clear that anime is capable of moving viewers on many levels—aesthetic, visceral, emotional, and intellectual. This is true of all good art of course, but it is not something that in the West most viewers expect from cartoons. In fact, it may well be that the medium itself may actually be an aid in rendering anime more accessible. This is possible partly because, as mentioned previously, "anime style" transcends obvious racial and cultural signification that might create barriers to viewer identification. As one fan put it, "The more the art is abstracted, the more we can relate to it as realism."

Furthermore, the nonreferential nature of the medium can lead the artist/director toward genres that are particularly universal, most notably science fiction and fantasy, which, perhaps not coincidentally, are the two most popular anime genres among anime fans in America. Although, thanks to recent developments in computer graphics and special effects, Hollywood directors are increasingly turning to live-action science-fiction and fantasy films, these are still extremely expensive and time-consuming projects compared to their animated equivalents. Also, as many viewers have noted, Hollywood directors seem, if anything, to be increasingly making the stories simply vehicles for special effects rather than vice versa.

Fantasy and science fiction are genres that are usually categorized in contrast to realism, just as animation and comics are seen as caricatures rather than realistic. Despite this widespread impression, one of the most strikingly consistent responses to the question of why anime is popular in America has been that, as one young female fan put it, "Anime is more realistic [than Hollywood products]." When fans say this, they are of course not referring to big eyes or blue hair, dragons, or spaceships, but to the story lines and characters. As one respondent explains, "Characters are given an immense amount of depth and background and their motivations are explored. They feel more real than most characters in American media (both animated and not)." The favorite anime programs and films of fans were often discussed in terms of characters and their development. Thus as one fan said of the gothic fantasy *Vampire Hunter D*, "What I really liked, beyond the enticing characters, however, was that few of them were entirely good or evil. It made them more real."

The ability of characters to develop in more complex ways is related to the narrative structure of most anime television series. Instead of being composed entirely of discrete episodes, as has been the case in much of American television, anime series often have a long narrative arc over many episodes, allowing for much more complex interplay among the characters and for the development of interesting backstories on the part of the major characters. Or as a fan of the immensely popular and long-running space fiction saga *Gundam Wing* put it, "The characters grow in their personalities, moving from beings selfish or mission oriented to more compassionate or having a purpose beyond missions."

Identificatory Fantasies

Not only did fans find anime characters fascinating and emotionally affecting, to the majority of the fans interviewed they were also potentially objects of identification. Sometimes characters served as "extensions" of the fan's self and other times as idealized role models for the development of a fan's identity. In either case, the relative ease with which so many fans identified with cartoon characters in fantasy settings again might come as a surprise to an older generation of Western viewers. For example, even if there were adults in the 1940s who identified with Mickey Mouse's predicament as the sorcerer's apprentice in Walt Disney's *Fantasia*, they would be most unlikely to ever consciously acknowledge this. This unease would be due not only to Mickey's cartoon nature, but to the fantastic situation of the cartoon itself (Mickey borrows the sorcerer's hat and transforms his broom into a servant with predictably tumultuous results).

By the late twentieth and early twenty-first centuries, however, the borderline between the fantastic and the real has become much more permeable. If anything, as scholars from Bruno Bettelheim on have shown, mythic and fantastic characters, precisely because of their archetypal quality, are particularly good vessels for identification.[12] The modes and tropes of fantasy (and its related genre, science fiction) such as metamorphosis, supernatural powers, or apocalypse, can work as metaphors for the human condition in ways that are often far more effective than apparently "realistic" situations where too many specific details can actually distance the reader or viewer.

This is of course not true for every viewer. One thirty-eight-year-old viewer, when asked, "Do you identify with any anime characters?" answered logically (if unimaginatively), "No, because how many anime have a middle-aged family man as its hero?" On the other hand, a sixty-year-old IRS agent commented, "I'm not a teenage girl, but I really identify with the situations, the day to day life." Indeed, most (but by no means all) of the respondents who answered "yes," were in their teens and twenties, although even among that group there was skepticism. One young woman protested, "Yaargh! Why do you ask those questions? They're cartoons!" Although she did go on to say, "Maybe I see myself in a few of these characters." However, among those who responded negatively, there were many who, when asked to discuss their favorite anime films and series, talked about them in ways that suggested a notably high degree of engagement with the cartoons. As the "middle-aged family man" suggested, "If you mean do I empathize with the characters, yes, with the better written or at least more comprehensively categorized ones."

The fans' abilities to identify/empathize with anime characters probably also have a great deal to do with the enormous range of anime. Since roughly 50 percent of all cinema and television output in Japan is animated, the anime industry functions quite similarly to Hollywood in the breadth of the products it creates. Thus anime genres include everything from sports to romance to mystery, although, as mentioned, the stories are often narrated through the mega-genres of fantasy or science fiction. A high school student in Utah summed up the protean nature of anime in the following description: "Anime is funny. It's tragic. It's scary. It's provocative. It's romantic. It's sci-fi. It's action. It does everything that movies do in a slightly different way."

Some fans are self-conscious about identification with both anime characters and as anime fans. One respondent explained, "[I feel that people see me] as a member of a group mentality that has rejected its own culture in favor of foreign 'cartoons.'" However, as this correspondent goes on to say, "Because so many people from other cultures are able to identify with anime, it suggests to me that some of the structural differences are superficial."

Given the variety of characters and genres, it is not surprising that there were varied forms of identification among the fans. Sometimes these "identifications" are lighthearted. As one forty-four year old responded, "Yes, because my friends give me nicknames from anime when they see similarities between my personality and that exhibited by a character (e.g., David from *Prince of Tennis*, because of my bad puns)." A young male student mentions how he identifies with the lead character from the romantic comedy *Love Hina*: "I always try and do the right thing but a lot of the time things backfire on me and I end up looking like a fool. (Luckily no one punches or kicks me as much as they do him)."

At other times, identifying with an anime character is clearly inspiring. This seems particularly (but not exclusively) the case with members of the MML. A Canadian female novelist identified with the eponymous heroine of Miyazaki's first major film, *Nausicaa of the Valley of Winds* (*Kaze no tani no Nausicaa*), even to the point of wearing a Nausicaa costume to a sci-fi convention at a time when the character was still "obscure," explaining that "Nausicaa was strong, caring, and able to grow and change as she recognized better outlooks and solutions to the challenges facing the people of her world." Another member of the MML commented, rather intriguingly, "I think I would identify with the whole of Irontown in [*Princess*] *Mononoke* actually; they are industrial people as I am (I'm trained as a chemical engineer), they do chemistry (steel making is full-fledged chemistry), and they are struggling for their dignity and independence." Another MML member mentioned how both she and her daughter identified with Kiki, the struggling young witch in Miyazaki's *Kiki's Delivery Service*, to the point where the daughter spent a junior year on her own in Japan, just as Kiki goes off for a year to manage by herself in a foreign city.

Among non-MML fans, a number of younger people gained inspiration from the heroes of adventure and action tales, such as Naruto of the currently popular ninja adventure series *Naruto*, seeing in Naruto's rigorous training a model for their student life. As one fan put it, "Right now I identify with Naruto a lot. I'm a college student with tests and projects constantly looming ahead, and I'm always trying to learn and perfect new skills. I'll often look to Naruto for motivation, since he's a guy who always works hard and pushes himself to get everything done and to do it as best he can." Similarly, a young high-school student identified with Luffy, the main character from the extremely popular pirate fantasy *One Piece*: "He personifies many of the values that I try to live by, that loyalty to your friends is very important and that one should try to have fun and be more carefree in life." On a more serious note, a male computer science major identified with Kenshin, the conflicted samurai protagonist of the *Rurouni kenshin* series, in that Kenshin is a "hero" in a series that "explores many interesting moral, social and psychological questions."

Besides Miyazaki heroines, female characters who inspired fans especially included Utena, the gender-bending heroine of *Revolutionary Girl Utena*, the feisty but vulnerable Faye Valentine of *Cowboy Bebop*, and Usagi/Serena from *Sailor Moon*, one of the first anime series to have girls as superheroes. A secretary from the Midwest mentioned how, as a young woman, watching *Sailor Moon*, "I felt empowered. Usagi was the first female superhero I ever saw whose power was a 'feminine' power. Like an awakening goddess, she does not gain her strength by being like a man." One fan appreciated Utena because she "stands up for her rights and helps others when they need it." Regarding Faye, one fan saw her as "tough and independent," and another characterized her as someone who "deals with the same issues as many women and has a strong personality and a voice but still remains feminine and womanly, which I don't know if have figured out completely."

Fan identifications in general are often related to wishful thinking and to nostalgia, and this is true in the case of anime fans as well. A thirty-four-year-old homemaker mentions that she "sometimes envies the female characters [in anime] because of the unexpectedness and adventure in their lives. [For example], in *Inuyasha*, Kagome [the female protagonist] gets to travel through time, and her actions are needed, and she gets to journey around the country learning about life at that time." A young woman at Smith College mentioned how she enjoyed action fantasies because as a child she could not do sports, commenting, "I would still love to learn archery or swordsmanship but, due to a shoulder injury, I am no longer fit to participate the way I would have liked to. By watching these characters I can in a sense live through what I was never allowed to do."

For others, certain anime evoke a bittersweet nostalgia. A male in his twenties mentioned how much he identified with the protagonist of the high-school romance series *Karekano*: "From internal feelings to the situation where he and Miyazawa take their relationships further (the act of touching her breast, then withdrawing in hesitation and self-chastisement) . . . there are a number of things similar to my own feelings and to my own experiences in high school."

Especially in the case of Miyazaki films, fans connected certain texts and characters with childhood and innocence. As one MML fan put it, "*My Neighbor Totoro* appeals to my inner child in a way that I cannot really explain. . . . There's something inside me that is somehow in sync with this movie." Another older male member of the list found that he "identi[fies] with Mei and Satsuki in *Totoro*. I can remember feeling the way they feel when I was their ages." Similarly, a twenty-year-old male member of the list identifies with Mei and Satsuki: "When I was younger I was always searching for animals and creatures in the woods near my house and wanted adventures like theirs." A Chinese Canadian graphic designer mentions how she "can relate to aspects of both girls' personalities (dogged determination mixed with fear in dealing with new experiences)," but also goes on to say how a less well-known Miyazaki film, *Whispers of the Heart* (*Mimi o sumaseba*), reminded her of "how [she] fell in love with [her] husband while traveling in Tokyo and Kyoto—brings back so many good memories."

Perhaps the most frequent form of identification was on a more complicated level, one that allowed the viewers the chance to explore the difficulties of constructing a social identity during the tumultuous periods of adolescence and young adulthood. One respondent described this process in the following satirical manner: "Yes, I the geeky subculture inhabitant, find a lot of similarity between myself and the main male character of anime X, who is socially awkward, but who possesses powers that have not been revealed fully (e.g., Akira, Naruto, Urotsukidoji, etc.)." Despite the cynicism, the respondent has a vital point: it is certainly the case that a large number of anime (probably the majority of anime that are popular in the West) revolve around young people who often possess special powers (or sometimes are just particularly strange or geeky!) that differentiate them from the mainstream.

This kind of story is of course not unique to anime and manga. Coming-of-age stories involving young people finding their places in the world are archetypal to every culture throughout history, from the Sumerian epic *Gilgamesh* to the recent American soap opera, *The O.C.* As a thirty-one-year-old fan writes thoughtfully:

> I think it is easy to identify with the youth and adolescent characters of animes [sic] like *Spirited Away* and *Evangelion*. Of course it is easy enough to make the charge of arrested development of the creators and/or fans. But youth also presents unique opportunities, as adolescents we are intensely aware of the conflicts and confusions in life. It can be easier to portray honesty and vulnerability in an adolescent character, which makes them more sympathetic. And childhood and adolescence provide a natural allegorical connection to the path of transformation that any good character to must go through for a story to be effective.

Judging by the large number of respondents who identified with adolescent characters, it appears that anime is particularly effective at portraying the conflicts and confusions of life. The majority of characters cited were from fantasy and science-fiction anime. These included such fairly recent series as *Fruits Basket, Inuyasha, Full Metal Alchemist, Cowboy Bebop, Furikuri, Haibane Renmei,* and somewhat older "classics," particularly the epic science-fiction series *Neon Genesis Evangelion* and the cyberpunk masterpiece *Ghost in the Shell*. Overwhelmingly, however, the respondents mentioned how "real" the situations and characters seemed to them.

This returns us to my point that fantasy can provide concrete metaphors for human emotional states in ways that may have more impact than would a realistic portrayal. For example the extremely popular fantasy series *Ranma 1/2* introduced a character named Ryoga who went on long would-be romantic journeys but always ended up getting incredibly lost. A 25 male engineering student appreciates this "lostness" from a metaphysical point of view, saying "I identify with characters such as Ryoga from *Ranma*—the painfully shy, eternally lost nice guy who, despite good intentions, never seems to get ahead."

In anime the "path of transformation" mentioned by the thirty-one-year-old respondent is sometimes a literal "transformation." Thus, one of the most frequently cited series was the very popular romantic comedy fantasy *Fruits Basket*, in both its manga and anime form. *Fruits Basket* revolves around an orphaned schoolgirl, who becomes a housekeeper for a largely male wealthy family, all of whom are suffering from a curse—they transform into a creature from their birth year in the Chinese zodiac when they are embraced by a person of the opposite sex. Most episodes contain a scene of metamorphosis and these transformations are lavishly depicted and can sometimes be quite frightening. Fascinatingly, however, none of the respondents mentioned the fantastical nature of the series. It is the human psychological elements that compel them. A female college students sums up the story's appeal to her in the following lengthy response:

> I think I identify with the characters who feel isolated from other people. It is a very real isolation, where they go through everyday life but carry around this problem, which can either be as a light as "Oh, is my crush going to notice me today?" Or as heavy as "Tomorrow I'll need to sacrifice myself to save the world." A lot of the characters from *Fruits Basket* are like that. They go through these emotionally difficult times but try to act like it doesn't matter because on some level they think that no one else will understand. I think that's sort of a real life way to feel because I don't think there is anyone out there who hasn't had a moment when they think that no one else could possibly understand how awful or wonderful that moment is to them.

Rather than dwelling on the bizarre and sometimes frightening physical metamorphoses of the characters, this respondent concentrates on their complicated psychological states, mentioning their "emotionally difficult times" and how they feel that "no one else will understand." Implicitly, the respondent understands that the bestial transformation is a metaphor for inner alienation, and she describes this condition as a "real life way to feel." Another respondent, a student at Smith, mentioned how one character in *Fruits Basket* "caught my eye because, as result of teasing, she lost her ability to speak. I know how it feels to be teased so I really felt for poor little Kisa." Though she notes that Kisa turns into a tiger on occasion, the fan's emphasis is on the character's human emotions. Similarly, a fan of the series *Full Metal Alchemist* never mentions that the series is set in a parallel universe in which people practice alchemy with sometimes terrifying results, preferring instead to describe it as a work "about humanity and the world."

Another fantasy/science-fiction series that drew empathy was the imaginative and zany *FuriKuri*. This work includes an attractive space alien (Haruko), a robot that grows from the head of the protagonist (Naota), and numerous scenes of disaster. Yet fans responded to the series in terms of its human issues. "Growing up is hard, " as one young male commentator put it, referring to Naota's problems (the robot in the head being only one of the most obvious). A female high school student from Utah noted that "I probably identify most with Naota from [FuriKuri] because he's going through a directionless phase until he meets Haruko, who becomes a new and exciting friend. That is much more human and typical of being a teenager than being chosen as a pilot in war or other conflicts"

Despite suggesting that war anime were not "typical," this student then goes on to acknowledge her love of *Neon Genesis Evangelion*, a 1996–97 series and film about young people trying to save the world which is still considered by many fans as the "definitive anime." Again, however, although most fans love the extraordinary battles between humans and aliens and the series' brilliant overall vision of apocalypse, it is the human story involving the young people (or "children" as they are called in the script), that ultimately grips these viewers. As the student describes it "[Evangelion]has all kind of themes which are easy to relate to in a very appealing and beautiful way. It has something for everyone." Or as the 16 year old previously quoted says, "No anime has surpassed it yet. . . . I love *Eva* because of the complexity of the characters and them finding their identities as people. It was the perfect age to make the children 14–15 because that's when a lot of self-exploration and identity happens. You care about and love the characters because you get to know them." Perhaps my favorite exposition of *Neon Genesis Evangelion* and one that marvelously sums up the series' varied appeal was from an older fan who explained that:

> "It has themes of the painful transition from youth to adulthood, or conflicts with the roles our parents play in our lives, as well as deeper eschatological themes and inquiry about the ultimate destination of our technological culture. That these ideas are presented in a package of giant robots, monsters and frankly puerile "Fan service" components of adolescent sexuality and humor make it a unique experience."

This explanation evokes the richness and complexity of *Neon Genesis Evangelion*'s world, effectively illustrating why viewers could relate to so many elements in the series.

A slightly more recent science-fiction series that evoked almost as much passionate identification as *Neon Genesis Evangelion* is *Cowboy Bebop*.[13] A near-future narrative concerning a group of mismatched interstellar bounty hunters, this series garnered accolades for a number of special elements, including its imaginative and powerful music score(s), and its unique narrative format, which one respondent described as "a wonderful hybrid of cinematic genres, borrowing from noir, western, melodrama traditions founded in classic

Hollywood cinema, plus quality writing." As with so many other popular series, however, *Cowboy Bebop*'s most important appeal for many viewers was its small cast of complex, endearing, and remarkably "real" characters, including the two main bounty hunters, Spike Spiegel, whose laid back "cool" manner hid a complex past, and Faye Valentine a voluptuously beautiful young woman who combined a sometimes prickly independent spirit with a rather touching vulnerability. As with many anime characters, some fans found a touch of gender ambiguity to Faye and Spike, no doubt another part of the appeal to young people working on their own issues of gender construction.

A female student who "played with armies instead of princesses when she was little" acknowledged identifying with "both Spike and Faye . . . they are all conflicted and have secrets and lost loves and great stories in their pasts." A "Jewish American working film critic" said of *Cowboy Bebop* "it truly puts you through a meat grinder, an emotional wringer, and at times you feel as truly somber and lifeless as Spike Spiegel does."A female film major at USC explicitly acknowledges the isolation of the characters as a major reason for identifying with them, not only from her own point of view but as an anime fan in general noting that, "I feel akin to virtually all the characters in *Cowboy Bebop*, the villains included. I think that so many anime fans feel themselves to be not so much outcasts as misfits . . . *Bebop* epitomizes that sentiment through the characters and the situations presented."

If the drifting interstellar crew of the *Bebop* becomes almost a metaphor for anime fans, does this suggest something about anime itself? Is it too simply an example of transnational cultural flows, looping across the twenty-first-century universe but not belonging to any one place in particular? Some anime commentators, including those involved in the production of anime, have commented that it can be a "*mukokuseki*" (stateless or nationless) product.[14] Certainly the fantasy and science-fiction settings of many of the most popular anime seem to bear this out, plus the aforementioned "anime style" of art. The fact that fans from around the world can identify and empathize with these characters also seems to suggest that the cultural origins of anime are far less important than its universal aspects. In this regard, anime may be seen as a culturally "odor free" product, to use Iwabuchi's term.

For the aforementioned reasons, my initial assumption when I began researching anime fandom was that "Japan" or "Japaneseness" would not be an important element in anime's attraction. The more I spoke to fans and went to conventions, however, I began to question this. Eventually I decided to include the following two questions regarding Japan in my questionnaire: Has your interest in anime led you to an interest in Japan? If yes, in what way? And what is your impression of Japan from anime? Much to my surprise, a strong majority (depending on the period, from 65–75 percent) answered "yes" to the first question with a notable minority (almost 10 percent) answering "no" because, as one respondent put it, "It's the other way round. My love of Japanese culture led me to anime."

Given that Americans are considered by the rest of the world (and often by ourselves) as a parochial people uninterested in anything beyond our borders, these answers were not only unexpected, but thought provoking as well. Obviously anime fans do not represent a majority of Americans, but the fact that anime fans are increasingly becoming mainstream does suggest that Americans can indeed be open to and even intensely interested in foreign cultures. Furthermore, from the point of view of fandom in general, these answers suggested a high degree of agency on the part of the fans. Rather than passively consuming an entertainment product, these fans were inspired to know not only more about the product, but also about its cultural origins. In the case of anime fandom, one can argue that learning about Japan (as opposed to just knowing about anime) added to the fan's cultural capital. Mastering a foreign language or simply gaining knowledge of a foreign culture can be a genuinely empowering activity. As one fan said dryly, "If you know something about a foreign culture, you look knowledgeable."

The "yes" answers ranged from moderate interest as in "Yes, I'd like to learn more about Japanese history," to intense enthusiasm. One thirty-one-year-old Minnesotan wrote, "Yes, I am working on getting an art degree so I can move to Japan and get work in the animation field. I love the whole culture and the people of Japan. I read about Japan, from its history to its current popular culture."

Some respondents were not quite so enthusiastic. Many wanted to visit Japan but frequently added that they would not necessarily want to live there. Some had already gone to Japan as a result of their interest in anime. A seventeen-year-old high school student who was also from the Midwest wrote, "As soon as I arrived in high school I took the Japanese language. This is my fourth year. I began this whole inner search on how could something so brilliant (anime) come from a culture that, I had learned up until then, was considered very cruel, strict, Godzilla-ridden and old-fashioned. During my studies everything caught my interest. I even had the most wonderful experience to go to Japan and go to a regular high school for one month." For this student anime was a road to revelation, allowing her to leave stereotypes behind, and a literal road to another culture, since she actually spent time in Japan as an outgrowth of her interest.

Similarly, a half Chinese, one-fourth German, and one-fourth Scottish-Irish woman wrote, "Anime did spark my interest in Japan, mostly because I was curious as to what kind of culture could create something like this. I could tell there were a lot of little cultural nuances that I wasn't registering so I started learning the culture because of that. This led me into a general interest in the culture and history of Japan." The respondent's awareness that she was not "registering" all the "little cultural nuances" also suggests her awareness of the significance of anime's Japanese origins.

Given the generally high level of interest in Japan, it was perhaps not surprising that a large number of respondents were either studying or had studied Japanese. As a twenty-one-year-old woman explained, "I decided once, when I realized that I wasn't able to get more episodes of a show I liked, that I would need to learn Japanese to understand what happened next." Many fans mentioned that they "watch anime to improve their Japanese," and a graduate student in computer sciences crowed, "You'd be amazed by how many words I learned because [of watching anime subtitled]. I'm guessing I have a vocabulary of about 150–200 words by now." Another explained that his "ultimate goal" in learning Japanese was to watch anime without subtitles.

What was perhaps more surprising were those who went beyond the language. As one young woman wrote, "I started reading, looking things up, and began to realize what an amazing culture it was." Respondents mentioned learning about history because of samurai shows like *RurouniKenshin*, or studying Japanese religion because of their fascination with the gods and demons depicted in *Inuyasha*. Several mentioned cooking favorite anime dishes. One female fan, a twenty-one-year-old librarian, went so far as to relate, "I've also learned to cook dishes that I have seen on anime shows. I have been told that I make the best miso soup and Japanese pancakes this side of Tokyo!"

For some respondents, interest in anime led to an interest in Japanese society in general. One woman wrote, "I notice when Japan is in the news now. I couldn't tell you the names of any major political figure in Canada at the moment, and it's the country next door. On the other hand, for a while last summer, I knew the names of several important figure in Japanese politics. Eek. It also affects entertainment news."

Perhaps even more intriguingly (and hearteningly), interest in anime has led some fans to develop an interest in other cultures in general. A Hispanic computer science major wrote, "I am much more interested in Japanese culture than before I gained an interest in anime. It in a way opened my eyes to how different areas can be different yet similar too. It's not just Japan that I gained interest in; I seem more interested in the notion of new cultures in general. I like to compare the differences and similarities."

Since "Japan" as a fantasy world has been a part of Western cultural perceptions since the nineteenth century, I was curious to see what impression respondents had gained of the country through anime. Here the answers varied considerably. Not surprisingly, a large number (probably 50 percent) of answers veered toward levity.

As one respondent put it, "If I were to gain my impression of Japan only from anime I would think that all the guys are clueless but make great robot pilots and all the women are ultra-cute and have magic powers." In a similar vein, another older respondent noted that "[Japan is] an interesting place. Every girl under nineteen wears a sailor suit, except when she transforms into a princess, and giant robots are lurking around every corner to save/destroy the world."

On the other hand, this person goes on to say, "Seriously, though, the reflection of Japanese culture is obviously stylized, but what it portrays is clearly a very layered and ancient culture. The various rituals, religious observances, architecture, weapons and so forth, both explicitly shown and implied, show accretion and adaptation over hundreds of years. Japan strikes me as a place where the very ancient and the ultra-modern can be found in close proximity, at times coexisting harmoniously and at times uneasily"

Another thoughtful response came from a Korean American student at Amherst College, who wrote:

> [Japan] is a place that is capable of referring to the Bible and to popular culture in one breath. I love the fact that it levels a lot of the cultural hierarchies in interesting ways. It is also a place that is covertly sexual/sensual, and it's a country that does not do things halfway. Looking at the incredible number of themes that are discussed in anime, I also argue that it's a place that is unsure about its national identity. . . . Japan constantly questions its societal norms and stereotypes (even as certain anime fall into stereotypes themselves.) In some ways it seems to be running from something.

An African American female fan wrote, "[Japan] has a whole tradition of swords and legends to draw from that the West does not have. And no matter what time period is depicted in anime there is always a belief that those who stray from the norm can be brought back. Moreover, anime is not afraid to confine males and females to traditional roles and those who venture out of their assigned roles are given characteristics of the other side." Such thoughtful responses suggest that anime can give a richer picture of Japanese society than might be expected. Far more than the nineteenth-century Japonisants, the contemporary anime fans frequently seem aware of the contradictory and complex elements that make up Japanese society. Not surprisingly, some had gone on to study Japan through anime. A student at Amherst, for example, mentioned writing his senior thesis on nostalgia in Miyazaki's film *Spirited Away*.

Inevitably there were some respondents who tended to idealize Japan just as Van Gogh had done over a century earlier. But these idealizations were usually based to a certain extent on reality. For example, two art students mentioned separately that they perceived anime studios as more "hands on" than American ones, giving the example of Hideaki Anno, the director of *Neon Genesis Evangelion*, who, as one respondent said, "just did what he wanted to do." Some brought up Japanese values, both aesthetic and social, that they admired. One person described Japan as a "very elegant culture," while another said she saw the Japanese as "gentle and unassuming."

Some saw the culture as more "spiritual," meaning in some cases that "they believe in another world beyond our own and separated from the traditional Christian-centric ideologies." Other fans saw the country as "more progressive than the U.S. They embrace change. They love technology." Others lauded Japan for being a "community-oriented society." One person pointed out that "in the credits for Anime one rarely sees an individual listed as producing credit and instead sees these positions filled with committees or companies, suggesting that Japan still values the importance of cooperation and working together far more than the U.S." A twenty-two-year-old male saw Japan as a society that "values cooperation and sacrifice as opposed to the survival-of-the-fittest mentality [seen] in the majority of Americans."

Some respondents had drawn less positive impressions from anime. A female art student's impression was that "conformity is desirable, while being different is viewed as negative. (In anime whenever a character develops some unusual power or whatever, they spend a lot of time wishing they were 'normal.')" A thirty-six-year-old librarian agreed with the conformity description, basing her knowledge particularly on *Cowboy Bebop* and *Sailor Moon*. She wrote, "I get the hint that Japan is a lot more group-oriented than the U.S. Okay, the characters in *Cowboy Bebop* are probably supposed to be wild, free, and independent, but I note that most of them aren't terribly happy. *Sailor Moon* especially, beats you over the head with the 'you have power when you have friends' theme. And all those school uniforms suggest a much higher level of conformity than American high school dress codes do." Others found aspects of anime that contradicted previous stereotypes: One fan wrote, "I am shocked at how modernization has cut them off from their culture. Somehow I thought that they still went around reciting poems about the Full Moon when the cherry blossoms came out."

A number of fans mentioned what they perceived as a more relaxed Japanese attitude toward sexuality. One person wrote, "My feeling is it's a far more open society than the U.S. in regards to discussion of sexuality." Others cheered what they felt was a lack of "political correctness" in Japanese society that they saw reflected in the male-female relationships in anime.

A large number of fans noted the apocalyptic cast to many anime, pointing out that "Japan gets blown up a lot." A few went more deeply into this theme. One male student suggested that he felt it showed that "the scars of World War II are still with them."

Most fans, of course, were highly aware that anime was only one approach to Japan (and a very distinctive one at that). As a thirty-six-year-old female writer/secretary put it, "Anime doesn't show us what Japan is: it shows us what Japan dreams. I hesitate to claim any real knowledge of a country I've never personally visited. However, I think it's safe to say that the Japanese, regardless of how they appear on the surface, are romantic dreamers at heart. And so are Americans. This may be our deepest bond."

The fact that this woman could find a "deep bond" between America and Japan, despite "what appears on the surface," suggests that immersion in anime is far more than a fascination with the exotic. At least for the fans described here, it seems to be a way to construct a more complex identity vis-a-vis the twenty-first-century world. The compelling stories and characters of anime offer the fans a chance to explore their own dreams (and nightmares) in settings that are both familiar and strange. And for the many who became interested in Japan, their fascination allows them to interact on a surprisingly deep level with another culture, from knowing the names of Japanese political figures to cooking Japanese cuisine. Especially for fans such as the young woman who "had never even set foot in Mexico," such knowledge and interaction can be extremely empowering. Rather than the traditional Orientalist construction of the West empowering itself by oppressing or patronizing the Eastern Other, these fans gain agency through discovering and then identifying with a society that they clearly recognize as having both universal and culturally specific aspects.

Douglas Kellner, among many others, has argued that the "postmodern" identity is a "fluid" one in which "identity becomes a freely chosen game, a theatrical presentation of the self, in which one is able to present oneself in a variety of roles, images and activities,"[15] and gives the examples of celebrities such as Madonna who are constantly reinventing themselves. On the one hand, anime fans seem to partake in that fluidity, both in the ease with which they identify with cartoon characters and with their willingness to engage with an alien culture (not to mention their fondness for dressing as anime characters at conventions). And yet, a strong impression I gained throughout my interviews and surveys was that most fans are actually quite sure of who they are, and they see both fandom and their engagement with anime as a way to augment their core selves rather than to fundamentally change their identity.

While many scholars have discussed the possibility of the loss of cultural identity in a globalizing world, anime fans seem quite capable of embracing a variety of identifications without losing their own sense of themselves. In their case, fandom is not simply a form of compensation for the pressures of daily life but a way of responding to some of those pressures for their own pleasure and enlightenment.

Sandvoss has suggested that a sense of *Heimat* (the German word for home) is an extremely important aspect of fan culture, providing the deteritorialized and decentralized modern self with a transitory sense of "belonging."[16] Certainly this sense of communality holds true for anime fans as well. But I might also suggest that anime fandom in particular, precisely because it is not a fandom around an indigenous cultural product nor one that engages with live-action characters, can also provide a healthy bit of estrangement from a world that sometimes can become a little too familiar. As Ulf Hamerz points out, "[especially to young people] home is bit of a prison."[17] Anime allows its fans to "leave home" for a little while to discover aspects of home at a different destination.

8

In Search of Sacred Space? Anime Fandom and MiyazakiWorld

What I think the various fan subcultures do is provide a space for community. They allow people of diverse background and experience to form bonds around a common interest. They let people know that they are not alone in their likes and their passions. Fan subcultures provide the sense of belonging that used to be common among most American communities and families prior to the 1980s. Today kids are raised by day cares and public schools. Parents are too busy working and building careers to devote significant time for family building and family life. Kids are just one of the many entries on the day planner.... Fan subcultures help to provide a space for community where people can come and be accepted for who they are. In a society as fragmented as America has become, fan subcultures can provide an oasis for the weary soul.

—Thirty-eight-year-old utility company tech supporter and member of the Miyazaki Mailing List

Miyazaki's film is about social interaction, historical context, responsibility and coordination within a society. Towards the end, the story is about a certain consensus—a group coming together to agree and rally around a certain set of values, experiences, goals.

—Mike, a member of the Miyazaki Mailing List

Q. What's the fascination of Hayao Miyazaki?
A. Even though Hayao Miyazaki is so successful, he seems to prefer to work hard and earnestly with people rather than distancing himself from people with walls of money and bureaucracy. He shares his wonderful stories of hope and courage with his audiences. He earnestly cares for the environment and helps young and old people share the enthusiasm for the real and imaginary parts of nature as large as a forest full of Catbuses and as small as a tree under which one Totoro stands in the rain.

—Michael Johnson, owner of the Miyazaki Mailing List

The previous chapter attempted to give a portrait of anime fans in general and discover what sort of elements attract them to the medium. As we saw, these elements included a range of aesthetics, narratives, and world views that appealed to Americans as more rich and compelling than what was available in their own popular culture. In this final chapter on fandom, I want to delve into a very specific anime fan group, the fans of Studio Ghibli, and touch particularly on the question of values and how for many of these fans, the values of Studio Ghibli have offered something different and richer than those of contemporary American society.

In his landmark book Bowling Alone: The Collapse and Revival of American Community (2000), the political scientist Robert Putnam charts the increasing decline of what social scientists term "social capital" in contemporary American society. Chronicling the fading of civic groups, union organizations, church socials, and sports clubs, Putnam paints a picture of American society (and by inference, other postindustrial societies) as growing ever more disconnected and fragmented. The book makes a strong case for how these trends lead to alienation and passivity, including offering a melancholy vision of 2010 where future Americans will spend their leisure time "sitting passively alone in front of glowing screens."[1] While Putnam does acknowledge the potential role of the Internet as a facilitator of communication, quoting sociologist Barry Wellman, who maintains that "computer-supported social networks sustain strong, inter-mediate and weak ties that provide information and social support in both specialized and broadly based relationships,"[2] he also worries that overuse of the Internet will lead to "single strand" cybercommunities that in turn generate "Cyberbalkanization" in which individuals speak only to a circle of "like-minded intimates."[3]

This chapter examines one such "single strand" cybercommunity, the Miyazaki Mailing List, an international group of fans devoted to the works of Miyazaki Hayao, Japan and arguably the world's greatest living animator. The chapter will discuss this group not only in terms of its status as an Internet community, but also in relation to anime fan culture overall, one of the fastest grow-ing subcultures in the world today, and finally, in relation to the question of Japanese "soft power," in this case what Douglas McGray defines as "the art of transmitting certain kinds of mass culture."[4]

I have chosen the Miyazaki Mailing List (MML) for a variety of reasons: First, it is one of the oldest and most continuous groups of Internet anime fans, beginning at Brown University by Steven Feldman in 1991 and now being run out of Seattle, Washington by Michael Johnson. Second, it is a particularly artic-ulate, engaged, and varied group, encompassing a wide range of ages, a fair number of female participants, and representing a notable range of countries from Australia to Belarussia. Finally and most importantly, the objects of the group's interest, Miyazaki, his partner Takahata Isao, and everything related to its animation studio, Studio Ghibli, comprise an impressively rich range of materi-als from which to draw discussion. These materials include approximately twelve feature films, including the American Academy Award–winning *Spirited Away*, a number of television series, and a new and immensely popular museum, the Ghibli Museum in Tokyo. Most important of all are the less tangible aspects of what I call MiyazakiWorld, an overt ideological agenda encompassing environmentalism, humanism, what might be called "Ghibli (or Miyazaki) family values," and a concern with presenting works of a psychological and moral complexity, unusual not only in animation, but also in most cinematic offerings today.

These latter concerns are particularly interesting in relation to the global transmission of cultural values. In "Japan's Soft Power and Public Diplomacy," Seiichi Kondo, a Japanese diplomat, argues that "the Japanese do not find it easy to project their ideas in the form of values. Japan's ideas are better conveyed by being translated into cultural products through the mediation of feelings than by being translated into logical strings of words through the mediation of language."[5] In fact, Studio Ghibli films contain much articulate and intelligent dialogue and some memorable phrases (perhaps the most famous one is the exhortation, "to see with eyes unclouded," from Miyazaki's 2001 film *Princess Mononoke*). It is probably true, however, that initially the extraordinary beauty of the artwork (Miyazaki still does his original drawings by hand), the sumptuous music, and the gripping stories first attract the viewer. Once attracted to MiyazakiWorld, however, the viewer is often drawn further in by the subtle but rich emotional palette (giving rise to a far more complex range of emotions than most Hollywood films), the three-dimensional characterizations of the protagonists, (who are frequently female), and the willingness to deal with a variety of powerful themes, from environmental and social collapse (*Future Boy Conan, Nausicaa, Princess Mononoke, Spirited Away, Grave of Fireflies, Ponpoko*) to heartfelt coming-of-age tales (*Only Yesterday, Totoro, Kiki's Delivery Service, Spirited Away*). Even in simpler, more child-oriented fantasies, the studio never fails to evoke what the *New Yorker* in a recent profile on Miyazaki calls "a sense of wonder."[6]

From the point of view of fan studies, there is one other particularly intriguing aspect of the MML, and this is how in many ways they differ, if not necessarily from most anime fans, from critical and conventional expectations of the kind of people who comprise fandom. Reviewing the literature on fandom, one is struck by how much space and energy is spent dealing with the issue of what Lisa Lewis calls the "fan pathology," the sense that "fans operate from a position of cultural marginality."[7] As Lewis says of how fandom is presented in cinema, "Fandom is overwhelmingly associated with adolescence or childhood, that is, with a state of arrested development or youth-oriented nostalgia. Furthermore, the fan impulse is presented as feminine."[8]

MML fans on the whole do not fit this stereotype not only because many in the group are older, male, and well educated, but because their online discussions reveal them to be notably mature and thoughtful people whose attraction to Studio Ghibli products seem less a case of "arrested development" or "youth-oriented nostalgia" than a considered response to the complexities and problems of the contemporary world. In fact, on finishing a rough draft of this chapter and reviewing the literally hundreds of pages of discussion I had examined, I became aware that I was drawing something more than a portrait of a particular fan community (and indeed some members of the MML resist even being called fans). Instead, the words and thoughts of the members came to constitute a portrait of our contemporary millennium society, at least as seen by thoughtful people hoping to do the right thing in the face of a world that seems increasingly captured by consumer capitalism, the desires of the powerful (and the concomitant alienation of the powerless), and frightening environmental problems. The fact that these are all problems explored in detail in the works of both Miyazaki and Takahata is of course why they are drawn to Studio Ghibli's output.

As such, I cannot argue that the MML members are exactly "typical" fans, but in a sense they are typical in their atypicality, at least among anime fans. As mentioned, in my research into anime fandom over the last ten years, I have found it increasingly difficult to draw a portrait of any one typical anime fan, especially as anime has become more and more pervasive in American culture. What was once, even five to ten years ago, a rather small and tight-knit community, largely male, frequently Asian American, and most often found on either of the coasts or else in big cities, has blossomed into a remarkably diverse group of fans, ranging over a wide age demographic and geographical breadth (including very enthusiastic aficionados in the heartland states) and with a remarkable span of political and religious beliefs (from conservative Evangelical Christians to a self-described "Atheist/Shintoist anarchist").

This chapter will attempt to draw a profile of the MML and show how the mailing list itself has become a form of virtual community. This community is more than just a fantasycape for the purpose of pure entertainment. It might, in fact, be called a "sacred space," based on Roger Aden's theory of "sacred place" in fan communities.[9] This space is a site for fans not only to discuss their specific interests in Ghibli products, but also to deal with larger philosophical, intellectual, and political issues arising from the Ghibli oeuvre and Miyazki's pronouncements and occasionally emotional and personal ones as well. Just as fan conventions provide fellowship and solidarity by offering a means for fans to interact in a liminoid space outside of their "regular" lives, the MML provides a liminoid virtual space where fans can enjoy the fellowship of others who appreciate visiting MiyazakiWorld, a world that is frequently seen by the members as more ethically, aesthetically, and intellectually appealing than the world around them.

Aden describes these virtual visits on the part of fans in general to their favorite fictional sites (such as Tolkien's Middle Earth or George Lucas's *Star Wars* fantasies) as "symbolic pilgrimages" in which "individuals ritualistically revisit powerful spaces that are symbolically envisioned through the interaction of story and individual imagination."[10] Indeed, the members of the MML sometimes jocularly refer to making "pilgrimages" to the new Studio Ghibli Museum in Tokyo, but it is their imaginative interaction with the sacred space of Studio Ghibli films that particularly concerns me here. By interacting with others who share their interest in appreciating and interpreting MiyazakiWorld, the members participate in actively constructing "mattering maps" or, more simply, what

Mihaly Csikszentmihalyi terms the "making of meaning,"[11] which, among other things, includes "learning to unite with other entities around us without losing our hard-won individuality."[12]

While MiyazakiWorld is not as all-encompassing as the realm of *Star Wars*, which Will Brooker describes as "for some people . . . the most important cultural text of our lives . . . a culture: a sprawling detailed mythos they [the fans] can pick through with their eyes closed,"[13] it too can be said to represent a detailed alternative reality that, as Joli Jensen says of fan culture in general, can present "an implicit critique of modern life."[14] It should be emphasized, however, that Studio Ghibli's works, while often fantasies, are far from simply escapist. In comparison to the *Star Wars* offerings, they are often much more downbeat, eschewing the grand heroics and triumphant endings that are crucial to Lucas's universe (and to much of Hollywood cinema in general).

Even in comparison to anime fandom in general, the MML community has a particularly intimate quality to it. We have mentioned the article in *Wired* magazine that described the anime community as among the earliest adopters of the Internet. This is certainly the case for the MML, a large percentage of who are involved with computers and technology around the world. As Will Brooker says of *StarWars* fandom in relation to the Internet, "the Internet enabled many fans to take their first step into a larger world."[15] Even among dedicated anime fans, however, the MML stands out not only for its longevity, high volume of traffic, and international makeup, but also for the generally high and remarkably civil level of discussion.[16] While the members may not be physically in a room interacting around a scratchy tenth-generation videotape (as the original anime fans were forced to do back in the early 1980s), the sense of immediacy, the enthusiasm and depth of the discussion, and the palpable feeling of fellowship on the part of many of the fans suggests that in some ways they still are gathered together. In fact, a number of MML members actively shy away from conventions and more typical fan activities, citing their dislike for the commercialism and frivolity of these engagements.

Of course even in the MML, commercial aspects of MiyazakiWorld also play a more important role than perhaps they used to. Postings from fans include many references to finding Miyazaki collectibles, such as the various dolls in the shape of Totoro, a cuddly spirit-animal who is one of Miyazaki's most felicitous creations; key chains with figures from *Spirited Away*; and vintage posters from *Nausicaa*, Miyazaki's first major film and one for whom the actual net part of MML is named (Nausicaa.net). Furthermore, virtually all the members are concerned with getting the latest and best DVD releases from Studio Ghibli (a number of threads concern the question of when a release will appear on the market and how attainable it is).

On the whole, however, commercial and marketing aspects are small in comparison to other types of discussion, which can range from a dispute over the frame counts of a particular scene to intense interactions over the philosophy, imagery, and overall message of a particular film. In fact, rather than calling them "consumers," a term often used in the literature of fandom,[17] I would prefer to call the Miyazaki fans "appreciators and interpreters," since so much of their discussion is on an emotional and intellectual level rather than a material one.[18]

This brings me to one of the basic questions concerning fandom, which is, what do the fans get out of their fan behavior? In the case of the MML, the more specific question would be, what is it about the imagined community that I call MiyazakiWorld that attracts such a variety of people from around the world? This question is particularly intriguing for two reasons: the first is the fact that, like other fantasies such as those of George Lucas and perhaps Gene Roddenberry, the creator of *Star Trek* (or on the literary front, J. R. R. Tolkien), MiyazakiWorld offers a definite worldview, even to some extent an ideology. And we can assume that, to some degree or another, the fans are responding to it.

Much work has been done on the notion of fandom as a form of compensation for the disappointment of the quotidian world. This notion is not always presented negatively. Roger Aden speaks of fandom as a form of escapism that is "purposeful play in which we symbolically move away from the material world to an imaginative world that is in many ways a *response* to the material"[19] As the MML's list owner, Michael Johnson, says of anime in relation to U.S. animation, "American cartoons browbeat the viewer with pithy platitudes and morals-of-the-story. Japanese cartoons engage the viewer and let or force hir [*sic*] to watch actively and arrive at hir [*sic*] own conclusions" What is intriguing here, and this brings up the second reason why MiyazakiWorld is so interesting, is that Americans, Europeans, South Americans, and Asians feel comfortable engaging in an imaginative world created by a Japanese director and targeted, initially at least, at an exclusively Japanese audience. In an age of increasing fragmentation and growing nationalism, what is it about Miyazaki's message that has struck a chord with so many people around the globe?

Part of the answer to the second question is undoubtedly related to the increasing influence of Japan's soft power worldwide. Certainly, Miyazaki's popularity is linked with the general rise of interest in anime over the last decade. To explain the depth, breadth, and longevity of Miyazaki's popularity, however, is a more complicated task involving both his fans and the nature of MiyazakiWorld.

It should be mentioned first of all that Miyazaki is hugely popular in his own country. Many of his films, including his three most recent, have been record breakers at the box office, appealing across generations and genders. The richness of his imagination plus his essentially wholesome vision make his works perfect for family viewing. It is, therefore, on the one hand, not surprising that Miyazaki's films should be appreciated internationally to some degree. What is interesting, however, is that, at least among the members of the MML, their favorite works of his are often the most "Japanese" of his oeuvre, specifically *My Neighbor Totoro, Princess Mononoke*, and *Spirited Away*.

We have mentioned Iwabuchi's suggestion that one reason for the proliferation of Japanese popular culture is that it has been rendered "culturally odorless"[20] through creating products such as Hello Kitty or Pikachu, whose origins cannot easily be traced back to Japan. To a certain extent, many of Miyazaki's early works do take place in relatively "odor free" cultural contexts, in some

Figure 10 A family of Miyazaki fans pose with a favorite character

cases post apocalyptic future worlds (*Future Boy Conan, Nausicaa*) or European-esque fantasy worlds (*Kiki's Delivery Service, Porco Rosso*). But this certainly cannot be said of the three mentioned previously, all of which deal with Japanese traditions, the Japanese landscape, and (in *Princess Mononoke*'s case) Japanese history. It should also be noted that a number of members of the MML list also particularly love the films of Miyazaki's partner, Takahata Isao, such as *Grave of Fireflies, Only Yesterday*, and *My Neighbor Yamada*, all of which are clearly specific to Japanese culture.

We need to go beyond the "odorless" explanation to understand the appeal of MiyazakiWorld. One way to do this is to examine the makeup of the MML. I have developed the following portrait based partly on information provided by Michael Johnson; partly on my own years as a "lurker" on the list and a detailed examination of discussions that took place from January to April of 2003 (not coincidentally, the period when *Spirited Away* won the Academy Award and the war in Iraq began); and partly on the responses I received to a questionnaire mailed out by my research assistant, Michael Roemer, in February and March of 2005. The questionnaire was my standard questionnaire that I have been using over the last five years to survey anime fans throughout the country, but with a few MML-specific questions added. Although the list membership technically comprises over one thousand members, only a relatively small percentage of these are active on the list. In any given week, perhaps ten members are actively vocal with another ten chiming in more occasionally. Michael Roemer and I received sixty-four questionnaire responses from the list, and, although self-selected from my own observation of the list over time, they seemed to be a reasonably representative sample.

To anyone with knowledge of fandom in general or anime fandom in particular, one of the most surprising aspects of the MML is the relatively older age of the members: 26 percent of the fans were between forty and forty-nine years old, 23 percent of them were between thirty and thirty-nine years old, and 14 percent were between ages fifty and sixty. The group of twenty to twenty-nine year olds was the second largest, however, comprising 25 percent of the respondents. And the remaining 10 percent were between sixteen and eighteen years old. While these results may partially be explained by the possibility that young people are less likely to fill out questionnaires, the age demographic accorded well with the members' own *perceptions* of themselves as an older, more mature group than the average anime mailing list.

The older ages of the fans may also be responsible for the fact that our respondents were 75 percent male. Although in the early days of fandom, anime fans tended to be overwhelmingly male,[21] this has changed enormously over the last several years. Background as to race and nationality was a little more complicated to ascertain, since non-American list subscribers sometimes did not identify themselves ethnically. Of the American members, thirty identified themselves as white, while there were four Asian Americans, one African American, and one American Hispanic. The other twenty-three (40 percent of the total respondents) were not Americans, but, judging by their names and countries represented (five from Australia, four from Canada, two from Sweden, two from France, and one from each of the following countries: Mexico, Ireland, Spain, Belarussia, Norway, and Brazil), it seems reasonably safe to conclude that these members were largely Caucasian. (although there was one self-identified Chinese-Australian), another slight surprise since, early on at least, many members of anime clubs were Asian American, and, at least on the West Coast, Asian Americans still constitute a fairly high percentage.

Also intriguing was the relatively high education level of the respondents. 45 percent (twenty-five) had received a bachelor's degree, 20 percent (eleven) had received a master's degree, and 5.45 percent (four) had doctorate degrees. This statistic also accords well with the members' perceptions of themselves as "better educated" and "more informed" than the average anime fan group. As one respondent, a fifty-year-old female artist, put it, "I think they are more intelligent and polite. They can argue without rancor for the most part. They cite scholarly examples, they are loyal to the genre. They're a lot more fun and cheerful than most grownups!" Another member called the list, "an island of sanity and fascinating discussion in wild anarchy that was the world of the usenet and nowadays, message boards."

Initially less surprising was the most represented occupation: 33 percent were in computers and engineering (and 39 percent had majored in computer sciences or engineering in college). This statistic accords well with profiles of science-fiction fans, many who have a technology background. But perhaps more interesting was the variety of other occupations represented. These included a video producer, two stay-at-home mothers, a number of artists (or students majoring in art), an attorney, a janitor/translator, a retired helicopter pilot, and a worker for the IRS. The large variety of occupations and interests seems much in accord with the face of anime fandom in general. Although technology workers and artists are probably still somewhat overrepresented in comparison to the general population, the increasing pervasiveness of anime and the increase in female fans has led to a much broader representation of occupations and interests.

But I also suspect that the wide variety of occupations may have something to do with Miyazaki's appeal that can be seen as both broad and specific. The superior aesthetic quality of his and Takahata's films undoubtedly attracts artists and designers. The relatively wholesome nature of Studio Ghibli's stories, plus their emphasis on children, clearly attracts a family audience. A number of respondents mentioned that they were parents who enjoyed watching the films with their children, although, as one person wryly remarked, "My children are grown now and I can't use them to hide behind." Finally, Miyazaki and his partner's concerns about the state of the world, the environment, and the future resonate with thoughtful people regardless of occupation.

The stereotype of fans in general has often been that they tend to be on the edges of society, resolutely nonmainstream. In my interviews with Midwest fans, however, I have been interested to see a relatively high (although by no means the majority) percentage of conservative fans, including fundamentalist Christians. My questionnaire for the MML included a section on religious beliefs, and here too the results were somewhat surprising. Although 54 percent could be described as liberal to leftwing (twenty-seven democrats and three socialists), 9 percent were center to Republican, one person was a libertarian, and 22 percent (mostly the younger respondents) described themselves as having no politics at all. In terms of religions, results varied widely as well: 21 percent were practicing Christians (including two members of the Church of Latter Day Saints), almost 20 percent were atheists (including one "atheist with some Ghiblist influences"), and 20 percent said they had no religion or were agnostic, while 28 percent said that they had some religious feelings but did not belong to an organized faith (a number of these mentioned an interest in Buddhism or Shintoism), and one respondent was a practicing Jew. Interestingly, a number of respondents reported having been raised in a strong religious faith (generally Jewish or Catholic), but had lost faith over the years.

The respondents were more in agreement when it came to the question of how they saw their beliefs in relation to American mainstream values and what they thought were the good and bad aspects of American culture. A totel of 68 percent saw themselves as outside of American mainstream values, while 26 percent saw their values as mainstream, and 6 percent (presumably foreign) said they did not know. The answers to the questions about values were often very intense and elaborate. The most often cited negative aspects of America were consumerism and/or materialism, with various permutations of "arrogant" or "bullying" following close in second. (It should be noted that while the non-American residents were often critical of the United States, the harshest critiques were from *American* respondents, including one who noted "feeling ashamed of being American.")

Often these responses were some of the longest in the questionnaire. One person summed up the negatives as "anti-intellectual bias, the problems of bigotry and sexism, the loss of community, the loss of the value of the family, and tendency to think of those we disagree with as the enemy." A fifty-two-year-old bureaucrat/attorney cited "familial breakdown, lack of community ties, lack of genuinely humane values, arrogance, selfishness," while a forty-eight-year-old bookseller (also male) mentioned "selfishness, short-sightedness, smugness, religiosity, hostility to the imagination." One respondent, a forty-one-year-old female novelist, described the worst aspects of American society as "[Americans] attempting to enforce a system of privilege that finds poverty and human suffering acceptable, so long as the results are that they live a wealthy life that supports and leaves unchallenged their sense of righteousness in holding their privileged position." Another woman, a forty-seven-year-old software engineer, brought up "rampant anti-intellectualism, an incredible over-regard for money and material things, a lack of respect for or interest in other cultures—parochial and arrogant." A conservative respondent, a twenty-three-year-old Mormon tech support worker, mentioned that Americans are "lazy and self-centered."

The previous statements are illuminating in light of Roger Aden's theory concerning how the "imaginative world [of the fans] is a *response* to the material" (i.e., outside world). In contrast to an America (and also, as some of the members readily admit, much of the industrialized world) that is viewed as materialistic, bullying, narrow, self-centered, and in danger of losing all human connection, MiyazakiWorld, as shown not only in the films of Studio Ghibli, but also in interviews with Miyazaki and Takahata, is seen as expansive, open to new possibilities—be they ideas or new creations—family oriented, and, to use one of the members' favorite words, "humanistic." Where America and other industrialized societies are perceived as bent on destroying the environment, the human soul, the family, and community, MiyazakiWorld is seen to be about cherishing traditions, family ties, and natural beauty. This cherishing is never pursued simplistically or sentimentally, however. Many of Studio Ghibli's films have at least a metaphorical apocalyptic subtext, but the final message is always one of at least the *possibility* of hope and redemption on the part of ordinary human beings.

One consistently sees in both the questionnaire responses and in conversational threads a feeling that Miyazaki and Takahata value down-to-earth human values, as opposed to technological or commercial values. Thus, one respondent commented on an early Miyazaki film, *Laputa: Castle in the Sky*, that "the film delves deep into the flaws of what high technology may bring to mankind in today's world." A long-running thread from around the time of *Spirited Away*'s opening in America concerned whether Miyazaki was attacking American consumer values or those of the Japanese when he showed the parents of the heroine transform-ing into literal pigs of consumption. After much discussion, one member summed up what seemed to be the general consensus: that "concern about glut-tony in *Spirited Away* was about consumption and greed. . . . Any supposedly civilized culture would rue losing its traditions and watching their people become ignorant of the things that should be cherished."

The comments on the positive elements of American culture and society were more uniform but also in line with a worldview that we might expect from fans of Miyazaki. Both American and non-Americans found U.S. society to be optimistic, energetic, and (somewhat surprisingly, given the many criticisms of "bullying") altruistic. A French doctoral candidate wrote approvingly that Americans "don't seem to shy away when it comes to faith." Many commented on the tolerance and diversity of American society, although a significant minority saw Americans as "not open to accepting different cultures," as a twenty-six-year-old Chinese American responded.

This minority view may tie into an aspect of fandom that is often noted among scholars of fan theory and that is the feeling, on the part of some fans at least, of being an outsider from a mainstream society that they see as bullying or rejecting on a personal level. A thirty-six-year-old Spanish journalist described himself as "a music fan, cinema fan, anime fan," but went on to insist, "I will never kick in the face another person because they cannot love anime films, and soccer fanatics can use these kind of attitudes." Many other members seemed comfortable in describing themselves in terms that could be considered pejora-tive. One respondent summed himself up as a "nerd, otaku, trekkie, goth witch, net junkie," and a number of others simply answered "nerd" or "geek."

On the other hand, another member described himself more prosaically as a "married nearly-middle-aged father of two who lives in the suburbs and works in the movie business." Many others, however, saw themselves in very positive terms and in ways that seemed particularly appropriate for Miyazaki fans. These included "a pragmatic romantic," a "bit of a dreamer," "someone who likes unique and unusual things," "a little more culturally aware than most," and "a science/technical major (recent UC Berkeley graduate) with a foreign back-ground, a rationalist/technical technological mindset, and a strong attraction toward the humanist message (e.g., Hayao Miyazaki, Isao Takahata, Yoshitoshi Abe's *Haibane Renmei* series, and from literature, Charles Dickens, Ursula Leguin, Phillip Pullman." This last self-description that notes an interest in other "world-building" artists (*Haibane Renmei* is an anime series that takes place in a fantasy world that people go to after death) again suggests that these highly colored fantasy realms are both compensations for and critiques of a less satisfying real world.

At the same time, it should be emphasized that members of the list are not simply escaping a disappointing reality. Many are extremely aware of the prob-lems of the real world and see in Miyazaki's environmental and humanist mes-sage a call for action. One respondent described himself as "a research scientist who values peace, justice, and wanting to make this a better world." A majority of respondents mentioned the environment as being the most significant issue of the day. As a female thirty-year-old Swedish student writes, "I think the environment question is the most important one for our survival as a species and is likely to remain so for the next hundred years at least." Miyazaki and Takahata's emphasis on environmentalism is seen as something that could change the world. A twenty-two-year-old Norwegian student suggested that "Miyazaki Sama [sama is a highly honorific form of Japanese address] puts messages in his story that I believe is something the world should listen to."

Overall, however, the MML does not see MiyazakiWorld ideology as being simplistic. One of the major threads of discussion throughout the lifetime of the MML has been Miyaaki's approach to good and evil. Many consider one of Studio Ghibli's major offerings to society to be precisely the lack of a clear-cut vision of good versus evil. One twenty-two-year-old French student compared Studio Ghibli with American animation, saying that "the difference . . . may come from Miyazaki (and Ghibli) producing movies that display real imaginative universes and do not need to show violence, eroticism and Manicheanism to please the audience . . . thus, people who like Ghibli may have a more reflective approach to animation." When a member of the list mentioned that "one of the most refreshing aspects of this movie *Spirited Away* is that Good and Evil are not delineated with simple and obvious cues that we often get from pop culture," a number of members leapt in to say that one of the attractions of Studio Ghibli offerings was the fact that they refuse to paint characters as purely good or purely evil. As one respondent said in another context, "Miyazaki's films contain too much ambiguity towards concepts of good and evil to be understood as recognizably didactic."

Clearly it is Miyazaki's and Takahata's willingness to entertain a worldview that acknowledges the ambiguity of life but at the same time exists within a moral framework that is one of MiyazakiWorld's major attractions. For example, David, in answer to another member's maintaining that "Christian themes abound in *Spirited Away*." asserted that "these themes are much older than Christianity itself" and cites "baptism/redemption/resurrection/temptation/healing/love" as being "all over the place in every religion and culture, popular stories, myths, legends, etc. What makes SA [*Spirited Away*] universal is precisely the fact that despite its very 'localized' settings and characters (everything is clearly by/for Japanese), it manages to tap into universal themes where everyone will recognize themselves."

Not all the discussion is on such an abstract level. One of the most passionate and emotionally resonant threads that I have seen occurred against the background of the beginning of the Iraq War, a war described by one member as "the elephant in the doorway throw[ing] a shadow on everything."

A young male student wrote to talk about his feelings of shame and powerlessness for being unable to do anything about the war beyond organizing teach-ins on his campus. In an affecting passage, he wrote, "Considering how Miyazaki's words are amongst those who have brought me to tears even before the bombs started falling, I wish Miyazaki could see these words." The response from the MML was swift and heartfelt. Laying aside their own personal politics, many of them framed their words of encouragement in terms of what they thought Miyazaki could offer. One respondent wrote the following:

> One of [Miyazaki]'s talents as a director and a writer is in his ability to make us examine our own views of the way things are, the way they should be and what we should do towards those ends. In *Princess Mononoke* the forest-god is killed despite the best efforts of the main characters. The death of the forest god resulted in a devastating catastrophe that looked as though it would undo all that was done in the course of the film. Yet his death ... was merely the beginning of a new era, with the promise of learning from the past and forging a new world.... The heroes don't always have to be the ones saving the world, they can be the ones that live every day doing for others what they would hope for themselves. Sacrifice isn't always glorious, but it is often necessary, and that is another Miyazaki lesson.

Another member responded, "The issue of power and powerlessness is an interesting one and perhaps there is even a Miyazaki connection to be made here ... we all have the ability to clean up some little corner of our world in some small way. We all have the ability to love. Mei and Kiki and Chihiro are not heroes because they have whole-heartedly devoted themselves to some giant CAUSE ... but because they do their best to be decent to those around them."

Akito, a member from Japan, recommended "a book of human's liberation" that Miyazaki had cited as an essential influence on him. Jonathan, who described himself as proud to be an American and an Italian, told him to "think about Nausicaa for a moment: Their valley was one of the few safe places on earth. They were surrounded by hostile nations. The toxic jungle was creeping up on them. Yet did they fear? No!"

Sharon, a long time member, went back to Miyazaki's own dialogue, telling the student that "in *Princess Mononoke* even with death happening all around them, even though San thought the world was over, Ashitaka corrected her that it was not over because they were still alive. Live like Ashitaka and see with eyes unclouded. He didn't regret being human, he didn't regret being cursed. Don't regret being who you are."

The responses of the fans described in this article reveal how the appeal of MiyazakiWorld becomes far more than enjoyable entertainment. While Miyazaki and Takahata may use specifically Japanese settings and (sometimes) characters, their themes and images are universal enough to touch people around the globe. In this they resemble other creators who have attracted great fandom, from J. R. R. Tolkien to J. K. Rowling of the *Harry Potter* series. More than Tolkien or Rowling, however, Miyazaki and Takahata revel in ambiguity and what might be considered a non-Western world view in which good and evil are not always clearly delineated, and the only appropriate response is to continue to look at the world "with eyes unclouded."

The fact that fans around the world find this viewpoint compelling suggests as much about the contemporary period as it does about Miyazaki. Roger Aden has suggested that fans sometimes appreciate fandom because it allows them to "break the rules," or at least offers an opportunity to see "how the rules limit us."[22] In the case of Miyazaki fans, particularly his Western ones, it is possible to speculate that Miyazaki's subtle and complex world view allows them to "break the rules" of Western culture, to go beyond the Hollywood happy endings, or the need for a defined good and evil, and embrace the world in all its ambiguity, heartbreak, and hope. By creating and interacting in their own "sacred space" on the Internet, the fans are able to produce a form of community which, in its emotional supportiveness, intellectual atmosphere, and passionate zeal to improve the world, ironically echoes the larger "sacred space" of MiyazakiWorld itself.

9

Conclusion:
From Fans to Fandom

A final vignette: It is September 2005. My daughter and I walk through the blazing summer heat of the old port town of Shimoda on Japan's Izu peninsula. In a sense this is where it all began. Shimoda is where in 1856 the first American consulate was established under a man named Townsend Harris. This was the beginning of Japan's return to full-fledged intercourse with the outside world and the beginning of the West's impressions of the country. Inevitably, there were problems as the two cultures began to deal with each other. One of Harris's interpreters was murdered by a samurai activist, enraged at what he considered to be Japan's capitulation to outside pressure. Harris himself engaged in a "romance" with one of the local women, Okichi, only to abandon her when he moved on to Edo. She died a broken alcoholic, scorned by her fellow countrymen.

One hundred and forty-nine years later, these stories have become the stuff of spectacle. My daughter and I visit Okichi's grave, hidden away in the temple shadows from the merciless sun, and head on to Ryosenji, the temple where the Treaty of Amity and Commerce, opening up the first Japanese ports, was concluded with Commodore Perry and the Japanese ambassador. There are very few tourists around, and the whole town seems eerily quiet. Down by the harbor, it is another matter, however. Sailing proudly on the azure blue waters is a gleaming ship, a replica of one of the Black Ships that formed Perry's small armada when he first forced his way into Japanese waters in 1853 and threatened the island with Western cannons. This ship, we discover when we board has no working weapons. It is a tourist ship designed for a harbor cruise on which one sees beautiful landmarks and tunes in to a few bits and pieces of history.

Once again we are in the space of fantasy and spectacle. In this case it is the Japanese who have converted an event of seismic geopolitical significance into a path to pleasure and play. This is no criticism. Rather, it is a source of hope when destroyers are transformed into pleasure ships, even if it has taken a century and a half to accomplish this.

When I first began the research for this book, I had several fundamental questions, the most salient being: what similarities existed between the Japanese popular-culture boom of our current millennium and the Japan waves that had occurred at other moments over the past 150 years? Was the recent rise of Japanese popular culture simply a result of "globalization," the product of a world in which technology made transcultural flows ridiculously easy at the same time as it created entertainment networks desperate for cultural product to feed the hungry desires of a world wide audience? In other words, is the current Japan wave a genuinely new phenomenon, or is it another, more contemporary version of "Japonisme"?

Perhaps inevitably, my answer is a qualified "yes" to both hypotheses. On the one hand, there are aspects of the present Japan boom that seem to me quite unique in that they could only have occurred in contemporary society. These elements include three major factors: the mass basis of the phenomenon, the speed and intensity at which the boom has spread, and the depth of its penetration, not simply geographically into most corners of the globe, but also psychologically into the minds and even identities of its most fervent adherents, the fans of anime and manga.

To examine these factors a little more closely, the "mass" culture that we now take for granted is largely a result of economic and technological growth that has allowed many more people more affluence and more leisure, while at the same time developing the technological instrumentalities (newspapers, radio, cinema, television, the Internet) to give them something to do with their time and money. It is highly doubtful that anime at least could ever have had the impact it achieved had it not been for the advent of the VCR, the DVD, and the Internet. Manga too, since it is dependent on translation, benefited from technology that allowed enthusiasts to obtain their favorite manga from Japan (sometimes over the Internet), scan it into their computers at home, and access multiple dictionaries and other information sites to help with the actual translation.

Speed and accessibility are also of course highly dependent on the technology that allows fans virtually instant access to their fan objects. Even though Tokyo is six thousand miles away, fans are now able to download yesterday's episode of Japan's most popular anime in a matter of minutes. When Gabriel, the yaoi fan interviewed in Chapter 5, mentioned his need for "instant gratification," his humorous self-deprecation had an element of truth. Fans no longer have to wait months for their favorite titles to become available.

Not only are anime and manga speedily available, but the fan can now share his or her pleasure (or complaints) online and around the world. This brings me to the third factor, that of depth of penetration. Geographically this means that anime and manga can be found all over the world from South Africa to Russia. As Yulia Mikhailova relates, manga and anime were virtually unknown in Russia until the 1990s. As Internet use spread among college students, Russian fans (who also called themselves otaku) were able to find each other and share their enthusiasm.[1]

With the Internet, anime and manga fans no longer need to feel alone. Through technology they can easily find each other, enjoy each other's opinions, and, as we saw in the chapter on Miyazaki fandom, support each other through emotionally tumultuous moments. When I began my research into anime, many interviewees told me that they felt very much isolated in their hobby, fearing that if they mentioned their fandom their peers would tease them. Although that aspect still exists to some extent, most fans seem more and more willing to proclaim their interests. This is partly a chicken-and-egg issue—the more the number of fans increases, the more they feel comfortable acknowledging their fandom—but the Internet is also responsible for giving them a new level of security. As Tran, the head of Drama Queen, says, "The Internet gives you a really sheltered vision of how many people are interested in [*yaoi*]."

The increasing presence of the virtual and the simulated in modern society may also be considered one of the factors in the increasing acceptance of anime and manga. The younger generation in particular is used to being a part of a world in which the boundaries between real and unreal are increasingly permeable. As we saw in Chapter 7, anime and manga fans are genuinely willing to identify with anime and manga characters on a deep and personal level. Thus, they are not only appropriating aspects of another culture for purposes of pleasure, but they are also integrating them into their identities as well.

Ironically, the world that technology has brought about—from cyborgs to nuclear apocalypse—may also be one of the reasons behind anime's popularity. Although as we have seen, anime and manga range across a vast amount of thematic material, science fiction and fantasy are among the most important genres and are particularly beloved among Western fans. As I argue elsewhere, fantasy and science fiction are especially appropriate genres for exploring and illuminating the chaotic events, rapid changes, and shifting identities that characterize the contemporary world.[2] It is perhaps no coincidence that after the events of 9/11, anime and manga fandom increased all the more. Anime and manga, such as *Akira*, *Neon Genesis Evangelion*, and *Nausicaa of the Valley of the Wind*, all engage directly with apocalyptic themes in ways that can be simultaneously haunting, disturbing, and uplifting. At the very least, however, they allow viewers and readers to engage with and perhaps even work through their own nightmares of catastrophe.[3] Furthermore, the popularity in the West of such anime cyberpunk science-fiction narratives as *Ghost in the Shell* (ironically, inspired partly by *Blade Runner*) or *Serial Experiments Lain* attest to the fact that anime and manga help us to work through our fear concerning technological change and human isolation as well.

On the other hand, there are also clear links between the current Japan boom and those that have gone before. It is useful to consider what "globalization" actually means. As Anthony Hopkins defines it, "Globalization involves the extension, intensification and quickening velocity of flows of people, products and ideas that shape the world. It integrates regions and continents; it compresses time and space; it prompts imitations and resistance. The results alter and may even transform relationships with and among states and societies across the globe."[4] Hopkins also goes on to point out that "it is not simply the result of a dominant center activating lesser peripheries, but is jointly produced by all parties to the process."

By this definition, it is obvious that we live in a globalizing world, but it is less obvious that this world or this period is unique. In one sense, "globalization" has been going on since human beings started to migrate. Even if we discount early migration or trade routes such as the Silk Road, surely the advent of the clipper ship in the nineteenth century followed by the steamship, the train, and the airplane (not to mention the overwhelming engine of imperialism itself) were all crucial agents in promoting the extension, intensification, and quickening velocity of flows of people, products, and ideas throughout the world. It may be argued that technology has enormously changed the speed of globalization, but I believe that it is also arguable that the nineteenth century was also undergoing its own globalization process, perhaps more slowly but with perhaps at least as many changes and challenges as we confront today.

One of these changes was the beginnings of mass culture as, in Europe and America, the middle class began to grow and with it, a culture of consumption. However, the mass culture that we talk about today has an infinitely broader geographical and social reach. It touched virtually anyone with access to a radio or the department stores and arcades that stocked the "millions" of fans, paper lanterns, and kimono fabrics, guaranteeing that the Japan boom went well beyond the elite—such as the Goncourt brothers and the bohemian society of the Impressionists and their descendants—to reach any consumer (especially perhaps the female consumer who was beginning to have more power by this period) with a little money and a desire to have something different on the walls of their front parlor.

Newspapers and journals (such as *Artistic Japan*) and particularly their advertisements helped spread the interest in Japan, if not as quickly as the Internet, still rapidly enough in urban areas that many types of people quickly became aware of the new "craze." We remember the description of how the initial Japan craze spread "like gunpowder to a lighted match," obviously an exaggeration but one that suggests how rapidly fads could develop even more than a century ago. Finally, we have seen how the great expositions and world's fairs provided a site of spectacle and pleasure where millions of ordinary people could see, touch, and even taste Japan.

We can see that in certain ways, Japonisme and the current fascination with Japanese culture are not so dissimilar from each other. But what about the third major element—depth of penetration, especially on a psychological level? Given what we have seen of the strong degree of identification and engagement on the part of anime and manga fans, it seems safe to conclude that contemporary aficionados of Japanese popular culture are not only appropriating it, but also integrating it into their own lives, sometimes at quite a profound level. Can we say the same of the enthusiasts of the nineteenth and twentieth centuries?

The answer to this is a bit complicated. On the one hand, it seems reasonable to say that most of those caught up in Japonisme, from the artists who were influenced by it, to the middle classes who consumed cheap Japanese decorations, primarily regarded Japan as an exotic visual source of pleasure and aesthetic inspiration. Furthermore, compared to the highly participatory and grassroots nature of contemporary fandom, earlier Japan booms may seem less interactive. Yet we should remember that even at the beginning of Japonisme, aficionados were grouping together for dinners and events revolving around a shared love of things Japanese that involved a genuinely creative level of participation. We might also remember Frank Lloyd Wright's "print parties," where he actively used the prints as teaching materials for his disciples. Most importantly, it should be emphasized that in this case, "aesthetic inspiration" had ultimately revolutionary significance to Western art. As should be clear from Chapter 1, the discovery of Japanese art would change the colors, designs, compositions, and subject material of Western artists forever. Ultimately, as I have argued, it ushered in a new way of approaching reality that may not be totally different from the way Japanese animation and manga have begun to affect contemporary notions of the real.

At this point in the nineteenth century, however, such revolutionary changes were restricted to artists. What about the middle-class European or American? Besides the pleasure of collecting and decorating, it is also true that there was a vogue for dressing up in Japanese clothing for reasons of fashion or to appear in tableaux vivants. But the reasons here do not seem to have much to do with identification with another culture so much as the sheer joy of reveling in the beautiful fabrics and designs of the Far East (and sometimes the Middle East and India, as well). This is not to discount the enjoyment of the visual. As we have said, pleasure is an important component in the West's approach to Japan, but we cannot say that these enthusiasms changed the values or philosophy of the average middle-class person.

There are major exceptions to this last statement, however, and they are worth remembering. We have seen how Van Gogh and Hearn idealized and at certain points identified with Japan to the point of affecting how they lived and reacted to the world. The fact that their idealizations were in some ways mistaken does not mean that the influence was any less profound. Japan gave them hope, inspiration, and comfort, at least for a time, and galvanized them to make changes in their lives of great importance.

Japanese religion in the form of Buddhism and Zen Buddhism in particular has also affected the lives of many Westerners on a deep level. Again, there were undoubtedly inaccuracies in the way Westerners understood Japanese religion, but it is clear that millions of Americans and Europeans over the last century found in Buddhism a source of genuine enlightenment and spiritual solace. We can remember Monet's ethereal water lilies with their vision of nature melting into infinity, or Kerouac and Snyder's vision of a "Dharma revolution." Even though Kerouac ultimately retreated from Buddhism, his dissemination of the religion affected the lives and world view of hundreds of thousands of young Americans from the 1960s onward. Snyder himself seems to have been able to integrate Buddhism into his life and poetry in a creative and organic fashion.

Perhaps the fundamental question concerning today's aficionados of Japanese popular culture and those who went before them is, how important is Japan in relation to anime and manga fandom? Are the fans thinking about Japan when they read manga, go to cons, or dress in costume? When I started my research, I assumed that the answer would be "not very," assuming that most enthusiasts were consuming these products of Japanese culture simply because they enjoyed their special qualities without thinking much about the country that produced them.

To my surprise, however, I discovered that the "Japaneseness" of anime and manga (if not perhaps Hello Kitty or other cute characters) was an essential aspect of the media's appeal to many fans. Of course this is not true in every case,[5] but as we have seen in the previous chapters, the number of fans who study Japanese, read up on Japanese history, and travel to Japan (or wish they could) is surprisingly high. While some idealize Japan in certain regards, on the whole I found their impressions and expectations of the country to be quite realistic.

At the same time, it must be acknowledged that anime and manga, while they contain and express strong Japanese elements, are also media that are inherently separated from the "reality" of even live-action film and television. The characters in anime and manga are both "Japanese" and at the same time "nationless." Or, more accurately, they belong to the world of animation and caricature, of fantasy and unreality to the highest degree. Thus, when a non-Japanese enjoys or identifies with a character, he is identifying within a highly distinctive fantasyscape that combines elements of "real" Japan within a cartoon imaginary. Again, we can perhaps say that the nineteenth-century Japonisants were engaging with an imaginary world of woodblock prints, or the readers of Waley's translation of Genji were entering the imagination of a long dead woman writer.

As I argued in Chapter 7, however, the media of cartoon and animation seem to me to be particularly interesting in terms of the identificatory process. Because of the relative lack of ethnic, national, and sometimes gender characteristics and the lack of limitations of the laws of the physical and material, the world of animation and manga seems to me to be a uniquely emancipating one. The fans who enter into it are not necessarily trying to "become" Japanese in the sense that Hearn and Van Gogh were. Rather they are participating in what may be a genuinely new and unique culture, one that may become increasingly salient as the century continues. Freed from material constraints, anime and manga offer an endless of array of possibilities to a world that seems increasingly fettered by the intractable realities of ethnic, religious, and national identifications. Anime and manga are truly sites of play, in the best sense of the term, where participants can engage on the most creative of levels.

The idea of "play" in relation to the realities of cultural identifications returns us to Said's theory of Orientalism. We have seen in various episodes throughout this book that Japan's relations with the West have indeed included classically "Orientalist" moments in which Japan has been clearly treated as the submissive, racially and culturally inferior Other, most obviously in the Allied propaganda of World War II. More subtly, but equally stereotypically, Japan became the mysterious, threatening, and "sneaky" Other to many Americans during the trade wars of the 1970s and 1980s. But, as I hope this book has demonstrated, Japan has also served (perhaps also stereotypically) as a model of a superior culture, from the aesthetic admiration heaped on it in the nineteenth century by the Western cultural elite to the fascination with Japanese business and society that surfaced during Japan's period of unprecedented economic success.

It is the current Japan boom, however, that most intriguingly complicates Said's argument, returning us to the question of how important "Japan" is in relation to this particular historic moment. In a sense, anime and manga fandom can be seen as a transcultural hybrid resulting from new technologies and an increasingly globalized world, one that spans not only geographic cultures but also the cultures of the "real" versus the "simulated" or the "virtual." Japan is a crucial element of this hybrid, but it is an element that is part of a larger imaginary, that of animation and cartoon and perhaps fantasy in general. It is certainly conceivable that anime and manga, as they become increasingly part of the global marketplace, may even begin to lose some of their more distinctively "Japanese" elements.

In that case, what can we say about Japan's place in the Western imagination in the twenty-first century? It is certainly safe to say that Japan remains a very strong presence in terms of its soft power. Anime and manga are not only popular in themselves, but have influenced and affected Western artists as well. The most famous example of this is the Wachowski Brothers' film trilogy of *The Matrix*, which, as they themselves acknowledge, was inspired partly by the Mamoru Oshii anime *Ghost in the Shell* (in itself as mentioned, owing a debt to Ridley Scott's *Blade Runner*). But there are many other examples worthy of mention. Some artists clearly see animation as a medium that can express things more dramatically and more creatively than live action. Linkin Park's intense and disturbing music video, *Breaking the Habit*, for example, shows a suicidal jump from a building to a car in reverse, underlining the despairing tension and passion of the song's lyrics. Quentin Tarantino's landmark film *Kill Bill (1)* uses an extended anime sequence (as with Linkin Park, created by a Japanese animator) to show what was an exceptionally bloody and violent sequence, even for a Tarantino film. Through his use of animation, Tarantino was able to create a visual symphony of violence that would surely have been unwatchable had it been filmed in live action.

Anime and manga inspire in term of content and character as well. Some of the fanfiction I have read is as good as anything put out by major publishing houses, with three dimensional characters, quirky situations, and highly imaginative plot lines. I will also never forget an extraordinarily moving antiwar music and anime video that was built around carefully chosen scenes from *Neon Genesis Evangelion*. On the "high culture" plane, Linda Stein, a New York sculptor, creates provocative and inspiring female figures based on the heroine of Miyazaki's blockbuster film, *Princess Mononoke*. The Japanese artist Takashi Murakami, whose famous "superflat" movement, based partly on anime and manga design and characters and partly on traditional Japanese aesthetics,[6] has created great excitement in the world of Western artists.

Japan itself is still an important subject for movie makers. *Kill Bill* also includes some stunning live-action sequences set in Japan, or rather the "Japan" familiar to Tarantino from martial arts films or anime. Other recent films such as *The Last Samurai* and *Memoirs of a Geisha* show that traditional Japanese stereotypes are alive and well. Although visually stunning, neither film unfortunately goes much beyond these stereotypes to create nuanced characters, preferring instead to indulge in the myth of the noble, tragic samurai[7] and the geisha as the embodiment of feminine mystery and eroticism.

Two other recent films, however, have given a more thought-provoking picture of modern Japan. Though far from adulatory, Sophia Coppola's *Lost in Translation* (2003) and Alejandro Inarritu's *Babel* (2006) at least show a reasonably realistic complex view of a modern society in which human connection is extremely hard to achieve. Not totally dissimilar from William Gibon's cyberpunk extrapolations, Japan in these films seems to epitomize the ultimate in alienated modernity, symbolized with haunting intensity by the young deaf girl in *Babel* who can only connect through her desperate sexuality. Although, on the one hand, the equation of the sexual with a Japanese women (none of the other female characters in the film are depicted in this manner) seems to echo the tendency discussed in Chapter 4 to eroticize the Japanese female, the character in *Babel* is shown with subtle three dimensionality as a deeply human and vulnerable young woman.

The depiction of the male characters is also interesting. Far from being the supermen depicted in *Rising Sun*, the Japanese in these two films (especially *Babel*) come across as conflicted and sometimes impotent human beings. As my former colleague, Nancy Stalker, points out, it is interesting that in *Lost in Translation*, one of the male characters introduces himself as "Charlie Brown," the pathetic character from the comic strip *Peanuts*. Fascinatingly, as she also points out, there is another "Charlie Brown" character in *Kill Bill* as well.

Perhaps what is most intriguing about both *Babel* and *Lost in Translation* is how Japan's role seems to be to exemplify urban technological society in sometimes very grim form. While the American characters in *Lost in Translation*, who are the film's real focus, are shown occasionally looking for "traditional Japan" in the form of shrines and ikebana, their relationship mainly takes place against a Japan that is a clearly modern, technologized society. Seen through the characters' eyes, Japan is efficient, beautifully put together, and yet somehow empty. This is even more the case with *Babel*, in which the Japanese characters seem, even more than the American couple played by Brad Pitt and Cate Blanchett, to epitomize all the most alienating aspects of contemporary society, from the disaffection between the generations to a perverse sexuality that offers no hope of genuine human connection.

Whether this will continue to be Japan's image throughout the next century is impossible to know. What does seem definite is that Japan's soft power is here to stay. Once again we return to the questions asked at the beginning of this book, which might be summed up as, Why Japan (as opposed to other non-Western countries)? By now, some of the answers may be discernable, but it is worth looking at them from a long-term perspective.

It seems to me that Japan's comparatively more equal status vis-à-vis the West was based on two interconnected forces—hard power and soft power. The importance of Japan's hard power in relation to that of any other non-Western country cannot be overestimated. As we saw, even from the beginning of the Japonisme craze, commentators were aware that the Japanese were not only bringing their arts, but also their intelligence, their curiosity, and their warships into the West. Japan's subsequent military victories and imperialist expansion provoked not only racist reactions, but also a respect and admiration very different from the condescension experienced by the colonized non-West. The postwar era in which Japanese economic power became a dominating factor in its relationship with the West was another example in which Japan (until the other East Asian nations began to catch up) again provoked admiration (although again mixed with racism and resentment).

Japan was thus a force to be reckoned with from very early on in its relations with the West. Westerners might inveigh against them, implement racist laws (such as the American immigration acts of the early twentieth century), and demonize them during World War II, but the fact was that Japan was not going away. Nowadays, the world looks to China with some of the mixed feelings that Japan once provoked, but at this point, it is China's military and economic strength, rather than its extraordinary civilization, that is the dominant image in the Western mind.

In contrast, Japan was able to maintain its image as a cultural force throughout its period of military and industrial strength. The reasons for this are both simple and complex. Part of it was timing. As we have seen, at one point Europeans and Americans saw in Japan and its "artistic" and "nature-loving culture" an escape from the deepening bleakness of industrialized society. Furthermore, the burgeoning of mass culture in the form of the new middle class and new consumption patterns favored the export of exotic but appealing Japanese goods that found their way into houses across both Europe and the United States. Aided by astute Japanese scholars and promoters, Japanese culture seemed both appealingly different but also accessible. In the twentieth century, Zen Buddhism, aided again by Japanese promotion, helped appeal to another generation of Westerners disaffected from modern life. Finally, in the contemporary period, the cuteness of Japanese toys offers comfort in an alienating age, while anime and manga, with their sophisticated but humane explorations of technological and environmental tragedy and apocalyptic trauma, offer not simply an escape, but a chance to work through contemporary concerns in ways that are both memorable and pleasurable.

We return once again to the concepts of "pleasure" and "play." While Japanese culture also offers philosophical thought and artistry of grandeur, in some ways it also offers particularly accessible forms of pleasure. It is worth noting that the woodblock prints that spearheaded the artistic revolution in the West were very much popular cultural products in their native land. Zen, at least in the terms that the West learned about it, seemed to have more to do with intuition, love of nature, and poetic anecdotes, rather than the challenging texts of other religions. Japanese literature from *Genji* on is world renowned not for its epic depictions of society, but for its extraordinary lyric beauty and its subtle and moving explorations of human psychology. Both these aspects, I would submit, are on display in anime and manga, as well as a sophisticated and attractive visual aesthetic.

At the risk of essentializing, then, I would suggest that in an industrialized world that increasingly privileges pleasure and the inner self as opposed to the martial, the civic, or the epic, Japanese culture works particularly well. The permeabilities of the boundary between the material and the fantasy, the concrete and the unreal, hinted at in Japanese art's influence on the West, explored in terms of the higher truths sought in Buddhism, and literalized in Japanese animation, also appear to have struck a chord at just the right moment. As Western thought turns away from Cartesian reality to embrace the uncertainties and flexibilities of a world with fewer and fewer master narratives, Japanese culture, with its tolerance of ambiguity and ephemerality, might be a particularly apt vehicle with which to confront the complexities of the current period.

Love of Japan also brought aficionados together. From the dinner parties in nineteenth-century Paris to the cons in twenty-first-century America, Japanese cultural products inspired moments of community throughout the West and beyond. Perhaps the most distinctive collectivity of interests at the moment is the yaoi community where fans are brought together to explore new ways of communicating, playing, and living. We began this book with a portrait of a woman, Monet's wife, dressed in a kimono. We know what Monet thought of Japan and Japonisme, but what did she think? Was her participation in the portrait a form of play or simply a kindness to her husband? Certainly her slightly flirtatious smile as she stares out at us suggest that she is enjoying the experience. What would she have thought of the young women translators who work in the yaoi community, or the women who spend weeks developing their costumes to parade in at the cons? We will never know, but we might guess that she would welcome their enthusiasm, their enjoyment, and their participation in a world that allows the potential to interact on many levels with a culture that might have begun as unfamiliar and Other but is now increasingly part of our own—a harbinger of genuine interactivity and interconnectedness in an increasingly globalizing world.

Notes

Introduction

1. Ronald Inden, *Imaginging India* (Bloomington: Indiana University Press, 1990), 68–69.
2. Jean Laplanche and J. B. Pontalis, quoted in James Donald, ed., *Fantasy Cinema* (London: British Film Institute, 1989), 6 passim.
3. Some of the most interesting critiques of Said include Aijaz Ahmad, "*Orientalism* and After: Ambivalence and Metropolitan Location in the Work of Edward Said," in *In Theory: Classes Nations, Literatures*, Aijaz Ahmad, ed. (London: Verson, 1992), 159–219; Rey Chow, *Writing Diaspora: Tactics of Intervention in Contemporary Cultural Studies* (Indianapolis: Indiana University Press), 1993; and J. J. Clarke, *Oriental Enlightenment: The Encounter Between Asian and Western Thought* (London: Routledge, 1997). Ronald Inden and Breckinridge and van der Veer extend Orientalism to South Asian Studies in, respectively, Ronald Inden, *Imagined India* (Bloomington: Indiana University Press, 1990); and Breckenridge and van der Veer, *Orientalism and the Postcolonial Predicament* (Philadelphia: University of Pennsylvania Press, 1993).
4. Susan Pointon, "Transcultural Orgasm as Apocalypse: Urotsukidoji; The Legend of the Overfiend," *Wide Angle* 19, no. 3 (July 1997): 45.
5. Joseph Nye, *Soft Power: The Means to Success in World Politics* (Cambridge, MA: Public Affairs, 2004), 5.
6. Roger Owen, quoted in Zachary Lockman, *Contending Visions of the Middle East: The History and Politics of Orientalism* (Cambridge: Cambridge University Press, 2004), 183.
7. Edward Said, *Orientalism* (New York: Vintage Books, 1978), 42.
8. Clarke, *Oriental Enlightenment*, 209.
9. John M. MacKenzie, *Orientalism, History Theory and the Arts* (Manchester: Manchester University Press, 1995), 126–27.
10. Said, *Orientalism*, 25.
11. Clarke, *Oriental Enlightenment*, 9.
12. Mihaly Csikszentmihalyi, *Flow* (New York: Harper Perennial, 1990), 3.
13. Camille Pissarro, February 27, 1895, letter to his son Lucien, in John Rewald, ed., *Camille Pissarro: Letters to His Son Lucien* (Boston: MFA, 2002), 207.

14. Arjun Appadurai, *Modernity at Large: Cultural Dimensions of Globalization* (Minneapolis: University of Minnesota Press, 1996), 33

15. MacKenzie, *Orientalism*, 89.

16. Ibid., 77.

17. Matt Hills, *Fan Cultures* (London: Routledge, 2002), 90.

18. Ibid., 111.

19. Ronald Inden, *Imaginedg India* (Bloomington: Indiana University Press, 1990), 38.

20. For example Brian Reading, a British economist, writes in his book *The Coming Collapse* about the "Hara Kiri Economy," using language of a rather extreme kind, such as describing Japan's "grotesque" tax system or calling Japanese democracy a "monstrosity" (*Japan: The Coming Collapse* [London: Orion Books, 1992], 286). While these are certainly attention-getting terms, one cannot help wondering whether Reading would have used them concerning another European nation.

21. Andrew Leonard, "Heads Up, Mickey," *Wired* 3, no. 4 (April): 1995.

22. Christopher Benfey, *The Great Wave: Gilded Age Misfits, Japanese Eccentrics and The Opening of Old Japan* (New York: Random House, 2002), 104.

23. Ibid., 245.

24. Koichi Iwabuchi, *Recentering Globalization: Popular culture and Japanese Transnationalism* (Durham, NC: Duke University Press, 2002), 7.

25. Jennifer Robertson, *Takarazuka: Sexual Politics and Popular Culture in Modern Japan* (Berkeley: University of California Press, 1998), 98.

Chapter 1

1. The title of this chapter is from the late nineteenth-century novelist, Joseph Conrad. Conrad was linked to modernism and his work was also occasionally described as "Impressionistic." In using this particular quotation, I wish to underline my argument that Japanese art was one of the major factors in the nineteenth century that helped to change the way Western artists "saw" the world.

2. Virginia Spate and Gary Hickey, "Monet and Japan," exhibition catalogue from the National Gallery of Australia (London: Thames and Hudson, 2001), 4–5.

3. Eric Hobsbawm, *The Age of Capital: 1848–1875* (New York: Vintage, 1975), 271.

4. G. d'Olby, quoted in "Monet and Japan," 202.

5. Marius Chamelin, quoted in ibid., 202.

6. Charles Bigot, quoted in ibid., 202.

7. Simon Boubee, quoted in ibid., 23

8. Ibid., 202.

9. Spate and Hickey, "Monet and Japan," 22.

10. Lionel Lambourne, *Japonisme: Cultural Crossings between East and West* (New York: Phaidon, 2005), 116.

11. Ibid., 111.

12. Eliza Rathbone and Johanna Halford-Macleod, *Art Beyond Isms: Masterworks from El Greco to Picasso in the Phillips Collection* (London: Third Millennium, 2002), 120.

13. Spate and Hickey, "Monet and Japan," 25.

14. Oscar Wilde, *The Decay of Lying*, in *The Complete Works of Oscar Wilde* (New York: Doubleday, 1923), 22, 54–53.

15. Ernest Chesneau, "Le Japon à Paris," *Gazette des Beaux Arts* 18 (1878): 385 (my translation).

16. Ibid., 386.

17. Ibid., 387.

18. Ibid.

19. Ibid., 391.

20. Ibid., 393.

21. Ibid., 387.

22. Siegfried Wichmann, *Japonisme: The Japanese Influence on Western Art since 1858* (London: Thames and Hudson, 1981), 19.

23. Gabriel Weisberg, Introduction to *The Origins of Art Nouveau: The Bing Empire*, ed. Weisberg, Becker, and Posseme (Ithaca, NY: Cornell Univerisity Press, 2005), 18.

24. Wichmann, *Japonisme*, 9.

25. Wiesberg, "The Creation of Japonisme," in *The Origins of Art Nouveau*, 52.

26. Edmond de Goncourt, quoted in Lewis Galanteane, ed., *The Goncourt Journals* (New York: Doubleday, 1937), 265.

27. Ibid., 120.

28. Edmund de Goncourt, quoted in Becker and Phillips, trans., *The Goncourt Journal: Paris and the Arts* (Ithaca, NY: Cornell University Press, 1971), 83–84.

29. Ibid., 157–58.

30. Ibid., 238.

31. Chesneau, "Le Japon à Paris," 387–88.

32. Ibid., 388.

33. Wiesberg, "A Family Affair," in Weisberg, Becker, and Posseme, eds., *The Origins of Art Nouveau*, 16.

34. Weisberg, "The Creation of Japonisme," in Weisberg, Becker, and Posseme, eds., *The Origins of Art Nouveau*, 45.

35. Ibid., 59–60.

36. *Artistic Japan* 1, no. 6 (1888): n.p. These quotations come from the "List of plates" at the end of the journal on unnumbered pages.

37. Siegfried Bing, "The Japanese as Decorators," *Artistic Japan* 1 (1888): 4.

38. Ary Renan, "Hokusai's Mang-wa," *Artistic Japan* 9 (1888): 3.

39. Ibid., 88.

40. Ibid., 89.

41. Ibid.

42. Ibid., 90.

43. Renan, "Hokusai's Mang-wa," 100.

44. Spate and Hickey, "Monet and Japan," 2.

45. Ronald Pickvance, *Van Gogh in Arles* (New York: Harry Abrams, 1984), 282–83.

46. Ibid., 283.
47. Spate and Hickey, "Monet and Japan," 11.
48. Claude Monet, quoted in Lambourne, *Japonisme*, 48.
49. Jules de Goncourt, quoted in "Monet and Japan," 5.
50. Spate and Hickey, "Monet and Japan," 37.
51. John House, *Monet: Nature into Art* (New Haven, CT: Yale University Press, 1986), 59.
52. Ibid.
53. Ibid.
54. Spate and Hickey, "Monet and Japan," 55.
55. Ibid., 57.
56. Ibid.
57. Ibid, 60.
58. Debora Silverman, *Van Gogh and Gauguin: The Search for Sacred Art* (New York: Farrar, Strauss and Giroux, 2000), 36.
59. Ibid., 39
60. Ibid., 43.
61. Vincent Van Gogh in a letter to his brother Theo, in *The Complete Letters of Vincent Van Gogh*, vol. 3 (Greenwich, CT: New York Graphic Society), 55.
62. Gauguin, quoted in Silverman, *Van Gogh and Gauguin*, 32.
63. Van Gogh in a letter to his brother Theo, in *The Complete Letters*, 66.
64. Van Gogh in a letter to his sister, in *The Complete Letters*, 443.
65. Van Gogh quoted in Derek Fell, *Van Gogh's Women: His Love Affairs and Journey into Madness* (New York: Carrol and Graf, 2004), 116.
66. Rathbone and Halford-Macleod, *Art Beyond Isms*, 132.
67. Elisa Evett, *The Critical Reception of Japanese Art in Late Nineteenth Century Europe* (Ann Arbor, MI: UMI Press, 1982), xv.
68. Ibid.
69. Ibid., 104.
70. Van Gogh, quoted in Naomi Maurer, *The Pursuit of Spiritual Wisdom: The Thought and Art of Vinent Van Gogh and Paul Gauguin* (Cranbury, NJ: Associated University Presses, 1998), 3.
71. Emile Bernard, quoted in Maurer, *The Pursuit of Spiritual Wisdom*, 3; emphasis original.
72. Ibid., 4.
73. Eric Hobsbawm, *The Age of Capital 1848–1875* (New York: Vintage, 1975), 253.
74. Ibid., 254

Chapter 2

1. John Berendt, *The City of Falling Angels* (New York: Penguin, 2005), 149.
2. Christopher Benfey, *The Great Wave: Gilded Age Misfits, Japanese Eccentrics and the Opening of Old Japan* (New York: Random House, 2003), 48.
3. Ibid., 109.
4. Lafcadio Hearn, *Glimpses of Unfamiliar Japan* (London: Jonathan Cape, 1927), 37.

5. Ibid.
6. Wm. Roger Louis, *Ends of British Imperialism: The Scramble for Empire, Suez, and Decolonization* (London: I. B. Tauris, 2006), 39.
7. Ayako Hotta-Lister, *The Japan-British Exposition of 1910: Gateway to the Island Empire of the East* (Richmond, VA: Japan Library, 1999), 201; emphasis added.
8. Christine M. E. Guth, *Longfellow's Tattoos* (Seattle: University of Washington Press, 2004), 30.
9. Ibid.
10. The story of Charley Longfellow's obsession with Japan is a fascinating one. There is even, as with Hearn, a hint of the modern day otaku in his concern for collecting, dressing in Japanese costume, and creating what Guth calls "a private world." Guth, *Longfellow's Tattoos*, 187.
11. Beatrice and Sydney Webb, quoted in John Walter de Gruchy, *Orienting Arthur Waley: Japonism, Orientalism, and the Creation of Japanese Literature in English* (Honolulu: University of Hawaii Press, 2003), 41.
12. When *The Mikado* was revived yet again for a performance in London in the 1990s, the "gentlemen of Japan" were dressed as "city gentlemen" (i.e., stockbrokers, bond traders, bankers, and the like) all wearing identical suits and bowler hats. Although not as colorful as the conventional kimono-clad ensemble of traditional *Mikado* performances, these modern "gentlemen" effectively conveyed how differently Japan was perceived at the end of the twentieth century in contrast to the previous century.
13. Carol Ann Christ, "The Sole Guardians of the Art Inheritance of Asia: Japan and China at the 1904 St. Louis World's Fair," *positions* 8, no. 3 (2000): 676.
14. Robert Rydell, *All the World's a Fair* (Chicago: University of Chicago Press, 1984), 4.
15. Christ, "The Sole Guardians," 675.
16. Ibid., 680.
17. Quoted in Paul Greenhalgh, *Ephemeral Vistas: The Expositions Universelles, Great Exhibitions and World's Fairs, 1851–1939* (Manchester: University of Manchester Press, 1988), 96–97. The quote is taken from John MacKenzie, *Propaganda and Empire: The Manipulation of British Public Opinion, 1880–1960* (Manchester: University of Manchester Press, 1985). According to Greenhalgh, phrenology was so popular that there were even mass consumption magazines devoted to it.
18. Hotta-Lister, *The Japan-British Exposition of 1910*.
19. Ibid., 61.
20. Ibid., 92.
21. Ibid., 130.
22. Ibid., 121.
23. Lafcadio Hearn, *Glimpses of Unfamiliar Japan* (Tokyo: Charles E. Tuttle, 1976), 9.
24. Ibid., 8.
25. Ibid.
26. Hearn, *Glimpses of Unfamiliar Japan*, 9.
27. Steven Caton, *Lawrence of Arabia: A Film's Anthropology* (Berkeley: University of California Press, 1999), 148.

28. In fact, as a number of commentators point out, while Hearn could be critical of the Japanese, he was never arrogant and often criticized other Westerners for what Dawson describes as their "cultural blindness." Carl Dawson, *Lafcadio Hearn and the Vision of Japan* (Baltimore: Johns Hopkins University Press, 1992), 35.

29. Benfey, *The Great Wave*, 217.

30. Jean Temple, *Blue Ghost: A Study of Lafcadio Hearn* (New York: Jonathan Cape, 1931), 16.

31. Hearn, *Kokoro* (Boston: Charles Tuttle, 1972), 208.

32. Undoubtedly in "The Conservative," Hearn is also projecting his own opinions and revelations onto the Japanese character and, on a deeper level, his identification with a person in exile from his own culture. It is perhaps not surprising that one of his favorite Japanese legends was the legend of Urashima Taro, a kind of Japanese Rip Van Winkle, but without the happy ending. For when Urashima returns after a three-hundred-year enchanted sojourn, he opens a casket that causes him to age and dies immediately. In one essay, Hearn writes about returning to his favorite city of Matsue and recognizing his own visage in an aged Urashima Taro mask worn by a woman whom he had asked to dance the legend of Urashima Taro for him (Dawson, *Lafcadio Hearn*, 28).

33. Ibid., 17.

34. Russell W. Belk, *Collecting in a Consumer Society* (London: Routledge, 1995), 90.

35. Dawson, *Lafcadio Hearn*, 152.

36. Hearn, *Glimpses of Unfamiliar Japan*, 2.

37. Ibid., 8.

38. Ibid.

39. See Isabella Bird, *Unbeaten Tracks in Japan*. Bird's experiences are interesting to compare with those of the many male adventurers who came to Japan during this period. Another interesting recollection of Japan by a female Westerner may be seen in *Clara's Diary*, written by an American woman who married a Japanese man (ed. M. William Steele).

40. Benfey, *The Great Wave*, 93.

41. Susan Stewart, *On Longing: Narratives of the Miniature, the Gigantic, the Souvenir* (Durham, NC: Duke University Press, 1993), 112.

42. Ibid.

43. Ibid., 113.

44. Quoted in Beongchon Yu, *An Ape of the Gods: The Art and Thought of Lafcadio Hearn* (Detroit: Wayne State University Press 1964), 189.

45. Lafcadio Hearn, *Japan: An Attempt at Interpretation* (Rutland, VT: Tuttle, 1955), 14–15, 33.

46. De Gruchy, *Orienting Arthur Waley*, 57.

47. Arthur Waley, quoted in Ivan Morris, ed., *Madly Singing in the Mountains: An Appreciation and Anthology of Arthur Waley* (London: George Allen and Unwin, 1970), 133.

48. Carmen Blacker, "Intent of Courtesy," in Morris, ed., *Madly Singing*, 24.

49. Hubert Waley, "Letter to Ivan Morris" in Morris, ed., *Madly Singing*, 124.

50. Alison Waley, "Letter to Ivan Morris" in Morris, ed., *Madly Singing*, 115.

51. Ibid., 116.

52. De Gruchy, *Orienting Arthur Waley*, 119.

53. "The Saturday Review," quoted in De Gruchy, *Orienting Arthur Waley*, 126.

54. De Gruchy, *Orienting Arthur Waley*, 152.

55. Earl Miner, *The Japanese Tradition in British and American Literature* (Princeton, NJ: Princeton University Press, 1958), 63.

56. Review of the first volume of *The Tale of Genji* (1925), in *The New Republic*, quoted in De Gruchy, *Orienting Arthur Waley*, 127.

57. Ibid., 120.

58. Conrad Aiken, quoted in Miner, *The Japanese Tradition*, 183.

59. Ibid., 114.

60. Transcript of a party talk recorded by Wright's secretary, Eugene Masselink, quoted in Julia Meech, *Frank Lloyd Wright and the Art of Japan: The Architect's Other Passion* (New York: Harry N. Abrams, 2001), 231.

61. Vincent Scully Jr., *Frank Lloyd Wright* (New York: George Brazillier, 1960), quoted in Meech, *Frank Lloyd Wright*, 264.

62. Thomas E. Talmadge, *The Story of Architecture in America* (New York: Norton, 1936), 229. Quoted in Meech, *Frank Lloyd Wright*, 19.

63. For a discussion of Japan's influence on northeast American intellectuals and the popularity of the tea ceremony, see Benfey, *The Great Wave*, 75–108 passim.

64. Judith Snodgrass, *Presenting Japanese Buddhism to the West* (Chapel Hill: University of North Carolina Press, 2003), 29.

65. Ibid., 17.

66. For a discussion of the tokonoma's influence on Frank Lloyd Wright, see Kevin Nute, *Frank Lloyd Wright and Japan* (New York: Van Nostrand Reinhold, 1993), 61.

67. Frank Lloyd Wright, *The Japanese Print: An Interpretation* (Chicago: Ralph Fletcher Seymour Co., Fine Arts Building, 1912), quoted in Meech, *Frank Lloyd Wright*, 70.

68. Ibid.

69. Wright, *An Autobiography* (New York: Horizon Press, 1977), 229.

Chapter 3

1. Philip K. Dick, *The Man in the High Castle* (London: Penguin Books, 1962), 31.

2. Ibid., 10–11.

3. Ibid., 12; emphasis original.

4. England and France maintained a complex relationship with Japan in the postwar period. For the English, the memory of the brutal treatment by the Japanese of English and Aznac prisoners of war remained a wound that was difficult to transcend. French intellectuals, on the other hand, saw certain aspects of Japanese ideology as offering an alternative to what they increasingly saw as American political hegemony. For further discussion of the

French relationship with Japan in the postwar period, see Douglas Slaymaker, ed., *Confluences: Postwar Japan and France* (Ann Arbor: University of Michigan Center for Japanese Studies, 2002).

5. The ambivalent emotions many Japanese felt toward Americans included gratitude, humiliation, and hatred. Several of Japan's best writers have explored this difficult relationship in their writings, especially Kenzaburo Oe, Nobuo Kojima, and Akiyuki Nosaka, some of whose writings have been translated into English.

6. For further discussion about the complex set of cultural transactions that Godzilla represents, see Takayuki Tatsumi, "Waiting for Godzilla: Chaotic Negotiations between Post-Orientalism and Hyper-Orientalism," in *Transactions, Transgressions, Transformations: American Culture in Western Europe and Japan*, ed. Fehrenbach and Poiger (New York: Berghahn Books, 2000), 224–37. Also see William Tsutsui, *Godzilla on My Mind* (New York: Palgrave Macmillan, 2004); and William Tsutsui, ed., *In Godzilla's Footsteps* (New York: Palgrave Macmillan, 2006).

7. Dave Barry, *Dave Barry Does Japan* (New York: Ballantine, 1992), 7.

8. William Gibson, "My Own Private Tokyo," *Wired*, September 9, 2001, p. 9.

9. Sonia Ryang, *Japan and National Anthropology: A Critique* (New York: Routledge Curzon, 2004), 28.

10. Ibid., 35.

11. Jack Kerouac, *The Dharma Bums* (New York: Penguin Books, 1976), 39.

12. Ibid., 97–98.

13. It should be noted that the first Buddhist temples in America were founded at the turn of the twentieth century by Japanese immigrants in Hawaii and California.

14. J. J. Clarke, *Oriental Enlightenment: The Encounter Between Western and Asian Thought* (London: Routledge, 1997), 89.

15. Henry Clarke Warren, quoted in Thomas Tweed, *The American Encounter with Buddhism 1844–1912: Victorian Culture and the Limits of Dissent* (Bloomington: Indiana University Press, 1992), 96.

16. Suzuki also wrote a considerable amount about Zen's relationship to the Japanese love of nature, even linking it to the New England Transcendentalist tradition of Henry David Thoreau and Ralph Waldo Emerson. This approach no doubt helped to "domesticate" Zen for American consumption. Some commentators have seen a link between Zen and Japanese nationalism but, on the whole, Suzuki's interpretation of Zen seems to be viewed in largely positive terms. See James Heisig and John Maraldo, *Rude Awakenings: Zen, the Kyoto School, and the Question of Japanese Nationalism* (Honolulu: University of Hawaii Press, 1995), 27. See also Judith Snodgrass, *Presenting Japanese Buddhism to the West* (Chapel Hill: University of North Carolina Press, 2003), 259–77.

17. For example, see Kamo no Chomei's "The Ten Foot Square Hut," in *The Ten Foot Square Hut and Tales of the Heike* (Rutland, VT: Tuttle, 1972), describing a monk's celebration of the transient beauties of nature and simultaneous denigration of worldly desires. In fifteenth-century Japan, a form of painting developed known as *shosaiga* (paintings for the study), usually depicting a Zen priest's study or hermitage at the bottom with a poem written in beautiful calligraphy on the top of the picture. See *Zen Painting and Calligraphy:*

Museum of Fine Arts Boston (Greenwich, CT: New York Graphic Society, 1970), 108–9.

18. Kerouac, *Dharma Bums*, 102.
19. Ibid., 13.
20. Ibid., 58.
21. Ibid., 58–59.
22. In fact, Regina Weinreich quotes more recent American haiku poets who suggest that Kerouac may have actually been writing *senryu*, a sister genre that deals with human nature rather than Nature. Much of later American haiku seems to follow this pattern as well. See Jack Kerouac, *Jack Kerouac Book of Haikus*, introduction by Regina Weinreich (New York: Penguin Poets, 2003), xxix.
23. Kerouac, *Dharma Bums*, 71.
24. Ibid., 83–84.
25. Ibid., 84.
26. Ibid., 85.
27. Ibid., 244.
28. Ibid., 18.
29. Ibid.
30. Ibid., 102.
31. Gary Snyder, "Epigraph" to *The Back Coutntry* (New York: New Dirctison, 1957). For further discussion of Basho's effect on American and English poets and translators, see Haruo Shirane, *Traces of Dreams: Landscape and Cultural Memory and the Poetry of Basho* (Stanford, CA: Stanford University Press, 1999), 41–48.
32. Charles Strain, "The Pacific Buddha's Wild Practice: Gary Snyder's Environmentalist Ethic," in *American Buddhism: Methods and Findings in Recent Scholarship*, ed. Duncan Williams and Christopher Queen (Richmond, UK: Curzon Press, 1998), 148.
33. Snyder, *The Real Work: Interviews and Talks 1964–1979* (New York: New Directions, 1980), 123.
34. Bob Steuding, *Gary Snyder* (Boston: Twayne, 1976), 65.
35. Kerouac, *Dharma Bums*, 157.
36. *Time*, quoted in Dennis McNally, *Desolation Angel* (New York: Delta, 1990), 255–56.
37. Shoji Yamada, "Zen: An Imagined Soft Power," unpublished paper presented at the Interrogating Japan's Soft Power Conference, February 25, 2006. On *Zen and the Art of Diaper Changing*, Yamada comments dryly, "While I stand in a certain kind of flabbergasted awe at her ability to bring Zen into a discussion of diaper changing, as a parent who has raised children there is something strangely convincing in the author's statement that "a baby too is a kind of koan." (7). Yamada also points out that some of these books, such as *Zen and the Art of the Internet*, have been translated into Japanese *minus* the word "Zen" in the title, suggesting to him that the Western understanding of the term "Zen" would be quite difficult to convey to a Japanese readership.
38. *Haikusine* (Houston: Lazywood, 2000). The book is described as "217 Food Poems by Texans Who Love to Eat and Feed their Heads," and includes such useful compositions as the following by Janice Adell Rossen:

> Desperately lonely
> Talk loud on cell phone, bleating
> Hang up, friend and eat

39. Mary Kay Witte, *Redneck Haiku* (Santa Monica, CA: Santa Monica Press, 2003), 41.
40. Issues of Western masculinity versus that of the Japanese male are prefigured in the extremely popular novel and television series *Shogun* in the late 1970s and 1980s. *Shogun* traces the story of an Englishman named Blackthorne (based on a real person) who is shipwrecked in Japan and ultimately becomes an advisor to the would-be shogun Toranaga (the historical Tokugawa Ieyasu). Both book and series contain a wealth of (sometimes inaccurate) detail that introduced many Americans of a new generation to a "samurai Japan." What is perhaps particularly intriguing about *Shogun* is that it shows a Westerner in a consistently supportive, albeit important, role. This may be related to the fact that during this period (as opposed to the late 1980s), Japan's new rise to power was still largely viewed with respect rather than fear.
41. Michael Crichton, *Rising Sun* (New York: Alfred Knopf, 1992), 258.
42. Bill Powell, "Don't Write Off Japan," *Newsweek*, no. 919 (1992): 48.
43. The Vapors, "Turning Japanese," from http://www.songmeanings.net.
44. Ezra Vogel, *Japan as Number One: Lessons for America* (Cambridge, MA: Harvard University Press, 1979), ix.
45. Ibid, 3.
46. Ibid., 235.
47. See ibid, 97–130, passim. It is perhaps not surprising that *Japan as Number One*, in its translated version, was a best seller in Japan. Not only did the book seem to confirm Japanese superiority, but it also suggested that certain vaunted aspects of American identity—such as the emphasis on individualism—actually had deleterious effects, an implication that must have been profoundly satisfying to many Japanese who had grown up under the American Occupation.
48. Crichton, *Rising Sun*, 30.
49. Ibid., 74.
50. Ibid., 73.
51. Ibid., 45.
52. Ibid., 225.
53. Ibid., 63.
54. Ibid., 229.
55. Ibid., 70.
56. To some extent, *Rising Sun* skewers self-absorbed American womanhood in the tradition of Michener's *Sayonara*. But unlike *Sayonara*, the reader is not given a self-sacrificing Japanese woman as an alternative. Instead we are presented with Theresa Asakuma, a research scientist who helps the detectives and who is characterized as another victim of the Japanese. Of mixed blood and with a crippled hand, Asakuma grows up doubly ostracized by Japanese society and has an understandably negative opinion toward them as a result. Crichton's portrayal of Japanese racism and prejudice here is undoubtedly

accurate, but it should also be noted that, with the partial exception of Eddie Sakamoto whose goofy charm comes across particularly vividly in the film, the Japanese characters are shown as uniformly stolid and unpleasant, hardly a "balanced" portrayal.

57. In Dominic Alessio's discussion of race in *Blade Runner*, he suggests that "what we could be witnessing . . . is a fear of displacement at home by the Other," pointing out that *Blade Runner's mise en scene* with its "jumbling mass of Chinese, Japanese, and Arabs, with the city's culture dominated by Japanese corporations such as Atari, Chinese food vendors, and Eastern belly dancers . . . could be a reflection of American grumbling during the Reagan Presidency about U.S. trade imbalances with Japan and illegal Latino immigration to California." Dominic Alession, "Redemption, 'Race,' Religion, Reality and the Far-Right: Science Fiction Film Adaptations of Philip K. Dick," in *The Blade Runner Experience*, ed. Will Brooker (London: Wallflower Books, 2005), 60–61.

58. William Gibson, *Neuromancer* (New York: Ace Books, 1984), 3.

59. Gibson, "Modern Boys and Mobile Girls," *Observer*, April 1, 2001.

60. Gibson, *Idoru* (New York: Berkley, 1996), 121.

61. Ibid., 121.

62. Ibid., 236.

63. Ibid., 331.

64. Fredric Jameson, "Progress versus Utopia or Can We Imagine the Future?" *Science Fiction Studies* 9, no. 2 (1982): 152.

65. In an interview in *Salon*, Gibson explains how *Idoru* was the first time he consciously extrapolated from "where we are today." In this case Gibson built on his knowledge of "idoru" culture in Japan where "assembly-line girl singers" are turned out to lip synch for their adoring fans and "took it one step further" only to discover, after he had finished the book, that the Japanese actually had created a "virtual idol" known as "Kyoko Date."

66. Gibson, *Idoru*, 293.

67. In an article for *Wired*, Gibson refers to Tokyo as "my handiest prop shop . . . sheer eye candy. You can see more chronological strata of futuristic design in a Tokyo streetscape then anywhere else in the world. Like successive layers of Tomorrowlands, older ones showing through when the newer ones start to peel." Gibson, "My Own Private Tokyo," *Wired* 9, no. 9 (2001).

68. Sharon Stockton "The Self Regained: Cyberpunk's Retreat to the Imperium," *Contemporary Literature* 36, no. 4 (Winter 1995).

69. Gibson, "My Own Private Tokyo."

70. Kerouac, *Dharma Bums*, 61–62.

71. Gibson, *Idoru*, 383.

Chapter 4

1. The title of this chapter is taken from a description of *Madama Butterfly* by Rosalind Morris, "M. Butterfly: Transvestism and Cultural Cross Dressing in the Critique of Empire," in *Gender and Culture in Literature and Film East and*

West, ed. Masivsut, Simson, and Smith (Honolulu: University of Hawaii Press), 42.

2. While Otomo is listed as the director for "Magnetic Rose," many of the themes in the episode seem to be the work of the screenwriter, Satoshi Kon. For further discussion of "Magnetic Rose," see my article, "Excuse me, who are you? Women, Performance, and the Gaze in the Films of Kon Satoshi," in *Cinema Anime*, ed. Steven Brown (New York: Palgrave, 2005).

3. Theresa de Lauretis, "Popular Culture, Public and Private Fantasies: Femininity and Fetishism in David Cronenberg's *M. Butterfly*," *Signs* 24, no. 2 (Winter 1999): 325.

4. Dorinne Kondo, "*M. Butterfly*: "Orientalism, Gender and a Critique of Essentialist Identity," *Cultural Critique* 16 (Autumn 1990): 10.

5. Even more depressing is the fact that young Western men still react to the "Butterfly" persona so enthusiastically. Unearthing the Web site "Young Dude's Guide to Japan," Sheridan Passo gives us the following disturbing comments from a modern-day Pinkerton:

> Wouldn't it be great if you could just find girls who weren't all '90s modern woman and female supremist [*sic*], talking like a guy and about their right to have the best orgasm they can, reading books about the 100 ways to achieve their career aims, and crushing the men on their way to the top. Wouldn't it be nice just to find a kind, polite girl who wasn't actually that worked up about women's state in society, just didn't really mind that the world is pretty much male-dominated, and actually quite enjoyed simply getting on with it, getting the most out of what life offers them. Someone who is ultra-feminine, of the surfer chick mentality, and sexy as well. Well, that's Japanese girls, dude!

Quoted in Sheridan Prasso, *The Asian Mystique* (New York: Public Affairs, 2005), 151.

6. Kondo, *M. Butterfly*, 8.
7. *Oxford English Dictionary* (New York: Avon Books, 1986).
8. Geoffrey Nowell-Smith, quoted in Sue Thornham, *Passionate Detachments* (New York: Hodder and Stoughton, 1997), 47.
9. Ibid., 48.
10. Pierre Loti, *Madame Chrysanthemum* (New York: Boni and Livright), 44.
11. Ibid., 97.
12. Ibid., 191.
13. Ibid., 65.
14. Ibid., 122.
15. Ibid., 67.
16. Ibid., 59.
17. Ibid., 44.
18. Ibid., 180.
19. Ibid., 173.
20. Ibid., 167.
21. Ibid., 217.
22. Ibid., 222.

23. Ibid., 223.

24. Ibid.

25. L. Illica, G. Giacosa, R. H. Elkin/Giacomo Puccini, *Madame Butterfly*, on (opera.stanford.edu/Puccini/Butterfly/act1), 1.

26. Ibid., 31.

27. Ibid., 6.

28. Loti, *Madame Chrysanthéme*, 44.

29. Puccini, *Madame Butterfly*, 29.

30. As Bram Dijkstra points out, the nineteenth century was the age of the beautiful dying female, celebrated in poetry, art, literature, and theater. Bram Dijkstra, *Idols of Perversity: Fantasies of Feminine Evil in Fin de Siècle Culture* (Oxford: Oxford University Press, 1986), 51–63.

31. Leslie Downer, *Madame Sadayakko: The Geisha Who Seduced the West* (New York: Review Books, 2003), 150.

32. Puccini, *Madame Butterfly*, Act I, Parts 2 and 3.

33. Gina Marchetti, *Romance and the "Yellow Peril"* (Berkeley: University of California Press, 1963), 78–79.

34. Ibid., 88.

35. James A. Michener, *Sayonara* (Greenwich, CT: Crest, 1974), 8.

36. Ibid.

37. Ibid., 168.

38. Ibid., 106

39. Ibid.

40. Ibid., 97.

41. Ibid., 104.

42. Ibid., 57.

43. Just in case his readers could not figure this out on their own, Michener includes a scene early on in the novel when a drab American female secretary tells Gruver of her jealousy of Japanese girls who have taken all the American men, explaining, "They all have the same secret. . . . They make their men feel important" (ibid., 49).

44. Ibid., 208.

45. Ibid.

46. Ibid., 102.

47. One particularly disturbing aspect of the novel is Kelly's propensity toward violence including slapping Katsumi when she disappoints him.

48. Bosley Crowther, "Sayonara," *New York Times*, December 6, 1957.

49. Michener, *Sayonara*, 107.

50. Marchetti, *Romance and the "Yellow Peril,"* 131.

51. Ibid., 143.

52. Ibid., 137.

53. Crowther, "Sayonara."

54. John Powers, "The Art of Seduction," *Vogue*, no. 08449 (December 2005): 348.

55. For a discussion of these romantic comedies, see Napier, *Anime from Akira to Howl's Moving Castle* (New York: Palgrave Macmillan, 2005).

56. Annalee Newitz, "Magical Girls and Atomic Bomb Sperm: Japanese Animation in America," *Film Quarterly* 49, no. 1 (Fall 1995): 5.

57. Ibid.
58. Ibid., 6.

Chapter 5

1. Robert Fenelon, "Talkin' 'Bout My Star Blazers Generation," *Animerica* 3, no. 8 (1995).
2. Douglas McGray, "Japan's Gross National Cool," *Foreign Policy* (May/June 2002): 44.
3. See Joseph Nye Jr., *Bound to Lead: The Changing Nature of American Power* (New York: Basic Books, 1990).
4. Heide Fehrenbach and Uta G. Poiger, Introduction to *Transactions, Transgressions, Transformations: American Culture in Western Europe and Japan* (New York: Berghan Books, 2000), xxix.
5. Woodrow Phoenix, *Plastic Culture: How Japanese Toys Conquered the World* (Tokyo: Kodansha, 2006), 40.
6. See Sharon Kinsella, "Cuties in Japan," in *Women, Media, and Consumption in Japan*, ed. Skov and Moeran (Honolulu: University of Hawaii Press, 1996). See also Anne Allison, *Millennial Monsters* (Berkeley: University of California Press, 2006), 15–18 passim.
7. David Buckingham and Julian Sefton-Green, "Structure, Agency and Pedagogy in Children's Media Culture," in *Pikachu's Global Adventure: The Rise and Fall of Pokemon*, ed. Joseph Tobin (Durham, NC: Duke University Press, 2004), 20.
8. Ibid., 21.
9. Koichi Iwabuchi, "How 'Japanese' is *Pokemon*?" in *Pikachu's Global Adventure: The Rise and Fall of Pokemon*," ed. Joseph Tobin (Durham, NC: Duke University Press, 2004), 69.
10. Ibid., 67.
11. Allison, *Millennial Monsters*, 12.
12. Christine Yano, "Panic Attacks: Anti Pokemon Voices in Global Markets," in Tobin, ed., *Pikachu's Global Adventure*, 130.
13. Ibid.
14. Ibid.
15. Matthew Allen, "*South Park* does Japan: Going Global with Chimpokomon," in *Popular Culture, Globalization and Japan*, ed. Allen and Sakamoto (New York: Routledge, 2006), 37.
16. Ibid., 45.
17. Mark Bloch, "Seizure-inducing *Pokemon* Heads for U.S.," quoted in Yano, "Panic Attacks," 129.
18. For a discussion of *Overfiend*'s impact on the perception of anime in the West, see Helen McCarthy and Jonathan Clemens, *The Erotic Anime Movie Guide* (Woodstock, NY: Overlook, 1998), 82–88.
19. John Tulloch and Henry Jenkins, *Science Fiction Audiences* (London: Routledge, 1995), 144.
20. Evelyn Dubocq, quoted in Fiona Ng, "Shojo Girls," *Bus* (Fall 2004).

21. For discussions of "slash" fanfiction in America see Constance Penley, "Brownian Motion: Women Tactics, and Technology," in *Technoculture*, ed. Penley and Ross (Minneapolis: University of Minnesota Press, 1991); and Sharon Cumberland, "Private Uses of Cyberspace: Women, Desire, and Fan Culture," in *Rethinking Media Change: The Aesthetics of Transition*, ed. Thornburn and Jenkins (Cambridge: Massachusetts Institute of Technology Press, 2004).

22. Henry Jenkins, "Quentin Tarantino's *Star Wars*? Digital Cinema, Media Convergence, and Participatory Culture," in Thornburn and Jenkins, eds., *Rethinking Media Change*, 287–89 passim.

23. Sharon Cumberland, "Women, Desire, and Fan Culture," in Thorburn and Jenkins, eds., *Rethinking Media Change*, 275.

Chapter 6

1. Lawrence Grossberg, "Is There a Fan in the House? The Affective Sensibility of Fandom," in *The Adoring Audience*, ed. Lisa Lewis (London: Routledge, 1992), 278.

2. Victor Turner, *Dramas, Fields, and Metaphors: Symbolic Action in Human Society* (Ithaca, NY: Cornell University Press, 1974), 143.

3. Ibid., 239.

4. Henry Jenkins, *Textual Poachers* (New York: Routledge, 1992), 282.

5. Quoted by Heather, one of the organizers of Conduit, a sci-fi/anime convention in Utah.

6. Ben Malbon discusses the "oceanic" and "ecstatic" feelings that members of the "clubbing" subculture get from dancing while taking drugs, describing "'altered states' which include . . . euphoria, happiness and joy characterized by a transitory, unexpected, valued and *extraordinary* quality of rare occurrence and magnitude in which an altered sense of consciousness is temporarily experienced." See Ben Malbon, "Moments of Ecstasy: Oceanic and Ecstatic Experiences in Clubbing," in *The Subcultures Reader*, ed. Ken Gelder (New York: Routledge, 1997), 491. While I do not think that drug use is particularly high in anime/manga fan culture (if anything, according to one con organizer, it has gone down as the average fan age has gotten younger), I cannot help wondering if at least cosplayers, while they parade around the convention, also experience a similar form of transitory euphoria related to the pleasure of performing an unusual but satisfying activity in a secure alternative environment.

7. In his book *Godzilla on My Mind*, William Tsutsui recalls pestering his parents to dress him up as his hero, Godzilla, for Halloween. Unfortunately, while Godzilla was quite a star on screen by that period, the idea of a Godzilla as a Halloween costume had not caught on. As Tsutsui sadly notes, "My third-grade classmates and their parents either did not know who Godzilla was or did not recognize what a four-two light green sack with a very odd nose was meant to represent." See William Tsutsui, *Godzilla on my Mind* (New York: Routledge, 2004), 2. The evening ended badly with "Godzilla" returning home with his tail between his legs.

8. For a discussion of the themes and content of *HaibaneRenmei*, see Napier, *Anime from Akira to Howl's Moving Castle* (New York: Routledge, 2005).

9. Homi K. Bhabha, "Of Mimicry and Man: The Ambivalence of Colonial Discourse," in *The Location of Culture* (London: Routledge, 1994), 92.

10. Ibid.

11. Milly Williamson, "Vampires and Goths: Fandom, Gender and Cult Dress," in *Dressed to Impress: Looking the Part*, ed. William Keenan (New York: Berg, 2001), 145.

Chapter 7

1. Francois Mitterrand, quoted in Michael Skovmand and Kim Christian Shrøder, *Media Cultures: Reappraising Transnational Media* (London: Routledge, 1992), 6.

2. Ibid.

3. Ulf Hedetoft, and Mette Hjort, Introduction to *The Postnational Self*, ed. Hedetoft and Hjort (Minneapolis: University of Minnesota Press, 2002), xv.

4. Tamar Liebes and Elihu Katz, *The Export of Meaning: Cross-Cultural Readings of Dallas* (London: Oxford University Press, 1990), 133.

5. Ibid., 80.

6. Ibid., 134.

7. Ibid.

8. Cornell Sandvoss, *Fans: The Mirror of Consumption* (Cambridge: Polity, 2005), 102.

9. Ibid., 7.

10. Roger Aden, *Popular Stories and Promised Lands: Fan Cultures and Symbolic Pilgrimages* (Tuscaloosa: University of Alabama Press, 1999), 34.

11. Scott McCloud, *Understanding Comics: The Invisitble Art* (New York: Harper Collins, 1994), 29–34.

12. See Bruno Bettelheim, *The Uses of Enchantment: The Meaning and Importance of Fairy Tales* (NewYork: Vintage, 1977), 45–66.

13. For a discussion of the content and themes of *Cowboy Bebop*, see Napier, *Anime from Akira to Howl's Moving Castle: Experiencing Contemporary Japanese Animation* (New York: Palgrave, 2005).

14. See Ueno Toshiya, *Kurenai no metarusutsu: anime to iu senjo* (Tokyo: Kodansha, 1998), 141–44. Also see Oshii Mamoru, Ueno Toshiya, and Ito Kazunori, "Eiga to wa jitsu wa animeishon datta," in *Eureka* 28, no. 9 (August 1996): 77–78.

15. Douglas Kellner, *Media Culture: Cultural Studies, Identity and Politics between the Modern and the Postmodern* (London: Routledge, 1995), 246–47.

16. Sandvoss, *Fans*, 64.

17. Ulf Hannerz, "Where We Are and Who We Want to Be," *Postnational Self*, ed. Hedetoft and Hjort (Minneapolis: University of Minnesota Press, 2002), 218.

Chapter 8

1. Roger Putnam, *Bowling Alone: The Collapse and Revival of American Community* (New York: Simon and Schuster, 2000), 11.
2. Ibid., 171.
3. Ibid., 178.
4. Douglas McGray, "Japan's Gross National Cool," *Foreign Policy* (May/June 2002): 48.
5. Seiichi Kondo, "Japan's Soft Power and Public Diplomacy," paper presented at the conference "Soft Power: National Assets in Japan and the United States." Sponsored by the Abe Foundation, February 25, 2005, p. 4.
6. Margaret Talbot, "The Auteur of Anime," *The New Yorker* (January 17, 2005): 66.
7. Henry Jenkins, *Textual Poachers* (New York: Routledge, 1992), 26.
8. Lisa Lewis, "Fan Stories on Film," in *The Adoring Audience: Fan Culture and Popular Media*, ed. Lisa Lewis (London: Routledge, 1992), 158.
9. Roger C. Aden, *Popular Stories and Promised Lands: Fan Cultures and Symbolic Pigrimages* (Tuscaloosa: University of Alabama Press, 1999), 91–94 passim.
10. Ibid., 69. Aden defines "liminoid" in relation to the more well-known "liminal," as a phrase "used to describe the increasingly optional ritual experiences found in industrial and postindustrial societies" (82).
11. Mihaly Csikszentmihalyi, *Flow: The Psychology of Optimal Experience* (New York: Harper and Row, 1990), 214–40.
12. Ibid., 240.
13. Will Brooker, *Using the Force: Creativity, Community and Star Wars Fans* (New York: Continuum, 2002), xii.
14. Joli Jenson, "Fandom as Pathology: The Consequences of Characterization," in *The Adoring Audience: Fan Culture and Popular Media*, ed. Lisa Lewis (London: Routledge, 1992), 9.
15. Brooker, *Using the Force*, xiv.
16. Credit for the "civilized" quality of the discussion must go, at least in some part, to Michael Johnson, the list owner. As was clear from his conversation with me (January 2005) and in the rules that he set up to govern the list, Michael is extremely conscious of wanting to promote a free-flowing, friendly, and polite environment. As he says, "I don't tolerate irresponsible behavior on the list." Michael's examples of undesirable behavior include everything from poor spelling and grammar, to "flaming, spamming, spoofing, or trolling." It is clear from the other list members' comments that the framework is much appreciated. Over half of the respondents, when asked to compare the MML with other anime fans, mentioned the civilized atmosphere. Or as one member, a Canadian stay-at-home mother, put it, "MML members seem invariably polite and respectful." On the other hand, consistent with what Matt Hills sees as the "performance" aspect of Internet fandom (Matt Hills, *Fan Cultures* [London: Routledge, 1992], 179), some members report being occasionally turned off by the more "pretentious" (i.e., literary, philosophical, or psychoanalytic discussions) that certain members of the group enjoy engaging in.

17. Hills discusses the notion of fans as "specialist" consumers or even "ideal" consumers. Hills, *Fan Cultures*, 29.
18. MML fans also strike me as particularly culturally sophisticated. A recent thread (in the fall of 2006) developed around the question, "What would Miyazaki be like if he was born in America?" The answers ranged considerably (one person likened him to Bill Gates!), but they all showed an appreciation and awareness of how different cultural factors can mold the individual to achieve very different things.
19. Aden, *Popular Stories*, 6.
20. Koichi Iwabuchi, "How 'Japanese' is Pokemon?" in *Pikachu's Global Adventure*, ed. Joseph Tobin (Durham, NC: Duke University Press, 2004), 7.
21. In Annalee Newitz's 1994 study of West Coast anime fans, she concluded that about 86 percent of the members of California university clubs were male. See annlee Newitz, "Anime Otaku: Japanese Animation Fans Outside Japan," *Bad Subjects* 13 (April 1994): 161. In my study of anime fans, I found that between 76 to 85 percent (depending on what group I was surveying) were male. See Susan Napier, *Anime from Akira to Princess Mononoke: Experiencing Contemporary Japanese Animation* (New York: Palgrave Macmillan, 2001), 247.
22. Aden, *Popular Stories*, 9.

Chapter 9

1. Yulia Mikhailova, "Apocalypse in Fantasy and Reality: Japanese Pop Culture in Contemporary Russia," in *In Godzilla's Footsteps*, ed. Tsutsui and Ito (New York: Palgrave, 2006), 185.
2. See Napier, "Introduction: Why Anime?" in *Anime from Akira to Howl's Moving Castle* (New York: Palgrave, 2005).
3. Roland Kelts draws a direct line between 9/11 and the increase in popularity in anime and manga. Interview with author at the Park Hyatt Hotel, Tokyo, May 2006. He also points out that, given the traumatic and transformative events of the contemporary period, "you start to believe that fresh ways of narrating the world, new styles of seeing, are not merely plausible but inevitable." Roland Kelts, *Japanamerica* (New York: Palgrave MacMillan, 2006), 27.
4. Anthony Hopkins, "Introduction," in *Global History: Interactions Between the Universal and the Local*, ed. Anthony Hopkins (New York: Palgrave Macmillan, 2006), 3.
5. Whereas I was surprised by the number of fans who were interested in Japan, Antonia Levi saw an opposite trend. In her case she was disappointed in the lack of Japan interests among the fans she surveyed. To my mind our different findings may be related to different expectations: I anticipated very little interest and was astounded and gratified by the level of knowledge and enthusiasm about the culture that I found. Levi started her research expecting a great deal of interest and found her expectations disappointed. See Levi "The Americanization of Anime and Manga: Negotiating Popular Culture," in *Cinema Anime*, ed. Steven Brown (New York: Palgrave Macmillan, 2006).

6. An exciting exhibition at the Boston Museum of Fine Arts in 2001 entitled "Made in Japan" juxtaposed Murakami's work with older pieces from the museum's collection to effectively display the continuities in his oeuvre.

7. The Japanese actor Takakura Ken, as a samurai lord is able to give some three dimensionality to his performance.

Bibliography

Aden, Roger. *Popular Stories and Promised Lands: Fan Cultures and Symbolic Pilgrimages*. Tuscaloosa: University of Alabama Press, 1999.

Ahmad, Ahjaz, ed. "Orientalism and After: Ambivalence and Metropolitan Location in the Work of Edward Said." In *Theory: Classes, Nations, Literatures*, edited by Ahjaz Ahmad. London: Verso, 1992.

Alessio, Dominic. "Redemption, 'Race,' Religion, Reality and the Far Right: Science-Fiction Film Adaptations of Philip K. Dick." In *The* Blade Runner *Experience*, edited by Will Brooker. London: Wallflower Books, 2005.

Allen, Matthew. "*South Park* Does Japan: Going Global with *Chimpokomon*." In *Popular Culture, Globalization, and Japan*, edited by Matthew Allen and Rumi Sakamoto. New York: Routledge, 2006.

Allison, Anne. "Cuteness as Japan's Millennial Product." In *Pikachu's Global Adventure: The Rise and Fall of* Pokemon, edited by Joseph Tobin. Durham, NC: Duke University Press, 2004.

———. *Millennial Monsters: Japanese Toys and the Global Imagination*. Berkeley: University of California Press, 2006.

Appadurai, Arjun, ed. *Globalization*. Durham, NC. Duke University Press, 2001.

———. *Modernity at Large: Cultural Dimensions of Globalization*. Minneapolis: University of Minnesota Press, 1996.

Ball, John. *Miss One Thousand Spring Blossoms*. Boston: Little Brown and Company, 1968.

Barry, Dave. *Dave Barry Does Japan*. New York: Random House, 1992.

Barthes, Roland. *Empire of Signs*. New York: Hill and Wang, 1992.

Belk, Russell. *Collecting in a Consumer Society*. London: Routledge, 1995.

Belson, Ken, and Brian Bremner. *Hello Kitty: The Remarkable Story of Sanrio and the Billion Dollar Feline Phenomenon*. Singapore: John Wiley and Sons, 2004.

Benedict, Ruth. *The Chrysanthemum and the Sword*. Boston: Houghton Mifflin, 1989.

Benfey, Christopher. *The Great Wave: Gilded Age Misfits, Japanese Eccentrics, and the Opening of Old Japan*. New York: Random House, 2003.

Berendt, John. *The City of Falling Angels*. New York: Penguin, 2005.

Bettelheim, Bruno. *The Uses of Enchantment*. New York: Vintage Books, 1977.

Bhabha, Homi K. "Of Mimicry and Man." In *The Location of Culture*, edited by Homi K. Bhabha. London: Routledge, 1994.

Bing, Siegfried. "The Japanese as Decorators." *Artistic Japan* 1 (1884).

Bird, Isabella. *Unbeaten Tracks in Japan*. London: Virago Press, 1984.

Blacker, Carmen. "Intent of Courtesy." In *Madly Singing in the Mountains: An Appreciation and Anthology of Arthur Waley*, edited by Ivan Morris. London: George Allen and Unwin, 1970.

Breckenridge, Carol A., and Peter van der Veer, eds. *Orientalism and the Postcolonial Predicament: Perspectives on South Asia*. Philadelphia: University of Pennsylvania Press, 1993.

Brooker, Will. *Using the Force: Creativity, Community, and Star Wars Fans*. New York: Continuum, 2002.

Buckingham, David, and Julian Sefton-Green. "Structure, Agency, and Pedagogy in Children's Media Culture." In *Pikachu's Global Adventure: The Rise and Fall of Pokemon*, edited by Joseph Tobin. Durham, NC: Duke University Press, 2004.

Buruma, Ian. *The Missionary and the Libertine: Love and War in East and West*. London: Faber and Faber, 1996.

Caton, Steven. Lawrence of Arabia*: A Film's Anthropology*. Berkeley: University of California Press, 1999.

Chesneau, Ernest. "Le Japon à Paris." *Gazette des Beaux Arts* 18 (1878): 385–93.

Chow, Rey. *Writing Diaspora: Tactics of Intervention in Contemporary Cultural Studies*. Bloomington: Indiana University Press, 1993.

Christ, Carol-Ann. "The Sole Guardians of the Art Inheritance of Asia: Japan and China at the 1904 St. Louis World's Fair." *positions* 8, no. 3 (2000): 675–709.

Clarke, J. J. *Oriental Enlightenment: The Encounter between Asian and Western Thought*. London: Routledge, 1997.

Clavell, James. *Shogun*. New York: Dell, 1975.

Conant, Ellen. Refractions from the Rising Sun: Japan's Participation in International Exhibitions 1862–1910." In *Japan and Britain: An Aesthetic Dialogue: 1850–1930*, edited by Tomoko Sato and Toshio Watanabe. London: Lund Humphries, 1991.

Cooper, Michael. *They Came to Japan*. Berkeley: University of California Press, 1982.

Crichton, Michael. *Rising Sun*. New York: Alfred Knopf, 1992.

Crowther, Bosley. "Sayonara." *New York Times*, December 6, 1957.

Csikszentmihalyi, Mihaly. *Flow: The Psychology of Optimal Experience*. New York: Harper Perennial, 1990.

Cumberland, Sharon. "Private Uses of Cyberspace: Women, Desire, and Fan Culture." In *Rethinking Media Change: The Aesthetics of Transition*, edited by David Thorburn and Henry Jenkins. Cambridge, MA: MIT Press, 2004.

Daniels, G. *Britain and Japan: Themes and Personalities 1859–1991*. London: Routledge, 1991.

Dawson, Carl. *Lafcadio Hearn and the Vision of Japan*. Baltimore: Johns Hopkins University Press, 1992.

De Gruchy, John W. *Orienting Arthur Waley: Japonism, Orientalism, and the Creation of Japanese Literature in English*. Honolulu: University of Hawaii Press, 2003.

Dick, Philip K. *The Man in the High Castle*. London: Penguin Books, 1962.

Dijkstra, Bram. *Idols of Perversity: Fantasies of Feminine Evil in Fin de Siècle Culture*. Oxford: Oxford University Press, 1986.

Donald, James, ed. *Fantasy Cinema*. London: British Film Institute, 1989.

Dower, John. *Embracing Defeat: Japan in the Wake of World War II*. New York: W. W. Norton & Company, 1999.

———. *War without Mercy: Race and Power in the Pacific War*. New York: Pantheon, 1986.

Downer, Lesley. *Madame Sadayakko: The Geisha Who Seduced the West*. London: Review Press, 2003.

Edwards, Holly. *Noble Dreams and Wicked Pleasures: Orientalism in America, 1870–1930*. Princeton, NJ: Princeton University Press, 2000.

Evett, Elisa. *The Critical Reception of Japanese Art in Late Nineteenth-Century Europe*. Ann Arbor, MI: UMI Research Press, 1982.

Fehrenbach, Heide, and Poiger, Uta G. Introduction to *Transactions, Transgressions, Transformations: American Culture in Western Europe and Japan*, edited by Heide Fehrenbach and Uta G. Poiger. New York: Berghan Books, 2000.

Fenelon, Robert. "Talkin' 'Bout My Star Blazers Generation." *Animerica* 3, no. 8 (1995): n.p.

Flaubert, Gustave. *Flaubert in Egypt*. London: Penguin Books, 1972.

Galanteane, Lewis, ed. *The Goncourt Journals*. New York: Doubleday, 1937.

Gibson, William. *Idoru*. New York: Putnam, 1996.

———. "Is Japan Still the Future?" *Wired* 9, no. 9 (September 2001), http://www.wired.com/wired/archive/9.09/japan.html.

———. "Modern Boys and Modern Girls." *The Observer*, April 1, 2001.

———. "My Own Private Tokyo." *Wired* 9, no. 9 (September 2001), http://www.wired.com/wired/archive/9.09/gibson.html.

———. *Neuromancer*. New York: Ace Books, 1984.

Gilbert, W. S., and Arthur Sullivan. *The Mikado*. In *The Complete Annotated Gilbert and Sullivan*, edited by Ian Bradley. Oxford: Oxford University Press, 1996.

Golden, Arthur. *Memoirs of a Geisha*. New York: Vintage, 1997.

Goncourt, Edmund de, and Jules de Goncourt. *The Goncourt Journal: Paris and the Arts*. Ithaca, NY: Cornell University Press, 1971.

———. *Manette Salomon*. Paris: Union Générale Editions, 1979.

Grossberg, Lawrence. "Is There a Fan in the House? The Affective Sensibility of Fandom." In *The Adoring Audience: Fan Culture and Popular Media*, edited by Lisa A. Lewis. London: Routledge, 1992.

Guth, Christine. *Longfellow's Tattoos: Tourism, Collecting, and Japan*. Seattle: University of Washington Press, 2004.

Hammond, Phil. *Cultural Differences: Media Memories; Anglo-American Images of Japan*. London: Cassell, 1997.

Hampton, Christopher. *The Ginger Tree*. London: Faber and Faber, 1989.

Hannerz, Ulf. "Where We Are and Who We Want to Be." In *The Postnational Self*, edited by Ulf Hedetoft and Mette Hjort. Minneapolis: University of Minnesota Press, 2002.

Hearn, Lafcadio. *Glimpses of Unfamiliar Japan*. Tokyo: Charles E. Tuttle, 1976.

———. *Japan: An Attempt at Interpretation*. Rutland, VT: Charles E. Tuttle, 1955.

———. *A Japanese Miscellany*. Tokyo: Charles E. Tuttle, 1967.

———. *Kokoro*. Tokyo: Charles E. Tuttle, 1972.

———. *Kotto*. Tokyo: Tut Books, 1972.

Hedetoft, Ulf, and Mette Hjort. Introduction to *The Postnational Self*, edited by Hedetoft and Hjort. Minneapolis: University of Minnesota Press, 2002.

Heisig, James, and John Maraldo. *Rude Awakenings: Zen, the Kyoto School, and the Question of Japanese Nationalism*. Honolulu: University of Hawaii Press, 1995.

Hills, Matt. *Fan Cultures*. London; Routledge, 2002.

Hobsbawm, Eric. *The Age of Capital: 1848–1875*. New York: Vintage, 1975.

———. *The Age of Empire: 1875–1914*. New York: Vintage Books, 1989.

Hopkins, Anthony. Introduction to *Global History: Interactions between the Universal and the Local*, edited by Anthony Hopkins. New York: Palgrave, 2006.

Hopkins, A. G., ed. *Global History: Interactions between the Universal and the Local*. New York: Palgrave, 2006.

Hotta-Lister, Ayako. *The Japan-British Exposition of 1910: Gateway to the Island Empire of the East*. Richmond, VA: Japan Library, 1999.

House, John. *Monet: Nature into Art*. New Haven, CT: Yale University Press, 1986.

Illica, G. Giacosa, R. H. Elkin, and Giacomo Puccini. *Madame Butterfly*. http://opera.stanford.edu/Puccini/Butterfly.

Inaga, Shigemi. "Claude Monet. Between Impressionism and Japonism." In *Monet and Japan*, edited by Virginia Spate and Gary Hickey. London: Thames and Hudson, 2001.

Inden, Ronald B. *Imagining India*. Bloomington: Indiana University Press, 1995.

Iwabuchi, Koichi. "How 'Japanese' Is *Pokemon*?" In *Pikachu's Global Adventure: The Rise and Fall of Pokemon*, edited by Joseph Tobin. Durham, NC: Duke University Press, 2004.

———. *Recentering Globalization: Popular Culture and Japanese Transnationalism*. Durham, NC: Duke University Press, 2002.

Jameson, Fredric. "Progress versus Utopia or Can We Imagine the Future?" *Science Fiction Studies* 9, no. 27 (July 1982): 147–58.

Jenkins, Henry. "Quentin Tarantino's *Star Wars*? Digital Cinema, Media Convergence, and Participatory Culture." In *Rethinking Media Change: The Aesthetics of Transition*, edited by David Thorburn and Henry Jenkins. Cambridge, MA: MIT Press, 2004.

———. *Textual Poachers*. New York: Routledge, 1992.

Jenson, Joli. "Fandom as Pathology: The Consequences of Characterization." In *The Adoring Audience: Fan Culture and Popular Media*, edited by Lisa Lewis. London: Routledge, 1992.

Kamo no Chomei. "The Ten Square Foot Hut." In *The Ten Square Foot Hut and Tales of the Heike*, edited by A. D. Sadler. Tokyo: Tuttle Books, 1972.

Katz, Elihu. "Viewers Work." In *The Audience and Its Landscape*, edited by James Hay, Lawrence Grossberg, and Ella Wartella. New York: Westview, 1996.

Kelts, Roland. *Japanamerica: How Japanese Popular Culture Has Invaded the United States*. New York: Palgrave, 2006.

Kerouac, Jack. *The Dharma Bums*. New York: Penguin, 1976.

———. *On the Road*. New York: Penguin, 1976.

Kinsella, Sharon. "Cuties in Japan." In *Women, Media, and Consumption in Japan*, edited by Lise Skov and Brian Moeran. Honolulu: University of Hawaii Press, 1995.

Kipling, Rudyard. *Kim*. London: Penguin, 1987.

Kojima, Nobuo. "The American School." In *Contemporary Japanese Literature: An Anthology of Fiction, Film, and Other Writing since 1945*, edited by Howard Hibbet. New York: Alfred Knopf, 1977.

Kondo, Dorinne. "M Butterfly: Orientalism, Gender, and a Critique of Essentialist Identity." *Cultural Critique* 16 (Autumn 1990): 5–29.

Kondo, Seiichi. "Japan's Soft Power and Public Diplomacy." Paper presented at the conference "Soft Power: National Assets in Japan and the United States." Sponsored by the Abe Foundation. February 25, 2005.

Lambourne, Lionel. *Japonisme: Cultural Crossing Between East and West*. New York: Phaidon, 2005.

Lauretis, Theresa de. "Popular Culture, Public and Private Fantasies: Femininity and Fetishism in David Cronenberg's M. Butterfly." *Signs: Journal of Women in Culture and Society* 24, no. 2 (Winter 1999): 303–34.

Leask, Nigel. *British Romantic Writers and the East: Anxieties of Empire*. Cambridge: Cambridge University Press, 2004.

Leonard, Andrew. "Heads Up Mickey." *Wired* 3, no. 4 (April 1995), http://www.wired.com/wired/archive/3.04/anime.html.

Levi, Antonia. "The Americanization of Anime and Manga: Negotiating Popular Culture." In *Cinema Anime*, edited by Steven Brown. New York: Palgrave, 2006.

Lewis, Lisa. "Fan Stories on Film." In *The Adoring Audience: Fan Cultures and Popular Media*, edited by Lisa Lewis. London: Routledge, 1992.

Liebes, Tamar, and Elihu Katz. *The Export of Meaning: Cross-Cultural Readings of Dallas*. London: Oxford University Press, 1990.

Lockman, Zachary. *Contending Visions of the Middle East*. Cambridge: Cambridge University Press, 2004.

Lori, Pierre. *Madame Chrysanthemum*. New York: Boni and Livright, n.d.

Louis, Wm. Roger. *Ends of British Imperialism: The Scramble for Empire, Suez, and Decolonization*. London: I. B.Tauris, 2006.

Mabuchi, Akiko. "Monet and Screen Painting." In *Monet and Japan*, edited by Virginia Spate and Gary Hickey. London: Thames and Hudson, 2001.

MacDonald, Galassi, and Ribeiro MacDonald, eds. *Whistler, Women, and Fashion*. New Haven, CT: Yale University Press, 2003.

MacKenzie, John M. *Orientalism: History, Theory, and the Arts*. Manchester: Manchester University Press, 1995.

Malbon, Ben. "Moments of Ecstasy: Oceanic and Ecstatic Experiences in Clubbing." In *The Subcultures Reader*, edited by Ken Gelder. New York: Routledge, 1997.

Marchetti, Gina. *Romance and the Yellow Peril*. Berkeley: University of California Press, 1993.

Mathy, Jean-Philippe. "From Sign to Thing: The French Literary Avant-Garde and the Japanese Difference." In *Confluences: Postwar Japan and France*, edited by Doug Slaymaker. Ann Arbor: University of Michigan Monograph Series, 2002.

Maurer, Naomi. *The Pursuit of Spiritual Wisdom: The Thought and Art of Vincent Van Gogh and Paul Gauguin*. New York; Associated University Presses, 1998.

McCarthy, Helen, and Jonathan Clements. *The Erotic Anime Movie Guide*. Woodstock, NY: Overlook, 1994.

McCloud, Scott. *Understanding Comics: The Invisible Art*. New York: HarperPerennial, 1994.

McCray, Douglas. "Japan's Gross National Cool." *Foreign Policy* (May/June 2002).

McNally, Dennis. *Desolation Angels: Jack Kerouac, the Beat Generation, and America*. New York: Delta, 1990.

Meech, Julia. *Frank Lloyd Wright and the Art of Japan: The Architect's Other Passion*. New York: Harry N. Abrams, 2001.

Michener, James. *Sayonara*. Greenwich, CT: Fawcett Crest, 1974.

Mikhailova, Yulia. "Apocalypse in Fantasy and Reality: Japanese Pop Culture in Contemporary Russia." In *In Godzilla's Footsteps*, edited by William Tsutsui and Michiko Ito. New York: Palgrave, 2005.

Miner, Earl. *The Japanese Tradition in British and American Literature*. Princeton, NJ: Princeton University Press, 1958.

Morris, Rosalind. "M Butterfly: Transvestism and Cultural Cross Dressing in the Critique of Empire." In *Gender and Culture in Literature and Film East and West*, edited by Nataya Masavisut, George Simson, and Larry E. Smith. Honolulu: University of Hawaii Press, 1993.

Napier, Susan. *Anime from* Akira *to* Howl's Moving Castle*: Experiencing Contemporary Japanese Animation*. New York: Palgrave, 2005.

———. "Appendix: The Fifth Look; Western Audiences and Japanese Animation." In *Anime from* Akira *to* Princess Mononoke*: Experiencing Contemporary Japanese Animation*. New York: Palgrave, 2000.

———. "Excuse Me, Who Are You? Performance, the Gaze, and the Female in the Works of Kon Satoshi." In *Cinema Anime*, edited by Steven Brown. New York: Palgrave, 2005.

Newitz, Annalee. "Anime Otaku: Japanese Animation Fans outside Japan." *Bad Subjects* 13 (April 1994): 1–12.

———. "Magical Girls and Atomic Bomb Sperm: Japanese Animation in America." *Film Quarterly* 49, no. 1 (Fall 1995): 2–15.

Ng, Fiona. "Shojo Girls." *Bust* (Fall 1994).

Nosaka, Akiyuki. "American Hijiki." In *Contemporary Japanese Literature: An Anthology of Fiction, Film, and Other Writing since 1945*, edited by Howard Hibbet. New York: Alfred Knopf, 1977.

Nute, Kevin. *Frank Lloyd Wright and Japan*. New York: Van Nostrand Reinhold, 1993.

Nye, Joseph. *Bound to Lead: The Changing Nature of American Power*. New York: Basic Books, 1990.

———. *Soft Power: The Means to Success in World Politics*. New York: PublicAffairs, 2004.

Okakura Kakuzo. *The Book of Tea*. Tokyo: Tuttle, 2001.

Ooshi, Mamoru, Ueno Toshiya, and Ito Kazunori. "Eiga to wa jitsu wa animeishon datta." *Eureka* 28, no. 9 (August 1996).

Ouchi, William. *Theory Z: How American Business Can Meet the Japanese Challenge*. Reading, MA: Addison Wesley, 1981.

Penley, Constance. "Brownian Motion: Women, Tactics, and Technology." In *TechnoCulture*, edited by Constance Penley and Andrew Ross. Minneapolis: University of Minnesota Press, 1991.

Phoenix, Woodrow. *Plastic Culture: How Japanese Toys Conquered the World*. Tokyo: Kodansha, 2006.

Pickvance, Ronald. *Van Gogh in Arles*. New York: Harry Abrams, 1984.

Pirsig, Robert. *Zen and the Art of Motorcycle Maintenance*. New York: Bantam, 1975.

Pissarro, Camille. *Letters to His Son Lucien*. Edited by John Rewald. Boston: MFA Publications, 2002.

Pointon, Susan: Trans-Cultural Orgasm as Apocalypse: Urotsukidoji; The Legend of the Overfiend." *Wide Angle* 19, no. 3 (1997): 41–63.

Porter, Dennis. *Haunted Journeys: Desire and Transgression in European Travel Writings*. Princeton, NJ: Princeton University Press, 1991.

Powell, Bill. "Don't Write Off Japan." *Newsweek*, no. 919 (1992): 48.

Powers, John. "The Art of Seduction." *Vogue* 08449 (December 2005).

Prasso, Sheridan. *The Asian Mystique: Dragon Ladies, Geisha Girls, and Our Fantasies of the Exotic Orient*. New York: Public Affairs, 2005.

Putnam, Robert. *Bowling Alone: The Collapse and Revival of American Community*. New York: Simon and Schuster, 2000.

Radway, Janice. *Reading the Romance: Women, Patriarchy, and Popular Literature*. Chapel Hill: University of North Carolina, 1991.

Rathbone, Eliza, and Johanna Halford-Macleod. *Art Beyond Isms: Masterworks from El Greco to Picasso in the Phillips Collection*. London: Third Millennium, 2003.

Reading, Brian. *Japan: The Coming Collapse*. London: Orion Books, 1992.

Renan, Ary. "Hokusai's Mang-wa." *Artistic Japan* 9 (1888): 87–101.

Robertson, Jennifer. *Takarazuka: Sexual Politics and Popular Culture in Modern Japan*. Berkeley: University of California Press, 1998.

Ryang, Sonia. *Japan and National Anthropology*. London: Routledge/Curzon, 2004.

Rydell, Robert. *All the Worlds a Fair*. Chicago: University of Chicago Press, 1984.

Said, Edward. *Culture and Imperialism*. New York: Alfred Knopf, 1993.

———. *Orientalism*. New York: Vintage Books, 1979.

Sandvoss, Cornel. *Fans: The Mirror of Consumption*. Malden, MA: Polity Press, 2005.

Shapiro, Michael. *Japan in the Land of the Brokenhearted*. New York: Henry Holt and Company, 1989.

Shirane, Haruo. *Traces of Dreams: Landscape, Cultural Memory, and the Poetry of Basho*. Stanford, CA: Stanford University Press, 1998.

Silverman, Debora. *Van Gogh and Gauguin: The Search for Sacred Art*. New York: Farrar, Straus, and Giroux, 2000.

Skovmand, Michael, and Kim Christian Shrøder. *Media Cultures: Reappraising Transnational Media*. London: Routledge, 1992.

Slaymaker, Douglas, ed. *Confluences: Postwar Japan and France*. Ann Arbor: University of Michigan Monograph Series, 2002.

Snodgrass, Judith. *Presenting Japanese Buddhism to the West*. Chapel Hill: University of North Carolina, 2003.

Snyder, Gary. *The Back Country*. New York: New Directions, 1957.

———. *The Real Work: Interviews and Talks 1964–1979*. New York: New Directions, 1980.

Spate, Virginia, and Gary Hickey, eds. *Monet and Japan*. Exhibition catalogue from the National Gallery of Australia. London: Thames and Hudson, 2001.

Staiger, Janet. *Media Reception Studies*. New York: New York University Press, 2005.

Steuding, Bob. *Gary Snyder*. Boston: Twayne, 1976.

Stewart, Susan. *On Longing: Narratives of the Miniature, the Gigantic, the Souvenir.* Durham, NC: Duke University Press, 1993.

Stockton, Sharon. "The Self Regained: Cyberpunk's Retreat to the Imperium." *Contemporary Literature* 36, no. 4 (Winter 1995): 588–612.

Strain, Charles. "The Pacific Buddha's Wild Practice: Gary Snyder's Environmentalist Ethic." In *American Buddhism: Methods and Findings in Recent Scholarship.* Richmond, UK: Curzon Press, 1998.

Suzuki, D. T. *Zen and Japanese Culture.* Princeton, NJ: Bollingen Press, 1953.

Talbot, Margaret. "The Auteur of Anime." *The New Yorker,* January 17, 2005.

Tatsumi, Takayuki. "Waiting for Godzilla: Chaotic Negotiations between Post-Orientalism and Hyper-Occidentalism." In *Transactions, Transgressions, Transformations: American Culture in Western Europe and Japan,* edited by Heide Fehrenbach and Uta Poiger. New York: Berghan Books, 2000.

Temple, Jean. *Blue Ghost: A Study of Lafcadio Hearn.* New York: Jonathan Cape, 1931.

Thornham, Sue. *Passionate Detachments.* New York: Hodder and Stoughton, 1997.

Treat, John. *Great Mirrors Shattered: Homosexuality, Orientalism, and Japan.* Oxford: Oxford University Press, 1999.

Tsutsui, William. *Godzilla on My Mind: Fifty Years of the King of Monsters.* New York: Palgrave, 2004.

Tsutsui, William, and Michiko Ito, eds. In *Godzilla's Footstep: Japanese Pop Culture Icons on the Global Stage.* New York: Palgrave, 2006.

Tulloch, John, and Henry Jenkins. *Science Fiction Audiences.* London: Routledge, 1995.

Turner, Victor. *Dramas, Fields and Metaphors: Symbolic Action in Human Society.* Ithaca, NY: Cornell University Press, 1974.

Tweed, Thomas. *The American Encounter with Buddhism, 1844–1912: Victorian Culture and the Limits of Dissent.* Bloomington: Indiana University Press, 1992.

Ueno, Toshiya. *Kurenai no metarusutsu: anime to iu senjo.* Tokyo: Kodansha, 1998.

Van Gogh, Vincent. *The Complete Letters of Vincent Van Gogh.* Vol. 3. Greenwich, CT: New York Graphic Society, n.d.

Van Wolferen, Karel. *The Enigma of Japanese Power: People and Politics in a Stateless Nation.* London: MacMillan, 1989.

Vogel, Ezra. *Japan as Number One: Lessons for America.* Cambridge, MA: Harvard University Press, 1979.

Waley, Alison. "Letter to Ivan Morris." In *Madly Singing in the Mountains: An Appreciation and Anthology of Arthur Waley,* edited by Ivan Morris. London: George Allen and Unwin, 1970.

Waley, Arthur. *The No Plays of Japan.* New York: Grove Press, n.d.

———. *The Tale of Genji.* New York: Random House, 1962.

Waley, Hubert. "Letter to Ivan Morris." In *Madly Singing in the Mountains: An Appreciation and Anthology of Arthur Waley,* edited by Ivan Morris. London: George Allen and Unwin, 1970.

Weinreich, Regina, ed. *The Jack Kerouac Book of Haikus.* New York: Penguin Poets, 2003.

Weisberg, Gabriel. "The Creation of Japonisme." In *The Origins of Art Nouveau: The Bing Empire,* edited by Gabriel P. Weisberg, Edwin Becker, and Evelyn Posseme. Ithaca, NY: Cornell University Press, 2005.

Whitney, Clara. *Clara's Diary: An American Girl in Meiji Japan*. Tokyo: Kodansha, 1979.

Wichmann, Siegfried. *Japonisme: The Japanese Influence on Western Art since 1858*. London: Thames and Hudson, 1981.

Wilde, Oscar. *The Decay of Lying*. In *The Complete Works of Oscar Wilde*. New York: Doubleday, 1923.

Williams, Simon. *Emotion and Social Theory: Corporeal Reflections on the (Ir)Rational*. London: Sage, 2001.

Williamson, Milly. "Vampires and Goths: Fandom, Gender, and Cult Dress." In *Dressed to Impress: Looking the Part*, edited by William Keenan. New York: Berg, 2001.

Wilson, Rob, and Wimal Dissanayake. *Global\Local*. Durham, NC: Duke University Press, 1996.

Witte, Mary Kay. *Redneck Haiku*. Santa Monica, CA.: Santa Monica Press, 2003.

Wright, Frank Lloyd. *An Autobiography*. New York: Horizon Press, 1977.

Yamada,Shoji. "Zen: An Imagined Soft Power." Paper presented at Interrogating Japan's Soft Power, conference at the University of Texas, February 2006.

Yano, Christine. "Panic Attacks: Anti-*Pokemon* Voices in Global Markets." In *Pikachu's Global Adventure: The Rise and Fall of* Pokemon, edited by Joseph Tobin. Durham, NC: Duke University Press, 2004.

Yu, Beongcheon. *An Ape of the Gods: The Art and Thought of Lafcadio Hearn*. Detroit: Wayne State University Press, 1969.

Index